T0125212

Promises, Performance, and Prospects

Antonio Martino

Promises, Performance, and Prospects

Essays on Political Economy 1980–1998

Antonio Martino

Edited and with a Foreword by Dwight Lee

Liberty Fund
Indianapolis

Amagi books are published by Liberty Fund, Inc.
a foundation established to encourage study of the
ideal of a society of free and responsible individuals.

The cuneiform inscription that appears in the logo and serves
as a design element in all Liberty Fund books is the earliest-known
written appearance of the word "freedom" (*amagi*), or "liberty."
It is taken from a clay document written about 2300 B.C.
in the Sumerian city-state of Lagash.

The essays in this volume express the thoughts and opinions of the
author, and should in no way be construed as reflecting the views
of the Italian government.

Printed in the United States of America

07 06 05 P 5 4 3 2 1

Library of Congress Cataloging-in-Publication Data

Martino, Antonio, 1942–
Promises, performance, and prospects: essays on political economy
1980–1998/Antonio Martino; edited and with a foreword by Dwight Lee.
p. cm.
Includes bibliographical references and index.
ISBN 0-86597-563-9 (paper: alk. paper)
1. Economic policy. 2. Italy—Economic policy. I. Lee, Dwight R. II. Title.
HD87 .M2757 2005
330—dc22 2004065012

LIBERTY FUND, INC.
8335 Allison Pointe Trail, Suite 300, Indianapolis, Indiana 46250-1684

TO CAROL

Contents

Foreword ix

PART 1. TAX REVENUES INCREASE AND GOVERNMENT INCREASES MORE

Italy's Lesson: Higher Taxes, Bigger Deficit 3

Italy's Tax Follies 7

Tax Issue Comes into Focus in Italy 11

Invisible Taxation: The Growth of Italy's Leviathan 15

Budget Deficits and Constitutional Constraints 28

PART 2. HOPES BETRAYED

Statism at Work: A Lesson from Italy 51

The Leaning Tower of Statism 65

Free Education or Educational Freedom? 68

Italian Socialists Warm to Vouchers 83

The Welfare State: Lessons from Italy 90

Taxation and Liberty in the European Welfare State 104

Solving the Global Public Pensions Crisis: The Italian Case 129

Is Social Justice a Myth? 136

Tales from the Public Sector: Inside the Labyrinth 148

Tales from the Public Sector: Red Tape all'Italiana 152

PART 3. GOING UNDERGROUND

The Underground Economy 157

Another Italian Economic Miracle? 177

PART 4. FANTASIES COLLIDE WITH REALITY

Was Keynes a Keynesian? 199
The Modern Mask of Socialism 218

PART 5. MONEY AND EUROPE

Toward Monetary Stability? 241
Nationalism, Money, and Europe 257
European Monetary Union: A Fatal Mistake? 267
A Monetary Constitution for Ex-Communist Countries 283

PART 6. THE FUTURE OF FREEDOM

A Comment on "Nineteen Eighty-four: A False Alarm?" 313
Are We Winning? 318
Liberalism in the Coming Decade: The Role of the Mont Pèlerin Society 329

Index 345

Foreword

This book consists of editorials, articles, and talks written by Antonio Martino between 1980 and 1998. The subject matter can be generally described as political economy, and more narrowly (and precisely) described as Italian economic concerns from a classical liberal/public choice perspective. The Italian focus is a useful one. Many of the political and economic problems facing Italy, and discussed by Martino, were worse than those facing the other industrialized democracies, especially during the earlier part of the period covered. But these same problems were endemic in all the industrialized democracies, with other countries catching up and passing Italy in terms of these problems by the end of the twentieth century. Although Martino's discussion in most chapters is motivated by the situation in Italy, his analysis is germane to problems that, to one degree or another, face all advanced democratic countries.

Martino's discussion highlights classical liberal principles of political economy that transcend the particulars of time and place. From Adam Smith to James Buchanan, the insights of political economists have been motivated by, and illustrated with, contemporary concerns that keep recurring in only slightly different guises. In 1980, when Martino was writing the earliest of the chapters contained here, the statist/Keynesian experiment had been running to mostly rave reviews from the political elite for several decades, but unmistakable evidence was accumulating that its performance had fallen far short of the promises. Government spending and budget deficits were expanding rapidly around the world, both in real terms and as percentages of national incomes, despite escalating tax burdens; inflation was debasing the major world currencies; and employment levels were rising—a combination of events that was beginning to destroy the Keynesian consensus.

By the late 1990s, the intellectual foundation being used to justify government control over the economy had largely crumbled. Socialism had either collapsed without pretense, as in the former Soviet Union, or been redefined to mean a move toward increased reliance on free markets, as in China. The classical liberal understanding of the benefits of limited government and free markets, almost completely lost by the end of World War II, experienced a genuine intellectual resurgence over the period of the articles in this volume. The articles published (in many cases republished) here provide a window on that resurgence by a scholar whose life has both contributed to and been greatly influenced by classical liberal thought.

Antonio Martino's classical liberalism can hardly be described as mainstream in Italy, but Martino's grandfather and father were classical liberals and successful politicians. His grandfather, also Antonio Martino, was the mayor of Messina at various intervals from 1899 to 1919, retiring from politics in opposition to the Fascist takeover. His father, Gaetano Martino, was a physician and a scientist who became one of the most prominent figures in post–World War II Italian politics. As Italy's minister of foreign affairs from 1954 to 1957, he played a major role in organizing the meetings that culminated in the 1957 Treaty of Rome, an early step toward European integration. Like his grandfather and father, Antonio did not start out as a politician, although given his family background, political issues were surely important in his intellectual development. Born in Messina in 1942, Martino graduated from the University of Messina Law School in 1964 and in the same year became an instructor of economics in the law school at the University of Rome. He took leave from the law school from 1966 to 1968 to pursue graduate studies in the department of economics at the University of Chicago, where he was a student of Milton Friedman and George Stigler. Martino remained at the University of Rome, serving as professor of economics (holding the chair of monetary history and policy from 1979 to 1992) until 1994, when he took parliamentary leave. He retired from the University of Rome in 2002.

As an academic, Martino was well known in Italy, and elsewhere, for his classical liberal views and positions on public policy. He frequently contributed to Italian and international magazines, he published numerous academic articles and twelve books, he was a frequent guest on Italian and international radio and television programs, he was highly sought after as a speaker by organizations from Italy to New Zealand, and he served as an academic adviser to think tanks around the world. From 1988 to 1990, he was president of the Mont Pèlerin Society, an organization of classical liberals founded in 1947 by Friedrich A. Hayek, and he has received a host of academic honors. Because, or maybe in spite of, Martino's well-known classical liberal views and recommendations, he was elected to Parliament in 1994, where he remains a member—being reelected in 1996 and 2001. He has served at the highest level of the Italian government, as minister of foreign affairs in the first Berlusconi government from May 1994 to January 1995 (the same position his father held forty years earlier) and as the minister of defense since June 2001 in the second Berlusconi government.

The chapters in this volume have been organized into six parts, each concentrating on a particular issue, or a set of related issues, that together tell a story of the promises and failures of government attempts to improve economic performance by expanding its control over the economy.

The first part ("Tax Revenues Increase and Government Increases More") discusses the government budget situation in Italy during the mid-1980s and contrasts this situation with that of the previous two decades with some comparisons with the United States. In 1981, the cost of government, measured as a percentage of national income, was 40 percent higher in Italy than in the United States. Italy's fiscal background raises a number of questions, not all dealt with in great depth in this opening section. What, for example, explains the explosion in government growth, and why did it occur when it did? Is there any evidence that the additional spending could be justified by improvements in government services? What is the connection between inflation and government taxation and spending? Are there ways of ensuring that fiscal decisions better reflect the social costs and benefits of government expenditures? Are large deficits a measure of fiscal irresponsibility or a means of controlling irresponsible government spending? Martino begins to address some of these questions in the last chapter in this part, "Budget Deficits and Constitutional Constraints." But most of these questions, and others, are considered in the following parts.

The title of the second part ("Hopes Betrayed") provides more than a hint of Martino's response to one question in the previous paragraph: Are the increased government spending and taxes justified by better government services? In addressing this question, Martino first considers the outcomes of more government spending and asks if they are worth what they cost. He points out, for example, that despite large increases in spending on education, schools and universities are overcrowded and perform poorly; and despite large increases in spending on poverty programs sufficient to eliminate poverty (if the money had gone to the poor), the poor remain. Martino observes that even prominent members of the Italian Socialist party (which had advocated nationalizing all economic activity, with the possible exception of barbershops) were beginning to express doubts about the outcomes of statist policies by the late 1980s.

Martino also draws on the public choice literature that provides a process explanation for excessive government. He points out that the political process enables organized interest groups to capture concentrated benefits and spread the costs over the general public. The result is that most of the benefits are considered, most of the costs are ignored, and government spending is increased beyond efficient limits.

Martino has a short personal story ("Inside the Labyrinth") in part 2 that illustrates what is commonly recognized as a problem with government—the problem of red tape. There has to be some form of accountability in the use of scarce resources. When they are allocated through markets, prices, profits, and losses impose accountability so effectively that little, if any, red tape is required. When we resort to government allocation, however, markets aren't typically available (or allowed) to impose accountability, and it has to be imposed in another way. Bureaucratic red tape—clumsy, inflexible, and excessive—is a very poor substitute for market accountability, but it results inevitably from the lack of market accountability. And the same process that Martino argues is generating too much government also generates the red tape.

Part 2 is the longest in the book, containing an analysis of several areas in which government has increased its involvement. Throughout part 2, Martino argues that the left's hopes invested in a larger and more active government were destined to be dashed. The higher the tax rate on income and profits, and the more extensive and detailed the regulations on business, the more motivation people have to move into the underground economy, which is the topic of the two chapters in part 3. As Adam Smith pointed out in *The Theory of Moral Sentiments,* advocates of government controls (men of systems) like to see people as pieces on a chessboard with no principle of motion other than what government authorities mandate. People have their own principles of motion, however, and will leave the chessboard (go underground) when government mandates are not to their liking.

As Martino points out, we cannot know exactly how large the underground economy is, but we can estimate its size. One interesting method of estimation that Martino discusses is to examine the ratio of currency to national income. Two things happen as more people shift into the underground economy: (1) the need for currency increases as more exchanges take place without leaving a paper trail (although this is not as important in Italy as in other countries because checking accounts in Italy are secret—or were in the early 1980s); (2) the official measures understate national income and overstate unemployment. Martino points out, among other things, that Keynesian-motivated attempts to fine-tune the economy with monetary and fiscal policy, difficult under the best conditions, are particularly difficult when the authorities cannot accurately measure what they are trying to fine-tune—the national income. Martino recognizes that the underground economy mitigates some of the harmful consequences of government laws, but he favors changing the laws, not breaking them.

In part 4 ("Fantasies Collide with Reality"), Martino considers how advocates of state control over the economy have reluctantly modified their views as evidence contrary to their hopes became too obvious to ignore. In the chapter "Was Keynes a Keynesian?" Martino points out that Keynes was not a socialist and disagreed with many views and recommendations of his "Keynesian" followers. Martino contends that Keynes was himself badly confused about important issues, particularly the effects of money on the real economy and the connection between money and inflation, and his confusion is largely responsible for

Keynesians' embracing many policies with which Keynes would have disagreed.

Following the chapter on Keynes, Martino considers how "The Modern Mask of Socialism" has been changed by its encounter with reality. From advocating the abolition of private ownership and total state control of the economy, respectable statists began shifting in the 1950s and 1960s to the softer socialism of Keynesianism, which saw government exerting somewhat less direct control over the economy through the "stabilizing" influence of monetary and fiscal policy. By the late 1970s, the combination of persistent, and escalating, inflation and high unemployment (a combination that the Keynesian model simply couldn't explain) was discrediting the claims of the Keynesian finetuners. In the 1980s, the economic successes of deregulation, privatization, and tax cutting in restoring balanced economic growth in advanced countries, and the dramatic contrast between those developing countries that relied largely on markets and those that suppressed markets through detailed state control, further reduced the confidence of socialists. And the collapse of the Soviet Union and its control over its Eastern European satellites made it almost impossible to remain both credible and socialist. Martino argues, however, that the rhetoric regarding socialism has changed much more than has economic policy. Government controls over economic decisions in many areas have actually increased despite the results of those controls. As James Buchanan has said, "Socialism is dead, but leviathan lives on."

The importance of money and monetary policy, with an emphasis on the European situation, is the topic of part 5. In the opening chapter in this part, "Toward Monetary Stability?" Martino points out that, although the connection between monetary growth and changes in the general price level is one of the best-established relationships in economics, supposedly good economists write entire books on inflation and never mention the quantity of money. And although central bankers commonly comment on the importance of monetary growth, more often than not their decisions ignore that importance. Martino sees the difficulty of maintaining stable, predictable, and noninflationary monetary growth as a symptom of a more fundamental problem, excessive monetary growth and budget deficits, which put pressure on the monetary authorities to monetize the debt. This argument had more credibility in the early 1980s, when Martino wrote this chapter, than it may appear to now. Since the early 1980s, government budget deficits have generally remained high, and have escalated in some countries, but inflation rates have declined. Large deficits don't have to be monetized, and central bankers can resist the political temptation to monetize them, especially when the public is aware of the connection between monetary growth and inflation through the persistent efforts of respected economists. But the inflationary temptations created by large budget deficits should not be ignored. As Martino points out, the story of government management of the money supply is "a very long story," and not one that inspires much optimism about monetary stability.

The next two chapters consider the prospects for a common European currency, the euro, before it was introduced. Martino presents arguments both for and against the euro, concluding that the most important consideration in whether a common currency will be an improvement over national currencies is the monetary constitution, in which the key consideration is rules versus discretion. He sees discretionary monetary policy as the source of monetary instability at the national level, and sees this as a bigger concern when monetary policy is determined at the European level. Martino also considers the pros and cons of an interesting way of introducing the euro.

In the final chapter in this part on monetary policy, Martino argues that the resource misallocations that result from monetary instability particularly harm countries making the transition from socialism. These countries urgently need monetary constitutions that greatly reduce the discretion of political authorities over monetary growth. Martino believes that agreeing on the need for such a constitution is more important than its exact formulation. He considers possible monetary constitutions based on the gold standard, Friedman's constant monetary-growth rule, and competing currencies, pointing out that none is perfect and that reliance on markets and limits on government are preconditions for any successful monetary constitution.

In a short final part, Martino speculates on the "Future of Freedom." The first of the three chapters in this part is a comment on Orwell's *Nineteen Eighty-four* (actually a comment on a book review of the book) written in, not surprisingly, 1984, before the collapse of the Berlin Wall and the liberation of Eastern Europe. Martino defends *Nineteen Eighty-four* against the charge that its prophecy was wrong. He counterargues that *Nineteen Eighty-four* was important because it predicted something that was not inevitable. As Martino says, "When the outcome is inevitable, prophecy is essentially useless." One is reminded of Schumpeter's observation in his preface to *Capitalism, Socialism and Democracy:* "The report that a given ship is sinking is not defeatist. Only the spirit in which this report is received can be defeatist: The crew can sit down and drink. But it can also rush to the pumps." Classical liberals rushed to the pumps, and their success in preventing a deluge of statism from completely swamping the private sector in more and more countries made it reasonable for Martino to ask in the next chapter, "Are We Winning?" Martino is moderately optimistic because (1) ideas and political rhetoric have dramatically shifted in favor of free markets and limited government, and (2) policy victories have been achieved in the form of deregulation, privatization, and marginal tax reductions. But he worries that these victories can be easily reversed, since the fundamental constitutional reforms needed to resist the unrelenting pressures for more government have not been achieved.

Martino continues his combination of moderate optimism and worried vigilance in the last chapter, "Liberalism in the Coming Decade," written after the fall of the Berlin Wall but before the collapse of the Soviet Union. He worries that the loss of faith in socialism has not been accompanied by an increased understanding and appreciation of markets or reduced pressure for more government. But ending on a more optimistic note, Martino emphasizes the importance of ideas. Keynes was right on the importance of ideas, but because of the power of correct ideas he was only partly right when he said that in the long run we are all dead. Martino tells us that Keynes and Marx are indeed dead, both physically and through their intellectual influence, but classical liberal thinkers such as John Locke, Adam Smith, and David Hume live on through the power of their ideas.

The struggle between the forces for freedom and those for more state control continues in many arenas and on many margins. There will never be a final victory for freedom, but neither will there be a final defeat. Just as flowers will always find openings to grow even if we attempt to pave over the entire earth, human freedom will always find openings through which to flourish despite attempts to suppress it. Martino's work can be considered nourishment for those flowers of freedom that can never be completely paved over by the forces of statism.

Dwight Lee

Part 1

Tax Revenues Increase and Government Increases More

Italy's Lesson: Higher Taxes, Bigger Deficit

Those who, like Walter Mondale, worry about the magnitude of the U.S. federal deficit and advocate tax increases as an indispensable step toward the deficit's reduction might benefit from the experience of other countries that have experienced similar problems. One such country is Italy.

According to International Monetary Fund figures, in 1980 the government deficit in Italy amounted to 37,138 billion lire, or 11 percent of the gross domestic product. To get a proper idea of the magnitude of such a deficit, one must put it in perspective of the U.S. government's 1983 deficit of $195 billion, which amounted to a "mere" 6.1 percent of America's gross national product. A U.S. deficit equal to 11 percent of its GNP would have amounted to over $350 billion.

In other words, the Italian deficit of 1980 was a staggering figure, requiring (if one is to follow Mr. Mondale's logic) the most drastic fiscal measures. If tax increases are needed to reduce a deficit equal to 6.1 percent of GNP, obviously they must be essential when the deficit is nearly twice that percentage.

Higher and Higher Taxes

And an increase in taxes is what Italy got: From 1980 to 1983 the total tax revenue increased 90 percent in nominal terms, jumping from 39.8 percent of GDP to 47.8 percent. This is indeed an extremely large increase, made all the more painful by the fact that there was

Originally published in *The Wall Street Journal,* October 25, 1984, and reprinted with permission.

no increase in real GDP over the same period. While real income remained constant, taxes increased rapidly, absorbing an additional 10 percent of GDP in four years.

These figures should dispose of the fallacy according to which Italians, being ingenious tax evaders, do not pay taxes. In fact, direct (mostly income) tax revenue showed the largest increase: 121 percent, going from 11.2 percent of GDP in 1980 to 15.7 percent in 1983. Indirect tax revenue (from value-added tax and the like) increased 77 percent, going from 10 percent of GDP in 1980 to 11.2 percent in 1983. Finally, social security "contributions" showed an 80 percent increase, from 14.5 percent of GDP to 16.4 percent. Only non-tax revenue remained constant at slightly more than 4 percent of GDP.

As I predicted in these pages last August, the increase in taxation and the proposals for further increases are beginning to result in an *open* tax rebellion by Italians. For example, two days ago, 90 percent of all stores in the whole country remained closed to protest a new tax package bill pending in parliament, and more of these manifestations of open tax resistance are to be expected in the future, as the traditional Italian way of opposing taxes—escape into the underground economy—becomes more and more difficult.

No one, as far as I know, has advocated such an extreme "remedy" for the U.S. budget deficit. That is ironic given that, as mentioned above, the Italian budget deficit in 1980 was almost twice as large as the U.S. budget deficit in 1983.

What results were achieved by such a substantial increase in taxes with respect to the need of reducing the Italian deficit? Contrary to the expectations of the deficit cutters, the Italian deficit has *increased* from 37,138 billion lire in 1980 to 88,522 billion lire in 1983—an increase of 138 percent. Even when inflation is taken into account, the deficit has increased in real terms by more than 51 percent, going from 11 percent to 16.5 percent of GDP.

The positive correlation between taxes and deficits is not confined to the experience of the past four years. Almost without exception, total tax revenue has increased every year in the last 10 years, in nominal terms, in real terms, and as a percentage of GDP. From 1974 to 1983, total tax revenue has increased sevenfold in nominal terms, and

80 percent in real terms, going from less than one-third of GDP in 1974 (32.8 percent) to almost one-half in 1983 (47.8 percent).

The effects of this gigantic increase in taxation on the deficit have been the opposite of what supporters of tax increases expect. The deficit has increased year in and year out, almost without exception, in nominal terms, in real terms, and as a percentage of GDP. From 1974 to 1983, the deficit has increased tenfold in nominal terms, and two and a half times in real terms, going from 8 percent of GDP in 1974 to 16.5 percent in 1983.

The obvious explanation for the failure of tax increases to reduce the deficit is that public expenditures have increased even faster than taxes. According to official figures, total public-sector spending increased 98 percent from 1980 to 1983, going from 165,400 billion lire in 1980 to 328,000 billion lire in 1983. To put things differently, while nominal GDP increased 197,161 billion lire, total public-sector spending increased 162,000 billion lire, which means that the increase in government spending absorbed 82.4 percent of the increase in nominal GDP. As a result, public spending jumped from 48.8 percent of GDP in 1980 to a staggering 61.2 percent in 1983. This means that real income net of public spending was 23.8 percent *lower* in 1983 than in 1980!

Had the Italian government followed the policy of attempting to reduce the deficit by keeping spending under control, the result might have been different. All that was needed was not a reduction in the absolute level of spending, nor even that spending be held constant. Rather, had spending been allowed to grow—but at a rate not faster than the growth of GDP, thereby keeping the ratio of public spending to GDP constant—the deficit (given the tremendous increase in taxes) would have been reduced to a mere 5,224 billion lire: less than 1 percent of GDP. Had the policy of spending restraint been followed without any increase in taxes as a percentage of GDP, the deficit would have been reduced from 11 percent to less than 9 percent. Obviously, the policy of restraint in spending is not only less painful but also more effective than that of increasing taxes.

A Bigger Deficit

What the Italian experience suggests is that tax increases have a perverse effect on the deficit. The "marginal propensity to public spending"—the ratio of the increase in spending over the increase in tax revenue—has very often been greater than a ratio of one, and this is true in other countries as well. This means that an increase in taxes may lead to an increase, rather than a decrease, in the deficit. Even though there is no strong a priori reason for this, the evidence suggests that a policy of tax increases is neither a necessary nor a sufficient condition for reducing the deficit, and that it has negative consequences on a country's economic vitality. Only by bringing government spending under control can a country hope to solve its financial problems, while at the same time allowing for economic prosperity and growth.

Italy's Tax Follies

News of the U.S. tax reform has been greeted here with reactions ranging from incredulity to envy. Even left-wing journalists usually critical of the Reagan administration have found it difficult to hide their approval of the reduction in income tax rates. Their point of view is not difficult to understand: The income tax burden on the Italian taxpayer was already substantially higher than that of his American counterpart, even before the reduction in the U.S. tax rates. For example, an Italian with a 1983 taxable income of $25,000 would have paid $6,946 to the government, while an American making the same would have paid out only $3,570 in 1984. True, translating income from one currency to another is difficult, with all the different deductions and types of taxes. But the difference is still large.

Furthermore, the magnitude of the American tax reform makes the "adjustment" in the structure of Italian income tax rates look silly. Comparing the Italian reform that changed nine income brackets with tax rates ranging from 18 percent to 65 percent to nine income brackets with rates ranging from 12 percent to 62 percent to the American reform is like comparing a small Fiat to a shiny Cadillac.

Things are made far worse in Italy by the bracket creep (or fiscal drag, as it is called here): According to a recent estimate, 45 percent of total income tax revenue for 1984 was due to the fiscal drag. The adjustments in tax rates that have been granted every now and then have offset only 30 percent of the potential impact of the combined effect of double-digit inflation and highly progressive income tax rates. In other words, the so-called reductions in tax rates have not

Originally published in *The Wall Street Journal Europe,* July 23, 1986, and reprinted with permission.

prevented the income tax burden from doubling: a gigantic unlegislated increase.

An Italian Myth

For the benefit of those who still believe in the myth that Italians, being ingenious tax evaders, do not pay taxes, let me add that from 1974 to 1985 total government revenue has increased almost nine times, from less than a third of Gross Domestic Product in 1974 to almost one half in 1985. Italians pay dearly for their government.

With such an exponential increase in tax revenue, some might surmise that Italy has succeeded in eliminating the deficit. As I have written in this paper before, however, this is not the case: According to International Monetary Fund figures, the deficit equalled 8.961 trillion lire in 1974 ($6 billion), and it skyrocketed to L121.332 trillion ($82 billion) in 1985. In that decade the deficit increased to nearly 18 percent of Gross Domestic Product from some 8 percent of Gross Domestic Product. Obviously the "marginal propensity to public spending" (the ratio of the increase in spending to the increase in revenue) is greater than one, so that when taxation increases so does the deficit.

Even more significant is that the Italian explosion in public-sector spending over the past five years has taken place not in response to a deliberate policy of government growth but *despite* the attempts of all governments to keep spending under control. From 1980 to 1985 public sector spending in real terms has increased by more than 35 percent. This growth has very important implications. If we define "private GDP" as "the amount of resources of the nation that people individually and separately decide about," or as the difference between total GDP and public spending, we come to the unpleasant conclusion that, from 1980 to 1985, "private GDP" has declined by more than 21 percent in real terms. According to official figures, "private" GDP in 1985 was 16 percent below its 1974 level.

Obviously public affluence is producing private scarcity: The growth of the share of GDP under bureaucratic-political control is reducing the amount of real resources under the direct control of individuals and their families. Here some might object, arguing that what the public sector absorbs through taxation it returns to society in the form of public services. I doubt that many Italians would be convinced by this, because there is a growing consensus that we don't get our money's worth from the government.

It may be, as Milton Friedman says, that the only reason we are still free is that we don't get all the government we pay for, but it is undeniable that much if not most of public-sector spending is simply wasted. Consequently, private provision of supposedly "free" public services is rapidly increasing: Police protection is now largely provided by the market; the number of out-of-court settlements and the amount of private arbitration is growing because of the unbelievable delays of "public" justice; private delivery of mail both within the city and between cities is a growth industry; and even some traditional welfare state activities are increasingly being supplied by the market, e.g., spectacular increases in private old-age pensions, disability pensions, and health insurance. Despite the obvious difficulty of charging for services that are supposed to be supplied free from the state, private provision of public services is flourishing.

The combined effect of rapidly increasing taxation and highly inefficient public services has resulted in several manifestations of open tax rebellion: Newspapers and magazines are routinely reporting on the phenomenon, and several groups are being organized to resist the continued increase in the tax burden and try to achieve reductions in the cost of government.

How are governments reacting to this potentially explosive situation? As suggested earlier, all governments in the past five years have tried to keep spending under control. Yet the results have been disappointing. Given their failure to reduce or keep expenditures constant, it now seems that recourse to Italy's Secret Weapon will prove unavoidable.

Let me illustrate. A few years ago, I was regularly commuting between Rome and Naples. According to official timetables, fast trains should have made the trip in one hour and 45 minutes. They were almost always late. To solve the problem, the management of the state railroads, having unsuccessfully tried to get the trains to arrive on time, resorted to the Secret Weapon: They changed the timetable, increasing the travel time from 1 hour 45 minutes to 2 hours 15 minutes. (Alas, it seems that this worked only temporarily; trains are now late even on the new timetable.)

Another example of the Secret Weapon is that of the exams that conclude pre-university education and allow students to enter the university. In the past they were very difficult, and a substantial number of those who took them flunked. The first solution was to improve the quality of secondary-school teaching, but this was easier said than done. Again the Secret Weapon was unleashed: Exams were made easier, and the number of students passing them jumped from something like 60 percent to the present 99 percent. The Secret Weapon strikes again.

Given the failure to keep public spending under control, it is only a matter of time before the Secret Weapon is brought out again: All that is required is an upward revision of the GDP figures. If you can't reduce spending, but you still want to reduce the ratio of spending to GDP, all you have to do is increase the GDP figure. Very simple, really.

Heartless Taxpayers

The revision of income figures has already been done once, in 1979, when in response to discussion about the size of Italy's underground economy the government statistical office increased GDP figures by 10 percent without really explaining the reasons for such a move. The usual well-informed sources maintain a similar upward adjustment in income figures is currently being considered.

I am convinced that the adjustment will occur, as it is undeniably beneficial: The ratio of public spending to GDP will be reduced, and so will the relative burden of taxation and the size of government deficit as a percentage of national income. At that point few people will deny that the financial situation has improved substantially, and only heartless taxpayers will have the courage to complain.

My only advice to our public statisticians is as follows: Don't be too modest, don't spoil the whole operation with a meager 10 percent increase. Think big: Nothing less than 30 percent will do.

Tax Issue Comes into Focus in Italy

Italy's tax revolution is entering a new and difficult phase. Things began to heat up late last year, with the turnout of more than 30,000 people at a demonstration in Turin opposing the present level of confiscatory taxation. Writing about that seminal event in *The Wall Street Journal,* I concluded: "There are signs that the political world will advise tax protesters to 'eat cake.'" Unfortunately, that prediction was soon confirmed by the proposed revision of the income tax structure, approved by the Italian government on Jan. 21.

The new system is undoubtedly a step in the right direction, but the change is trivial. Income tax brackets are reduced to eight from nine; rates that used to range from 12 percent to 62 percent should, according to the new scheme, range from 11 percent to 56 percent. Those who were hoping for a radical revision of the old structure have every reason to be disappointed. This will have important effects in the coming months and years, on both the economic and political levels. The tax issue is finally coming into focus in this country, and the real question is not whether but when it will overwhelm the current crop of politicians.

On a practical level, the new plan has several flaws. It does not eliminate bracket creep (or "fiscal drag," as it is called here) through the indexation of income tax brackets and deductions, as was advocated by economists of different schools. The paradox is that bracket creep violates the Italian constitution, which states: "No personal or patrimonial obligation may be imposed except on the basis of law." The in-

Originally published in *The Wall Street Journal Europe,* February 4, 1987, and reprinted with permission.

creased tax burden resulting from inflation and steeply graduated tax rates is not legislated by anybody. It is, therefore, a "patrimonial obligation" that no law has authorized. And it is not a minor "patrimonial obligation." According to one estimate, bracket creep accumulated since 1976 yielded 24,300 billion Italian lire in 1984, or 45 percent of total income tax revenue that year. (A dollar currently translates into 1,288 lire.)

Real Incomes to Drop

Tax rates that were introduced for the rich now fall, thanks to the combined effort of inflation and rate progression, on middle or low incomes. Taxpayers are starting to recognize that they are being exploited by a system that violates the constitution, and taxpayers are unlikely to be fooled, as often happened in the past, by small "reductions." They are well aware that this kind of window dressing not only fails to reduce their taxes, the minor reductions don't even prevent the tax burden from rising.

Take, for example, a net taxable income of L30 million for 1980, or $35,000 at the then-prevailing exchange rate. According to the tax structure of the time, such an income would have been subject to an income tax of L7,590,000, or 25.3 percent, and it would have faced a marginal tax rate—i.e., the rate on the next lira earned—of 35 percent. Under the proposed reform, the same *real* net taxable income in 1987 (L64 million, considering inflation) will have to pay more than L18 million in income tax, or 28.3 percent, and will face a marginal tax rate of 40 percent. Thus, despite two "reductions" in income tax rates, both the total tax burden and the marginal tax rate facing the *same* real income will have gone up. If the government's proposal is approved, real after-tax income would be lower in 1987 than in 1980. So it is hard to understand what the minister of finance, Bruno Visentini, had in mind when he claimed that his plan would result in a "tax reduction in real terms."

Mr. Visentini's plan does not even consider some small, but important, changes that have been advocated. For example, if a taxpayer ends up paying more than he should, according to Italian legislation, he must wait for many years until the government reimburses him. In the meantime, he must pay his taxes and cannot deduct his credit. This system is not only unfair to the taxpayer, it is also a bureaucratic burden and possibly a net cost for the government, because of bureaucratic costs and interest payments. But Mr. Visentini does not seem interested in allowing Italian taxpayers to "compensate" tax credits and tax liabilities. In short, considering the quality of the proposed "reform," it does not seem likely that taxpayers will feel satisfied.

New initiatives are being taken. For example, another demonstration is going to be held on March 22, this time in Genoa. According to some newspapers, it seems that the Genoa march will have a new feature. Marchers will gather, at the end of the speeches, in a large square, where there will be several trucks of the association of blood donors, and the marchers will donate their blood. The proposed slogan is "Better donate your blood than let the government suck it!"

Such grotesque elements in the revolt of Italy's taxpayers should not mislead the government. The tax revolt is a serious movement, and the government would be foolish to ignore it. The political world has so far reacted in a mixed way. This is in some ways understandable. On the one hand, many politicians see the anti-tax movement as a threat to the existing political apparatus, because the movement has no affiliation with any existing parties. On the other hand, a political party that could convince tax protesters of being seriously favorable to radical reform would reap substantial electoral benefits.

Politicians are further vexed by the fact that admitting that taxation is excessive would mean acknowledging that government spending has grown beyond an acceptable level. This is difficult for politicians under whom total government spending grew to 62.1 percent of gross domestic product in 1985 from 48.8 percent in 1980. Among various parties, the Christian Democrats seem willing to appease taxpayers; they feel, rightly, that the middle class has been badly hurt by bracket creep, and they'd like to do something about it. However, they are constrained both by the attitude of their partners in the coalition and by the fact that they've approved all the major spending decisions. The other coalition parties are divided. The Liberals openly support tax reform and promise to do something about it. Republicans and Socialists either deny that there is a tax problem or prefer to ignore the tax protests altogether.

Communists' Direction

It's almost as difficult for the opposition, both because the Communist Party has always voted for more public spending and because the Communists are reluctant to concede the failure of the welfare state. The Communists' latest strategy seems to call for some reforms in the right direction—the largest Communist union, the Italian General Confederation of Labor, for example, supports indexation of income tax brackets together with the introduction of new taxes on capital gains and a "wealth tax." Their ultimate goal would be to appease taxpayers without any reduction in either the absolute level of government spending or of explicit taxation.

At this point, Italian politicians would be well advised to ponder Edmund Burke's well-known remark: "To tax and to please, no more than to love and to be wise, is not given to men." And it's becoming ever more clear that if a political party really intends to increase its electoral support today, it must show its opposition to the present unacceptable level of taxation.

Invisible Taxation: The Growth of Italy's Leviathan

As long ago as 1892 Vilfredo Pareto noticed that Italy is acted on "by two predominant causes, Protection on the one hand and excessive State expenditures on the other." Italy's financial problems, he continued, "give us an idea of the state to which . . . other countries will come one day, if they do not stop in time on the dangerous course on which they have ventured."[1]

A country that has such a long history of statist exploitation of its citizens should provide a good case study for other nations that are pursuing similar policies. Indeed, our conclusion may be that statism, though so far triumphant in the policies of most Western democracies, might well be not only intellectually defunct but also (and more important) financially bankrupt. Statism has a past, albeit inglorious, but it has no future. It might be that despite the well-meaning but unsuccessful policies of "conservative" leaders, economic freedom will eventually prevail.

It is generally believed that Italians, being ingenious tax evaders, do not pay taxes, or that they pay much less than citizens in other countries. For example, as soon as every new government takes office (Italy has at least one change of government every year), it proclaims that it will solve any and every problem by resorting to a fight against tax evasion. The amount of taxes Italians evade thus becomes some kind of El Dorado, whose fabulous riches, if tapped, would provide benevolent politicians with a panacea for all economic ills of the country. Nor

Originally published in *Policy Review* 25, summer 1983, pp. 46–51, and reprinted with permission.

1. V. Pareto, "State Expenditures in Italy as Compared with the National Wealth," *The Economic Journal,* September 1892, pp. 561–64.

is this notion accepted only by official demagoguery; at times even academics entertain it. Thus, for example, Professor Richard Rose recently stated: "Historically, Italy has been the leader in nonpayment of taxes and there is little doubt that it still is at the head of the pack. One unpublished [Organization for Economic Cooperation and Development] report estimates that tax evasion there is as high as 27 percent of total reported income."[2]

Such a notion, which, as we shall see, is largely unfounded, is probably due to the misleading nature of the term *taxes.* The best example of the deceptiveness of that ghastly word is provided by the assertion of that Italian economist who publicly declared that there is no connection between taxation and freedom—as evidenced by the fact that the subjects of communist regimes pay little or no taxes (sic) and yet have no political freedom.

The idea that Italians are successful tax evaders is further strengthened by the belief that only people on fixed incomes pay their due. In fact, as has been repeatedly pointed out,[3] people on fixed incomes receive 70 percent of national income but contribute only 40 to 50 percent of the revenue from income taxes.

The truth is that visible taxes are only a fraction of the total cost of government. That is, even if one limits oneself to that part of the total cost of government consisting of pecuniary outlays, visible taxes are only a part of the story. As Professor Milton Friedman puts it: "The true cost of government to the public is not measured by explicit taxes but by government spending. If government spends $500 billion, and takes in through taxes $440 billion . . . who pays the difference? Not Santa Claus, but the U.S. citizen. . . . In effect, what you have are two kinds of taxes: the open, explicit taxes and the hidden taxes. And what's called a deficit is a hidden tax. . . . The thing we must keep our

2. R. Rose, "The Makings of a Do-It-Yourself Tax Revolt," *Public Opinion,* Aug.–Sept. 1980, especially pp. 13–14. For an analysis of the connection between tax evasion and the underground economy, see A. Martino, "Measuring Italy's Underground Economy," *Policy Review,* no. 16, pp. 87–106. [See pp. 177–95 of this volume.]

3. C. Cosciani, "La reforma del impuesto sobre la renta de las personas fisicas," p. 195; V. Visco, "Chi paga veramente le tasse in Italia," *La Repubblica,* January 12, 1983.

TABLE 1. *Public Sector Spending As a Percentage of Gross Domestic Product*

1960–1964	33.9%	1975–1979	48.0%
1965–1969	36.9	1980	50.3
1970–1974	40.0	1981	52.1

Source: A. Martino and E. Del Colle, "'Government push' e inflazione" (unpublished).

eye on is what government spends. That's the measure of the amount of resources of the nation that people cannot individually and separately decide about. It's a measure of the amount we turn over to the bureaucrats to spend on our behalf."[4]

If this is the case, then in order to have a correct measure of the cost of government—at least of that part that takes the form of pecuniary outlays—one cannot limit oneself to *explicit* taxes. For if this were so, it would be true that taxation in communist countries is low; instead one must look at government spending. Here, it becomes obvious that Italians, despite their ingenuity as tax evaders, do pay very dearly for their government—certainly no less than other nationals and much more than U.S. citizens.

Table 1 illustrates the pecuniary cost of government to the Italian taxpayer and its growth since 1960. According to one estimate, public sector spending absorbed 26.9 percent of national income in 1951;[5] by 1981 it had almost doubled to 52.1 percent. In thirty years we have gone from a situation in which government was absorbing slightly more than one-fourth of national income to one in which it absorbs more than one-half. This makes the cost of the Italian government some 40 percent higher—in relative terms—than that of the U.S. government (at all levels).[6] Thus, when we take inflation into account,

4. M. Friedman, "The Limitations of Tax Limitation," *Policy Review,* no. 5, pp. 7–14.

5. M. Fratianni and F. Spinelli, "The Growth of Government in Italy: Evidence from 1861 to 1979," unpublished paper. The authors' estimates differ from those in our table because they look at the ratio of government spending to net national income at current prices, rather than to gross domestic product.

6. J. T. Bennett and M. H. Johnson, *Better Government at Half the Price: Private Production of Public Services,* Caroline House Publishers, 1981, table 2, p. 5.

the per capita cost of government almost doubled from 1960 to 1970 (an increase of more than 92 percent) and almost doubled again from 1970 to 1981 (an increase of more than 93 percent).

In light of these figures, one might well ask how a nation of ingenious tax evaders has ended up sacrificing such a high percentage of its income to the tax man and allowed that percentage to grow so rapidly. To answer this, we must look at the factors that have allowed government to grow so rapidly to such enormous size with very little (if any) open resistance by the taxpayer. One explanation runs as follows:

> In order for taxpayers to oppose government growth, they must be aware of the share of the cost of government that falls on them. People, that is, must realize that *they* are paying for government spending; they must be aware of how much they are paying in taxes. In order for that to happen, taxes must be *visible*. . . . While this is true of some kinds of taxes, it is not true for all. Obviously, from the point of view of the government and of the politicians the preferred type of tax is that which people pay without realizing it, for that avoids the possibility of tax resistance and leaves people unaware of the cost of government. In Italy, most taxes are of this kind.[7]

Indeed, Italians bear the cost of government without being aware that they are paying for it. This is true of *explicit* taxes that are largely *invisible.* According to official figures, for example, income taxes in 1981 amounted to 14.2 percent of net national income. These are the most visible of all taxes, and they were low relative to national income. But even that percentage is misleading, since most people pay their income tax through withholding and are not, therefore, always aware of how much they are paying—everybody tends to think of his income in terms of the net figure. Indirect taxes amounted to 11.9 percent of net national income in 1981. These are almost perfectly invisible, as they are usually included in the prices paid by consumers. Finally, in 1981 social security contributions amounted to 16 percent of net national income; these too are highly invisible, as they are partly paid by the employer. Thus the employee is not aware of how much he is paying

7. A. Martino, *Constraining Inflationary Government,* Washington, D.C.: The Heritage Foundation, 1982, p. 49.

TABLE 2. *Government Deficits as a Percentage of:*

	Government Spending	Gross Domestic Product
1960–1964	5.7%	2.1%
1965–1969	9.7	3.8
1970–1974	18.4	7.5
1975–1979	25.3	12.2
1980	21.9	11.0
1981	25.7	13.4

through his employer. Of a total explicit fiscal pressure equal to 42.1 percent of net national income, therefore, it is not unreasonable to assume that less than one-fourth of it was visible, that is, paid by people fully aware that they were paying taxes.[8]

Explicit taxes are not, unfortunately, the end of the story. The other important component of the pecuniary cost of government is the deficit. Now, if our hypothesis is correct, we would expect that the growth of government has been accompanied (and made possible) by an increase in the deficit—the most invisible of all taxes. This is exactly what has happened.

As Table 2 clearly shows, the government deficit has been growing rapidly since 1960, both as a percentage of total public sector spending and as a percentage of national income. In 1960, for every million lire of public spending, 950,000 lire came from explicit taxes of one kind or another; in 1981, for every million lire of public spending, only 743,000 lire were paid for by explicit taxes—the rest was "financed" by the deficit. As a percentage of GDP, the deficit increased more than threefold from 1960 to 1970; and it again increased almost two and a half times from 1970 to 1981. Furthermore, all declines in the absolute size of the deficit (in 1961, 1967, 1969, 1976, and 1979) were invariably followed by sharp increases that more than offset the decline and con-

8. See *I conti degli Italiani*, vol. 16, ed. 1982, Instituto Centrale di Statistica, Roma.

firmed the rapidly growing trend. This makes one suspect that those five declines (out of twenty-two years) were the result of accounting gimmickry similar to the kind that has made New York City famous. In nominal terms the deficit was 140 times higher in 1981 than in 1960.

For the government, the deficit is the ideal tax for a variety of reasons. First of all, very few people even perceive it as a tax. Most people are under the delusion that deficit-financed public spending, like manna from heaven, means a benefit no one has to pay for, the proverbial free lunch. Second, no one can predict on an a priori basis who is going to bear the burden of the increased deficit. The final outcome depends on a variety of circumstances, including the way the deficit is financed, so that it is impossible to know ahead of time who is going to be hurt. And it is equally difficult to know a posteriori whether the deficit tax was paid in the form of inflation or in the form of the destruction of jobs produced by the crowding out of private productive investment. Finally, the cost of the deficit-financed increase in government spending is spread out among a large number of unaware taxpayers. Thus, it is absolutely impossible for them to trace the unpleasant consequences of inflation and slow growth to the deficit and see it as a tax.

It is obvious, however, that the growth of the government deficit cannot continue endlessly. It can very well be argued that a country whose deficit amounts to more than 15 percent of national income—as, according to provisional figures, Italy's did in 1982—has reached the upper limit.

The invisibility of taxes, of which the growth of the unlegislated deficit "tax" is the most conspicuous example, goes a long way in explaining how a country of ingenious tax evaders can end up sacrificing more than half of its income to the greed of politicians and bureaucrats. It is not, however, the whole story. After all, the growth in the cost of government has continued for a long time. People have had ample time to realize what the government was doing to them. Why haven't they rebelled?

Other factors, in addition to invisible taxes, have contributed to the Italian taxpayer's acceptance of an increased degree of statist exploitation. Paradoxically, one reason has been tax evasion. People who are lucky enough to be able to pay less for their government than they are required to do by tax laws are usually aware of it. They derive no little satisfaction from having succeeded in saving some money from the public waste for the benefit of their families and themselves. Such satisfaction might, in some cases, obscure the obvious truth that despite their success in evading, they are still paying more than before. In other words, they are aware of what they are *not* paying, but because of the invisibility of taxes, they are not aware of what they *are* in fact paying. Convinced as they are that they can personally "get away with it," they are often supporters of government growth—and of drastic punishment for tax evasion. It is also for this reason that my socialist friends, who during the course of the year vociferously support any and every increase in government spending, complain bitterly about taxation when the time comes to pay their income tax. They do not see the connection between spending and taxes, or they believe that the others should bear the cost of their favored statist policies. Therefore, when the day of reckoning comes, they condemn tax evasion even though they are far from innocent.

Delusions and Illusions

A less extravagant factor that might explain the absence of taxpayers' resistance to statist exploitation might be provided by some kind of "money illusion." Since nominal per capita income has increased year after year since 1960, people might have been deluded into believing that they were better off than before. Indeed, even if one takes the cost of government into account by deducting nominal per capita public sector spending from nominal per capita income, the resulting per capita "disposable income"—the amount of resources under private control[9]—has increased yearly since 1960, with only two exceptions. However, these two exceptions are so minor (in 1971 per capita disposable income was 0.35 percent below its 1970 level, and in 1975 it was 1.3 percent below its 1974 level) it is doubtful whether they were in fact noticed by the average Italian. In other words, even net

9. The author's term differs from the U.S. definition of disposable income, which describes private sector income less taxes but plus government transfer and interest payments.

of public spending, nominal per capita disposable income has always increased since 1960. This factor might have prevented the average Italian from asking himself how much government was costing him. However, this hypothesis holds true only if people are concerned with nominal income and disregard the erosion of their purchasing power due to inflation—that is, only if they suffer from money illusion.[10]

I have no doubt that money illusion has played a role with the majority of the people, but only for a limited period of time. After ten consecutive years of double-digit inflation, money illusion must have been eroded. Everybody should be aware that their *real* income is something different from their *nominal* income and that because of inflation one can make more money per year and still be worse off than before. A more fundamental explanation is required: "In terms of its purchasing power, Italy's GDP per head will probably be around $7,300 in 1982, almost equal to the probable $7,550 of Britain. Italy has been catching up fast. While Britain's GDP grew by an average of barely 1.6 percent in the five years to 1980, Italy's grew by an average of nearly 4 percent. That made it western Europe's fastest growing major economy, and it was achieved during the oil-shocked 1970s by the one big European country that has had to import nearly all its energy."[11]

Almost everybody agrees that economic growth is desirable. It can, however, have unpleasant implications, and not necessarily of the kind lamented by ecologists and assorted doomsayers. One such consequence of economic growth is that it hides the growth of statism from the taxpayer. While the Italian underground economy was busy making the country prosper and grow, politicians and bureaucrats were exploiting economic growth to their advantage to finance the rapid growth of public sector spending.

The average taxpayer, however, has not been aware of the increased degree of statist exploitation because, thanks to economic growth, his disposable income has increased even in real terms despite the rapid growth in public sector spending. In other words, taxpayers have had no strong incentive to become informed about their real tax burden

10. In nominal terms, effectively disposable income has increased very rapidly since 1960, despite the growth of public spending, because of inflation. Thus: 1960 = 100.0; 1970 = 239.8; 1980 = 944.4; 1981 = 1,071.8.

11. *The Economist*, Aug. 14, 1982, p. 11.

TABLE 3.

	Per Capita GDP (A)	Per Capita Public Sector Spending (B)	Per Capita Disposable Income (A–B)		Per Capita GDP (A)	Per Capita Public Sector Spending (B)	Per Capita Disposable Income (A–B)
1960	L 2,984,205	L 975,835	L 2,008,370	1971	L 5,330,688	L 2,206,905	L 3,123,783
1961	3,214,161	1,079,958	2,134,203	1972	5,495,080	2,258,478	3,236,602
1962	3,413,622	1,164,045	2,249,577	1973	5,893,014	2,439,708	3,453,306
1963	3,583,757	1,225,645	2,358,112	1974	6,025,598	2,398,188	3,627,410
1964	3,690,054	1,291,519	2,398,535	1975	5,775,637	2,720,325	3,055,312
1965	3,776,096	1,408,484	2,367,612	1976	6,161,516	2,852,782	3,308,734
1966	3,986,757	1,459,153	2,527,604	1977	6,298,315	2,922,418	3,375,897
1967	4,271,983	1,546,458	2,725,525	1978	6,528,724	3,401,465	3,127,259
1968	4,547,884	1,723,648	2,824,236	1979	6,789,206	3,292,765	3,496,441
1969	4,858,740	1,778,299	3,080,441	1980	7,017,332	3,529,718	3,487,614
1970	5,167,265	1,875,717	3,291,548	1981	6,961,160	3,626,764	3,334,396

All figures in constant 1981 prices. Source: A. Martino and E. Del Colle, *op. cit.*

because their personal real welfare was increasing. The situation is, however, changing, and it might very well be that past trends will not be allowed to continue. But look at the figures in Table 3.

Table 3 shows that real per capita GDP has increased since 1960 with only two exceptions, 1975 and 1981. Real per capita public sector spending has increased since 1960 with only two exceptions, 1974 and 1979.

During these twenty-two years, real per capita GDP increased substantially. In 1981 it was two and a third times greater than in 1960 (1960 = 100, 1981 = 233). Real per capita public sector spending, however, increased much faster. In 1981 it was almost four times greater than in 1960 (1960 = 100, 1981 = 371). The two declines in real per capita public sector spending have been small (−1.7 percent and −3.1 percent, respectively) and have been followed immediately by a vigorous resumption of the upward trend. As in the case of the deficit, it might well be that the two exceptions (in twenty-two years) to the rule that government spending—in real per capita terms—can only increase were more apparent than real, possibly due to accounting gimmickry. Be that as it may, what needs to be stressed is that even though real per capita income has been growing rapidly, per capita public sector spending has been growing much more rapidly.

The more important set of figures for our purposes, however, is that related to real per capita income net of public spending, what we have called real per capita disposable income. This figure measures the real value of the average Italian's income over which he has command. From 1960 to 1981 there have been six exceptions to the general rule of yearly growth in these figures—1965, 1971, 1975, 1978, 1980, and 1981. Over the whole period real per capita disposable income has increased 66 percent (1960 = 100, 1981 = 166). It would, however, be misleading to consider the declines as isolated exceptions to the general upward trend. To begin with, the first two declines were small (−1.3 percent and −5.1 percent, respectively), and they have been followed by a continuation of the rapid growth in personal welfare. The last four declines, instead, have been concentrated in the last seven years, and if taken together, they have been substantial. In particular, real per capita disposable income in 1981 was only marginally above its 1970 level (1.3 percent higher). In twelve years it had increased a meager 1.3 percent, compared with the 63.9 percent increase of the previous eleven years. Also, in 1981 real per capita disposable income was 8 percent below its 1974 level.

In other words, in the first two decades under consideration, the Italian economy grew vigorously. Real per capita income increased 62.8 percent from 1960 to 1969, and 31.4 percent from 1970 to 1979. Most of the increase, however, has been absorbed by an insatiable Leviathan so that the average Italian has seen the rate of growth of real disposable income go down. Although it increased 53.4 percent from 1960 to 1969 and 6.2 percent from 1970 to 1979, in recent years it has started to decline on a fairly regular basis. The reason for this is the explosive growth of public sector spending. From 1974 to 1981 real per capita income *increased* 15.5 percent while real disposable per capita income *declined* 8 percent. During the same period, real per capita public sector spending increased 51.2 percent, and the government deficit increased fivefold.

In terms of personal welfare, statism is pushing Italy back toward the levels that prevailed decades ago. It would seem highly unlikely that Italians will not notice such a pronounced phenomenon. As long as the real income under their control was growing year after year, it was understandable that they could be deceived by the invisibility of taxes and fail to notice the growth in the real cost of government. But now that the real income under their control not only fails to grow but is beginning to decline, they will have a strong incentive to become informed about the real cost of government and try to see through the invisibility of taxes. Furthermore, taxes are becoming less invisible, thanks to inflation and bracket creep. Income taxes amounted to 6.1 percent of net national income in 1970; they've increased to 14.2 percent in 1981. As a result, even labor union leaders are learning English terms and economic concepts and complain about the impact of the fiscal drag on their members.

The above figures show the prevailing conditions over the twenty-two-year period. Even though the country has grown rather satisfactorily, the rate of real per capita income growth dropped between 1970 and 1979 to 50 percent of its level in the previous decade. Government spending has grown much more rapidly in real per capita terms, so the percentage of GDP absorbed by government has been increasing. In 1981 it was 60 percent higher than in 1960. It seems obvious that such a tendency cannot continue very long when government (at all levels) already absorbs more than half of national income. Sooner or later, the tendency must change.

However, this is only part of the story. If one looks at the factors that have made government growth possible, one must conclude that not only is much more growth doubtful, but it is also unlikely to remain at its present levels. The first factor that allowed government to grow was the invisibility of taxes. This largely meant an increase in deficit-financed government spending; the percentage of government spending not financed by explicit taxes was more than five times higher in 1981 than in 1960. However, it is unlikely that the Italian government will be able to finance a deficit equal to 15 percent of GDP without disastrous economic consequences. In the past it was possible to bear extravagant government deficits without excessive damage because the savings rate was relatively high. At the beginning of the 1960s, Italians were saving roughly one-fifth of their income, thus allowing the government to borrow extensively from the market. The consequence was a somewhat slower rate of growth and some inflation to the extent that the government deficit resulted in an increase in the rate of growth of the quantity of money. On the other hand, while today the government deficit has exploded (in nominal terms, in real terms, and as a percentage of GDP), the savings rate has dropped sharply; the propensity to save has gone from 20.1 percent in 1961 to 9.7 percent in 1981. It is no longer possible, therefore, to finance the deficit in a noninflationary, nonrecessionary way. For the deficit to remain at its present level, the government has to crowd out private investment completely, or monetize the debt, speeding up inflation as a consequence, or—which is even more likely—do both of the above. The attempt to keep the deficit at its present level, therefore, would very likely lead to a sharp increase in stagflation—inflation-cum-stagnation, if not recession.

The decline in the savings rate must have come as a surprise to those Keynesian economists who relied on Keynes's prediction that as a rule a greater proportion of income will be saved as real income increases.[12] On the contrary, the increase in real per capita income has been accompanied by a decline in the proportion of income saved, so the increase in the government deficit, far from being expansionary (as it would be in a Keynesian world), is proving to be recessionary.

The decline in the savings rate cannot, as we have seen, be attributed to a decline in real per capita GDP. What then has caused it? Lack of opportunities open to small savers is not an explanation, for it has been going on for a long time. It might very well be that the decline in the savings rate has been produced by the decline in real disposable per capita income: Italians are becoming more aware of it. An interesting corollary of this hypothesis is that Italians do not consider government services part of their income, at least not to the extent of their cost. Given the proverbial inefficiency of their government, this is not surprising.

The first option open to the government is to leave the deficit at its present level and plunge the country into a serious inflation-cum-recession. The second alternative would be to try to reduce the deficit,

12. J. M. Keynes, *General Theory* (1936), New York, Harcourt, Brace & World, 1964, p. 97.

but this would involve a decrease in spending, or an increase in taxes, or both. If the government tries to maintain the present level of statist exploitation and refuses to cut spending, it will have to increase explicit taxes. Italians will, therefore, become more aware of the cost of government. Whether there is an increase in "slumpflation" (if the government leaves the deficit as it is) or an increase in explicit taxes (aimed at reducing the deficit), Italians will learn a healthy lesson on the costs of statism. The only way out of the dilemma would be a decline in spending. But, even assuming that such an option is open to governments with a very limited life expectancy, it is certainly not easy.

It can be argued that since the costs of a reduction in government spending come first, whereas the benefits come later, no rational government with a life expectancy of less than a year will engage in such a policy. The alternatives, however, are probably worse. No government wants to preside over a very serious economic crisis or enact a sharp increase in explicit taxes. No matter what policy is chosen, the damaging consequences of government growth can no longer be kept hidden from the public.

Things are made far worse for the government by the decline in real disposable per capita income because Italians now have an incentive to become better informed about the cost of government, and if they discover that more than half of their income goes to the tax man, it is doubtful they will approve. Furthermore, the decline in real per capita disposable income will also have a negative impact on the savings rate, which in turn will add to the problem. It would seem as if the long process of statist exploitation has finally come to an end: Statism is bankrupt.

It is hard to tell what form a tax rebellion might take in Italy: increased tax evasion, a protest vote, or what? But, as George III and Louis XVI would confirm, one can never tell how tax revolts will end.

Budget Deficits and Constitutional Constraints

Introduction

Budget deficits were regarded as the ultimate propellant of economic growth when, under the influence of the "Keynesian revolution," most economists believed that high employment and stability could be achieved through appropriate manipulations of the budget. In recent times, however, we have witnessed a reversal in the profession's conventional wisdom. Deficits are now being blamed for a lot of different economic problems: inflation, unemployment, slow growth, the stock market crash, high interest rates, balance of payments difficulties, instability of exchange rates, and a variety of other troubles.

While some of these criticisms are dubious or definitely unfounded, it is increasingly recognized that, whereas deficit-financed increases in public spending change the *structure* of total spending, by transferring funds from the private to the public sector, their impact on the *level* of aggregate demand may very well be negligible in most cases.

Be that as it may, what follows will be devoted to examining the following three theses:

1. Budget deficits make government growth easier. The possibility of running a deficit allows politicians to hide the cost of government from those who bear it.

2. Paradoxically, under different circumstances, the preoccupation with the size of the deficit may slow down the growth of spending. According to Professor Milton Friedman (1987, 1988), this is the case in the United States today. I maintain, however, that in the long run the

Originally published in *Cato Journal* 8, no. 3, winter 1989, pp. 695–711, and reprinted with permission.

"Friedman effect" is less important in slowing down spending growth than financial illusion is in accelerating it.

3. While constitutional constraints may ultimately prove ineffective, they are probably all we can hope for to (temporarily?) halt or slow down the increase in public-sector spending.

In analyzing these issues, I shall mostly draw on my country's experience. I am convinced, however, that the conclusions are not idiosyncratic in that they are broadly applicable to a variety of other countries. Italy seems to be the ideal candidate for the study of government deficits both because it ranks as number one among Western advanced democracies in terms of the deficit to GDP ratio, and because it has an admirable fiscal constitution that was intended to make the formation of budget deficits almost impossible.

The Problem

The single most significant feature of Italy's economy in the past 25 years is the growth of government spending, taxation, and budget deficits. In fact, Italy's problem is an extreme variation of a more general theme: "Public spending in the 24 industrial countries belonging to the Organization for Economic Co-operation and Development (OECD) is now about 43 percent of their gross domestic products. In 1960 . . . the ratio was only 29 percent." And, "in all industrial countries, taxes have risen as a proportion of GDP since 1965" (*The Economist,* June 1, 1985).

SPENDING

From 1960 to 1987 public-sector spending has increased 68 times in nominal terms, 489 percent in real terms (taking inflation into account), and it has gone from 32.7 percent of GDP to 52.2 percent. The process tends to accelerate: From 1980 to 1987 public-sector spending has increased 204 percent in nominal terms or 42.3 percent in real terms, and it has gone from 43.2 percent of GDP to 52.2 percent (see Table 1).

From 1980 to 1987 the increase in public-sector spending has absorbed 58.2 percent of the increase in GDP: For every million lire of additional product, 582,000 lire have gone to the government and

TABLE 1. *Public-Sector Spending in Italy*

	Billions of Lire		
	Current Prices	1987 Prices	Percent of GDP
1960	7,588	87,181	32.7
1965	14,591	132,032	37.3
1970	22,816	177,948	36.3
1975	57,816	263,439	46.1
1980	168,811	360,749	43.2
1985	431,183	477,429	52.9
1987	513,351	513,351	52.2

Source: Based on data from Banca d'Italia, 1988.

418,000 lire have been left to the private sector. It is worth noting that this spectacular increase has taken place at a time when all governments were giving the control of spending top priority in their programs. The results of their efforts have been disappointing, to say the least. Had spending remained constant in nominal terms from 1980 to 1987, in 1987 the budget would have shown a *surplus* of 238,084 billion lire; had it remained constant in real terms, the budget would still have had a *surplus* of 46,145 billion lire. Finally, had spending grown in proportion to GDP, net borrowing in 1987 would have amounted to 17,979 lire instead of 106,456 billion lire.

TAXATION

Contrary to popular mythology, Italy is a heavily taxed country. Italians may be ingenious tax evaders, but they end up paying more explicit taxes than taxpayers of other Western countries.

International comparisons are always difficult to make. However, this should not discourage us from making them. The figures in Table 2 should not be taken at face value; even with all caveats, however, they show how much more serious the problem of excessive taxation is in Italy compared with the other six members of the so-called Group of Seven (G7) and the average for OECD countries.

It is also interesting to note that the only country in which tax reve-

TABLE 2. *Tax Revenue as a Percentage of GDP, 1982–84 Average*

Country	Average Tax Rate (%)
France	44.61
Italy	40.72
United Kingdom	38.56
Germany	37.57
Canada	33.61
United States	29.52
Japan	27.08
"G7" Average	35.95
OECD	36.87

Source: Peleggi (1987, p. 14).

nue as a percentage of GDP exceeds Italy's—France—is in the process of revising its GDP figures upward, so that Italy may soon achieve the dubious honor of being the most heavily taxed country in the G7.

In addition to international comparisons, which are inevitably debatable, the severity of taxation in Italy is shown by the rapid growth of taxes over time. The figures in Table 3 show the rapid growth of public sector revenue since 1975. From 1975 to 1987 total revenue has increased more than ninefold in nominal terms or over 110 percent in real terms, and it has gone from 33.6 percent to 41.4 percent of GDP. The increase has been particularly exorbitant in income tax revenue: From 1975 to 1987, it increased almost 16 times in nominal terms or three and a half times in real terms, and the percentage of public spending it finances has gone from 14.6 percent to 26.7 percent. Finally, as for marginal rates, Italian taxpayers start facing a 26 percent marginal rate at an annual income of US$8,500.

MARGINAL PROPENSITY FOR PUBLIC-SECTOR SPENDING

The figures on public spending and revenue allow us to analyze the relationship between the two. Specifically, how public spending reacts to increases in revenue deserves investigation. The reason is obvious: From an ex post perspective, it is an arithmetic truism that if revenue increases while spending remains constant, the deficit is re-

TABLE 3. *Total Public-Sector Revenue in Italy*

	Billions of Lire		Percent
	Current Prices	1987 Prices	of GDP
1975	42,159	192,098	33.63
1976	55,778	217,514	35.61
1977	70,596	235,357	37.14
1978	85,454	253,985	38.45
1979	102,567	265,680	37.96
1980	134,315	287,031	34.40
1981	168,007	300,444	35.90
1982	209,308	321,330	38.40
1983	257,463	344,952	40.64
1984	288,793	349,067	39.68
1985	326,757	361,803	40.06
1986	369,031	386,010	40.90
1987	406,895	406,895	41.41

Source: Based on data from Banca d'Italia, 1988.

duced. What is true ex post need not be true ex ante: An increase in revenue compared to last year's need not reduce the deficit if in the meantime spending also increases. The net effect of an increase in revenue on the size of the deficit obviously depends on the size of the spending increase compared to the magnitude of the increase in revenue.

Borrowing a somewhat different Keynesian concept, what matters is the "marginal propensity for public-sector spending," the ratio of the increase in total government spending to the increase in tax revenue. This propensity is shown in Table 4 for the period 1975–87. The figures show that the marginal propensity for public-sector spending has been greater than one in every year except 1976 and 1986, averaging 1.3123 for the entire period: A 1,000,000 lire increase in revenue has on average resulted in a 1,312,300 lire increase in spending, and a consequent 312,300 lire increase in net borrowing. It further means that, even though revenue has increased every year, this has not resulted in a reduction of the deficit, because, with the exception of 1976

TABLE 4. *Italy's Marginal Propensity for Public-Sector Spending*

	dG	dT	dG/dT
1975	12,078	5,740	2.10
1976	13,195	13,619	0.97
1977	16,197	14,818	1.09
1978	21,843	14,858	1.47
1979	20,897	17,113	1.22
1980	38,863	31,748	1.22
1981	53,237	33,692	1.58
1982	51,021	41,301	1.24
1983	54,540	48,155	1.13
1984	46,628	31,330	1.49
1985	56,946	37,964	1.50
1986	41,669	42,274	0.98
1987	40,499	37,864	1.07

Note: dG = increase in public-sector spending, billions of lire; dT = increase in public-sector revenue, billions of lire; dG/dT = "government's marginal propensity to spend."
Source: Based on data from Banca d'Italia, 1988.

and 1986, the increase in revenue has always stimulated an even larger increase in spending.

As for the two exceptions, in those two years Italy's marginal propensity for public-sector spending was 0.97 and 0.98, respectively. This means that in 1976 and 1986 the increase in revenue has in fact resulted in a reduction in the deficit. However, a deficit reduction of 20 to 30 thousand lire has cost the Italian taxpayer one million lire. In the light of the evidence, increasing public revenue through higher taxation does not seem a very effective way to cut the deficit.

THE DEFICIT

The most spectacular increase has been that of the deficit. From 1961 to 1987 the deficit (in the IMF definition) has increased 319 times in nominal terms or over 28 times in real terms, and it has gone from 1.4 percent of GDP in 1961 to 11.6 percent in 1987 (see Table 5).

To get an idea of the size of Italy's deficit, we can compare it to the

TABLE 5. *Italian Government Deficit*

	Billions of Lire			Percent of Total
	Current Prices	1987 Prices	GDP	Public-Sector Spending
1951	388	5,315	3.74	n.a.
1956	330	4,030	2.02	n.a.
1961	357	4,015	1.38	4.10
1966	1,831	16,169	4.32	11.81
1971	4,757	35,298	6.94	16.77
1976	14,866	57,972	9.49	20.93
1981	53,296	95,308	11.39	24.00
1986	108,497	113,489	12.02	22.94
1987	113,899	113,899	11.59	22.19

Sources: For the deficit and the CPI: International Monetary Fund, *International Financial Statistics,* various issues. For GDP and public-sector spending: Banca d'Italia.

TABLE 6. *Government Deficit as a Percentage of GDP, 1987*

Country	Deficit as Percentage of GDP
Italy	12.6
Canada	4.9
France	2.7
United Kingdom	2.7
United States	2.4
Germany	1.5
Japan	0.9

Source: Roberts (1987, p. 5).

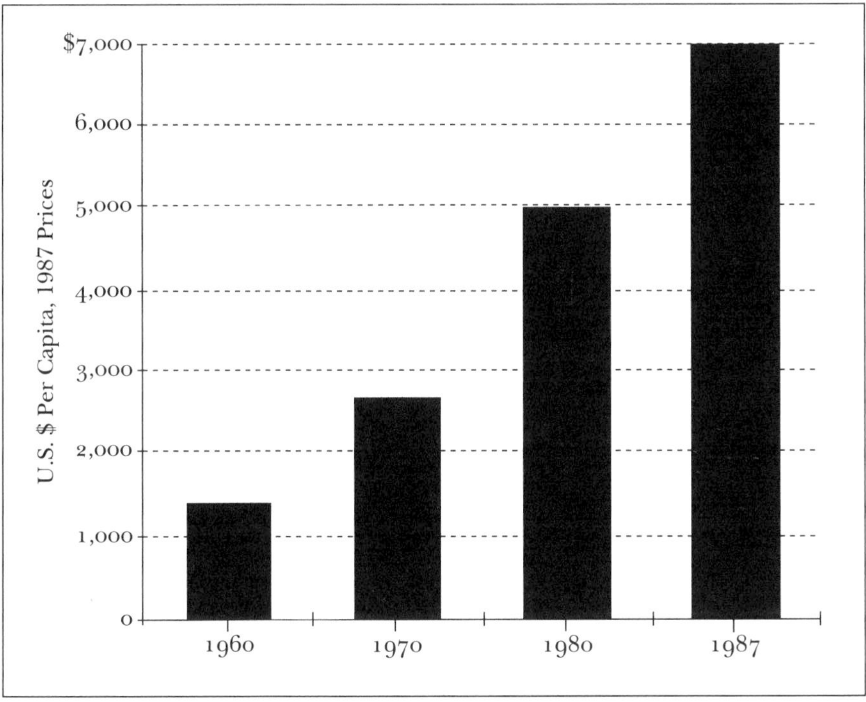

FIGURE 1. *Italy: Real Per Capita Cost of Government, 1960–87*
Source: Based on IMF and BI data.

U.S. deficit. In 1985 the U.S. deficit (in the IMF definition) reached a staggering $212.11 billion. Had the federal government run a deficit equal, in proportion to the country's GDP, to that of the Italian government, it would have reached $597.5 billion. This means that, in relative terms, the Italian deficit in 1985 was almost three times larger than the U.S. federal budget deficit. And this is an understatement because in America the total public-sector deficit is smaller than that of the federal government (as some state and local governments run budget surpluses).

According to the data in Table 6, the magnitude of Italy's public-sector deficit is substantially higher than that of any other country in the G7. Although the table refers to 1987, updating the table does not change Italy's position as the leading deficit nation in the G7.

The relationship between the deficit and government spending is

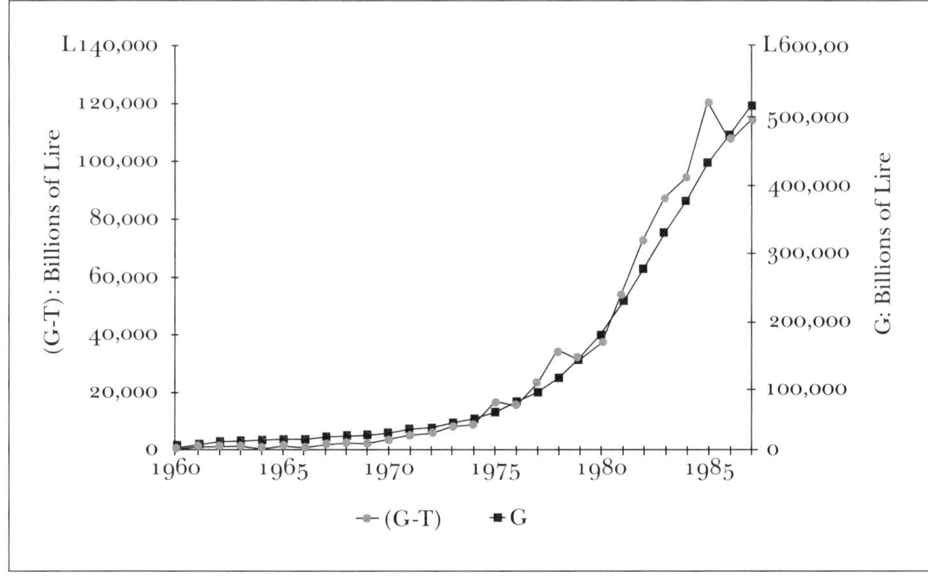

FIGURE 2. *Italy: Budget Deficit and Total Spending, 1960–87*
Source: Based on IMF and BI data.

illustrated in Figures 1 through 4. In real per capita terms, the cost of government in Italy has increased from US$1,410 in 1960 to US$6,986 in 1987 (Figure 1). The time pattern of the deficit has been remarkably similar to that of total spending both in absolute terms (Figure 2) and as a percentage of GDP (Figure 3). Finally, the deficit as a percentage of total spending has fluctuated along a rising trend (Figure 4).

PUBLIC DEBT

Not surprisingly, the need to finance growing annual deficits has resulted in the rapid increase of total public debt outstanding.

The figures in Table 7 illustrate the growth of public debt. As in the case of the deficit (see Table 5), total debt was reduced as a percentage of GDP until the mid-1960s. From then on it started to grow rapidly: In 1987 it was 68 times larger than in 1965 in nominal terms, and over 7 times in real terms. During the same period, public debt rose from 34.2 percent to 92.4 percent of GDP. According to a recent government paper, the correct ratio for 1987 is 97.2 percent, and it is supposed to rise to 120.7 percent by 1992. Per capita public debt in

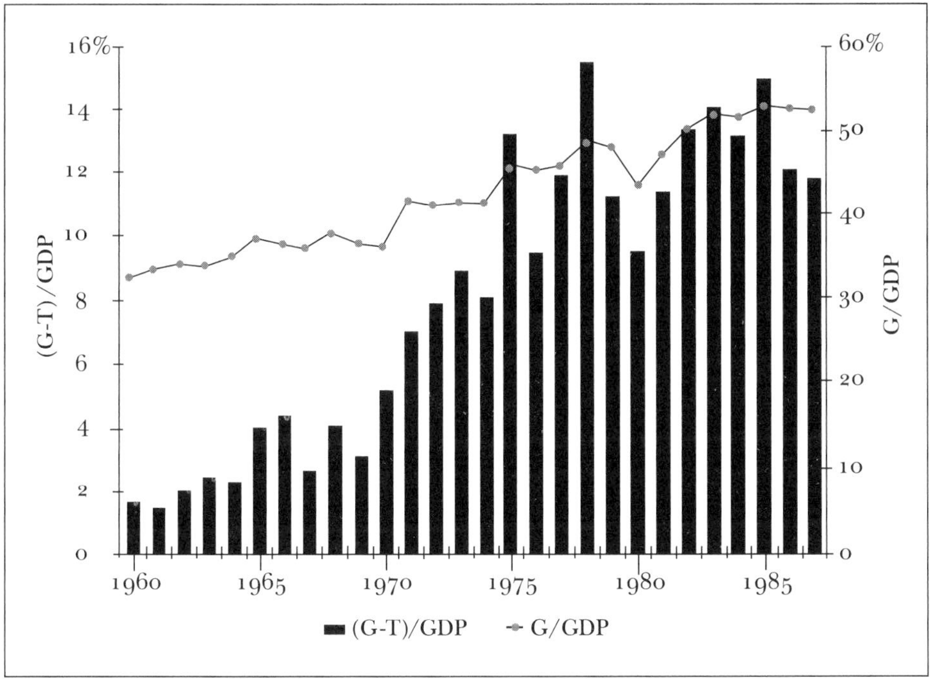

FIGURE 3. *Italy: Government Deficit and Spending as a Percentage of GDP*
Source: Based on IMF and BI data.

real terms (1987 prices) has risen from US$1,954 in 1966 to US$12,798 in 1987 (see Figure 5).

The deficit has also been a source of difficulties (and a scapegoat) for the monetary authorities, who are always prepared to blame the rapid rate of monetary growth on the size of the budget deficit. While in general monetary growth has been closely related to the increase in the deficit, the sharp reduction in the monetary growth rate in the past 8 to 9 years has been achieved despite the continued growth of the deficit. This fact seems to suggest that monetary policy can be effectively kept under control even in the face of large and growing deficits.

An Explanation

Gordon Tullock (1983) has maintained that we do not have a general theory of government growth, that all explanations of the rapid

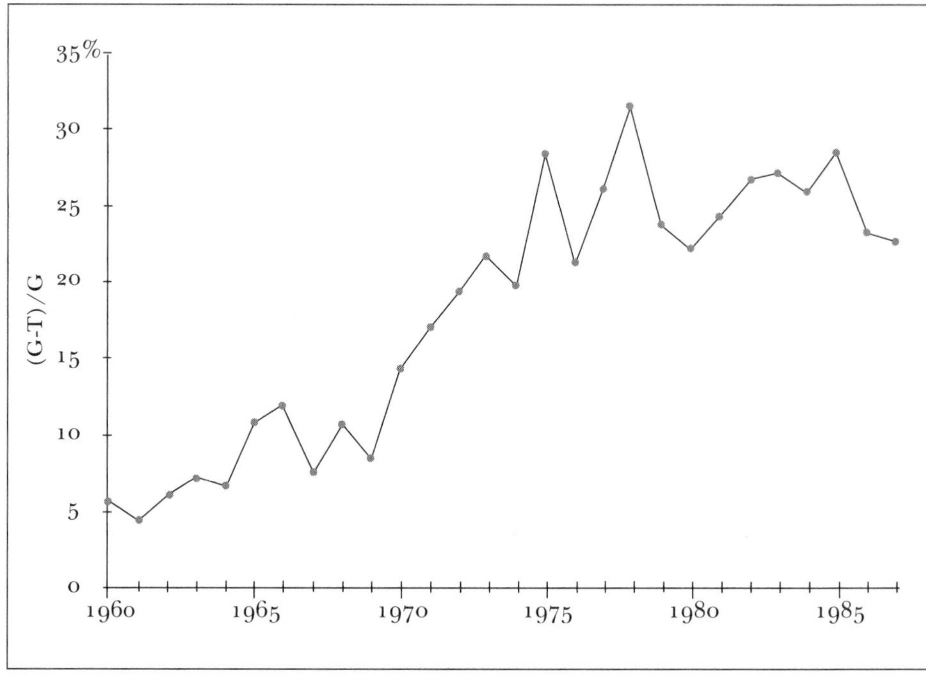

FIGURE 4. *Italy: Budget Deficit as a Percentage of Total Spending*
Source: Based on IMF and BI data.

increase in taxation and spending in the postwar era are contradicted by the evidence: What is true for a given country at one time is not true for another country or for another period of time. In a sense, this is true by definition: The circumstances and the prevailing intellectual climate vary from country to country and over time. It is also true that a general theory should apply equally well to past trends as to contemporary developments. There is no doubt that we do not have any satisfactory explanation for such a wide range of events. But in another sense we do have a theory of government growth that explains fairly closely the prevailing tendencies in Western democracies during the last 25 to 30 years. It is not new, but it is worth mentioning.[1]

The starting point of such an explanation is the existence of three asymmetries in the perception of costs and benefits of public spend-

1. The following explanation draws on my 1986 paper.

TABLE 7. *Italy's Public Debt*

	Billions of Lire			Billions of
	Current Prices	1987 Prices	Percent of GDP	U.S. Dollars 1987 Prices
1950	4,709	70,867	50.9	54.65
1955	7,300	91,765	48.6	70.76
1960	9,286	106,689	40.0	82.27
1965	13,378	121,139	34.2	93.41
1970	23,189	180,857	36.9	139.46
1975	67,087	305,682	53.5	235.72
1980	206,212	440,675	52.8	339.82
1985	654,261	724,433	81.2	558.63
1987	907,842	907,842	92.4	700.06

Sources: IMF, *International Financial Statistics, Yearbook 1987;* the 1987 figure is from Banca d'Italia, 1988.

ing. First, the democratic political process tends to favor decisions that result in benefits for a small group of beneficiaries where the cost is spread over a large number of taxpayers (or consumers). For example, a decision to confer a benefit of, let us say, $230 million to 1,000 beneficiaries (say, a subsidy to the domestic exporters of a given good) gives each one of them a $230,000 incentive to make sure the proposal is approved. On the other hand, if the cost of the bill is spread evenly over the entire U.S. population, it would cost each and every American citizen only $1. "In these circumstances the outcome is not in doubt: the spoliators will win hands down" (Pareto, 1896).[2]

The existence of such an asymmetry is confirmed by the realization that spending on public goods has not been the main factor behind the growth of total spending. Since public goods benefit the whole of society, they often lack a constituency lobbying for them, so that the growth of public spending is usually slower. There is further evidence of the existence of this asymmetry in the near-impossibility of reducing government spending, since the costs of the reduction would fall on

2. Quoted in Stigler and Friedland (1980).

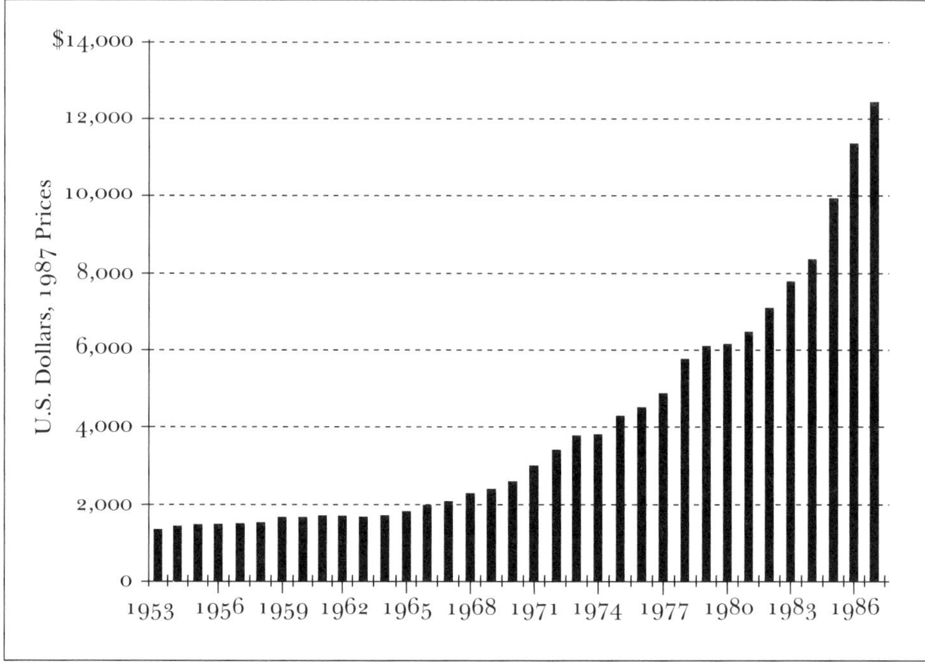

FIGURE 5. *Italy: Real Per Capita Public Debt, 1987 Prices*
Source: Based on IMF and BI data.

a small number of former beneficiaries, and the benefits would go to society as a whole.[3] Finally, it is obvious that the success of the first group of beneficiaries will provide an incentive for the formation of other groups, so that the asymmetry results in a process of government growth that continues over time.

The second asymmetry occurs because the political process tends to favor decisions based on visible benefits and invisible costs. The visibility of benefits guarantees the support for the proposal by the potential beneficiaries, while the invisibility of costs neutralizes the opposition of the taxpayer-voters who will bear them. In the previous

3. Compare Milton and Rose Friedman (1984, p. 42): "[There] is an asymmetry between the resistance to increasing the size of government and to decreasing it, between introducing new programs and dismantling them. An increase in the size of government is far less likely to run into concentrated and effective resistance—and, indeed, sabotage—than a decrease in the size of government."

example, while each one of the producers of the good has an incentive of $230,000 to be exactly informed about the effects of the subsidy for him, the value of the information for the individual taxpayer is only $1. In all likelihood, therefore, while the beneficiaries will know exactly how much they stand to gain from the proposal, those who bear its cost will (rationally) be ignorant of its impact on them.

Finally, the political process favors decisions that result in an immediate (even if small) gain whose cost (even if large) is paid in the distant future. This last asymmetry is particularly acute in Italy because, given the high instability of the executive (the average "life expectancy at birth" of Italian governments is less than a year), the time horizon of political decisionmakers tends to be very short. Governments generally tend to favor spending decisions that confer an immediate gain to some group in society, even if the future cost of the decision is substantial, because in all likelihood it will be borne by another government.

If this analysis is correct, we would expect government growth to be faster when public spending is financed by a device that spreads costs over large numbers of taxpayers, hides these costs from those who bear them, and produces immediate benefits at the expense of high (if not disastrous) consequences in the future. Such a device exists, and it is called a deficit. Its time pattern—in Italy, at least—confirms the preceding analysis beyond any doubt.

I must stress at this point that the validity of this analysis does not depend on the existence of an *uninterrupted* growth of the deficit. What happens is that, when the deficit reaches a certain amount, the need to reduce it—stressed with great vigor by fiscal conservatives of all political parties—results in higher taxation. It is quite possible, therefore, that the asymmetries will produce increases in the deficit followed by increases in explicit taxation, and a reduction in the deficit, and so on. (This, however, has not been the case in Italy, where the deficit has grown with almost no interruption: See Table 5).

The "Friedman Effect"

Milton Friedman (1987, 1988) has argued that the existence of a budget deficit may prevent government from increasing spending: "Most commentators bemoan the large budget deficit. I welcome it.

The deficit is the only thing that is forcing us to think seriously about how to control federal spending. The economic effect of the deficit is unquestionably bad, but the political effect of the deficit is good." And, more recently, "the deficit has been the only effective restraint on congressional spending."

Friedman was obviously referring to the situation in the United States in 1987. Given President Reagan's commitment not to increase taxation under any circumstance, the deficit is an effective deterrent to spending increases. However, if the U.S. president was not as concerned with excessive taxation as Mr. Reagan, the deficit, rather than restraining spending, would have provided a wonderful excuse for increasing taxation. Let's hope that the Bush administration will spare us conclusive evidence in favor of this assumption.

In other words, while I believe that the "Friedman effect" has been effective in the United States, I am convinced that it is not a lasting phenomenon. Sooner or later, perhaps after a change in government, the possibility of running a deficit will prove to be a force favoring the growth of spending rather than its containment.

This is so because, in the long run, the possibility of running a deficit allows the three asymmetries to operate unconstrained. In the words of James Buchanan (1983, pp. 17–18):

> Beneficiary groups, recipients of direct transfers or of governmentally financed programs, tend to be concentrated, organized, and capable of exerting influence over elected politicians. By contrast, taxpayer groups, those who pay taxes, tend to be widely dispersed and, indeed, tend to include almost everyone due to the fact that taxes are general rather than specific. As a result of the asymmetry, it becomes easier to get political decision makers to expand budgets than to contract them.

In other words, the asymmetries work unconstrained when budget deficits are possible, but they do not necessarily result in the uninterrupted growth of the deficit, because governments alternate between fiscal prudence and folly. What the asymmetries guarantee is that the reduction of the deficit will always take place at a higher level of taxation and spending rather than at a lower level. But it is still the *possibility* of running a budget deficit that makes it possible for spending to keep growing uninterruptedly.

Italy, the Constitution, and Keynes

An objection arises at this point. The structure of incentives affecting the behavior of voters, politicians, and taxpayers so as to promote the growth of government can be assumed to have existed ever since mass democracy was born. Why, then, did government deficits not start to increase in Italy until the early 1960s?

The extraordinary paradox of the Italian case is that Italy has a fiscal constitution that was intended precisely to avoid the kind of financial disorder we now experience, by forcing spending decisions to conform to a standard of financial responsibility. Unfortunately, the constitutional constraint did not succeed.

The cornerstone of Italy's fiscal constitution is the last paragraph of Article 81, which reads: "Every other law which involves new or greater expenditures must indicate the means to meet them." The intent of the authors of this article is made explicit in the published proceedings of the discussion that preceded its approval. Their aim was that of ensuring a responsible approach to spending decisions and a tendency toward a balanced budget. Since the previous paragraph of Article 81 forbids the introduction of new taxes and expenses in the budget law, the combination of the two principles should have resulted in a "rigorous constraint" on the formation of increases in the deficit. The meaning of the rule embodied in the last paragraph of Article 81 is unequivocal to anyone who reads the proceedings of the constitutional subcommittee; its implications are even clearer to economists familiar with the work of Knut Wicksell, who, as early as 1896, had recognized the need to couple spending proposals with specific plans for covering their costs as a way to achieve financial responsibility.

The constitutional constraint worked rather well until 1961. As shown in Table 5, from 1951 to 1961 the government deficit in Italy declined 8 percent in nominal terms or 24.5 percent in real terms, and as a percentage of GDP, it went from 3.74 in 1951 to 1.38 in 1961—a 63 percent decrease. The budget was not balanced, but the *tendency* was there: As a percentage of GDP, the deficit was cut substantially in the 1950s. Then the trend changed: From 1961 until today, the growth of the deficit is one of the few certainties of economic life. Why?

In my opinion, the answer is threefold. First, there is the impact of the "Keynesian revolution." As long as the "balanced-budget norm" prevailed, the formation of larger budget deficits was discouraged, and the constitutional constraint was enforced. Until 1961, there have been 12 cases of laws sent back to Parliament by the president of the Republic, who refused to sign them because they violated Article 81 of the constitution. After the political change of the early 1960s—the "opening to the left" (the formation of a government coalition including the Socialists)—and the advent of the "Keynesian revolution," the "balanced-budget norm" was replaced by the Keynesian mythology of deficit spending. The various presidents of the Republic did not avail themselves of their veto power, and the constitutional principle was no longer enforced. The working of the three asymmetries became unconstrained, and the budget deficit exploded.

The rapid growth of government can therefore be attributed to the combined effect of the system of political incentives typical of the democratic political process on the one hand, and the consequences of the "Keynesian revolution" on the other. The "decoupling" of decisions on spending and taxing, made possible by the abandonment of the "balanced-budget norm," has allowed taxation and spending to grow rapidly in response to the political pressures resulting from the three asymmetries mentioned above.

The evidence, in Italy at least, confirms the validity of Buchanan and Wagner's conclusion (1978, p. 27):

> The mounting historical evidence of the ill effects of Keynes's ideas cannot continue to be ignored. Keynesian economics has turned the politicians loose; it has destroyed the effective constraint on politicians' ordinary appetites to spend and spend without the apparent necessity to tax.
>
> Sober assessment suggests that, politically, Keynesianism represents a substantial disease that over the long run can prove fatal for the survival of democracy.

In addition to the deleterious consequences of Keynesianism, two more factors contributed to the abandonment of the constitutional rule. First is the general nature of the Italian constitution: an ambiguous, quixotic, and often unenforceable document. Second, the last paragraph of Article 81 could have been (and should have been) expressed in a more specific way, so that it could be either enforced or *openly* violated. As it happens, it has been possible to bypass it by "interpreting" it in a more flexible manner. For example, when a bill introduces an expenditure destined to continue in the future, politicians and "constitutional experts" maintain that the principle is respected if the law "indicates the means" to finance the expense for the first year, even if it ignores the necessity to raise the funds for the following years.

Conclusions

These last two factors could and should have been avoided: There is no reason why the Italian constitution should make delightful reading for anyone opposed to written constitutions. Also, the constitutional principle could have been phrased in a more explicit and binding way. It is impossible to tell a priori, however, if a better-worded rule within the framework of a meaningful constitution would have stood the test of the change in intellectual climate brought about by Keynesianism. But, on the other hand, we should probably avoid the extreme pessimism of Anthony de Jasay, who, in his admirable book (de Jasay 1985), likens constitutional rules to chastity belts: "With its key always within reach, a chastity belt will at best occasion delay before nature takes its course" (p. 187).

Even if the introduction of a constitutional rule is only a temporary remedy, in that, sooner or later, politicians will try to bypass it, it is the only chance a democracy has to contain the displacement of individual liberty by the growing leviathan. It is not accidental that, in the Western world, countries with a federal constitution or a constitutional rule (such as Switzerland, Finland, or the United States) are those that have the best record in the containment of government growth.

The Italian experience should teach other countries that a fiscal constitution is necessary. Indeed, if one agrees that the "Italian disease" is only a more acute form of the same illness that affects all Western societies, the need for a set of constraints on irresponsible spending decisions is an urgent one. It is the most a country can do to avoid falling into the kind of financial disarray that is currently plaguing Italy.

But the Italian experience also teaches another, less optimistic, lesson: Although monetary and fiscal constitutions are necessary, they are far from being a sufficient guarantee against excessive and irresponsible government. There is no such a thing as a foolproof legal device that can protect us forever. There is no substitute for our constant alertness, for our awareness of the threat posed to our freedom by an increasingly intrusive leviathan.

REFERENCES

Buchanan, James M. "I limiti alla fiscalità." In *La Costituzione Fiscale e Monetaria: Vincoli alla Finanza Inflazionistica.* Rome: CREA, 1983.

———. "Tax Reform as Political Choice." *Economic Perspectives* 1 (summer 1987): 29–35.

Buchanan, James M., and Richard E. Wagner. *The Consequences of Mr. Keynes.* Hobart Paper 78. London: Institute of Economic Affairs, 1978.

de Jasay, Anthony. *The State.* Oxford: Basil Blackwell, 1985.

Friedman, Milton. "Economists and Economic Policy." *Economic Impact,* no. 57, 1987.

———. "Why the Twin Deficits Are a Blessing." *Wall Street Journal Europe,* December 15, 1988.

Friedman, Milton, and Rose Friedman. *Tyranny of the Status Quo.* New York: Harcourt Brace Jovanovich, 1984.

Martino, Antonio. *Constraining Inflationary Government.* Washington, D.C.: Heritage Foundation, 1982.

———. "Italian Lessons on the Welfare State." *Economic Affairs* 6, June–July 1986, 18–25.

———. *Noi e il fisco, La crescita della fiscalità arbitraria: cause, conseguenze, rimedi.* Pordenone: Edizioni Studio Tesi, 1987.

Pareto, Vilfredo. *Cours d'Economie Politique.* 1896. Reprinted in *Sociological Writings.* Translated by D. Mirfin and edited by S. E. Finer. London: 1966.

Peleggi, G. "Il prelievo tributario in Italia: un confronto internazionale." In *Lo Stato Come Incassa.* Centro Studi Confindustria, 1987.

Roberts, Paul Craig. "Deficit USA, un fantasma che turba solo l'Europa." *Il Sole-24 Ore,* November 18, 1987, p. 5.

Stigler, George, and Clare Friedland. *The Year of Economists: 1980–81.* Chicago: University of Chicago Press, 1980.

Tullock, Gordon. "Esiste una teoria generale della crescita dello statalismo?" In *La Costituzione Fiscale e Monetaria: Vincoli alla Finanza Inflazionistica.* Rome: CREA, 1983.

Part 2

Hopes Betrayed

Statism at Work: A Lesson from Italy

1. On April 15, 1851, the great Italian liberal statesman Camillo Benso, Count of Cavour, delivered a speech in the Chamber of Deputies that was destined to be remembered. Said the Count:

> . . . the course of humanity is directed toward two goals, one political and the other economic. In the political order humanity tends to modify its institutions in order to bring an ever-increasing number of its members to participate in political power. In the economic order it clearly aims at the improvement of the conditions of the lower classes. . . .
>
> Two means are offered us in order to reach this goal (improving the conditions of the lower classes). All systems conceived in modern times . . . may be reduced to two. Some have faith in the principle of Liberty, in the principle of free competition, in the free development of moral and intellectual man. They believe that with the ever-increasing realization of this principle there must follow an increased well-being for all and especially for the less affluent classes. This is the school of the economists. . . .
>
> There is another school, professing absolutely different principles. It believes that the miseries of humanity cannot be relieved and that the conditions of the working classes cannot be improved except by restricting individual action ever more and by enlarging without limit the central action of the government. This, gentlemen, is the socialist school. . . . (Its) doctrines may be summarized as maintaining that it is the right and therefore the duty of the government to intervene in the distribution and employment of capi-

Talk given at Hillsdale College, October 29, 1980.

> tal, that the government has the mission and authority to substitute its will, which it considers more enlightened, for the free will of individuals (C. Benso Conte di Cavour, "In Defense of Free Trade," speech in the Chamber of Deputies, April 15, 1851).

One hundred and thirty years have passed since Cavour thus summarized the available political alternatives, but it seems to me that the choice is still between the "principle of Liberty" and its opposite, that of "enlarging without limit the central action of the government." I like to refer to this second alternative as "statism," leaving room for the ample variety of ideologies that have adopted and still adopt such a method. From this point of view, Communism, Nazism, Fascism, Socialism, and Interventionism are all species of the same genus: Statism.

It is not new to say that statism in various degrees has been the dominant philosophy even in the Free World during the past two or three decades. If we all suffer from the same disease, it might be worth comparing our own problems with those of other countries. From this point of view, I believe that the Italian experience can be illuminating for other countries in general and for the United States in particular. We are at a more advanced stage of the same illness: You, too, will get there unless you reverse your present trends.

Statism, like unhappiness, cannot be quantified. The best approximate indicator of the degree of statism is the percentage of the flow of resources absorbed by the public sector, i.e., the ratio of public sector spending to national income. This percentage has risen in Italy from 37 percent in 1960 to 44 percent in 1970 and is expected to be somewhere between 55 percent and 60 percent for fiscal 1980. This means that the average Italian must work from January to some day in mid-July for the government, and only the remainder of the year for himself and his family.

From 1951 to 1976 public spending in Italy increased 820 percent (*The Economist,* March 31, 1979, p. 86). During the forty-five minutes of my lecture the Italian government (at all levels, central and local) will spend more than $15 million; $338,453.82 every minute. Or $9.60 for every Italian every day (using the current exchange rate).

2. Before I proceed in illustrating the effects of statism in my country, let me stress one point: The ratio of public-sector spending to na-

tional income measures is what I would call, in Marxian terminology, the degree of "statist exploitation." I have always been puzzled by the fact that Marxists complain about capitalistic exploitation, which, if I understand correctly, is measured by the ratio of profits to national income, and remain silent about statist exploitation, the percentage of our income wasted by bureaucrats and politicians. And yet the former amounts at most to a few percentage points, whereas the latter corresponds to more than half of the average Italian's income.

It is important at this point not to forget that, according to Milton Friedman, "The true cost of government to the public is not measured by explicit taxes but by government spending. If government spends $500 billion, and takes in through taxes $440 billion . . . who pays the difference? Not Santa Claus, but the U.S. citizen. . . . In effect, what you have are two kinds of taxes: the open, explicit taxes and the hidden taxes. And what's called a deficit is a hidden tax. . . . The thing we must keep our eye on is what government spends. That's the measure of the amount of resources of the nation that people cannot individually and separately decide about. It's a measure of the amount we turn over to the bureaucrats to spend on our behalf." (*Policy Review,* no. 5, summer 1978, pp. 11–12).

This being said, when statist exploitation reaches the levels of, say, Italy or Great Britain, that has very important moral implications. I entirely agree with Robert Nozick when he says: "Taxation of earnings from labor is on a par with forced labor. . . . taking the earnings of *n* hours of labor is like taking *n* hours from the person; it is like forcing the person to work *n* hours for another's purpose.

"Seizing the results of someone's labor is equivalent to seizing hours from him and directing him to carry on various activities. If people force you to do certain work, or unrewarded work, for a certain period of time, they decide what you are to do and what purposes your work is to serve apart from your decisions. This process whereby they take this decision from you makes them a *part-owner* of you; it gives them a property right in you" (*Anarchy, State, and Utopia,* pp. 169–72).

Quite independently from considerations of efficiency and progress, statism is to be criticized on moral grounds, for a high degree of statist exploitation gives bureaucrats and politicians a property right on the average citizen's time that is incompatible with the moral basis of a free society. Obviously, if one is convinced, as I am, that anarchy is impossible, every society must suffer from some degree of statist exploitation. However, awareness of this fundamental moral problem on the part of the public is essential in preventing the government from growing beyond its proper domain.

3. The increase in statism in Italy took place in the early '60s, with the so-called political opening to the left, the move to a coalition including the Italian Socialist Party. Before that, during the '50s, when Italy was governed by a coalition including the Italian Liberal Party, there was the period of the Italian "economic miracle." In a climate of monetary stability—the annual rate of inflation from 1951 to 1960 ranged between 1.5 and 2 percent—with our balance of payments always in the black, our private enterprise, free-market economy produced a decade of uninterrupted growth. Income grew at the rate of 10.5 percent per year throughout the decade. Investments were growing at an annual rate of 9.8 percent. Employment was increasing, and the productive capacity of the country rose from the state of destruction and disarray that had followed the war to an unprecedented peak.

The change toward greater statism brought about by the "center-left"—the socialist-oriented government—from the early '60s on can best be illustrated by the government deficit. In 1951, at the beginning of the Liberal years, the government deficit totaled 388 billion lire, 3.99 percent of Gross Domestic Product. In 1960, it had declined in nominal terms to 382 billion lire, 1.76 percent of GDP. Then the center-left stepped in, and by 1970 the deficit had reached 3,226 billion lire: 5.56 percent of GDP. In 1975, it totaled 16,523 billion lire: 14.35 percent of GDP, and for fiscal 1980 it is expected to exceed 40,000 billion lire: 16.26 percent of GDP.

These figures should provide enough evidence to support my claim that Italy is an economic giant, on a par with the United States. Our $49 billion government deficit is only slightly below the size of the U.S. government's!

4. Financial irresponsibility on the part of the government is only the first, immediate consequence of statism; it isn't the only one. In order to finance such a deficit, massive borrowing is inevitable. Public debt has risen from 22,665 billion lire in 1970 to 137,973 billion lire in 1978. In the words of the governor of the Bank of Italy: "the

TABLE 1

Money (M_1) 1970–1978 = 100		Consumer Price Index 1972–1980 = 100	
1970	47.3	51.1	1972
1971	56.3	56.6	1973
1972	66.0	67.4	1974
1973	82.0	78.9	1975
1974	89.7	92.1	1976
1975	101.8	109.0	1977
1976	121.0	123.4	1978
1977	149.4	146.0	1979
1978	186.0	175.1	1980*

Sources: Banca d'Italia; ISTAT.
M_1 = currency + demand deposits, end of the year figures; * = estimate.

ratio of public debt to GNP has reached 70% at the end of 1978; it was roughly 45% in 1968–70" (*Relazione Annuale,* May 31, 1979). What this means is that the need to finance government deficit through borrowing results in the massive destruction of credit and in the "crowding out" of private productive investments. The destruction of new credit by public borrowing has averaged 58.5 percent per year from 1973 to 1978 (see *Tendenze Monetarie,* no. 34, July 2, 1979). The effect of this on productivity, employment, and growth needs no comment.

The government's financial irresponsibility has made monetary folly inevitable. The annual rate of growth of the quantity of money (M_2), which reached the 25 percent mark in the second half of 1975, has remained consistently within the 20–25 percent range since then. When money grows at the annual rate of 25 percent, when the quantity of money doubles every three to three and a half years, it is little wonder that prices aren't stable. Nineteen eighty will be the eighth consecutive year of double-digit inflation in Italy: something unprecedented in the peacetime history of the country.

It is of little comfort for the monetary economist that the quantity theory of money for Italy in the 1970s works perfectly in its most simplified, mechanical form with a two-year lag (see Table 1).

TABLE 2. *Number of Working Days Lost Through Industrial Stoppages Per 1,000 Employees Per Year, 1963–1978 Average*

Luxembourg	0.0
Holland	36.2
W. Germany	47.3
Denmark	206.3
Belgium	274.8
France	284.0
United Kingdom	499.8
Ireland	924.7
Italy	1,412.9

Source: Eurostat, *Occupazione e Disoccupazione,* July 1979.

5. Statism has also greatly contributed to trade unions' irresponsibility by making collective bargaining a political process dominated by demagogic considerations. As a result of this, and of foolish legislation that has in fact strengthened the monopoly power of the major unions, strikes have become such a common feature that Italy has earned the nickname "strikeland." The label is entirely appropriate: The average number of days of strike per 1,000 workers per year from 1963 to 1978 has been five times higher in Italy than in the other EEC countries (see Table 2).

Trade union pressures have resulted in wage increases that are generally considered to be excessive (nominal wage increases have been the highest in the EEC in recent years). Even the Marxist left in Italy today acknowledges that wage increases have been excessive . . . and they put the blame on labor unions. I find this paradoxical: Why blame those who *get* an excessive wage increase rather than those who *grant* it? If I get more than I should, that serves my interest. If a businessman pays labor services more than he should, he brings ruin upon himself. So why blame the unions? The truth is that if Italy has suffered from excessive wage increases, statism is to be blamed, not the unions. What has happened is that managers of public firms have willingly surrendered public money to the unions in order to buy social peace. This explains why public firms are almost all in the red and why we have had excessive wage increases.

6. The center-left also gave impetus to another socialist policy: that of direct state intervention in the economy. The first strategy that was tried was that of nationalization. However, the nationalization of electricity in 1963 was such an obvious disaster, both in terms of the cost of the operation and for its effects on the business, that *no one* today has the courage to advocate nationalization any more. This is a big change from the early 1960s, when the leader of the Italian Socialist Party, Francesco De Martino, interviewed on television, proclaimed that the platform of his party included the nationalization of *all* economic activities, with the only exception of barber shops!

State intervention today is seen in the form of indirect control of business through the giant state holding, IRI, and through the purchase of "problem firms." IRI has at times been quoted as a successful mixture of socialism and capitalism. While few people seem to remember that such a mixture is a Fascist invention—for IRI was born then—it is very hard to see where IRI's success is. From June 1977 to June 1978 IRI has lost 722 billion lire, approximately 1.5 million lire (= $1,830) for every worker employed. Alfa Romeo, the prestigious state carmaker, produces 200,000 cars per year . . . and it loses 200 billion lire per year, i.e., it loses roughly 1 million lire (= $1,235) per car! Let me remind you that IRI is Europe's largest industrial employer, with over 500,000 employees, so its failure is not a minor accident. So far, it has accumulated debts for 30,000 billion lire, or $34 billions, i.e., over $65,000 for every worker employed!

7. Statism has produced inefficiency on a large scale and has spread it throughout the economy. One of the reasons for this is the well-known distortion of incentives that is the inevitable companion of interventionism. Government intervention in the economy *inevitably* ends up penalizing success by overtaxing "obscene profits" and subsidizing failures (successful businesses don't need any subsidy). The result of this is that what Gaetano Salvemini said of Fascism can be applied to the Italian economy: "In actual fact, it is the State, i.e. the taxpayer who has become responsible to private enterprise. In Fascist Italy the State pays for the blunders of private enterprise . . . Profit is private and individual. Loss is public and social" (*Under the Axe of Fascism,* 1936, p. 416).

Before we move on to other effects of statism, let me give another two illustrations of the efficiency of statism. The first is that of the public dairy (Centrale del latte) in Rome. It sells milk at a politically enforced price, competing with private suppliers who succeed in making a profit while the public dairy, with 1,049 workers, has lost L14,280,000,000 (= $17,630,000) in 1978, that is, $16,800 per worker in one single year!

My favorite example of state efficiency is, of course, the post office. I very much doubt that Adam Smith, had he experienced the efficiency of the Italian post office, would have written that "the post office is . . . the only mercantile project which has been successfully managed by every sort of government." The appalling performance of the Italian mail has provided the world with reasons to laugh. On October 31, 1978, the general manager of the post office happily declared on television that absenteeism had dropped from 50 percent to 24 percent, and that "if you mail your Christmas cards now, there are good chances that they'll get delivered before Christmas"!

And, of course, everyone knows of the time when the Italian post office was either burning the mail or selling it for scrap, due to the lack of storage space for the backed-up mail accumulated during the strikes. Now it has solved that problem by combining two inefficiencies into one. The undelivered mail is put on freight cars that travel around the country until the strike is over. As a result of all of this, even government agencies (including the post office) resort to private delivery services and take advantage of the Vatican postal services or the Swiss for mail going abroad.

The case of the post office is my favorite because it allows me to infuriate my communist friends by quoting Lenin: "[We need] to organize the *whole* national economy like the postal system."!

8. Statism has produced widespread waste. I'm not referring here to the misallocation of resources created by government intervention, nor to the kind of waste that's usually associated with corruption. What I now maintain is that statism is a negative-sum game, in the sense that what society receives from the government is always and inevitably *less* than what society has been coerced to give to the government. The reason is quite simple: Government intervention operates by imposing costs on some groups in society in order to hand out benefits to other groups (or taxing the whole of society in order to give to everybody).

But, since the costs of transferring these resources is positive and increasing, the value of the benefits of government intervention is inevitably lower than the costs of government. And the difference grows with the growth of government. A good example of these costs is provided by the bureaucratic costs. Take redistribution: "Between 1960 and 1974, the total level of expenditure on social welfare programs in the United States increased $120 billion, from $50 billion to $170 billion. According to the Bureau of Census there are 25 million poor people in the United States, defined as people with an income level of $4,137 or less for a given year for a family of four. If that $120 billion—not the whole budget, just the increase—had simply been given to the poor, it would have given each and every one of them an annual stipend of $4,800 a year, or $19,200 for every family of four" (Arianna Stassinopoulos, "The Inflation of Politics and the Disintegration of Culture," *Imprimis,* March 1978).

The same is true in Italy: In 1975 the total cost of social programs was 22,200 billion lire. Had that money gone directly to the poor, even supposing that 20 percent of total population should be considered "poor," it would have given some 9 million lire for every family of four, well above the national average (9 million lire are roughly 11,000 dollars).

Clearly the benefits of government intervention are much smaller than the costs, and there are good reasons to believe that this form of bureaucratic waste increases with government.

9. I hope you will forgive me if I deliberately disregard another, very sad, consequence of statism: corruption. I will limit myself to say that I very much agree with Professor George Stigler when he says that "corruption has turned regulation into gold." This is true, although to a different extent, in every country. I'm not sure that statism is a sufficient condition for corruption, but it seems to me that it's a necessary one.

One of the many paradoxes of statism is that government intervention, advocated to remedy the supposed unjustices created by capitalism and to increase social justice, ends up creating undesirable and unjustifiable inequalities that could otherwise be avoided. Instead of remedying the unjustices of capitalism, statism creates most of the undesirable inequalities that plague our societies. It does this for three reasons. First of all, as already mentioned, distribution—i.e., the determination of relative wages—in a statist society is based on the political bargaining power of the various groups. The result is that relative wages do not reflect the contribution of the various groups to the production of national income, but are entirely based on their political strength. Thus, in my country you have the paradox of a doorman at the Parliament being paid twice as much as a university professor, or a street cleaner making more than a university-educated civil servant. The second reason behind the fact that a statist society inevitably produces undesirable inequalities is regressive redistribution. When government is limited, it is entirely possible to tax the (few) rich in order to give to the (many) poor. But as the degree of government intervention increases, that is no longer possible. The government ends up taxing everybody (including the poor) in order to give to everybody (including the rich). It's as if the state taxes the poor to give to the rich. This is the kind of regressive redistribution that is most evident in the financing of higher education, for example. But the same is clearly true of public transportation, when the price of the ticket is below its cost, and of the whole range of public services that benefit everybody and are financed out of general tax revenue. The third reason behind the undesirable redistributive effects of unlimited government is that government intervention is often supported in order to guarantee equality of access to essential public services. However, since the government usually fails to provide a satisfactory level of these services, what happens is that only the rich can afford to escape the inefficiency of the government programs and get what they need from private suppliers. The typical example is public education. The level of public education in state schools is so low that an increasing number of families send their children to private schools. However, this option is open only to the relatively well off. They can afford to pay twice for their children's education—once in taxes and once in fees—something that the poor cannot do. Introduced to guarantee "equality of entry," government intervention ends up producing "inequality of exit."

10. Another highly undesirable consequence of statism is that "state help kills self help": The higher the degree of government provision of services, the lower the individual sense of responsibility in these matters becomes. I shall never forget a program on Italian television

a few years ago. The commentator was interviewing the inhabitants of a high-rise complex that housed some eighty families. All the women interviewed were complaining because their children were often getting sick due to the fact that the water reservoirs on the roof were not covered. The resulting pollution of the drinking water was allegedly the cause of their children's diseases. They all blamed the city for this. No one even thought of the possibility of the eighty families' getting together and having the water reservoirs properly covered!

Another important negative consequence of statism has been the disruption of the social fabric. This is probably the most devastating of all the effects of excessive government. The danger was clearly perceived by John Stuart Mill, when he wrote:

> . . . the public, accustomed to expect everything to be done for them by the State, or at least to do nothing for themselves without asking from the State not only leave to do it, but even how it is to be done, naturally hold the State responsible for all evil which befalls them, and when the evil exceeds their amount of patience, they rise against the government and make what is called a revolution; whereupon somebody else, with or without legitimate authority from the nation, vaults into the seat, issues his orders to the bureaucracy, and everything goes on much as it did before; the bureaucracy being unchanged, and nobody else being capable of taking their place. (*On Liberty*, p. 114)

In today's world, the disruption of the social fabric for the reasons indicated by Mill takes the form of terrorism.

Few people seem to realize that the fundamental principle behind terrorism is the idea of the omnipotence of political power, a government of unlimited power and responsibility. It is a variation of the old confusion between intentions and realizations. If the government can do all it wants to do, if realizations inevitably follow intentions, doesn't it follow that social problems are the result of bad intentions? Isn't it true that all social ills are the intended consequence of the action of evil men? And if so, shouldn't the solution be found in the elimination of the wicked? Terrorism is a logical outcome of statism.

For example, distribution, the idea that it is the government's right and duty to distribute the so-called social pie (presumably fallen from heaven), when widely accepted, leads to the inevitable generalization of envy and the disruption of the social fabric. If what I have has been given to me by the government, handed down to the subject by a benign owner, what will inevitably follow is that I shall start hating my neighbour, for I will naturally become convinced that I'm getting too little and that he is getting too much. Convinced that the sovereign is giving me a raw deal, I will then try to change the government, using any means at my disposal, for that will appear to me to be the only way to improve my situation, to increase my lot. David Hume was very well aware of this when he wrote:

> In a perfect theocracy, where a being, infinitely intelligent, governs by particular volitions, this rule (to assign the largest possession to the most extensive virtue) would certainly have a place. But were mankind to execute such a law; so great is the uncertainty of merit, both from its natural obscurity, and from the self-conceit of each individual, that no determinate rule of conduct could ever result from it; and the total dissolution of society must be the immediate consequence. (1751, as quoted by S. Brittan and P. Lilley, *The Delusion of Incomes Policy,* 1977, p. 12).

11. The list of the undesirable consequences of statism is endless, but I shall limit myself to two further considerations. The first is that statism has destroyed the state. What I mean is that, paradoxically, today we have *too much* state in terms of cost, *too little* state in terms of results. Don't misunderstand me: I'm very well aware of the fact that the only reason we are still free is because we don't get all the government we pay for. I certainly do not want any more government. What I mean is that by engaging itself in tasks it cannot and should not perform, the government has neglected its proper duties, its institutional functions. It is trying to do what it should not do, and it is not doing what it should do. When I hear that the number of private bodyguards in Milano is greater than the number of policemen, I do not rejoice. Even if it proves the superiority of the private provision of public goods, it is undoubtedly a tragic symptom of the decadence in the quality of civilized life that has been imposed upon us by statism.

I apologize to those of you who believe in anarchy. I have a great respect for your intellectual case. However, for reasons that would be too long to state now, I'm not an anarchist. I believe that there are things that should be done by the government, things that only the government can do. The enforcement of law and order, the administration of justice, foreign defense, the protection of life, liberty and property, are all things, which in my opinion, the government should do. In my country, as in other countries, the performance of the state in these areas has deteriorated steadily with the increase in statism. I believe this to be one of the worst effects of statism: the destruction of the state and its resulting incapacity to supply us the basics of civilized life.

12. All the undesirable consequences of statism that I have tried to summarize so far are the unavoidable result of a more fundamental problem, that is, that excessive government is incompatible with personal freedom, with basic human liberty, and personal responsibility. The superiority of the market process over the political process has been clearly summarized by Milton Friedman:

> The crucial point is this: in a *political* system, 51 percent of the people can control it. That's an overstatement, of course, since no government that's supported by only 51 percent of the people will do the same things that one supported by 90 percent of the people will do. But in a political system, everything tends to be a yes-or-no decision; if 51 percent vote yes, it's yes. A political system finds it very difficult to satisfy the needs of minority groups. It's very hard to set up a political arrangement under which, if 51 percent of the people vote one way and 49 percent the other way, the 51 percent will get what they want and the 49 percent will get what they want. Rather, the 49 percent will also get what the 51 percent want.
>
> In a *market* system, if 51 percent of the people vote, say, to buy American cars and 49 percent of the people vote to buy foreign cars and the government lets their votes be effective and doesn't impose tariffs, 51 percent will get American cars and 49 percent will get foreign cars (*Playboy* interview).

Any extension of the political process, therefore, inevitably reduces personal liberty. But I would dare go a step further. I believe that the market mechanism is not only more compatible with individual liberty than the political mechanism, but that it is also more democratic, more responsive to the will of the people. Every day, some 220 million Americans *vote* in an election that's repeated each day of the year. Each one of us when buying something worth, say, $10, has a $10 incentive to choose rationally. Mistakes are undoubtedly made, but the process is repeated every day, and we all end up learning from our own past mistakes. This is the most democratic and efficient process to determine "what this country needs." In a free society, "what the country needs" is nothing but what the people want. The market allows them to express individually their preferences in "elections" that are held every single day of the year. No political mechanism guarantees that.

Furthermore, I contend that liberty is more important than democracy, that no majority should be allowed to violate fundamental personal liberties. Suppose Stalin and Hitler had ruled under perfectly democratic rules, would we approve of their crimes? The basic human liberties that they violated are far more important than any voting procedure, no matter how "democratic."

We must fight against the tendency of government to grow beyond its proper domain. Indeed, we must roll it back to its traditional functions. Statism must be resisted not only because of its tragic economic failures, but above all because it endangers freedom and threatens the very survival of Western civilization. Let's not forget Albert J. Nock's warning:

> It is unfortunately none too well understood that, just as the State has no money of its own, so it has no power of its own. All the power it has is what society gives it, plus what it confiscates from time to time on one pretext or another; there is no other source from which State power can be drawn. Therefore, every assumption of State power, whether by gift or seizure, leaves society with so much less power; there is never, nor can be, any strengthening of State power without a corresponding and roughly equivalent depletion of social power.

The Leaning Tower of Statism

Political rhetoric is changing fast in Italy. Twenty-five years ago the country was moving away from the "center" government, which had presided over the economic miracle of the 1950s with a largely laissez-faire policy, toward a "center-left" coalition government, based on an alliance with the Socialist Party and the exclusion of the classical liberals. The slogans declared that liberalism, with its emphasis on the free market, was not enough. The economic miracle had to be replaced with a social miracle, and for that purpose "modern economic policy" had to supplant the traditional reliance on market forces.

The leader of the Italian Socialist Party, Francesco De Martino, declared on television that if his party won an absolute majority it would nationalize all economic activities, with the possible exclusion of barber shops. Statism, in other words, was the consensus of the overwhelming majority of politicians of almost all political parties. Those of us who dared to challenge the prevailing wisdom—which relied on deficit spending, national economic planning, nationalization, and direct government intervention—were labeled reactionaries and ignored by the new mandarins.

Statists of all parties have had a go at it: From 1960 to 1987, government spending increased 68 times in nominal terms—almost 6 times in real terms—climbing from one-third of gross domestic product to 52 percent. Despite a huge increase in revenue during the same period, the deficit exploded: from nearly 2 percent to 12 percent of GDP. In real terms (1987 prices), total public debt outstanding went from \$82.3 billion in 1960 to over \$700 billion in 1987. Regardless of how

Originally published in *Reason,* February 1989, p. 46, and reprinted with permission.

it is measured, government in Italy has grown very rapidly in the past quarter century.

The results of this spectacular growth seem to have disappointed its promoters, however. On July 12, 1987, the leftist weekly *L'Espresso* published a debate between Claudio Martelli, deputy leader of the Italian Socialist Party, and Achille Occhetto, then deputy leader (now leader) of the Italian Communist Party. In the course of the debate, Martelli said: "It's simple: both in the East and in the West we see the crisis of a philosophy that's been common to both social democrats and communists: statism." To which Occhetto replied: "I agree with you more than you do! . . . Statism, as you say, is the true burden which both social democrats and communists must avoid."

This is not an isolated episode. In his concluding speech at the Communist Party annual festival, Occhetto stressed that the party has "severely criticized the traditional statism of the working class." The productive energies of the country, he said, must be allowed to operate in the private sector, as well as in the public and cooperative sectors. Occhetto is clearly eager to distance himself from his party's traditional statist policies.

The new philosophy is also beginning to show in actual policy proposals. In presenting his plans for a new budget, Giuliano Amato, Socialist minister of the Treasury, advocated extensive privatization of government-controlled corporations, health care and other social services, communications facilities, and even postal services. Not surprisingly, some Liberal Party members suggested that Amato should be given honorary membership in their ranks.

It is too soon, however, for free-market advocates to celebrate. While the rhetoric has changed dramatically, policies have not changed much. No one seems to believe in socialism wholesale, but when it comes to socialism at the retail level, so to speak, the organized action of pressure groups inevitably results in yet more government intervention. For example, while there is general agreement that the National Health System has failed miserably (it is "the scandal of the century," says *L'Espresso*), the bureaucrats and their unions will make sure no one dismantles it anytime soon.

The real hope for the future of freedom in Italy rests more on arithmetic than on rhetoric: Statism is financially bankrupt. Interest payments on government debt amount to 15 percent of total public-sector spending. Taxation on labor income has reached 45 percent, and organized business and labor interests are beginning to protest high taxes. At the same time, government's failure is underscored by the tremendous success of private enterprises that compete with it.

Even government agencies resort to private carriers for reliable mail service. And according to CENSIS, an independent research institute, more than half of the people entitled to "free" public health care instead purchase it from private suppliers. Private health insurance is a growth industry and private schools are booming.

As Italy's financial problems get worse, the prospects for a free economy improve. The call for reform will be too strong to resist, and the new rhetoric of limited government will translate into policy.

Free Education or Educational Freedom?

Wherever is found what is called a paternal government, there is found state education. It has been discovered that the best way to insure implicit obedience is to commence tyranny in the nursery.—Benjamin Disraeli, 1874

Is Education a Public Good?

The idea that education is essential for the survival of a free and democratic society is deeply rooted in Western culture. Thus, limiting our analysis to modern times, the constitution of Massachusetts of 1780 states:

> Wisdom and knowledge, as well as virtue, diffused generally among the body of the people, being necessary for the preservation of their rights and liberties, and as these depend on spreading the opportunities and advantages of education in the various parts of the country and among the different orders of the people, it shall be the duty of the legislatures and magistrates, in all future periods of this commonwealth, to cherish the interest of literature and the sciences, and of all seminaries of them.

Even more explicitly, the Texas Declaration of Independence of 1836 proclaims:

> It is an axiom in political science that unless a people are educated and enlightened it is idle to expect the continuance of civil liberty or the capacity for self-government.

Talk given at the Mont Pèlerin Society Meeting, Viña del Mar, Chile, November 1981.

On the assumption that education must be regarded as a "public good," contemporary liberal thought has accepted the need for making it compulsory. Thus Professor Hayek has asserted:

> In contemporary society, the case for compulsory education up to a certain minimum standard is twofold. There is the general argument that all of us will be exposed to less risks and will receive more benefits from our fellows if they share with us certain basic knowledge and beliefs. And in a country with democratic institutions there is the further important consideration that democracy is not likely to work, except on the smallest local scale, with a partly illiterate people.[1]

Furthermore, the importance of education in a free society has been seen as justifying government financing of certain kinds of schooling. Thus Professor Friedman states:

> A stable and democratic society is impossible without a minimum degree of literacy and knowledge on the part of most citizens and without widespread acceptance of some common set of values. Education can contribute to both. In consequence, the gain from the education of a child accrues not only to the child or to his parents but also to other members of the society. . . . There is therefore a significant "neighborhood effect."[2]

Liberals have always been aware, however, of the threat posed to freedom by government intervention in education, which is often a sufficient condition for that abominable form of intellectual rape called indoctrination. John Stuart Mill's views on the matter ("A general State education is a mere contrivance for molding people to be exactly like one another") are well known and need not be repeated. But also, contemporary liberals have repeatedly warned us against such a danger: "[T]he more highly one rates the power that education can have over men's minds, the more convinced one should be of the danger of placing this power in the hands of any single authority"

1. F. A. Hayek, *The Constitution of Liberty,* Chicago, 1960, p. 377.
2. M. Friedman, *Capitalism and Freedom,* Chicago, 1962, p. 86.

(Hayek). Or "I know of no case on record in which a government has been able to inculcate ideas of the kind that are necessary to preserve a free society" (Friedman).

These warnings are especially important and meaningful for those of us who live in societies in which education is a quasi-monopoly of the state. The degree of indoctrination in state schools in Italy is such that many people see the importance of the family in making children forget what they learn in school. While state education becomes more and more a process of driving prejudices down the students' throats, it increasingly fails in providing the kind of basic knowledge that was supposed to justify its existence. The paradox is that state education in Italy was introduced in the second half of the nineteenth century as a guarantee of freedom from the Catholic Church's monopoly in education. (And the Church resisted such a move to the point of opposing the introduction of compulsory education and defending illiteracy.) Today, on the other hand, Catholic schools are often the only alternative to the kind of indoctrination prevalent in state schools.

Is Compulsion Justified?

It seems evident that education is at the same time a public good, to the extent that it provides people with the kind of knowledge that is essential for the survival of a free and democratic society, and a public "bad," when it amounts to indoctrination of values and beliefs that threaten the basis of a free society. Awareness of this problem has an extensive history of its own. Thus, in 1851, Arthur Schopenhauer warned:

> No child under the age of fifteen should receive instruction in subjects which may possibly be the vehicle of serious error, such as philosophy or religion, for wrong notions imbibed early can seldom be rooted out, and of all the intellectual faculties, judgement is the last to arrive at maturity. The child should give its attention either to subjects where no error is possible at all, such as mathematics, or to those in which there is no particular danger in making a mistake, such as languages.

More specifically to our point, it was awareness of the dangers of indoctrination of the kind that is inimical to freedom that led Ludwig von Mises to support the view that compulsory education should be limited to a few minimum requirements.

> In countries which are not harassed by struggles between various linguistic groups public education can work if it is limited to reading, writing, and arithmetic. With bright children it is even possible to add elementary notions of geometry, the natural sciences, and the valid laws of the country. But as soon as one wants to go farther, serious difficulties appear. Teaching at the elementary level necessarily turns into indoctrination. . . . On the high school level and even on the college level the handing down of historical and economic knowledge is virtually indoctrination. The greater part of the students are certainly not mature enough to form their own opinion on the ground of a critical examination of their teachers' representation of the subject.[3]

Even more radically, he allegedly advocated restricting compulsory education to the kind of knowledge required to read street signs!

The fact is that the case for making education compulsory is far from clear. First of all, it is evident that education confers a private benefit on the student which in the modern world is quite sizable. It is true that literacy today has ceased to have a market in itself, but it is also true that if one is illiterate and innumerate one can expect to find only the most menial and low-paid kinds of occupation. Obviously, it is in the people's own private interest to go to school, and it seems, therefore, useless to make education compulsory. This point has been confirmed by Professor E. G. West's studies that show, on the basis of historical evidence, that compulsory education was introduced, not because otherwise people would not go to school, but to serve the interest of teachers and bureaucrats.[4]

Secondly, the mere existence of a neighborhood effect, whose size might be quite small compared to the private benefit in the educa-

3. Ludwig von Mises, *Human Action,* Chicago, 1963, pp. 876–77.

4. E. G. West, *The Economics of Education Tax Credits,* Heritage Foundation, 1981, especially pp. 14–15.

tion "package," does not seem to justify compulsion. Certainly, pleasant "neighborhood effects" do not justify making it compulsory for beautiful women to dress well. (In this case, as in that of education, compulsion is also unnecessary, because it is in their private interest to dress well.)

Finally, and more to the point, to say that education must be made compulsory because it is essential for the survival of a free and democratic society seems on a part with the argument that we should ban the teaching of values and beliefs which threaten the survival of a free society. Should we ban *Das Kapital* and make *Free to Choose* compulsory?

In the light of my country's experience, I am convinced that the "social" value of education has been grossly exaggerated and somewhat misunderstood. It is true that, to the extent that education is a vehicle of politically meaningful values and beliefs, it conditions people's attitudes toward the political organization of society. But it is far from clear that the political views prevalent in the Italian educational system are of the kind that can contribute to making society freer, more stable, and more democratic. To a very large extent, the opposite is true: Schools instill values and beliefs that are inimical to the survival of a free and democratic society. It is my understanding that such is the case in many other countries as well.

Also, it is to be believed that the economic value of "education" has been exaggerated. After all, there is such a thing as useless knowledge. A substantial fraction of the things people learn in school has no effect on their earning capacity, and it is doubtful that it makes them more "educated," being exclusively a form of intellectual consumption.

This being said, it seems obvious that what the liberal supporters of compulsory education had in mind was not the kind of political indoctrination that is so common in our schools. What they meant is that there is a minimum amount of "objective knowledge"—reading, writing, arithmetic, and the ability to read street signs—that is essential for the survival of any complex modern society, and especially of a free and democratic one. It is the kind of knowledge "where no error is possible at all" or where "there is no particular danger in making a mistake," to use Schopenhauer's appropriate definition. From the point of view of this kind of knowledge, it is not implausible to believe that "education makes a people easy to lead, but difficult to drive; easy to govern, but impossible to enslave."

For this kind of knowledge, however, compulsion seems useless for the reason stated above, namely that these notions confer a private gain on the person who possesses them. Such a personal, private incentive makes compulsion unnecessary . . . and harmless. This would be a much better world if the only form of compulsion in existence were that which forced people to do what they would do anyway!

However, even if one does not oppose compulsion because it is essentially harmless, one should still try to make sure that compulsory education is limited and that it does not amount to the indoctrination of values and beliefs that are inimical to the survival of a free democracy. This is why I would favor, for example, a reduction of the years of compulsory education in my country—from eight to five years—and a rigorous specification of the kind of knowledge that must be transmitted to all students during the years of compulsory education.

In order to avoid misunderstanding, let me stress that the specification of the kind of knowledge I have in mind refers only to compulsory education. I obviously oppose any form of limitation or censorship on the years of schooling that come after compulsory education. As a liberal, I believe that after the years of compulsory education, people should be free to learn whatever they please, even if it is the kind of values and beliefs that are inimical to a free society. If the "consumers" of education want to learn, say, Marxism, in a free society it is the duty of the "producers" to supply them with what they want. I do not believe that there is any risk of generalized and homogeneous indoctrination in a free and competitive school system. Only unilateral indoctrination can result from the state's monopoly in education and the lack of competition in ideas that seems to be its inevitable companion. As Hayek has stressed, freedom is essential in the realm of ideas:

> Nowhere is freedom more important than where our ignorance is greatest—at the boundaries of knowledge, in other words, where nobody can predict what lies a step ahead. . . . [T]he ultimate aim of freedom is the enlargement of those capacities in which man surpasses his ancestors and to which each generation must endeavor to

add its share—its share in the growth of knowledge and the gradual advancement of moral and aesthetic beliefs, where no superior must be allowed to enforce one set of views of what is right or good and where only further experience can decide what should prevail.[5]

Financing Compulsory Education

The Italian school system is the most "statist" in Europe, that is, the one in which the percentage of students in state schools is the highest, between 92 and 93 percent.[6] Such a quasi-monopoly of state schools is often seen as a consequence of the fact that education is a public good that should, "obviously," be supplied by the state. Liberals need not be reminded that, even if one accepts the need for making education compulsory, this does not imply that the government should directly engage in supplying it. We have been aware of this non sequitur at least since 1859, the year John Stuart Mill's *On Liberty* was published.[7]

The true explanation for the extremely high percentage of students in state schools—a percentage, however, that seems to be declining at a rather rapid pace—is the well-known one connected with the way education is financed. Education in public schools is "free," that is, financed out of general tax revenue, whereas private schools charge fees. It is not surprising, therefore, that most parents show a preference for "free" public education. What is surprising is that there are private schools at all and that their share of the market is growing so fast that many people talk of a boom in private education.

The present system of financing compulsory education is (a) inimical to personal liberty, (b) inequitable, and (c) inefficient, and must, therefore, be changed. The crisis of our schools is due to the fact that the government is engaged in the business of supplying education and that the "public" money goes to the "producers," the schools, rather than to the "consumers," the students. Again, this confirms the validity

5. F. A. Hayek, op. cit., p. 394.

6. S. Valitutti, "Introduzione ai lavori," in *La Scuola Non Statale in Italia,* Napoli, 1978, p. 3.

7. J. S. Mill, *On Liberty* (1859), Appleton-Century-Crofts, New York, 1947, pp. 107–8.

of an old liberal idea. One needs only refer to Friedman's views on the matter that have been expressed in the last quarter of a century.[8] It might be worthwhile, however, to repeat this well-known analysis.

Public financing of compulsory education in the present form is inimical to personal liberty because it confers an unjustifiable advantage on public schools in their competition with private schools. Such an advantage tends to restrict the number of private schools, and it therefore restricts the number of choices open to individuals and their families. That a state monopoly in education is inimical to personal liberty can be easily seen by observing that it is typical of all totalitarianisms. Monopoly in education is a necessary condition for indoctrination, as it leaves no alternatives to "official" education. It is on a par with a state monopoly on information, but it might very well be much more dangerous for the survival of free intellects. A good example of the fact that the present system of financing compulsory education is incompatible with personal freedom is provided by religious education. It is obvious that if religious instruction is included in the package offered by state schools, this violates the liberty of nonbelievers or believers of other faiths. If, on the other hand, religion is not taught in public schools, it is the liberty of believers that is violated. The only liberal solution is that which would allow parents to choose whether they want their children exposed to religious teaching or not, and this is not possible when all (or most) schools must conform to the same general blueprint.

Public financing of compulsory education in the present form is inequitable. Given the poor and declining quality of public education, many people are now sending their children to private schools. However, this choice is open only to the relatively well off, who can afford to pay twice for their children's education (once in taxes and once in private school fees). The paradox is that public education, which was supposed to guarantee "equality of access" to this "essential public ser-

8. M. Friedman, *Capitalism and Freedom,* op. cit., chap. 6; M. and R. Friedman, *Free to Choose, A Personal Statement,* Harcourt Brace Jovanovich, New York, 1980, chap. 6; also E. G. West, *Economics, Education and the Politician,* The Institute of Economic Affairs, London, 1968; R. Harris and A. Seldon, *Pricing or Taxing?,* The Institute of Economic Affairs, London, 1976; A. Seldon, *Charge,* Temple Smith, London, 1977, especially part 2, chap. 4, pp. 61–82.

vice," has resulted, to use Lord Harris's appropriate definition, in "inequality of exit": Only the rich can afford to free themselves from the amenities of public indoctrination.

Public financing of compulsory education in the present form promotes inefficiency. Italian schools seem to confirm a general phenomenon: The cost per child is much higher in public than in private schools. But this is not, unfortunately, the end of the story. To the higher cost one must add a lower (and declining) quality. In 1978, the Milan Polytechnic ran a test on some 250 first-year students of engineering to ascertain their knowledge of basic mathematics. Fifty-six percent of these would-be engineers did not know what pi is. Not a great result after thirteen years of public schooling! Inefficiency is the only reassuring aspect of the Italian school system: As long as it lasts (and it is actually increasing), private schools will have a (growing) market and freedom will survive.

An obvious solution to the present crisis might be the well-known one of the voucher. It is not worth repeating what has already been said so often and so well by liberal scholars on the subject. I would only like to add two comments from an Italian perspective. The first is that, should we adopt a voucher system, I am convinced that rather than "add ons" we would have, at least at the beginning, a wide diffusion of rebates: The value of the voucher would be so much above the cost of education in private schools that schools would try to attract students by offering discounts on the voucher. The second, less optimistic, comment is that, as long as the state remains the largest employer and we keep on having that absurd institution that is the "legal value" of diplomas, we will need government controls over standards in order to prevent schools from issuing legal-value diplomas of little educational content.

The voucher would have to be personal and not negotiable; and it could only be spent in approved institutions. Its value would have to be higher for those schools that operate in very isolated communities where the small number of students makes the per-unit cost higher than in the rest of the country. Finally, it would be desirable to have a limited number of scholarships for exceptionally gifted students from needy families, so as to give them access to special programs suited to their higher-than-average ability.

The voucher system would restore freedom of choice in education for those who cannot afford it under the present system, and, by fostering competition among schools, it would provide an incentive to greater efficiency. Even if one grants, however, that the voucher would be more compatible with personal liberty, equity, and efficiency, the question remains of why should compulsory education be financed out of general tax revenue. One need not accept the notion that education is a public good in order to support the voucher. The fact is that the voucher seems to be the best way to move from the present system to one in which education is almost entirely financed privately, one, that is, in which the amount society spends on education is determined by individual decisions. By keeping the nominal value of the voucher constant, we would be reasonably sure that inflation and real income growth would render it meaningless in the future.

Financing Noncompulsory Education

In the Italian educational system, public financing is not limited to compulsory education but covers all levels of education, including the universities. The "public good" argument is even weaker here, and it is hard to find a justification for such an extension of public financing of education. As in the case of compulsory education, though to a greater extent, public financing of higher education is illiberal, inequitable, and inefficient.

It is easy to see why public financing is illiberal.[9] When the Soviet Union introduced a tax on the Jews who wanted to migrate to Israel, the general reaction was to interpret such a move as a manifestation of anti-Semitism. Anti-Semitism probably did play a role, but it was not the main cause of the Soviet authorities' decision. The true cause was public financing of higher education. What the Russian government was saying was: "The Russian taxpayer has paid for your education; what you know, therefore, does not belong to you, it belongs to the

9. On the relationship between public finance and academic freedom, *see* J. M. Buchanan, "Public Finance and Academic Freedom," in *What Should Economists Do?*, Liberty Fund, Inc., Indianapolis, 1979, chap. 14; and A. A. Alchian, "The Economic and Social Impact of Free Tuition," in *Economic Forces at Work*, Liberty Fund, Inc., Indianapolis, 1977, chap. 8.

state; if you want to leave the country, you must first give us back what belongs to us and not to you." That this was the logic of the decision is evidenced by the fact that the tax varied according to professional qualifications. From public financing of higher education to the repugnant notion that what I know does not belong to me, but belongs to the taxpayer, there is only a small and perfectly consistent step. Public financing of higher education would become a precondition of a property right in human beings on the part of the government.

But, someone might object, that's the Soviet Union; in our free democracies such a notion would obviously be rejected by everybody with great indignation. However, first of all there is no reason why public financing of higher education should always be seen as a gift from the taxpayer to the beneficiary. In the case of my country, the absurd restrictions imposed on those who want to take *their own* physical capital out of the country represent a bad omen. It would certainly not be surprising if in the future we'd have restrictions on the export of *human* capital properly belonging to the state because of public finance of higher education.

Only if I bear the cost of my own education, no one can question my property right in it. But as long as I receive it as a "gift" from the benevolent taxpayer, my property right in my knowledge can be questioned. This, in my opinion, is the strongest argument against "free" education.

Secondly, that public financing of higher education can be inimical to personal freedom even in a free democracy can be understood by looking at the Italian experience. The tremendous increase in the number of university students, in itself a consequence of public financing, has made the rationing problem dramatic. So far, the problem has just been ignored by legislators, with the wonderful effects in terms of efficiency that will be mentioned in what follows. But the overcrowding of our universities has also convinced many people of the need to introduce a *numerus clausus,* a ceiling on the maximum number of students per field of studies, to be determined by a national committee on the basis of an estimate of the country's needs in the various subjects. Now, it is obvious that a country that denies people the right to choose their future profession is not a free country. The decision of whether my child should become a doctor or a plumber in a free society properly belongs to him and to no one else. Furthermore, a little reflection on how such a national committee would actually work suggests that the consequence could only be that the children of the ruling political oligarchy would be allowed to attend the university in the subject of their own choice, whereas those who lack political clout would likely be discriminated against. The obvious reason for this is that there are no objective criteria on which to decide how many doctors, lawyers, or scientists "the country needs," so that the maximum number would be entirely arbitrary. Even more important, there are no objective criteria on which to decide who is more qualified for a particular specialization: There is no such a thing as objectively measurable merit.

Nor is the use of merit as a criterion desirable; as Hayek has suggested:

> a much sharper division between classes might come to exist, and the less fortunate might become seriously neglected, if all the more intelligent were deliberately and successfully brought into the wealthy group and it became not only a general presumption but a universal fact that the relatively poor were less intelligent.[10]

Public financing of higher education is also inequitable. As Friedman has repeatedly shown, it amounts to a form of regressive redistribution, where the cost of university education is borne by everybody, including the poor, and the benefit goes to people who, thanks to such a gift, will end up receiving a higher-than-average income during their lifetime. It is true that the government will get some of that money back because of progressive taxation, but the after-tax income of the university-educated man will still be higher than it would have been had he not received that education. To the extent that the cost is borne by (even poor) taxpayers, there is a transfer of resources from the poor to the middle class.

To the above argument middle-class, middle-income people tend to reply that university education does not necessarily increase earnings, that a plumber makes more money than a university-educated schoolteacher. (Such argument is invariably brought out by schoolteachers.) The argument is obviously wrong: if the *real* income of a schoolteacher

10. F. A. Hayek, op. cit., p. 383.

is not higher than that of a plumber, why doesn't he stop teaching and take up plumbing? If *money* income is all that matters, why are so many people going through university education in order to become teachers instead of going into plumbing? Even granting that plumbers have a higher *money* income than teachers, nonpecuniary factors must obviously make the teachers' *real* income equal to or higher than that of the plumber, or there would be a movement of teachers into plumbing. (It is, I believe, a general rule, valid in all countries but hard to understand, that most people dislike plumbers and feel that they are making "too much" money.)

Finally, public financing of higher education promotes inefficiency. The Italian university system vividly illustrates the disastrous consequences of public financing when coupled with a mistaken notion of "democracy." The fact that university education is "free," coupled with the idea that in a democracy anybody should be allowed to get ("free") a university degree, and stay in school as long as he pleases, has swollen the student population to an incredible extent, while the number of faculty members and the availability of resources have failed to adjust to the increase in the number of students. The results have been devastating. When I started to teach at the University of Rome in 1964, the total student population was roughly 50,000 on a campus that was built for a maximum of 15,000. Today, the total number of students at the University of Rome is in the neighborhood of 140,000 on the same campus and with roughly the same number of faculty members. This explains why Italian universities have been defined as institutions where students don't study, teachers don't teach, and researchers do anything but research. The reasons for this unfortunately accurate description of the appalling situation of our universities are fairly obvious. Given the number of students and the existing facilities, it is fortunate that attendance is only in the order of 5 percent. Students, therefore, do not attend classes, but rather prepare for exams by studying textbooks at home. Teachers, on the other hand, have an excellent justification for not devoting too much time to teaching since their lectures benefit only a tiny fraction of the total student population. Finally, since salaries are hopelessly inadequate, you can't blame university professors if they devote more time to making a living by moonlighting than they do to teaching and research. In the light of the general situation, it is not surprising that Italian universities are in a state of crisis; what is surprising is that they work at all, even if only for a small minority of dedicated students, teachers, and researchers.

It seems evident that the rationing problem is at the root of the state of crisis of Italian universities, because the present system has simultaneously increased the demand for university education and reduced the supply of it. Only a system of rationing by prices—that is, making students pay a tuition equal to the cost of education—can prevent resorting to the *numerus clausus* and solve the present crisis. The solution, that is, can be found in changing the system of financing higher education. One possible way out of the present mess is that of moving from a generalized system of public finance to a combination of vouchers at the secondary school level, student loans and scholarships at the university level, and an increasing role of private payments for higher education. Such an arrangement should guarantee the transition from the present system to one in which noncompulsory education would be financed exclusively by the beneficiaries.[11]

Conclusion

In Italy, as in many other Western countries, education is (a) compulsory up to a certain level, (b) financed out of general tax revenue, and (c) supplied by the state under quasi-monopoly conditions. I have tried to show that the case for compulsory education is even weaker than many liberal thinkers believe. However, even if one accepts the need for compulsion, this does not justify a direct role of the state in education. Here the problem of financing education is linked with the problem of who should supply it.

The Italian experience confirms an old and well-known story: Education is not a "free" good. "Free" education, financed out of general tax revenue, is inimical to educational freedom, it is inequitable, and it promotes inefficiency. Those who believe in the importance of an efficient, equitable, and free educational system must become aware

11. E. G. West seems to favor tax credits over vouchers: see *The Economics of Education Tax Credits,* op. cit. I am not sure that such a proposal could be made workable in a country such as Italy, where indirect taxes are the main source of tax revenue.

of the fact that the solution to present problems is inseparably and inescapably linked to the way education is financed. We should move toward a system of pricing, of private financing of education. For as long as we have "free" education, we are not going to have freedom in education, and it is highly doubtful that we can have "education" at all.

Italian Socialists Warm to Vouchers

Since its foundation in 1892 the Italian Socialist Party (PSI) has been made up of two components: the libertarian and the traditional statist. The two "souls" of Italian socialism have managed to coexist within the same party at the cost of a compromise that has often made the party platform unintelligible. But in the past 40 years the statist branch has been in control, at least as far as one could tell from the political platform. In the early 1960s PSI was advocating widespread nationalization, central planning, confiscatory taxation, aggressive deficit spending, etc.—the usual array of Marxism-cum-Keynesianism. The change inside the PSI is a remarkable example of a change for the better, of a rediscovery of the party's libertarian tradition ignored by its leaders for many decades.

The most notable example of this change has recently been provided by Claudio Martelli, the deputy leader of the PSI, whose position within the party is made even more influential because the leader of the PSI, Bettino Craxi, is prime minister. Claudio Martelli is a young (under-40) socialist who, unlike many of his predecessors, seems to have realized that the "holy writs" of traditional socialism are hopelessly inadequate for today's world and its problems.

Martelli recently demonstrated his openness to new ideas and his respect for the libertarian tradition of Italian socialism by advocating education vouchers in Italy. He did not specify in his original statement how and when they should be introduced, but his suggestion, coming from the deputy leader of the party of the prime minister, ex-

Originally published in *Economic Affairs,* August–September 1986, pp. 47–49, and reprinted with permission.

ploded like a bomb in the stagnant world of Italian politics. For weeks almost all Italian newspapers carried editorials on the subject. Needless to say, the majority of the comments were critical of the voucher idea, but their quality was so poor that one could not help feeling that most of the participants in the debate had never heard of education vouchers before, so that they did not know what they were talking about. Many comments were based on the belief that the voucher idea had been *invented* by Martelli and were proudly ignorant of the enormous literature on the subject.

Their ignorance was entirely unjustified. Aside from the numerous English-language publications on the subject, education vouchers had been advocated in Italy for many years, so that even those who could not read English should have been aware of the proposal.[1]

Some of the criticisms were simply meaningless. For example, Sylos Labini, a self-defined socialist economist, violently (and vulgarly) accused Martelli of supporting a violation of the Italian constitution. His argument was that the voucher idea violates the third paragraph of article 33 of the Italian constitution, which says that "Organized groups and private persons have the right to establish schools and educational institutions without burden to the state."[2] But it is obvious that, if such a constitutional provision has any meaning (which is doubtful), it is that private schools may not be *established* with taxpayers' money. Furthermore, as Martelli pointed out, there is no reason that the transfer of funds from taxpayers to the government, and

1. For example, Milton Friedman's *Capitalism and Freedom* as translated into Italian almost 20 years ago: *Efficienza economica e libertà,* Vallecchi Editore, Florence, 1967. More recently, some economists have been advocating education vouchers: for example, my "La questione finanziaria della scuola non statale," in *La scuola non statale in Italia,* Fratelli Conte Editori, Napoli, 1978, pp. 121ff. Furthermore, the Centro Ricerche Economiche Applicate (a free-market institute based in Rome) has devoted two publications to vouchers: *Il finanziamento dell'istruzione in una libera democrazia,* CREA, Rome, 1982; *Il buono-scuola,* CREA, Rome, 1985.

2. Norman Kogan, *The Government of Italy,* T. Y. Crowell, New York, 1962, p. 193. The ambiguity of the English translation should not be blamed on the translator: The entire Italian constitution is very ambiguously phrased, and most of its 139 articles are unquestionably meaningless. The entire document makes delightful reading for anyone opposed to written constitutions.

from the government to the schools should be considered consistent with the constitution (even though, says Martelli, "it produces inequity and inefficiency"), whereas the transfer of funds from the government to the consumer, and from the consumer to the schools should be considered incompatible with the constitution. In essence, what Martelli is saying is that there is no reason that existing direct subsidies to private schools should be considered constitutional, whereas subsidies going to students and their families should not. Finally, a voucher scheme can be established in such a way as to *reduce* total government spending on education, and it would be very hard to argue that even in this case vouchers would violate the constitution. Martelli went even further than this, arguing that, if necessary, socialists were certainly not afraid of changing the constitution.

Three more criticisms are worth mentioning. The first will prove unintelligible to most non-Italian readers: according to Franca Falcucci, the Christian-Democrat minister of education, and Salvatore Valitutti, a Liberal former minister of education, vouchers would be incompatible with the "legal value of diplomas." This "legal value" of diplomas is one of those Italian ideas that are very hard to explain to people who are not lucky enough to live in Italy. It seems to mean that the government certifies that all diplomas conform to a politically predetermined standard. And, the argument goes, vouchers, by promoting competition and diversity, would not guarantee that all diplomas conformed to such a standard. The argument is unconvincing: first of all, given existing diversities, the quality of diplomas already varies tremendously depending on the school that grants them. Secondly, it is entirely possible to have a voucher scheme combined with the provision that, in order to be entitled to receive vouchers, schools should conform to some minimum (and nondiscriminatory) standard. Finally, the diversity and experimentation that vouchers would make possible is one of their strongest advantages. Only dogmatic statists can believe that there is such a thing as "the" right curriculum, equal for everybody, and known only to the superior wisdom of education bureaucrats and politicians. And there is no reason that, if vouchers are indeed incompatible with the "legal value," we should not get rid of this meaningless notion.

The second criticism is particularly notable because of its source.

According to Salvatore Valitutti, the Liberal former minister of education, the voucher "would transfer the decision of which schools should survive to the family." And, continues this remarkable Liberal, it is not argued that families would guarantee the survival of the "most socially needed" schools. But the true liberal is convinced that only the people can decide what is "socially needed." In the political, as in the economic, market, the liberal believes that "consumer sovereignty" is far more important than the vested interests of producers. Secondly, how can anyone trust the wisdom of citizens, in their capacity of voters, to choose the right political outcome, and simultaneously distrust their judgement, in their capacity of parents, to choose the right school for their children? If anything, there are excellent reasons to believe that voters' decisions will be far more careless than parents'. If my child's future is at stake, I have every reason to be well informed on existing options and to try to make the best possible choice. On the other hand, since no election has ever been decided by one vote, I have no such incentive to be well informed when casting my vote.

The third argument against vouchers is undoubtedly the strongest. If we have vouchers and competition, it has been claimed by several of the participants in the debate, we cannot guarantee the stability of employment of teachers and bureaucrats. Today, most teachers and all bureaucrats in Italy enjoy life tenure: once hired, they cannot be fired. As a result, they are living testimony to Adam Smith's wisdom, because their interest is

> set as directly in opposition to [their] duty as it is possible to set it. It is the interest of every man to live as much at ease as he can; and if his emoluments are to be precisely the same, whether he does, or does not perform some very laborious duty, it is certainly his interest, at least as interest is vulgarly understood, either to neglect it altogether, or, if he is subject to some authority which will not suffer him to do this, to perform it in as careless and slovenly a manner as that authority will permit.[3]

The concentrated, visible, and immediate interest of bad teachers and bureaucrats has very good chances of prevailing over the diffused,

3. *The Wealth of Nations,* Cannan edition, p. 718.

invisible, and long-term interest of society. It is because of this contrast that vouchers have had so few and isolated successes, and it is because of it that it is very difficult to reform the schools in a liberal direction.[4]

Yet it is one thing to say that from a *positive*—objective—point of view the opposition of teachers' unions and bureaucrats poses a formidable threat to the introduction of vouchers, and quite a different thing to *oppose* vouchers on the grounds of the opposition of vested interests. The hostility of tenured teachers and bureaucrats is clearly aimed at protecting a privilege at the expense of the general interests of society. What they are trying to protect is the inefficiency and laziness of many of their peers at the expense of consumers and taxpayers. To consider such a position acceptable (from a *normative* point of view) would mean to accept the view that the whole educational system should be geared to serve the interests of people who work in it, even though they are inefficient, rather than those of the students, their families, and the future progress of society.

Furthermore, good teachers would *gain* from the change. Today they are grossly underpaid—the same as their less-qualified colleagues. In a competitive environment, their salaries would very likely increase substantially. Moreover, the number of good teachers would also increase: many of the not-so-good of today would be motivated by a working system of incentives to improve the quality of their performance.

Of the other criticisms, one is probably worth mentioning: the idea that since most existing private schools are Catholic, vouchers would benefit Catholic schools. Here, two elements of the argument are noteworthy. First, it is taken for granted that, with freedom of choice, students would move away from state schools and into private ones. Obviously, critics are convinced that state schools *are* inefficient and incapable of reforming themselves—an excellent argument *for* vouchers! Secondly, some people oppose vouchers because they oppose other people's values. They do not claim that the present system is superior to the voucher scheme, but they object to the possibility of other people getting what they want from the schools (a Catholic education for their children). This line of reasoning is, of course, incom-

4. This problem is brilliantly analyzed by Gordon Tullock, "No Public Choice in State Education," *Economic Affairs* 6, no. 4, 1986.

patible with the "rules" of a free society. A state monopoly of education may be essential to the survival of a totalitarian state; a free democracy can do without such a paternalistic and authoritarian institution.

Some support came from readers who sent letters to newspapers supporting vouchers. One of them correctly said that the freedom of the press would not be guaranteed by a system based on a single publicly financed newspaper and that, likewise, the freedom of education was certainly not protected by a single state supplier of "free" schooling. Some came from liberals,[5] but it is worth emphasizing the support coming from the socialist camp.

The first interesting argument for vouchers coming from a Socialist was that of Francesco Forte, a public-choice economist and member of the present government for the Italian Socialist Party.[6] According to this most influential "new Socialist" economist, there is no reason that "public goods" should be supplied by the state. If politicians want to make sure that some "essential" services are supplied to everybody, the best way is to provide people who cannot afford to pay with purchasing power, and leave it to the market to produce the particular service under competitive conditions. The voucher idea, therefore, could be extended, according to Forte, to the provision of housing, health, prescription drugs, etc. Such an argument is unlikely to be considered novel by readers of *Economic Affairs,* but it is remarkable coming from a member of the PSI.

But the most interesting defense of the voucher idea from the socialist camp was supplied by Claudio Martelli himself.[7] The deputy leader of PSI defended the voucher scheme from the point of view of equity, efficiency, cost-effectiveness, and freedom of choice. People familiar with the argument *for* vouchers would not have learned much from his article, but they could not have avoided admiring the vigor and rigor of his argumentation. Few liberals could disagree with his conclusion that "the strategy of competing diverse educational institutions is the only one that is capable of revitalising, diversifying and 'au-

5. For example, G. Miglio, "Una carta di credito per andare a scuola," *Il Sole–24 Ore,* March 4, 1986. Professor Miglio is a Catholic *and* a liberal. Cf. also Antonio Martino, "In cerca del 'buono' Stato," *Il Sole–24 Ore,* June 6, 1986.

6. Cf. "'Buoni scuola' per una buona scuola," *Il Giornale,* March 7, 1986.

7. "Questa scuola sta andando in malora," *La Repubblica,* March 9–10, 1986.

tonomising' public schools." There is no reason that "a private structure should not perform a public service."

I hope that the liberal trend in Italian socialism comes to an end soon. Considering the indifference toward liberal ideas of my fellow members of the Italian Liberal Party, if Italian socialists continue to advocate liberalizing reforms, I might consider joining their party. And it would be disastrous for me: not having been a Socialist at 20, I have proved to be heartless; if I became Socialist at 40, I would prove to be brainless.

The Welfare State: Lessons from Italy

If you stop meddling with people they take care of themselves.
If you stop commanding people they behave themselves.
If you stop imposing on people they become themselves. —*Lao-tze*

Foreword

According to Nobel Laureate in Economics Lawrence R. Klein,[1] in the year 2000 real per capita GDP in Taiwan will roughly equal that of Italy. I believe that the projection may prove to be conservative; if present trends continue, the Republic of China may achieve that result sooner. In order for this to happen, however, it must try to avoid making the mistakes that have brought Italy's extraordinary economic growth almost to an end. For this reason I believe Italy's experience with the welfare state can be quite relevant to Taiwan's future.

Intentions vs. Results

Welfare states around the world are subject to growing criticism. Their "free" benefits are proving to be increasingly costly, and the burden of taxation needed to finance them is widely regarded as unbearable. Furthermore, the quality of services provided by the state is generally considered unsatisfactory so that an increasing number of people, even though entitled to "free" state services, prefer to resort

Talk given at a program at National Taiwan University, Republic of China, November 23–24, 1987, unpublished.

1. See "Foreword," *Models of Development,* edited by Lawrence J. Lau, ICS Press, San Francisco, 1986, p. xiii.

to private provision, thus paying these services twice (once in taxes, once in fees).

At face value, judging from the alleged goals of their programs, the ideals of supporters of state welfare seem lofty and noble. Who wants to see sick people go without medical care, or old people destitute, or children of poor families forgo their education, etc? The apparent loftiness of the ideals of the welfare state makes rational discussion of its desirability very difficult. If supporters of state provision of welfare services aim at "social happiness and justice," doesn't it follow that those who disagree with them intend to achieve social *un*happiness and *in*justice? Furthermore, if their goals are ignoble, why should we bother arguing with them?

I think that in this, as in many other cases, it is essential to distinguish between intentions and results. "Economists have always concerned themselves with the unintended effects of human action. Indeed, economics can be defined as the study of such unintended effects. Politicians, on the other hand, seldom pay any attention to such secondary effects, concentrating instead on the immediate, intended consequences of their decision. A good example of this contrast is provided by the wonderful story of a little town in Abruzzi, Italy, that was plagued by a large number of vipers. The local politicians thought it wise to attempt to solve the problem by offering a reward for any viper killed. The unintended effect of their action was, as any economist could easily have predicted, an increase in the supply of vipers—peasants started breeding vipers in their basements."[2]

No matter how noble and enlightened the goals of the welfare state, rational discussion mandates that we concentrate on its results. As it happens, however, the historical origin of comprehensive welfare is far from noble, as it is generally ascribed to Bismarck's 1881 attempt to undermine the popularity of the Social Democrats. Considering its conception and its performance, it can be said of the welfare state that, like the mule, it has "neither pride of ancestry nor hope of posterity."

In what follows, I'll try to illustrate the abysmal, and by now gen-

2. A. Martino, "Measuring Italy's Underground Economy," *Policy Review,* no. 16, p. 87. [See pp. 177–95 of this volume.]

erally recognized, failure of Italy's welfare state, which is only a more extreme example of a general phenomenon.

The Financial Crisis

Over the last one hundred years government expenditure has grown much faster than the national product in virtually all industrialized countries. In the 1960s and 1970s this process has been gaining speed. From 1960 to 1980, for example, total government outlays in the OECD have on average increased as a percentage of Gross Domestic Product from 28.5 percent to 39.3 percent. As a result, taxes take an ever larger share of national income, and increasing government borrowing portends even higher taxes in the future. As government controls an ever larger part of national expenditures, the liberty of the individual citizen is successively eroded. The liberal state is increasingly displaced by the welfare state.—Roland Vaubel, 1984

The most important aspect of Italy's present economic condition is the state of near-bankruptcy of government finances. To a very large extent, financial difficulties are due to the growth of the welfare state. Furthermore, the same factors that have produced the increase in welfare spending are responsible for the growth in spending for other reasons. Let me illustrate.

A. GOVERNMENT SPENDING

From 1960 to 1986, public-sector spending has increased 62 times in nominal terms, 397 percent in real per capita terms, and it has gone from 32.7 percent of Gross Domestic Product (GDP) to 52.4 percent.

In recent years, despite the commitment of all governments to control the growth of expenditures, the process has accelerated: From 1980 to 1986, public-sector spending has increased 176 percent in nominal terms, 40.8 percent in real terms, and it has gone from 43.5 percent of GDP to 52.4 percent.

It is worth noting that the increase in public expenditures has absorbed 60 percent of the increase in GDP: For every million of additional product, 600,000 have gone to the government, 400,000 have been left to the private sector.

The figures in Table 1 illustrate the dimensions of the problem: In 1986 average per capita public-sector spending has reached US$6,093—US$24,372 for the average family of four!

TABLE 1. *The Per Capita Cost of Government: 1960–1986 in Real Terms: 1986 Prices*

1960	L1,656,000	100	US$1,227
1970	L3,127,000	189	US$2,316
1980	L5,840,000	353	US$4,326
1986	L8,225,000	497	US$6,093

TABLE 2. *Tax Revenue as % of GDP: An International Comparison 1982–1984 Average*

Italy	40.72
France	44.61
Germany	37.57
United Kingdom	38.56
Canada	33.61
U.S.A.	29.52
Japan	27.08
"G7" average	35.95
OECD	36.87

Source: G. Peleggi, "Il prelievo tributario in Italia: un confronto internazionale," in *Lo Stato Come Incassa*, Centro Studi Confindustria 1987, p. 14.

B. TAXATION

From 1960 to 1986 public-sector revenue has increased 51 times in nominal terms, 370 percent in real terms, and it has gone from 31.1 percent of GDP to 41.2 percent.

Even in this case the process accelerates: From 1980 to 1986, public-sector revenue has increased 173 percent in nominal terms, 35.3 percent in real terms, and it has gone from 34.6 percent of GDP to 41.2 percent.

International comparisons are always difficult to make. However, this should not discourage us from making them. The figures in Table 2 should not be taken at face value; even with all caveats, however, they show how much more serious the problem of excessive taxation is in

Italy compared with the other six members of the so-called Group of Seven (G7) and the average for OECD countries.

It is also interesting to note that the only country in which tax revenue as a percentage of GDP exceeds Italy's—France—is in the process of revising its GDP figures upward, so that Italy may soon achieve the dubious honor of being the most heavily taxed country in the Group of Seven.

The increase has been particularly exorbitant in income tax revenue: From 1975 to 1986, it has increased fourteen times (+1,275 percent) in nominal terms, almost three times in real terms (+220 percent), and the percentage of public spending it finances has gone from 14.6 percent to 24.75 percent. Finally, as for marginal rates, Italian taxpayers start facing a 26 percent marginal rate at an income of US$8,500.

C. THE DEFICIT

"Despite" the rapid growth in tax revenue, the government deficit has increased at an exponential rate.

In the twenty-five years since 1961, the government deficit in the International Monetary Fund definition has increased over 300 times in nominal terms, 29 times in real terms, taking inflation into account, and it has gone from 1.5 percent to 12.1 percent of GDP.

The increase in the deficit is not due to "insufficient" taxation (whatever that means). As we have seen, tax revenue has increased very rapidly in the past decades. The obvious cause of its growth is the explosion of public spending, despite all political promises. From 1980 to 1986, all governments, as previously mentioned, have pledged to bring spending under control; the results have been disappointing, to say the least.

Had public-sector spending remained constant in nominal terms from 1980 to 1986, the budget would have reported a surplus of almost 200,000 billion lire in 1986. Had it grown so as to offset the influence of inflation, thus remaining constant in real terms, the 1986 budget would have shown a surplus of 26,017 billion lire. Had it grown faster than inflation but no faster than nominal GDP, so as to keep the ratio constant, the 1986 deficit would have amounted to 20,808 instead of 108,497 billion lire. A very modest policy of *containment* of spending

TABLE 3. *The Deficit*

	Billions of lire		
	Current Prices	1986 Prices	As % of GDP
1961	357	3,786	1.5%
1971	4,757	33,282	6.9%
1981	53,296	91,164	11.4%
1986	108,497	108,497	12.1%

Source: International Monetary Fund, *International Financial Statistics.*

growth would have brought the deficit under control in seven years. But even that modest policy could not be implemented.

This is not a peculiarly Italian phenomenon: In several other countries the control of public spending seems impossible. Neither the Reagan administration nor the governments of Mrs. Thatcher have been very successful in curbing public spending. The reasons for this appear obvious if one accepts the following analysis.

An Explanation

Gordon Tullock maintains that we do not have a general theory of government growth, that all explanations of the rapid increase in taxation and spending in the post–World War II era are contradicted by the evidence. What is true for a given country at one time is not true for another country or for another period of time. In a sense, this is true by definition: The circumstances and the prevailing intellectual climate are different from country to country, and they vary over time. Also, it is true that a *general* theory should apply equally well to past trends as well as to contemporary developments. There is no doubt that we do not have any satisfactory explanation for such a wide range of events. In another sense, I believe that we do have an explanation that adequately accounts for the prevailing tendencies in Western democracies in the last twenty-five to thirty years. Such a theory is not new and it may not be as *general* as we would like, but it is worth considering.

I believe that the starting point of such an explanation is the existence of three asymmetries in the perception of costs and benefits of public spending. First, the democratic political process tends to favor decisions that result in benefits for a small group of beneficiaries and whose cost is spread over a large number of taxpayers (or consumers). For example, a decision to confer a benefit of, let us say, $230,000 each to 1,000 beneficiaries (say, a subsidy to the domestic exporters of a given good) gives each one of them a $230,000 incentive to make sure the proposal is approved. On the other hand, if the cost of the proposal is spread evenly over the entire U.S. population, it would cost each American citizen only $1. "In these circumstances, wrote Pareto in 1896, the outcome is not in doubt: the spoliators will win hands down."

The existence of such an asymmetry is confirmed by the fact that spending on public goods has not been the main factor behind the growth of total spending. Since public goods benefit the whole of society, they often lack a constituency lobbying for them, so that the growth of public spending is usually slower. Also, the existence of this asymmetry is evidenced by the near-impossibility to *reduce* government spending, because the costs of the reduction would fall on a small number of former beneficiaries, while the benefits would go to society as a whole. The failure of several Western governments to reduce public spending confirms such a hypothesis. Finally, it is obvious that the success of the first group of beneficiaries will provide an incentive for the formation of other groups, so that the asymmetry develops into a process of government *growth* over time.

The second asymmetry results from the fact that the political process tends to favor decisions based on *visible* benefits and *invisible* costs. The visibility of benefits guarantees the support for the proposal by the potential beneficiaries, while the invisibility of costs neutralizes the opposition of those who bear them. In the previous example, while each one of the producers of the good has an incentive of $230,000 to be exactly informed about the effects of the subsidy for him, the value of the information for the individual taxpayers is only $1. In all likelihood, therefore, while the beneficiaries will know exactly how much they stand to gain from the proposal, those who bear its cost will (rationally) be ignorant of its impact on them.

Finally, the political process favors decisions that result in an *immediate* (even if small) gain whose cost (even if large) is paid in the distant *future.* This last asymmetry is particularly acute in Italy because, given the high instability of the executive (the average "life expectancy at birth" of Italian governments is less than a year), the time horizon of political decision makers tends to be very short. Governments generally tend to favor spending decisions that confer an immediate gain to some group in society, even if the future cost of the decision is substantial, because in all likelihood it will be borne by another government.

If the above analysis is correct, we would expect government growth to be faster when public spending is financed by a device that (a) spreads costs over a large number of taxpayers; (b) hides these costs from those who bear them; (c) produces immediate benefits at the expense of high (if not disastrous) consequences in the future. Such a device exists, and it is called a deficit. Its time pattern—in Italy, at least—confirms the preceding analysis beyond any doubt.

Let me stress at this point that the validity of the above analysis does not depend on the existence of an *uninterrupted* growth of the deficit through time. What happens is that, when the deficit reaches a certain level, the need to reduce it—stressed with great vigor by fiscal conservatives of all political parties—results in higher taxation. It is quite possible, therefore, that those asymmetries produce increases in the deficit followed by increases in explicit taxation and a reduction in the deficit, and so on. (This, however, has not been the case in Italy, where the deficit has grown with almost no interruption.) In the words of James Buchanan:

> Beneficiary groups, recipients of direct transfers or of governmentally-financed programs, tend to be concentrated, organized, and capable of exerting influence over elected politicians. By contrast, taxpayer groups, those who pay taxes, tend to be widely dispersed and, indeed, tend to include almost everyone due to the fact that taxes are general rather than specific. As a result of the asymmetry, it becomes easier to get political decision-makers to expand budgets than to contract them.[3]

3. See "I limiti alla fiscalità," in *La Costituzione fiscale e monetaria,* CREA, Rome, 1983, pp. 17ff.

In other words, those asymmetries work unconstrained when budget deficits are possible, but they do not necessarily result in the uninterrupted growth of the deficit, because governments alternate between fiscal prudence and folly. What the asymmetries guarantee is that the reduction of the deficit will always take place at a higher level of taxation and spending rather than at a lower level. But it is still the *possibility* of running a budget deficit that makes it possible for spending to keep growing uninterruptedly.

Welfare for Whom?

The preceding analysis explains the growth of public spending when deficits are possible. It should also help in understanding two propositions about the welfare state which have not been given adequate attention. I'd like to point out that

1. Welfare programs serve the interests of some bureaucrats and politicians far more than they help the intended beneficiaries;

2. Because of the opposition of the concentrated, immediate, and visible interests of bureaucrats and politicians, once a welfare program is introduced, it is almost impossible to dispose of it.

A. THE SIZE OF THE PROBLEM

It is difficult to quantify the total dimension of Italy's welfare system, because it is run by various levels of government (central, regional, provincial, and municipal) and by different agencies. However, even if we limit ourselves to the item "social spending" in the public-sector budget, which can be used as a proxy, its size and growth over time are undeniable.

As shown in Table 4, social spending has grown rapidly in the period 1980–1986, increasing almost threefold in nominal terms (+179 percent), and 38.5 percent in real terms. Its growth has been roughly equal to that of total spending, with this ratio remaining stable, but faster than GDP's growth, with that ratio increasing over the years.

More than the growth, however, it is the absolute amount that's remarkable. In 1986 social spending amounted to 153,447 billion lire, US$116,250,000,000 at the then-prevailing exchange rate. This money was supposed to go to those who needed it. Had it gone to the poorest

TABLE 4. *Social Spending: 1980–1986*

	Billions of lire		As a % of	
	Current Prices	1986 Prices	Total Spending	GDP
1980	54,990	110,805	32.38	14.08
1981	73,136	125,101	32.81	15.62
1982	88,935	130,615	32.41	16.31
1983	109,707	140,534	33.38	17.37
1984	121,805	140,813	32.52	16.90
1985	139,245	147,440	32.46	17.28
1986	153,447	153,447	32.73	17.15

Source: Banca d'Italia, *Appendice, Assemblea Generale Ordinaria dei Partecipanti,* 1987. Data in the first column are in billions of lire at current prices; in the second in billions of lire at 1986 prices; the last two columns measure "social spending" as a percentage of total public-sector spending and GDP respectively.

20 percent of total population, it would have amounted to an additional income of 13,460,000 lire (US$10,197) for each and every of the 11,400,000 Italians in the poorest 20 percent: US$40,788 for the average "poor" family of four. Had this happened, poverty would have completely disappeared, Italy would have become a country made up of exclusively affluent people. Poverty has not disappeared; alas, that money must have gone elsewhere.

B. WHO ARE THE TRUE BENEFICIARIES?

Nor is the case of social spending unique. Another interesting example is provided by "public" kindergartens in Rome, where the municipal administration spends in excess of 77 billion lire per year for its kindergartens that offer their services "free" to a population of 4,000 children. This means that the average cost per child to the taxpayer amounts to 19,250,000 lire (US$14,583). It is to be believed that the "official" beneficiaries of the public kindergartens' program would much rather have a grant of 4,000,000 lire, which would enable them to send their kids to the most exclusive private schools, than the "free" public kindergartens. If this solution was adopted, the taxpayer would save some 61 billion lire per year, with no loss of welfare for the "official" beneficiaries.

The previous analysis, however, explains why such a solution is not even considered: The benefit it would give to the taxpayer is diffused and invisible (very few taxpayers know how much the Rome kindergartens are costing them), while the cost of the proposal would fall on the politicians and bureaucrats presently employed by the program. Each one of them would bear a substantial loss from the repeal of the present system, and would likely be well informed about how much he stands to gain from its continuation. Therefore, even though public kindergartens are obviously uneconomic, it is safe to bet that they will remain in existence for a long time. The concentrated, organized, immediate, and visible interest of the bureaucrats will in all likelihood continue to prevail over the diffused, disorganized, and poorly perceived interest of society.

The same is true in a variety of other instances. Take the National Health System (NHS), for example. Its annual cost is in excess of 50,000 billion lire (some US$38 billion). Its performance is generally regarded as unacceptable, so that over 50 percent of those entitled to "free" public medical care resort to private care. Further, its per capita cost greatly exceeds the cost of private health insurance. There is no doubt that the intended beneficiaries of the NHS would be better off if they'd be given free private health insurance. Such a solution would also greatly benefit the taxpayer, especially if the free insurance would be means-tested. Such a revolutionary and generally beneficial reform, however, does not have a chance of being introduced, because it would be detrimental to the highly organized interests of the 600,000 politicians and bureaucrats presently employed by the NHS.

Furthermore, if the true beneficiaries of state welfare were those in need, i.e., the poor, why has welfare spending *increased* with income? Real income today is much higher and more evenly distributed than, let us say, twenty years ago. If the purpose of welfare spending were that of helping the poor, we should spend less today than we did twenty years ago. The fact that we are spending substantially more now than we did then provides additional evidence that welfare spending is not intended for the poor; its true aim is that of helping those (usually members of the middle class) who run the welfare programs.

Besides, state welfare in its present form tends to be universal: It taxes everybody (including the poor) in order to give to almost everybody (including the wealthy). It is as if it takes from the poor to give to the rich, and its aggregate net effect may well be regressive rather than progressive. If the well-being of the poor were the true goal, selective and means-tested benefits would replace today's universal (and highly inefficient) arrangement.

Finally, if the true purpose of welfare spending were that of helping the poor, the most effective solution would be that of direct cash transfers in the form of a supplemental income, a negative income tax, or some other such solution. Since cash transfers have never even been considered, one must conclude that it is the interest of the producers of "free" welfare services that present arrangements try to serve, not that of the poor, who in fact benefit far more from the spontaneous working of market forces than they do from the dubious generosity of the welfare state.

Considering these facts, it seems safe to conclude that, while it is doubtful whether state welfare in fact helps the poor, it does benefit those who run the programs intended to help the poor. Second, once a welfare program is established, it will survive any evidence of its undesirability because of the opposition to its repeal from politicians and bureaucrats. They are the true beneficiaries of state welfare.

Conclusion

Above this race of men stands an immense and tutelary power, which takes upon itself alone to secure their gratification and to watch over their fate. That power is absolute, minute, regular, provident, and mild. It would be like the authority of a parent if, like that authority, its object was to prepare men for manhood; but it seeks, on the contrary, to keep them in perpetual childhood: it is well content that the people should rejoice, provided they think of nothing but rejoicing. For their happiness such a government willingly labors, but it chooses to be the sole agent and the only arbiter of that happiness; it provides for their security, foresees and supplies their necessities, facilitates their pleasures, manages their principal concerns, directs their industry, regulates the descent of property, and subdivides their inheritance; what remains, but to spare them all care of thinking and all the trouble of living?—Alexis de Tocqueville, 1835

I believe that the evidence in Italy, as well as that of almost all other countries, shows that the "Bismarckian" welfare state has failed. While its inflating costs are threatening the financial solvency of several governments, its results are generally considered unsatisfactory. Disillusionment and frustration have replaced the generous but naive enthusiasm which had characterized its inception.

Also, it is increasingly recognized that comprehensive state welfare has had numerous undesirable side effects: the reduction of personal liberty and freedom of choice, a weakening of family ties, and a decrease in saving and capital formation. Last, but not least, state help has displaced self-help, making a large number of citizens addicted to public charity and incapable of looking after themselves and their families. The bureaucratization of society and the politicization of life which plague many Western democracies are to a considerable extent the result of the welfare state. The real problem now for most Western democracies is how to disentangle themselves from the welfare mess. The resistance of the various interest groups might well prove impossible to overcome.

Things could be easier for those countries that have not engaged in extensive welfare programs yet. They should benefit from the experience of other countries, and try to avoid repeating the same mistakes. Is there an alternative way to pursue the noble ideals of the welfare state, one that is immune from its astronomical costs and abysmal failures? To the extent that there is one, it is that of moving away from state provision of welfare services towards the "voucher society."

For example, this alternative was implicit in John Stuart Mill's 1859 analysis of schooling:

> If the government would make up its mind to *require* for every child a good education, it might save itself the trouble of *providing* one. It might leave to parents to obtain the education where and how they pleased, and content itself with helping to pay the school fees of the poorer classes of children, and defraying the entire school expenses of those who have no one else to pay for them.

Although vouchers have a long intellectual history, they are new and revolutionary in the practical sense. They have never been tried. The case for school vouchers is well known and needs no further illustration, but the same method could be used for health care, old age pensions, housing, and other services currently provided "free" by the welfare state.

Vouchers would go only to that fraction of population that lacks, through no fault of its own, the capacity to pay for some "essential" services. The vouchers could then be spent to purchase privately and competitively supplied health insurance policies, retirement policies, or housing. Bureaucratic costs would be substantially reduced, and the financial burden for the taxpayer would become manageable (provided the number of beneficiaries is kept judiciously small).

It seems to me that we must urgently look for a workable alternative to state welfare, lest its collapse destroy our free democracies.

Taxation and Liberty in the European Welfare State

Taxation of earnings from labor is on a par with forced labor. . . . Seizing the results of someone's labor is equivalent to seizing hours from him and directing him to carry on various activities. If people force you to do certain work, or unrewarded work, for a certain period of time, they decide what you are to do and what purposes your work is to serve apart from your decisions. This process whereby they take this decision from you makes them a part-owner *of you; it gives them a property right in you.—R. Nozick, 1974*

The Italian Case

Welfare states around the world are subject to growing criticism. Their "free" benefits are proving increasingly expensive, and the burden of taxation needed to finance them is widely regarded as unbearable. This general proposition is true to a different extent in different countries, and it is an interesting exercise to try to ascertain which country is winning the race to bankruptcy.

International comparisons, however, are difficult to make, and they are not always very significant, when they are not irrelevant.[1] The meaning of data and their reliability vary from country to country, and the adjustments needed to make the figures comparable are exceedingly complex.

There is a widespread notion that Italy is not a good example of an overtaxed country. First of all, it is said, Italians, being ingenious tax

Talk given at a program in Santa Fe, New Mexico, September 26–29, 1985, unpublished.

1. *See* A. Seldon, "Taxation in the United Kingdom," in *Taxation, An International Perspective,* W. Block and M. Walker, eds., The Fraser Institute, 1984, especially pp. 163ff.

TABLE 1. *Central Government Revenue and Expenditures: 1982 (as a % of GDP)*

	Revenue	Expenditures	Net Borrowing
Italy	42.1	54.3	11.9
France	47.9	50.8	2.9
West Germany	45.2	49.8	3.9
United Kingdom	44.0	45.6	1.6
Canada	40.1	47.4	5.5
Japan	30.7	35.6	4.1
U.S.A.	31.6	35.5	3.8

Source: Banca d'Italia, Assemblea Generale Ordinaria dei Partecipanti, *Relazione*, 1982, May 31, 1983, p. 198.

evaders, do not pay taxes.[2] Secondly, left-wing statists maintain that Italy's welfare system "lags behind" those of "more advanced" countries. This argument is not peculiar to Italy, as similar statements are made for other countries as well.[3] Finally, the quality of welfare benefits in Italy is unanimously regarded as unsatisfactory, and this leads some people to the conclusion that, therefore, Italy has "too little" state charity.

All of the above arguments are incorrect. If it is true that (some) Italians evade taxes, it is also true that they pay taxes to an extent that is unprecedented in the history of the country. Secondly, it is not true that Italy lags behind other countries: The ratio of public sector spending to GDP is among the highest in the world (Table 1).

Finally, if it is true that welfare services are disappointing, this does not mean that Italy has too little state charity, the low level of benefits being just another example of the well-known inefficiency of the public sector. A good example is provided by the Servizio Sanitario Nazionale (national health service). Despite its astronomical total cost—in the

2. *See* R. Rose, "The Making of a Do-It-Yourself Tax Revolt," *Public Opinion*, August–September 1980.

3. *See* Pechman's statement about the U.K. quoted in A. Seldon, op. cit., pp. 163–64.

TABLE 2. *Italy: Public Sector Revenue*

	Total		Tax Revenue		
	Nominal	As a % of GDP	Nominal	Real (1983 prices)	As a % of GDP
1974	36,648	33.1	32,025	125,703	28.9
1975	42,159	33.6	36,971	124,075	29.5
1976	55,778	35.6	49,265	141,553	31.4
1977	70,596	37.1	62,134	152,540	32.7
1978	85,454	38.4	75,857	166,064	34.1
1979	102,567	38.0	91,202	174,004	33.7
1980	135,064	39.9	121,133	190,677	35.8
1981	167,611	41.7	149,745	200,057	37.3
1982	209,199	44.4	188,686	216,489	40.0
1983	256,297	47.8	232,351	232,351	43.4

Source: Banca d'Italia, *Appendice*, Assemblea generale ordinaria dei partecipanti, 1983, March 31, 1984, pp. 47, 122. Nominal figures in billions of current lire; real figure in billions of 1983 lire.

neighborhood of 40,000 billion lire ($20 billions)—it is so inefficient that more than half of the population, even though entitled to "free" public health, prefers to resort to private care and pay twice (once in taxes, once in fees) for medical services.

It must also be mentioned that the *growth* of taxation in Italy has been extremely fast, and this makes the Italian case a particularly good illustration of the relationship between taxation and liberty. For all these reasons, and also because of obvious idiosyncrasies, I shall use the Italian experience as an illustration of the general case.

The Tax Burden

Table 2 illustrates the size and the growth of the tax burden in Italy from 1974 to 1983. During these ten years, total revenue has increased seven times, whereas GDP in 1983 was slightly less than five times its 1974 level. As a result, total revenue has increased from less than one-third of GDP in 1974 to almost one-half in 1983. The increase in revenue has come almost exclusively from tax sources; nontax revenue has remained roughly constant as a percentage of GDP during the whole period.

In nominal terms, tax revenue has increased more than seven times (+625 percent). However, this has been a decade of high inflation—the consumer price index has almost quadrupled from 1974 to 1983—so that real figures are more significant. Even taking inflation into account, the growth of tax revenue is enormous: from 1974 to 1983, real tax revenue has increased almost 85 percent, going from 28.9 percent of GDP to 43.4 percent.[4] The growth of the real tax burden has been markedly faster from 1980 to 1983 than in the previous years: In 1980 taxation was absorbing 6.9 percent more of GDP than in 1974. It had taken *seven* years to increase the tax burden by less than 7 percent of GDP; in the following *four* years, the increase was larger than in the previous seven: an extra 7.6 percent of GDP was absorbed by taxation.

The acceleration in the rate of growth of taxation from 1980 to 1983 cannot, obviously, continue for a long time. Given the absolute size of the tax burden, it is unlikely that the tendency will be allowed to continue. From 1980 to 1983, GDP has increased by 197,161 billion lire, tax revenue by 111,218 billions; in other words, the increase in taxation has absorbed 56.4 percent of the increase in GDP. As we shall see, things are much worse if one looks at the growth of public spending.

Public Spending

From 1974 to 1983 public-sector expenditures have increased over seven times in nominal terms, almost 83 percent in real terms, and they have gone from 41.3 percent of GDP to 61.2 percent in 1983. This is indeed an astronomical increase: in ten years the public sector has increased its share of the pie by an *extra* 20 percent. The absolute amount is also staggering: It means that the average Italian has worked

4. The discrepancy between these percentages and those in Table 1—both coming from the same source—will not surprise anybody: Banca d'Italia is, after all, a government institution. A more generous explanation might be that, as the figures in Table 2 have been published one year later than those in Table 1, there might have been a revision. The discrepancy is, however, quite small, and it does not alter the meaning of the data for our purposes.

TABLE 3. *Italy: Public-Sector Expenditures*

	Nominal	Real (1983 prices)	As a % of GDP
1974	45,738	179,528	41.3
1975	57,816	194,030	46.1
1976	71,011	204,035	45.3
1977	87,208	214,097	45.9
1978	109,051	238,731	49.1
1979	129,948	247,928	48.1
1980	165,398	260,354	48.8
1981	218,350	291,713	54.4
1982	274,598	315,060	58.2
1983	327,875	327,875	61.2

Source: Banca d'Italia, op. cit.

from January 1 to May 31 for the government in 1974, from January 1 to August 12 in 1983—an extra 73 days of "government exploitation"!

The figures in Table 3 also illustrate the acceleration in the rate of growth of public spending. In 1980 public-sector expenditures accounted for less than one-half of GDP; from 1980 to 1983 GDP has increased by 197,161 billion lire, whereas public spending has increased by 162,477 billion. This means that from 1980 to 1983 the increase in spending has absorbed 82.4 percent of the increase in GDP—a fantastic acceleration. It is worth mentioning that such an acceleration of public spending has taken place at a time when governments were proclaiming their determination to control the growth of spending. Indeed, that has been the number-one priority in all government programs in the past few years. The results have been disappointing, to say the least. Also, it must be stressed that such an increase in statism and the resulting increase in taxation have taken place during years of almost complete stagnation: From 1980 to 1983 there has been no appreciable increase in real per capita GDP.

Needless to say, the increase in spending has not been the result of an increased production of "public goods." Even those who do not share my view that the quality and quantity of public goods have actu-

TABLE 4. *Italy: Net Borrowing*

	Nominal	Real (1983 prices)	As a % of GDP
1974	9,090	35,680	8.2
1975	15,657	52,545	12.5
1976	15,233	43,769	9.7
1977	16,612	40,783	8.7
1978	23,597	51,658	10.6
1979	27,381	52,240	10.1
1980	30,334	47,749	8.9
1981	50,739	67,787	12.6
1982	65,399	75,036	13.9
1983	71,578	71,578	13.4

Source: Banca d'Italia, op. cit.

ally *declined* from 1974 to 1983 freely agree that they have certainly not increased by 83 percent during the decade. But we'll come back to this later.

The Deficit

The figures in Table 4 illustrate the growth of net borrowing—one of the ways to measure the government deficit. It can be seen that, with the (apparent?) exception of 1976, net borrowing has increased every single year in nominal terms throughout the decade. In 1983 it was almost eight times larger than in 1974 in nominal terms, twice larger in real terms, and it had gone from 8.2 percent of GDP to 13.4 percent.

The growth of the deficit disposes of a common fallacy: the idea that, in order to reduce the deficit, all that's needed is to increase taxes. As we have seen, taxation has grown very fast during the decade, and yet the deficit, rather than decreasing, has gone up by leaps and bounds. The reason is quite obvious: The "marginal propensity to public spending"—the increase in spending over the increase in revenue—has consistently been greater than one. The result is that when taxes go up so does the deficit.

In order to reduce the deficit, there is no alternative to a policy of limiting government spending. Had public spending not been *reduced,* not held *constant,* but *increased* in proportion to GDP from 1980 to 1983, it would have amounted to 261,521 billion lire in 1983 (48.8 percent of GDP). This would have resulted in net borrowing of 5,224 billion lire, instead of 71,578: less than 1 percent of GDP, instead of 13.4 percent. A very moderate policy of restraint—holding public spending constant in percentage of GDP—would have resulted in the lowest deficit in the history of the Republic of Italy. The reason for this spectacular success would have been the enormous increase in tax revenue during those four years. However, as we have seen, that opportunity has been wasted, and it is highly doubtful that it will present itself again.

The control of public spending is far more effective in reducing the deficit than the increase in taxation per se. Had total revenue remained constant as a percentage of GDP from 1980 to 1983, and had public spending also remained constant as a percentage of GDP during the same period, the deficit (as measured by net borrowing) would have amounted to 47,695 billion in 1983, rather than 71,578 billion. It would have been reduced by a third compared to its actual level. Even without any increase in taxation, control of public spending would have succeeded in containing the deficit.

The Public Debt

The cumulative effect of an uninterrupted series of budget deficits is reflected in the growth of public debt outstanding. In Table 5A the official figures of the public debt for the decade show an increase of 609 percent in nominal terms, a near doubling in real terms, and an increase of 47 percent in the ratio of public debt to GDP. The process has accelerated after 1983, and the ratio is presently greater than one, which means that public debt exceeds one year's income. Government officials, worried by the size of the debt and its growth, have recently announced their plan to reduce the ratio to GDP to one [sic] by 1988.

The growth of the public debt is an inevitable consequence of the budget deficit, and, as this has been going on for many years, so has the growth of the debt. According to International Monetary Fund fig-

TABLE 5. *A. Italy: Public Debt*

	Nominal	Real (1983 prices)	As a % of GDP
1974	63,885	250,758	57.7
1975	82,996	278,535	66.2
1976	101,651	292,073	64.9
1977	123,685	303,648	65.1
1978	157,466	344,720	70.8
1979	189,439	361,431	70.1
1980	226,798	357,005	66.9
1981	281,178	375,650	70.0
1982	359,157	412,079	76.2
1983	453,439	453,439	84.6

Source: Banca d'Italia, op. cit.

B. An International Comparison

	1979	1980	1981	1982	1983
Italy	70.1	66.9	70.0	76.2	84.6
Seven major industrial countries, average	42.0	42.9	44.0	47.9	50.8

Source: Banca d'Italia, op. cit.

ures, between 1961 and 1982, public debt in lire and foreign currencies soared almost thirty-fivefold. The most common type of government bonds is a BOT (pronounced "boat"), a Buono Ordinario del Tesoro, or ordinary treasury bill. So many have been issued that Italians joke they've become "BOT people."[5]

Both the size and the growth of public debt in Italy are unparalleled in other major industrial countries. Table 5B shows how much greater Italy's indebtedness is compared to the average of the seven major industrial countries.

5. *See* A. Martino, "Italy Risks Turning Bond Buyers into 'BOT' People," *The Wall Street Journal Europe,* February 7, 1984.

C. Italy: Interest Payments

	Nominal	As a % of GDP	As a % of Public-Sector Expenditures
1974	3,691	3.34	8.07
1975	5,285	4.22	9.14
1976	7,439	4.75	10.48
1977	9,664	5.08	11.08
1978	13,360	6.01	12.25
1979	16,046	5.94	12.35
1980	21,525	6.35	13.01
1981	29,465	7.34	13.49
1982	40,570	8.61	14.77
1983	50,137	9.36	15.29

Source: Banca d'Italia, op. cit.

It doesn't require much imagination to figure out that interest payments on such an astronomical public debt are high—in 1983 they accounted for over 70 percent of the deficit. Table 5C shows the growth of interest payments from 1974 to 1983: They have increased almost fourteen times in nominal terms, almost three times as a percentage of GDP—growing to an incredible near 10 percent, and they have almost doubled their ratio to public-sector spending. In 1983 interest payments accounted for more than 15 percent of total public-sector spending.

Given the size of the problem, some people are arguing for a tax on interest payments on government bonds, which today promise exemption from "all present and future taxes." Such is the state of financial disarray that these people are prepared to ignore the rules of basic honesty in the (vain) attempt to remedy the situation. They forget that it's hardly fair to blame the enormous size of the public debt on those who have agreed to lend money to the government. And considering the reasons for the huge rise in Italy's public deficit, it's clear that a tax on bonds wouldn't solve the problem. It is not unlikely that it might make matters worse.

Tax Evasion?

What has been said so far should suffice to dispel the notion that financial disarray in Italy is due to insufficient taxation—whatever *that* means. In fact, as mentioned before, in the past twenty-five years the growth in taxation has been accompanied by an *increase* in the budget deficit, rather than a decrease. In the light of this evidence, it would seem as if, in order to reduce the deficit, taxation should be reduced rather than increased.[6]

As for those who claim that taxation is not excessive, given the undeniable fact that the proportion of GDP absorbed by government has reached an all-time high, they should either view the history of the country as a long, gradual process toward the "right" level of taxation, or argue that there have been valid reasons for the rapid growth of the cost of government. In the first case, however, they should explain why we have historically always paid "too little" taxes and what is "right" about the present level of taxation. If they choose the second alternative, they should provide us with an acceptable analysis of the reasons that justify such a tremendous increase in taxation. Nobody, as far as I know, has even tried to answer these questions, and, as long as they remain unanswered, it seems fair to conclude that the growth of taxation is unjustified and its present level is unacceptable.

One of the reasons why many people still hold the view that, despite the rapid growth of recent years, taxation in Italy is low is based on what I would call the "Rose paradox." In a 1980 paper, Professor Richard Rose stated: "Historically, Italy has been the leader in nonpayment of taxes and there is little doubt that it still is at the head of the pack. One unpublished (Organization for Economic Cooperation and Development) report estimates that tax evasion there is as high as 27 percent of total reported income."[7]

Here the existence of tax evasion is taken as conclusive evidence

6. *See* A. Martino, "Italy's Lesson: Higher Taxes, Bigger Deficit," *The Wall Street Journal Europe*, October 25, 1984. [See pp. 3–6 of this volume.]

7. R. Rose, op. cit. See also A. Martino, "Invisible Taxation, The Growth of Italy's Leviathan," *Policy Review*, no. 25, pp. 46ff. [see pp. 15–27 of this volume]; A. Martino, "Italians Pay More Taxes Than They Think," *The Wall Street Journal Europe*, August 8, 1983.

that Italians don't pay taxes. Such a conclusion is a complete non sequitur of the premise. The fact is that tax evasion has always existed, and it would be surprising if tax laws did not take it into account. Our tax rates, in other words, have already been corrected to incorporate the probable degree of evasion. If Italians had paid that famous 27 percent of OECD-estimated evasion on top of what they in fact did pay in taxes in 1980, total public revenue in 1980 would have amounted to 66.9 percent of GDP. I don't know of anybody willing to justify that level of fiscal burden, and I'm sure that Professor Richard Rose would agree that 67 percent of GDP is an unacceptable high level of taxation. The existence of evasion, in other words, does not imply that Italians do not pay taxes, or that they pay little. It's true that the fact that they pay does not prove that they do not evade; but it is equally true that the fact that they evade does not mean that they do not pay. Despite their success as tax evaders, Italians do pay very dearly for their government. And, given the unreliability of estimates of tax evasion, it is a lot easier to assume that tax evasion exists than it is to quantify it.

Another reason that leads many observers to believe that taxation in Italy is low has to do with the so-called submerged or underground economy. The existence of unreported income, however, does not per se affect our analysis of the *growth* of taxation. If "true" income is higher than that recorded in official statistics, the ratio of tax revenue to GDP is lower than the recorded one. But this does not necessarily affect either the absolute level of taxation or its growth over time. Talks about the existence of the underground economy have misled many people to believe that taxation was not excessive and that there was ample room for more government growth.[8] The truth is that, considering the arbitrary upward revision in official income statistics of 1979 (a 10 percent increase), and the fantastic growth of taxation from 1979 and on, the share of income that goes unrecorded in official figures must have substantially declined in the past five years. I am also personally convinced that the government's "fight" against tax evasion has been rather successful in reducing the size of the underground econ-

8. I regret to say that I am guilty of such a crime, having written on the subject. See "Measuring Italy's Underground Economy," *Policy Review,* no. 16, Spring 1981, pp. 87ff. [See pp. 177–95 of this volume.]

omy, even though I cannot offer any conclusive evidence in support of such a belief.

Fraudulent Taxation

We are, however, left with a puzzle: How has a nation of ingenious tax evaders ended up sacrificing such a high percentage of its income to the tax man and allowed that percentage to grow so rapidly? One possible explanation runs as follows:

> In order for taxpayers to oppose government growth, they must be aware of the share of the cost of government that falls on them. People, that is, must realize that *they* are paying for government spending; they must be aware of how much they are paying in taxes. In order for that to happen, taxes must be *visible*. . . . While this is true of some kinds of taxes, it is not true for all. . . . In Italy, most taxes are (invisible).[9]

Table 6 illustrates the financing of public expenditures in Italy in the decade 1974–1983. The picture has changed somewhat over time. However, the basic fact remains: Most of the sources of revenue to finance public expenditures are of a "hidden" nature. This means that, by and large, Italians bear the cost of government without being aware that they are paying for it. In 1983, as we have seen, total public-sector spending amounted to 61.2 percent of GDP, and, judging from the absence of *open* manifestations of taxpayers' rebellion, the government had no problem in extracting that extravagant percentage of people's income from their pockets. How was that "miracle" accomplished?

The answer, in my opinion, must be found in the way public spending was financed. Direct taxation—the most visible form of taxation—yielded "only" 25.6 percent of total public spending. However, direct taxes are not perfectly visible; given the existence of withholding by the employer, Italians are used to thinking of their income in terms of the after-withholding, net figure, and they are not aware of how much they are paying in withholding tax through their employer. Indirect

9. A. Martino, *Constraining Inflationary Government,* The Heritage Foundation, Washington, D.C., 1982, p. 49.

TABLE 6. *Italy: Financing Public Expenditures*

	Direct Taxation		Indirect Taxation		"Social Contributions"		Other Revenue		Net Borrowing	
1974	6,949	(15.2)	10,870	(23.8)	14,206	(31.0)	4,623	(10.1)	9,090	(19.9)
1975	8,440	(14.6)	10,962	(19.0)	17,569	(30.4)	5,188	(9.0)	15,657	(27.1)
1976	12,334	(17.4)	15,021	(21.1)	21,910	(30.8)	6,513	(9.2)	15,233	(21.5)
1977	16,458	(18.9)	19,485	(22.3)	26,191	(30.0)	8,462	(9.7)	16,612	(19.1)
1978	22,408	(20.6)	22,368	(20.5)	31,081	(28.5)	9,597	(8.8)	23,597	(21.6)
1979	26,628	(20.5)	25,347	(19.5)	39,227	(30.2)	11,365	(8.7)	27,381	(21.1)
1980	38,045	(23.0)	34,128	(20.6)	48,960	(29.6)	13,931	(8.4)	30,334	(18.3)
1981	51,575	(23.6)	39,025	(17.9)	59,145	(27.1)	17,866	(8.2)	50,739	(23.2)
1982	67,229	(24.5)	47,680	(17.4)	73,777	(26.9)	20,513	(7.5)	65,399	(23.8)
1983	84,134	(25.6)	60,242	(18.4)	87,975	(26.8)	23,946	(7.3)	71,578	(21.8)

Source: Banca d'Italia, op. cit. All figures in billions of current lire. Figures in parentheses express the item as a percentage of total public-sector spending.

taxes amounted to 18.4 percent of public spending. Again, these are almost perfectly invisible: Few Italians are aware of the fact that the "price" of gasoline is in fact made out of indirect taxes equal to almost two-thirds of the total. "Social contributions" amounted to 26.8 percent of total public-sector spending. "Contributions" are in fact compulsory, so that they represent a payroll tax. But, as they are largely paid "by the employer," the employee is not aware of how much he is paying in taxes through his employer. Another typical example of hidden taxation.

Finally, net borrowing amounted to 21.8 percent of public spending. This is the most invisible of all taxes. Most people (including, alas, even professional economists) seem convinced that deficit-financed public spending is like manna from heaven, a benefit no one has to pay for.

Taking all these factors into consideration, it is not unreasonable to suppose that in 1983 80 percent of all taxes were invisible, which means that for every million lire of taxes paid by taxpayers aware of what they were doing, the government took another four million away from them without them being aware of it. This is, in my opinion, the single most important factor that has prevented a tax rebellion from taking place in Italy so far.

But this is not the main reason for objecting to the invisibility of taxes. The fact is that the visibility of taxes is an essential component of a truly democratic government. In a democracy, people must be aware of the cost of government, because *they* (and no one else) bear that cost. Government of the people means, among other things, that people must control their government. This is impossible when the cost of government is hidden behind a complex cobweb of invisible taxes, understood only by those who possess the kind of sophisticated knowledge required to see through. The decision of how much government to have, of what percentage of personal income should be turned over to the government (and what percentage should be left to the free choice of the individual), in a democracy naturally belongs to the people. A political system in which government surreptitiously takes over one-half of their income from the people, knowing that, if they were aware of it, they would not allow it to happen, is not only a fraudulent one, it is also an undemocratic one, because it violates the people's sovereignty.

Such a conclusion is confirmed by Article 75, Section 2, of the Italian constitution, which explicitly forbids resort to popular referendum "for tax laws or laws on the budget." Supporters of the constitutional prohibition explicitly justify its existence on the ground that Italians, if allowed to vote on tax issues, would repeal most, if not all, taxes. Obviously, they are ready to admit that taxation is regarded as excessive by the majority of the electorate.

Toward Greater Visibility?

There is something stealthy about the nature of the Italian welfare state, where invisible taxation is used to finance nonexistent benefits. A good example is that of "social spending." As we have seen, from 1980 to 1983 total public-sector spending has nearly doubled in nominal terms. Of all categories of public expenditures, social spending showed the largest increase, accounting for 31.7 percent of the increase in total spending.

In absolute terms the amount devoted to social spending was staggering: 105,051 billion lire ($70 billion at the then-prevailing exchange rate). This money should presumably have gone to the "poor." Now,

TABLE 7. *Italy: Individual Income Tax Rates*

up to $7,243	18%
from $7,244 to $15,802	27%
from $15,803 to $19,753	35%
from $19,754 to $25,020	37%
from $25,021 to $39,505	41%
from $39,506 to $79,010	47%
from $79,011 to $164,604	56%
from $164,605 to $329,208	62%
above $329,208	65%

Source: Ministero delle Finanze, mod. 740/84, Redditi, 1983, Dichiarazione delle Persone Fisiche, *Istruzioni per la compilazione.*

Income brackets have been converted into U.S. $ figures, using the average exchange rate for 1983, as reported in *International Financial Statistics*: $1 = L1,518.8.

assuming that one Italian out of five is poor (an obvious exaggeration), had those 105,051 billion lire gone to the 11,400,000 poor Italians, it would have turned them into affluent members of the upper middle class: Each one of them would have received 9,215,000 lire ($6,067), 36,860,000 ($24,268) for a family of four. Poverty would have disappeared from the country, Italians would have all been wealthy. Clearly, things did not work out that way, and the Italian poor have a hard time seeing the benefits handed out to them by the generosity of the welfare state.

The hidden nature of the Italian tax system is, however, diminishing: As the figures in Table 6 show, direct taxation has had the largest absolute increase, among the various sources of revenue, from 1974 to 1983. The reason for such a large increase in income tax revenue is, obviously, the bracket creep: the combined effect of inflation and steeply graduated tax rates that have pushed an increasing number of taxpayers into higher income brackets.

Table 7 shows the bracket tax rates on individual taxable income for 1983. It can be seen that even relatively modest incomes are subject to very high marginal rates: Income above $25,000, for example, is taxed at a marginal rate of 41 percent.[10] Taking inflation into account (1984 has been the twelfth consecutive year of double-digit inflation), it is not surprising that even trade union leaders are learning English terms and economic concepts, and they all complain now of the dire consequences of the "fiscal drag."

In fact, bracket creep, and not economic growth or explicit increases in tax rates, is largely responsible for the increase in direct tax revenue: from 1974 to 1983, it has increased twelve times in nominal terms, over 200 percent in real terms, and over 150 percent as a share of GDP.

The Growth of Government: An Explanation

Gordon Tullock maintains that we do not have a general theory of government growth, that all explanations of the rapid increase in taxation and spending in the post–World War II era are contradicted by the evidence: What is true for a given country at one time is not true for another country or for another period of time.[11] In a sense, this is true by definition: The circumstances and the prevailing intellectual climate are different from country to country and they vary over time. Also, it is true that a *general* theory should apply equally well to past trends as well as to contemporary developments. There is no doubt that we do not have any satisfactory explanation for such a wide range of events. In another sense, I believe that we do have a theory of

10. This makes the income tax burden due by an Italian taxpayer substantially higher than that of his American counterpart. For example, a taxable income of $25,020 for 1983 would have paid $6,946.27 in Italy—an average tax rate of 27.76 percent. The same income in the United States would have been subject to a federal income tax of $3,570 in 1984—an average tax rate of 14.27 percent. See J. A. Tatom, "Federal Income Tax Reform in 1985: Indexation," The Federal Reserve Bank of St. Louis *Review* 67, no. 2, 1985, p. 5ff. Comparisons are, however, very difficult to make: Translating incomes from one currency to another is tricky, account must be made for deductions and other kinds of taxes, etc. However, that difference is not meaningless.

11. G. Tullock, "Esiste una teoria generale della crescita dello statalismo?" in *La Costituzione Fiscale e Monetaria, Vincoli alla Finanza Inflazionistica,* CREA, Rome 1983, pp. 35ff.

government growth that explains pretty well the prevailing tendencies in Western democracies in the last twenty-five to thirty years. Such a theory is not new, but it is worth mentioning.

I believe that the starting point of such an explanation is the existence of three asymmetries in the perception of costs and benefits of public spending.[12] First of all, the democratic political process tends to favor decisions that result in benefits for a small group of beneficiaries and whose cost is spread over a large number of taxpayers. The recent proposal to increase the salary of Italian university professors, who are, I regret to admit, government employees, by an average of 10,000,000 lire each, gave each one of the 10,000 members of the profession an incentive of 10,000,000 lire a year to support the proposal. On the other hand, if the cost of the bill (100 billion lire) is spread evenly over the whole of society, each one of the 57,000,000 Italians will have an incentive to oppose the bill worth only 1,750 lire a year. "In these circumstances, wrote Pareto in 1896, the outcome is not in doubt: the spoliators will win hands down."[13]

The existence of such an asymmetry is confirmed by the fact that spending on public goods has not been the main factor behind the growth of total spending. Since public goods benefit the whole of society, they often lack a constituency lobbying for them, so that the growth of public spending is usually slower. Also, the existence of this asymmetry is evidenced by the near-impossibility to *reduce* government spending, because the costs of the reduction would fall on a small number of former beneficiaries, and the benefits would go to society as a whole. Finally, it is obvious that the success of the first group of beneficiaries will provide an incentive for the formation of other groups, so that the asymmetry results in a process of government *growth* that continues over time.

The second asymmetry results from the fact that the political process tends to favor decisions based on *visible* benefits and *invisible* costs.

12. *See* A. Martino, "Fraudulent 'Democracy,'" *Economic Affairs* 4, no. 1, 1983; A. Martino, "Toward Monetary Stability?" *Economia Internazionale* 37, nos. 1–2, 1984.

13. V. Pareto, *Cours d'économie politique,* 1896. In *Sociological Writings,* translated by D. Mirfin and edited by S. E. Finer, London, 1966, as quoted in *The Year of Economists: 1980–81,* compiled by G. J. Stigler and C. Friedland, Chicago, 1980.

The visibility of benefits guarantees the support for the proposal by the potential beneficiaries, while the invisibility of costs neutralizes the opposition of those who will bear them. In the previous example, while university professors are likely to know exactly how much they stand to gain from the approval of the bill, it is unlikely that any taxpayer knows how much the increase in university professors' salary will add to his own tax burden.

Finally, the political process favors decisions that result in an *immediate* gain (even if small) whose cost (even if large) is paid in the distant *future*. This last asymmetry is particularly acute in Italy because, given the high instability of the executive (the average "life expectancy at birth" of Italian governments is less than a year), the time horizon of political decision makers tends to be very short. Governments generally tend to favor spending decisions that confer an immediate gain to some group in society, even if the future cost of the decision is substantial, because in all likelyhood it will be borne by another government.

If the above analysis is correct, we would expect government growth to be faster when public spending is financed by a device that (a) spreads costs over large numbers of taxpayers; (b) hides these costs from those who bear them; (c) produces immediate benefits at the expense of high (if not disastrous) consequences in the future. Such a device exists, and it is called a deficit. Its time pattern—in Italy, at least—confirms the preceding analysis beyond any doubt.

Let me stress at this point that the validity of the above analysis does not depend on the existence of an uninterrupted growth of the deficit through time. What happens is that, when the deficit reaches a certain level, the need to reduce it—stressed with great vigor by fiscal conservatives of all political parties—results in higher taxation. It is quite possible, therefore, that those asymmetries produce increases in the deficit followed by increases in explicit taxation, and a reduction in the deficit, and so on. (As we shall see, this is not the case for Italy.) In the words of James Buchanan:

> Beneficiary groups, recipients of direct transfers or of governmentally-financed programs, tend to be concentrated, organized, and capable of exerting influence over elected politicians. By contrast, taxpayer groups, those who pay taxes, tend to be widely dispersed

TABLE 8. *Italy: The Deficit*

	Nominal	As a % of GDP
1951	388	3.6%
1961	357	1.5%
1971	4,757	6.9%
1981	53,210	13.4%
1983	88,522	16.5%

Source: IMF, *International Financial Statistics*, various issues. The IMF definition of the deficit differs from the "net borrowing" definition of Banca d'Italia. Hence the disprepancy with the figures of Table 4.

and, indeed, tend to include almost everyone due to the fact that taxes are general rather than specific. As a result of the asymmetry, it becomes easier to get political decision-makers to expand budgets than to contract them.[14]

In other words, those asymmetries work unconstrained when budget deficits are possible, but they do not necessarily result in uninterrupted growth of the deficit, because governments alternate between fiscal prudence and folly. What the asymmetries guarantee is that the reduction of the deficit will always take place at a higher level of taxation and spending rather than at a lower level. But it is still the *possibility* of running a budget deficit that makes it possible for government to keep growing uninterruptedly.

At this point, a problem arises. The incentive structure affecting the behavior of voters, politicians, and taxpayers in such a way as to promote government growth can be assumed to have been in existence ever since mass democracy was born. Why is it, then, that government deficits did not start to increase in Italy until the early 1960s?

The answer must be found in the impact of the "Keynesian revolution." As long as the "balanced budget norm" prevailed, the formation of larger budget deficits was discouraged: The deficit declined from 388 billion lire in 1951 to 357 billion in 1961, from 3.6 percent of

14. J. M. Buchanan, "I limiti alla fiscalità," in *La Costituzione . . .*, op. cit., pp. 17ff.

GDP to 1.5 percent. The 1950s were the decade of liberal governments, when the balanced budget norm embodied in the Italian constitution[15] was substantially respected. With the "opening to the left"—the formation of a government coalition including the Socialists—in the early 1960s, the balanced budget norm was replaced by the Keynesian mythology of deficit spending. The working of those three asymmetries became unconstrained, and the budget deficit exploded: 6.9 percent of GDP in 1971, 13.4 percent in 1981, 16.5 percent in 1983. The evidence—in Italy, at least—confirms the validity of J. M. Buchanan's and R. E. Wagner's conclusion:

> The mounting historical evidence of the ill-effects of Keynes's ideas cannot continue to be ignored. Keynesian economics has turned the politicians loose; it has destroyed the effective constraint on politicians' ordinary appetites to spend and spend without the apparent necessity to tax.
>
> Sober assessment suggests that, politically, Keynesianism represents a substantial disease that over the long run can prove fatal for the survival of democracy.[16]

Taxation and Liberty

If the preceding analysis is correct, the rapid growth of government in all European welfare states can be attributed to the combined effect of the system of political incentives typical of the democratic political process on the one hand, and the consequences of the Keynesian revolution on the other. The "decoupling" of spending and taxing decisions, made possible by the abandonment of the balanced budget norm, has allowed taxation and spending to grow rapidly over time in response to the political pressures resulting from the three asymmetries mentioned above.

This is true to a different extent of all European welfare states. With

15. For an analysis of Italy's fiscal constitution, see A. Martino, *Constraining Inflationary Government,* op. cit.

16. J. M. Buchanan and R. E. Wagner, "Democracy and Keynesian Constitutions: Political Biases and Economic Consequences," in *The Consequences of Mr Keynes,* The Institute of Economic Affairs, London, 1978, p. 27.

some opportune qualifications, what has been said about Italy can be repeated for other European countries as well. In the words of Roland Vaubel:

> Over the last one hundred years government expenditure has grown much faster than the national product in virtually all industrialized countries. In the 1960s and 1970s this process has been gaining speed. From 1960 to 1980, for example, total government outlays in the OECD have on average increased as a percentage of Gross Domestic Product from 28.5 per cent to 39.3 per cent. As a result, taxes take an ever larger share of national income, and increasing government borrowing portends even higher taxes in the future. As government controls an ever larger part of national expenditures, the liberty of the individual citizen is successively eroded. The liberal state is increasingly displaced by the welfare state.[17]

One of the peculiarities of the growth of taxation in Italy is its hidden and fraudulent nature. This has prevented active taxpayers' resistance, at least thus far. Again, this is not exclusive to Italy; the main function of budget deficits is precisely that of hiding the cost of government from those who bear it. And, to a different extent, budget deficits have played an important rôle in making the growth of government possible in all welfare states.

The deficit is a tax that falls on the whole of society, it is largely invisible—no one knows how much he will personally pay because of the deficit, and it is entirely arbitrary. I consider this to be the most important objection to deficit-financed public spending. In this, as in so many other matters, I entirely agree with Adam Smith:

> The tax which each individual is bound to pay ought to be certain, and not arbitrary. The time of payment, the manner of payment, the quantity to be paid, ought all to be clear and plain to the contributor, and to every other person. . . .
>
> The certainty of what each individual ought to pay is, in taxation, a matter of so great importance, that a very considerable degree of

17. R. Vaubel, "I fondamenti teorici dello stato assistenziale: un'analisi critica," in *La Crisi dello Stato Assistenziale,* CREA, Rome, 1984, p. 19ff.

> inequality . . . is not near so great an evil as a very small degree of uncertainty.[18]

Even though Adam Smith had a different problem in mind, his defense of the importance of certainty in taxation applies to the case of all forms of hidden taxation, including the deficit.

The existence of hidden taxation has made the growth of government easier. But that is not its only consequence; the most undesirable feature of the present system is that the ratio of government spending to national income is not decided by some authority subject to a clear and well-defined set of rules. The most important decision in fiscal matters—what percentage of national income should be turned over to politicians and bureaucrats—is neither trusted to an authority nor disciplined by impartial rules. Each individual spending proposal is examined in its own light, without any regard to other needs and goals. The ratio of GDP absorbed by government is then the unintentional outcome of the sum of thousands and thousands of spending decisions.

It is ironic that in an overtaxed country like Italy, relatively more importance is given by academics, journalists, and politicians to questions like "who should pay for an increase in taxation" or "how should more tax revenue be raised" than to the much more fundamental questions: "How much should people pay?" and "Who should decide what percentage of the national income should go to the government?" In other words, discussion on fiscal issues tends to center on the *distribution* of the tax burden and on the optimal *kind* of taxation, and it neglects the much more important issues of the desirable *level* of taxation and of the optimal decision-making *process* to determine the size of the fiscal burden in a democracy. Yet the last two questions are all-important.

One needs not repeat the old argument that a transfer of resources from A to B is morally acceptable if, and only if, A agrees to it, in order to understand how crucially important the decision-making process is in fiscal matters. In the words of Frederic Bastiat: "When a portion of wealth is transferred from the person who owns it—without his con-

18. A. Smith, *The Wealth of Nations,* E. Cannan edition, Modern Library, New York, 1937, p. 778.

sent and without compensation, and whether by force or by fraud—to anyone who does not own it, then I say that property is violated; that an act of plunder is committed."[19] Obviously, minimizing the extent of "legal plunder" by adopting some kind of procedure that could prevent taxation from growing beyond its "proper" level (let alone defining the "proper" level of taxation) should be a high-priority goal in a free democracy. Yet one hears very little discussion on this issue even in countries that, like the countries of Europe, are obviously overtaxed.

One of the most vivid illustrations of the relationship between the level of taxation and individual liberty is provided by Robert Nozick in the "Tale of the Slave." It illustrates the essence of what he calls *demoktesis,* or "ownership of the people, by the people, and for the people," and it can thus be summarized. Suppose there is a country where slavery is accepted. The slaves work for their owner, who gets all the product of their labor over and above the cost of keeping them alive.

Such an arrangement is not only morally repugnant, it is also inefficient, both because it presumably violates the principle of the division of labor, by denying slaves the choice of the occupation for which they have a comparative advantage, and because it deprives slaves of all incentives. Presumably because of efficiency considerations, the master decides to move to a different kind of arrangement. The slaves are now free to work on their own three days a week, but they are required to provide for their own needs and work on the master's farm the other four days.

This second arrangement is better than the first, but it is still inefficient, because slaves are still deprived of incentives in their work on their master's farm, and can only devote three-sevenths of their time to the occupation for which they have a comparative advantage. So the master moves to a third arrangement, allowing the slaves to work on their own seven days a week, provided they give him four-sevenths of their wages. This last situation is undistinguishable from the other two, even though more efficient: The slaves are still slaves and the master

19. F. Bastiat, *The Law* (1850), The Foundation for Economic Education, Irvington-on-Hudson, New York, 1974, p. 26.

master. Incidentally, four-sevenths are slightly more than 57 percent, a percentage that's very close to the incidence of taxation in most European welfare states![20]

The tale shows the relationship between taxation and liberty, by illustrating the principle that "taxation of earnings from labor is on a par with forced labor." I have elsewhere[21] referred to this phenomenon by calling it "statist exploitation"—in somewhat modified Marxian jargon. I have always been puzzled by the fact that Marxists complain about capitalistic exploitation, which—if I understand correctly—is measured by the ratio of profits to national income, and they remain silent about statist exploitation, the percentage of our income absorbed by bureaucrats and politicians. And yet the former amounts at most to a few percentage points, whereas the latter corresponds to over 60 percent of the average Italian's income.

Obviously, if one is convinced, as I am, that anarchy is impossible, some degree of statist exploitation is unavoidable. However, this does not mean that *any* degree of exploitation, any *level* of taxation, is compatible with personal freedom. What would the meaning of freedom be if the government would confiscate 100 percent of national income?

Conclusion

There is an inverse relationship between the level of taxation—the ratio of tax revenue to GDP—and individual liberty. Economic considerations about the undesirable consequences of high taxation aside, excessive taxation must be avoided. Under present conditions, in Italy as well as in other European welfare states, the level of taxation is neither planned by the deliberate decision of an authority nor trusted to some impartial rule. Furthermore, the structure of political incentives has so far resulted in the continuous growth of taxation over time. If allowed to continue, this process would wipe out individual freedom completely. Something must be done, as soon as possible, before it's too late. Changing the people in charge, as has been done in En-

20. *See* R. Nozick, *Anarchy, State, and Utopia,* Basic Books, New York, 1974, pp. 290–92.

21. "Statism at Work: The Italian Case," in *Champions of Freedom, The Ludwig von Mises Lecture Series,* Hillsdale College, Mich., 1981, p. 18.

gland, is at best a stopgap measure: The growth of taxation cannot be blamed on the conspiracy of evil and incompetent politicians; it has been the result of the "natural" working of the democratic process in the absence of an effective fiscal constitution.

In my opinion, that's the direction toward which we ought to move. As James Buchanan has stressed: "*A constitutionally imposed and defined fiscal and monetary framework is a necessary requirement for the viability of a tolerably free society.*"[22]

ADDENDUM. *Italy: 1984*

	Nominal	1983 Prices	As a % of GDP
Total Public-Sector Revenue	290,176	261,890	47.4
Public-Sector Expenditures	380,327	343,254	62.1
Net Borrowing	90,151	81,363	14.7
Public Debt	560,478	505,844	91.6

	Nominal	% of GDP	% of P.S.E.
Interest Payments	60,335	9.86	15.86

Financing Public Expenditures

	Direct Taxation	Indirect Taxation	"Social Contributions"	Other Revenue	Net Borrowing
1984	93,789 (24.7)	69,460 (18.3)	99,441 (26.1)	27,486 (7.2)	90,151 (23.7)

Source: Banca d'Italia, 1985.

22. J. M. Buchanan, "I limiti alla fiscalità," op. cit., p. 31.

Solving the Global Public Pensions Crisis: The Italian Case

The Jungle

The Italian public pension system is so complex that it has become customary to refer to it as "the pension jungle." Beyond the complexity of the jungle, however, one thing seems clear: The system in its present form is unsustainable and, unless it is drastically reformed, it is heading toward bankruptcy. It is no accident that in the past six years there have been three "reforms" (in 1992, 1995, and 1997) and one aborted attempt (in 1994). Considering the quality of these changes, it is fairly easy to make a prediction: The crisis in public pensions will continue to be central to the political debate for many years. I wouldn't be surprised if we'd continue having a pension reform every two years or so well into the next decade.

In Democracy Demography Is Destiny

The roots of the crisis in public pensions in Italy are similar to those elsewhere: The pay-as-you-go system is doomed because of demographic changes. Since the number of those who pay into the system is not increasing, while the number of beneficiaries is growing rapidly, the burden of the pension system on the individual worker is destined to grow to unbearable levels, or the amount of benefits must be drastically reduced. The "from cradle to grave" welfare state is collapsing, because there are too few cradles and not enough graves.

There are fewer cradles—Italy has the lowest fertility rate in the

Talk given in London, sponsored by Cato Institute and *The Economist*, December 8–9, 1997, unpublished.

world. In the late sixties the number of births in any given year was almost double that of deaths; from 1992 the two have become equal.[1] Also, the population is getting older: an astonishing 22.5 percent of total population is over 60.[2] It has been estimated that by 2020 the ratio of people over 60 to those aged twenty to fifty-nine will be 52 percent, the highest in Europe, more than double what it was in 1960.[3]

The burden of pensions is not only growing, it is also falling on a number of workers that's not increasing. In the 1950s there were 4.61 active workers for each pension in the major government pension scheme (INPS); in 1963 the number had declined to 2.62; today it's only 1.11.[4] The number of pensions is increasing very rapidly—from 1991 to 1994 it has gone from 16 to 17 millions—while the number of workers is not increasing. In fact, from 1990 to 1996 the number of employed workers has declined from 23,327,000 to 22,273,000—over one million fewer jobs in seven years.[5] In 1996, the labor force was 40.3 percent and employed workers only 35.4 percent of total population.[6] Finally, 68.6 percent of males fifty-five to sixty-four do not work, mostly because they've retired thanks to the "generosity" of our public pensions.[7]

Some people claim that the problem is less serious than it seems, because social spending in Italy is lower than in other European coun-

1. See Giovanni Palladino, "Italy: Regional Perspective, Investment Opportunities, Pension Issues," Malta, Sept. 18, 1997, unpublished paper. Catholic Italy has the dubious record of the lowest average number of children per woman: 1.26. See Giuliano Cazzola, *Le nuove pensioni degli italiani,* Il Mulino/Contemporanea 81, Bologna, 1995, p. 12. It has been estimated that in the period from 1995 to 2000, there will be 9.6 births, and 9.9 deaths per 1,000 inhabitants: see "Tutti i numeri per capire il mondo," *Panorama* and *The Economist,* The Economist, 1996, Italian translation, 1997, p. 17 and p. 64.

2. *L'Italia in cifre,* ISTAT, Rome, 1997, p. 3.

3. Erasmus, "Dallo spreco alla previdenza," in Giuliano Urbani, ed., *Il Buongoverno, Restituire lo Stato ai cittadini,* Vallecchi Editore, Florence, 1996, p. 321.

4. See Giuliano Cazzola, *op. cit.,* 1995, p. 10.

5. See Claudio Murero, "Mercato del lavoro e occupazione in Italia," unpublished paper, June 23, 1997.

6. Banca d'Italia, *Relazione 1996, Appendice,* Rome, 1997.

7. G. Palladino, *op. cit.* According to the same author, Italy's 68.6 percent of not-working males aged fifty-five to sixty-four compares to Germany's 54 percent, the U.S.A.'s 37 percent, and Japan's 28 percent.

tries.[8] However, from 1975 to 1996 social spending in Italy has increased over 18 times in nominal terms, 160 percent in real terms, and it has gone from 14.1 percent to 19.5 percent of GDP. If one adds that Italy has to face interest payments on a truly gigantic public debt—in 1996 interest payments equaled 10.9 percent of GDP—it's clear that there is no reason for merriment. It is true, however, that by far the most important cause of this colossal increase has been the increase in spending on pensions. Because of demographic tendencies, barring real reforms, the Italian ratio of pensions to GDP should rise to 25.6 percent in 2020, when the OECD average will be 15.1 percent.[9] "Italy's social spending is not especially profligate. As a proportion of GDP, the total is actually a little below the EU average. . . . But when it comes to pensions, Italy's figure, at 15% of GDP, is about one-third above the EU average. Moreover, the gap is widening: over the next couple of decades, Italy's pension spending as a proportion of GDP is set to rise more than anywhere else."[10]

Democracy and Demagoguery

The roots of the disarray of the public pension system must be traced back to the late 1960s when, thanks to favorable demographic tendencies, it looked as if the pay-as-you-go system could sustain any amount of demagoguery. It was at that time that the Italian pension system became one of the most generous in the world. A Socialist minister of Labor summarized his government's attitude to pensions by proclaiming that "a pension, like a cigar, cannot be denied to anybody."

This was especially true of disability pensions: they were not denied to anyone. In 1994 there were close to 4 million people drawing a disability pension.[11] In some cases, the pensions have been awarded without regard to whether the beneficiary was in fact disabled. Anecdotal

8. See, for example, Ornello Vitali, "L'insostenibile pesantezza del sistema italiano," *Ideazione,* Anno 3, no. 6, 1996, p. 183.

9. OECD, *Reforming Public Pensions,* Paris 1988, as quoted in G. Cazzola, *op. cit.,* 1995, p. 13.

10. "Age-old problem," *The Economist,* November 8, 1997, Italy Survey, p. 25.

11. G. Cazzola, *op. cit.,* 1995, p. 48.

evidence suggests that fraud and abuse are widespread: Not all of the disabled are impaired; witness the recent case of a professional photographer who was receiving a pension for the blind. Disability pensions have been one of the main tools of the patronage system, of the use of taxpayers' money to buy votes.

Another consequence of the philosophy of largesse has been the reduction of retirement age: the so-called seniority pensions, paid regardless of age after a given number of years in service.[12] For many years, government employees have been allowed to retire after nineteen years, six months and one day of work. But there were so many loopholes (for example, by paying some additional contributions, one could have the years of college considered as years of work) that it was possible to retire after fifteen years of actual work. It is thanks to this demagogic use of pensions that the peculiarly Italian phenomenon of "baby pensions"—people retiring in their forties—has become widespread. I personally know of people who have retired in their thirties (one in the late twenties), taking advantage of the generosity of the public pension system.

In general, one could retire after thirty-five years of work, regardless of age, or after fifteen years of work at age fifty-five for women, sixty for men. But there were exceptions to that rule (in fact, the number of exceptions is so high that it's not clear whether there is a rule at all). Even today, after three reforms, a government employee can retire at fifty-three, if he has paid contributions for thirty-five years, or at any age if he has paid for thirty-six years. According to this last reform, in the year 2004 the retirement age for government employees will be fifty-seven with thirty-five years of contributions, any age with thirty-eight years. And even these rules have exceptions—blue-collar workers, those who have entered the labor force at an early age, and other privileged groups enjoy more favorable conditions.

Nor has the generosity been confined to retirement age. The 1968 "revolution" meant a change from a "defined contribution" to a "defined benefit" system. The size of the pension was connected not to what the worker had contributed to the pension system, but to the salary received during the last three years of work (later this was in-

12. See *The Economist*, November 8, 1997, *op. cit.*

creased to five years). Thus we had the puzzling phenomenon of workers receiving substantial increases in their salary in the years preceding their retirement.

The Impossibility of Political Reform

The actual and projected financial problems of the public pension system are mind-boggling. On the one hand, its generosity has greatly contributed to the growth of the public debt: It has been estimated that no less than one-third of Italy's gigantic public debt is due to the pension system.[13] Even worse, if one takes into account the net value of claims on the public pension system, total public debt outstanding in 1995 increases from a meager 120 percent to a hefty 220 percent of GDP.[14] "Last year the OECD estimated that Italy's current pensions obligations amounted to four times its GDP, compared with an EU average of three times GDP."[15] On the other hand, it is obvious that, given the existing demographic tendencies, sooner or later the system in its present form will collapse. According to some experts, barring a drastic reform, in ten to fifteen years contributions would have to grow to 50 percent of workers' pay in order to sustain the burden of pensions. That percentage of contributions is highly unlikely to be accepted.

This is especially true since "social contributions" and other payroll taxes already account for over 50 percent of total labor costs. This huge tax on work has destroyed jobs in the official economy (the rate of unemployment, presently at 12.9 percent, is largely attributable to the payroll tax), it has made the creation of new jobs nearly impossible (in fact, as previously mentioned, the number of jobs in the 1990s has

13. See G. Palladino, "The Italian Pension System: Too Generous to Be Sustainable," unpublished manuscript, 1997, and *op. cit.*, p. 9.

14. Danilo Taino, "Scacco matto Ma allo Stato," *Corriere della sera, CorrierEconomia,* November 10, 1997, p. 7. The author refers to a study by Morgan Stanley Dean Witter Research based on OECD data. According to the same author, in order to avoid the collapse of the pension system, retirement age should be increased to seventy, or taxes should be increased by an amount equal to 30 percent of GDP. Needless to add, both "solutions" are highly unlikely to be adopted.

15. *The Economist, op. cit.*

declined by 1 million), and it has forced many small and medium firms to "go underground," to operate in the informal economy.

The fact that the system is unsustainable, however, does not guarantee that it will be reformed. Exactly the same forces that have made it expand against all common sense are now working against any possible reform. When in 1994 the Berlusconi government tried to reform the pension system, the political left and labor unions[16] joined forces and staged a gigantic demonstration. The Berlusconi reform was eventually abandoned. In 1995, the Dini government decided to negotiate its reform with the labor unions, with the result that it only produced cosmetic changes. Prodi has tried to remedy the inadequacy of the Dini reform but, because of violent opposition from the Refounded (but unrepentant) Communists, he had to give up. The alternative would have been the fall of his government.

All this explains my prediction that we'll continue to have at least one reform every two years: It looks as if no government will have the courage to deal with the crisis in public pensions. This is even more so because in Italy, Harold Wilson's wisdom that "a fortnight is a long time in politics," applies like in no other country. Given that the "life expectancy at birth" of our governments is in the order of ten months, it is unlikely that any government will adopt a policy that is unpopular in the short run and produces its beneficial effects in the long run.

Toward a Do-It-Yourself Pension Reform?

It is unlikely, however, that Italians will sit idle while their retirement income, entrusted to the enlightened hands of the government, fades away. Sooner or later, people will realize that public pensions will not materialize when needed, and, if they want to avoid destitution in their old age, they must act. So far, they have been prevented from providing for their old age through private pension funds for the simple reason that they do not exist. Legislation on private pension funds, introduced by the Amato government, goes back to April 1993. However, the unfavorable tax treatment discouraged the formation of

16. "pensioners . . . make up half of all trade union members," *The Economist, op. cit.*

funds. In August 1995, the Dini government revised the 1993 legislation, making it less difficult to create private pension funds. So far nothing has happened, but the first funds are expected to see the light soon.

If funds are allowed to come into existence, it is easy to predict that they will be extremely successful. It is now increasingly clear that with public pensions, the potential beneficiary has no guarantee that he will receive his pension—that depends on the state of public finances and other factors beyond his control. Even if he does receive it, he cannot predict at what age that will happen—that again depends on factors beyond his control, like the kinds of "reforms" the government will produce in the meantime. Finally, no one knows what kind of sum to expect: So far, public pensions have been extremely favorable for most people, but money is running short and one kind of inevitable reform will be the reduction of benefits.

Once it becomes clear that public pensions are clouded in uncertainty, people will start providing for themselves—a de facto privatization. Italy has one of the highest saving rates in the industrial world. After declining from 1975 to 1992, the ratio of savings to GDP has started to grow, but there still is room for further expansion. If this happens, most Italians will continue to pay for their bankrupt public pension system, receive little or no benefits from it, and resort to a private pension system for their retirement. It is no accident that members of Parliament do not use the official public pension system, preferring to resort to their own, "private" arrangement!

Is Social Justice a Myth?

1. The expression "social justice" and the prominent role it plays in contemporary political debate reminds me of Bertrand Russell's acute observation: "The most savage controversies are those about matters as to which there is no good evidence either way." Russell was undoubtedly right: wars are fought for religion, not for mathematics. In the case of social justice it can reasonably be argued that, had the expression been less void of empirical content, its role in contemporary political controversy would be far smaller than it is today.

According to Webster's New Dictionary of Synonyms, myth "varies considerably in its denotation and connotation depending on the persuasion of the user." Also, "the word is used to designate a story, belief, or notion commonly held to be true but utterly without factual basis."

On both grounds, social justice *is* a myth. The expression owes its immense popularity precisely to its ambiguity and meaninglessness. It can be used by different people, holding quite different views, to designate a wide variety of different things. Its obvious appeal stems from its persuasive strength, from its positive connotation, which allows the user to praise his own ideas and simultaneously express contempt for the ideas of those who don't agree with him.

If my goal is social justice, the goal of those who disagree with me is, obviously, "social *un*justice." They are evidently inspired by evil intentions, and their ideas are not worthy of a highly motivated man. This simple trick is very old, but it is still quite popular—as evidenced by the American "liberals'" frequent accusation of "lack of compassion" thrown at those who disagree with them.

The Heritage Lectures 7, Washington, D.C., 1982, pp. 23–35.

The expression "social justice" is more popular among advocates of statism than it is among individualists, as it is often used to justify (and praise) faith in the omnipotence of government. In this respect, it is intended to provide the moral justification for what Sir Karl Popper calls "holistic social engineering," which, he stresses, "is never of a 'private' but always of a 'public' character. It aims at remodeling the 'whole of society' in accordance with a definite plan or blueprint."[1]

It cannot be denied that advocates of social justice are quite often motivated by lofty ideals. Such is the case, for example, of those who are genuinely concerned about poverty and the need to do something about it. Their sincere compassion for the poor is undoubtedly a noble sentiment, and it deserves respect and admiration. However, their belief that the way to help the poor is that of remodeling the whole of society according to their preferred general plan is more likely to hurt everybody rather than to achieve their aim, helping the poor.

From this point of view, noble altruists confirm the wisdom of Henry D. Thoreau's famous remark: "There is no odor so bad as that which arises from goodness tainted. . . . If I knew for a certainty that a man was coming to my house with the conscious design of doing me good, I should run for my life."[2]

Supporters of social justice, though, are not always motivated by lofty ideals. Quite often their inspiration is less noble, as evidenced by the fact that many people illustrate the meaning of social justice by examples based on hate for those who have rather than on sincere compassion for the poor. In other words, the *un*justice is perceived not as consisting of the miserable conditions of the poor, but of the *difference* between poor and rich. The implicit implication is that the poor would be better off if the wealth of the rich were eliminated, *even if their own lot did not change!*

It is here that the myth produces its worst effects, because it leads to contempt for wealth on the one hand, and the "cult of poverty" on the other. As such, social justice is simply the rationalization of envy, and its unintended effects have been the erosion of the social fabric and the perpetuation of avoidable poverty.

1. K. Popper, *The Poverty of Historicism* (1957), 1974, p. 67.
2. H. D. Thoreau, *Walden, or, Life in the Woods* (1847), New York, 1970, p. 207.

This process whereby the rationalization of envy leads to praise of poverty and contempt of wealth has been brilliantly analyzed by Helmut Schoeck in his classic treatise on envy.[3] He stresses that, whereas the approach has very old ideological roots, its revival is "of purely Marxist origin" and it plays a very important role in Marxist criticism of Western societies. The paradox is, according to Schoeck, that many Marxists regard high incomes as "socially just" in the socialist society of scarcity, "unjust" in the affluent society of capitalism.

As for the criticism leveled against our affluent society, one can only agree with his conclusion:

> For more than ten years social criticism in Western industrial societies has been focused on their material achievements. Something simply *has* to be wrong *because* the times are so good. The suspicion that this criticism is neither profound nor well founded, but is due rather to an absence of other legitimate targets, is confirmed when we recall that in modern times social criticism has never yet commended a society for obliging its members to lead a poor and wretched existence (p. 210).

And as for the cult of poverty:

> Is there any valid reason why being miserable should bring one closer to the truth? The parables of the Bible may be largely responsible for this peculiar assumption—yet what is meant by truth has long since ceased to be religious or theological truth (where the above may indeed apply), but scientific, verifiable, pragmatic truth, and why this should be revealed to the man with an empty stomach and dressed in sackcloth, rather than to one who is well dressed and well fed, is not immediately apparent (ibid.).

This last remark reminds one of the role played by Christianity with its scenario of camels, needles, and wealthy men who couldn't go to Paradise, in spreading the cult of poverty. Little attention was given to the unintended consequences of the indictment of wealth as sinful and poverty as virtuous. While it is hard to understand why poverty

3. H. Schoeck, *Envy, A Theory of Social Behaviour* (1966), New York, 1972, especially chap. 13.

should be virtuous, for *anybody* can become poor if he wants to, the unintended effects of the praise of poverty are the diffusion of poverty and the ennoblement of envy. The fact is that only the production of wealth can reduce poverty, but, if poverty is *virtuous,* why should it be reduced? And if wealth is sinful, why should it be produced?

It was precisely this sort of reasoning that led F. W. Nietzsche to the extreme view that "Christianity has been the greatest misfortune of mankind." There is undoubtedly room for disagreement here, but that it is possible to misinterpret Christianity in such a way is evidenced by the views of the advocates of the so-called Christian social doctrine and by the present pope's politically motivated, but ill-advised, frequent criticism of "materialistic capitalism."

2. Social justice is very popular in the field of distribution. Indeed, it can be said that "distributive justice" is synonymous with "social justice." Even here, however, the meaning attributed to the expression varies considerably depending on the persuasion of the user. Only a small minority of those who advocate distributive justice interpret it as meaning "perfect equality" (whatever *that* means). No society has ever been based on absolute egalitarianism, and even communist countries operate on the basis of an unequal distribution of income. Nor is complete equality part of the communist faith: Stalin himself scorned what he labeled "petty bourgeois egalitarianism."

But if distributive justice does not mean perfect equality, what does it mean? It has been convincingly argued that the term *distribution* is, in a free society, meaningless. Thus Robert Nozick states:

> The term "distributive justice" is not a neutral one. Hearing the term "distribution," most people presume that some thing or mechanism uses some principle or criterion to give out a supply of things. Into this process of distributing shares some error may have crept. So it is an open question, at least, whether *re*distribution should take place; whether we should do again what has already been done once, though poorly. However, we are not in the position of children who have been given portions of pie by someone who now makes last minute adjustments to rectify careless cutting. There is no *central* distribution, no person or group entitled to control all the resources, jointly deciding how they are to be doled out. What

> each person gets, he gets from others who give to him in exchange for something, or as a gift. In a free society, diverse persons control different resources, and new holdings arise out of the voluntary exchanges and actions of persons. There is no more a distributing or distribution of shares than there is a distributing of mates in a society in which persons choose whom they shall marry. The total result is the product of many individual decisions which the different individuals involved are entitled to make.[4]

I believe that the best attempt to give a meaning to the expression "distributive justice" is that of John Rawls. Here we enter into a vast subject that has attracted the attention of social scientists in the past decades. It is a field which lies outside my professional interests, and I consider myself moderately incompetent on the subject. What follows are just a few doubts I have about Rawls's construction.

Rawls's thesis is that

> Persons in the initial situation would choose two . . . principles: the first requires equality in the assignment of basic rights and duties, while the second holds that social and economic inequalities . . . are just only if they result in compensating benefits for everyone, and in particular for the least advantaged members of society.[5]

If I interpret Rawls's analysis correctly, its aim is that of finding a set of principles that would ensure a definitive solution to the problem of distributive justice in any kind of society, forever.[6] It might be said that such an aim is, by its very nature, unattainable. The problem of distributive justice represents the essence of contemporary political debate, the qualifying element in the choice of the preferred politico-economic system. An unanimously accepted solution to the problem would ensure the realization of a "perfect" society, free from any kind of political or social conflict. This explains why the problem has so

4. R. Nozick, *Anarchy, State, and Utopia,* New York, 1974, pp. 149–50.

5. J. Rawls, *A Theory of Justice,* 1971, pp. 14–15.

6. Such is also the opinion of S. Gordon, "The New Contractarians" in *The Journal of Political Economy,* June 1976, p. 576. What follows is largely based on my article "Diversità è un valore," in *Le Ragioni della Giustizia,* Biblioteca della libertà, 1977, nos. 65–66, pp. 213–24.

much appeal to the social thinker, but it also suggests that probably a solution can never be found.

As Sir Karl Popper has taught us:

> . . . we shall always have to live in an imperfect society. This is so not only because even very good people are very imperfect; nor is it because, obviously, we often make mistakes because we do not know enough. Even more important than either of these reasons is the fact that there always exist irresolvable clashes of values: there are many moral problems which are insoluble because moral principles may conflict. There can be no human society without conflict: such a society would be a society not of friends but of ants.[7]

The fact that Rawls's aim is excessively ambitious, however, should not prevent us from analyzing his construction. The first problem to be solved is: Who are the "least advantaged members of society"? The expression suggests that there is an *objective* way to measure people's position in the distribution. Such an objective measure, however, does not exist, and it would be erroneous to think that it could be approximated by money income, because money income provides a very inaccurate, if not contradictory, indication of people's real income and welfare. And, if one correctly looks at *real* income, it is almost impossible to ascertain who the "least advantaged" members of society are.

Nonpecuniary factors—such as a pleasant job, a good climate, leisure, the possibility of spending time with friends and family, etc.—significantly influence personal welfare, but are not quantifiable. At times they are reflected in the money income—so that, for example, *ceteris paribus,* one would expect a pleasant job to pay less than an unpleasant one—but very often their influence on the size of money income is offset by other factors.

As an illustration of this point, take the case of a worker in Naples who makes 200,000 lire a month. He knows that if he moves to Milan he would be paid 500,000 lire a month for the same job. And yet he does not move. What does that mean? It means that for him the pleasure of living in Naples (rather than in Milan) is worth *at least* 300,000 lire a month. Otherwise he would move to Milan. Now, suppose our

7. K. Popper, *Unended Quest,* 1976, p. 116.

Rawlsian equalizer moves in. He looks at the money wage-differential and jumps to the conclusion that it is unfair to pay two workers different wages for the same job. "Equal pay for equal work" might be his slogan. So, he decides that both workers should be paid the same, regardless of *where* they work. If he does that though, he in fact introduces an unjustifiable inequality: in *real* terms, the worker in Naples now makes much more than the one in Milan. The effect of the "equalization" would obviously be that of creating unemployment in Naples and labor shortage in Milan. This is something the Italian government has not yet understood. They are puzzled by the fact that, whereas in the South they have far more applicants for a given bureaucratic job than positions available, in the North they can't fill all their positions. The explanation is quite simple: government employees are paid the same money wage regardless of where they work. But the point is that money income is not a good proxy of real wealth.

This problem is vividly illustrated by a famous parable reflecting Professor George J. Stigler's humor:

> Dr. John Upright, the young physician, devoted every energy of his being to the curing of the illnesses of his patients. No hours were too long, no demand on his skill or sympathies too great, if a man or child could be helped. He received £2,000 net each year, until he died at the age of 41 from over-work. Dr. Henry Leisure, on the contrary, insisted that even patients with broken legs be brought to his office only on Tuesdays, Thursdays, and Fridays, between 12:30 and 3:30 PM. He preferred to take three patients simultaneously, so he could advise while playing bridge, at which he cheated. He received £2,000 net each year, until he retired at the age of 84.[8]

If this is the case, we are left with no *objective* way to know who the least advantaged members of society are.

It seems to me that the most important feature of Rawls's approach is the fact that he believes that in the "initial situation," behind the "veil" of ignorance, everybody would accept his two principles as the basis for the definitive solution of the problem of distributive justice.

8. George J. Stigler, *The Theory of Price*, 3rd edition, 1966, p. 17n.

This seems to indicate that, in Rawls's world, the justification for his principles of justice is that they would be unanimously accepted in the initial situation. It seems to me that such a solution leaves room for two very important objections.

First of all, there is no guarantee whatsoever that Rawls's principles would be *unanimously* accepted in the initial situation. In order to argue that, one would have to assume that in the initial situation all individuals are *identical.* The veil of ignorance is not sufficient: Everybody must have the same attitude toward risk, the same political views, hold the same religious beliefs, etc. But if all individuals are *identical,* why isn't perfect equality the chosen criterion of distribution? On the other hand, if they are *not* identical, how can we assume that they would all agree with Rawls's principles?

Maybe *many* would agree, namely those who share Rawls's system of values, but nothing guarantees that unanimity would be reached. Just as an example, I would prefer this to Rawls's "difference principle": "Inequalities are unjust if, and only if, they result in a certain and demonstrable damage to someone (excluding the envious)." I believe that such a principle would be easier to enforce and much more compatible with individual liberty than the one suggested by Rawls, but of course there are many other possible criteria,[9] and nothing guarantees that in the initial situation one of them would be unanimously chosen.

The second objection is even more important. Even if we assume that Rawls's principles would be unanimously accepted in the initial situation, what guarantee do we have that the distribution that results from them would be forever accepted? How can we objectively prove that existing inequalities produce compensating benefits for the least advantaged members of society? Isn't it more credible that, even if the principles are unanimously accepted in the initial situation, the justice of the resulting distribution will always be challenged by at least some members of society?

However, these are not my main points of disagreement with Rawls's argument. The fact is that Rawls does not believe it just to allow the

9. For a summary of some of these, see S. Brittan and P. Lilley, *The Delusion of Incomes Policy,* London, 1977, especially pp. 196ff.

distribution of income and wealth to be affected by the "natural lottery" of individual talents and personal abilities. This instinctive repulsion for inequalities determined by personal qualities is hard to understand, especially considering that Rawls must be convinced of possessing a higher-than-average endowment of personal ability. What he fails to understand is that rarely, if ever, are differences in natural abilities are exclusive result of what he calls the "natural lottery." All talents are to a large extent the result of a combination of natural hereditary factors and of acquired skills.

Arthur Rubinstein presumably had a hereditary predisposition for music, but it was only thanks to daily practice (eight hours per day, every day—according to him) that he could become and continue to be the great pianist known to everybody. It is doubtful that he would have devoted so much work to that purpose if he had lived in a society based on Rawls's difference principles, that would have confiscated the result of his work, because it was partially due to the natural lottery. Anybody who has heard Rubinstein play knows that his talent has benefited everybody and has been a significant example of the immaterial nature of social wealth.

But this is not the point. Suppose that Rubinstein would have refused to play in public, that he would have developed his natural abilities exclusively for the benefit of those he liked and for himself. In such a case, obviously, his talent would not have produced compensating benefits for the least advantaged members of society. It would have been an obvious violation of Rawls's difference principle. What should have been done? Should he have been forbidden to play? And if so, what about the first principle, the principle of equal liberty?

This leads us to the fundamental objection to Rawls's construction, an objection that is valid for any kind of patterned, prefabricated system of distributive justice: Such systems are incompatible with individual freedom. This point has been stressed by several scholars, and it might be worth looking at their point of view in their own words.

As the late Harry G. Johnson has pointed out, freedom of choice produces inequalities:

> the exercise of the alternatives of choice provided to the citizen necessarily give rise to observed inequalities of income as convention-

> ally measured, and . . . efforts to prevent this outcome or to cancel it out by post facto income redistribution run the serious risk both of depriving the citizen of the benefits of freedom of choice and self-fulfillment and of eventually requiring a reversion to a more authoritative or totalitarian structure of the society and the state.[10]

Or, as Robert Nozick has stressed, liberty upsets the pattern, *any* distributive pattern. He uses the known example of supposing that Wilt Chamberlain signs a contract according to which he gets 25 cents for every ticket sold. "Let us suppose," says Nozick, "that in one season one million persons attend his home games, and Wilt Chamberlain winds up with $250,000, a much larger sum than the average income. . . . Is he entitled to this income? . . . Each of these persons *chose* to give twenty-five cents of their money to Chamberlain." If *they* were entitled to it, "didn't this include their being entitled to give it to . . . Wilt Chamberlain? Can anyone else complain on grounds of justice?" (p. 161). And he concludes: "The socialist society would have to forbid capitalist acts between consenting adults" (p. 163).

This is the fundamental point. If we allow freedom of choice, the individual spending decisions *continually* alter the distribution of income. No patterned, prefabricated distribution can last very long if freedom of choice is allowed. And this is true of *any* kind of distribution, be it based on equality or on inequality. In a free society, in a society, that is, where people are free to decide how to use their income, any observed distribution is the result of the previous process of exchanges and the starting point of a new process that will lead to a different distribution. If one wants to maintain the chosen distribution through time, therefore, one has to forbid "capitalist acts between consenting adults" and give up individual freedom of choice. If, on the other hand, one wants to preserve individual freedom of choice, one must give up the idea of maintaining a patterned distribution of income and wealth. This is not a recent discovery, as it was clearly understood by David Hume: "Render possessions ever so equal, men's different degree of art, care, and industry will immediately break that equality."

10. H. G. Johnson, *On Economics and Society*, 1975, p. 214.

All of this undoubtedly confirms that equality of any kind is incompatible with freedom. Sir Karl Popper states: ". . . freedom is more important than equality; . . . the attempt to realize equality endangers freedom; . . . if freedom is lost, there will not even be equality among the unfree."[11]

3. A free society needs not lack compassion for the poor. We can and must do something to help those who, through no fault of their own, earn an income that is below what society regards as acceptable. The best possible solution, in my opinion, would be to move from the present wasteful and bureaucratic system of governmental assistance to a comprehensive and automatic negative income tax system.

But we must also be aware of the threat posed to freedom by the myth of social justice. The only kind of justice that is compatible with a free society is, as Professor F. A. von Hayek has shown, commutative justice.

> Commutative justice means . . . a reward according to the value which a person's services actually have to those of his fellows to whom he renders them, and which finds expression in the price the latter are willing to pay. This value has, as we must concede, no necessary connection with moral merit. It will be the same, irrespective of whether a given performance was in the case of one man the result of great effort and painful sacrifice while it is rendered by another with playful ease and perhaps even for his own enjoyment. . . . Commutative justice takes no account of personal or subjective circumstances, of needs or good intentions but solely of how the results of a man's activities are valued by those who make use of them.[12]

We need not have an inferiority complex toward those who claim that they possess a superior formula of social justice—they are usually possessed by it. No country has ever succeeded in improving the material well-being of its members by rejecting the principles of a free economy and imposing a prefabricated blueprint of distribution on

11. K. Popper, *Unended Quest,* op. cit., p. 36.

12. F. A. von Hayek, *Studies in Politics, Philosophy, and Economics,* Chicago, 1969, pp. 257ff.

the whole of society. They have succeeded in making the rich worse off without improving the conditions of the poor, and in the process, they have often impaired the productive capacity of the whole economy.

But even more important is the fact that our free societies are the closest historical approximation to a minimal state that has been thus far realized, and, as R. Nozick aptly reminds us:

> The minimal state treats us as inviolate individuals, who may not be used in certain ways by others as means or tools or instruments or resources; it treats us as persons having individual rights with the dignity this constitutes. Treating us with respect by respecting our rights, it allows us, individually or with whom we choose, to choose our life and to realize our ends and our conception of ourselves, insofar as we can, aided by the voluntary cooperation of other individuals possessing the same dignity. How *dare* any state or group of individuals do more. Or less.

Tales from the Public Sector: Inside the Labyrinth

It will probably come as a surprise to those who are familiar with the grim statistics of Italy's explosive growth of government spending to know that the country has a very elaborate and sophisticated system of control of public expenditures. Compliance with the old principle "quod non est in actis . . ." in practice means that every decision must go through a long, complex procedure of certification, registration, classification, and control. The effects that this "advanced" system of formal guarantees has on the speed of spending decisions deserve illustration. Here is a personal experience.

In February 1970 I passed the national competition (*concorso*) for Assistant Professor in Economics, and the following month I was appointed Assistant Professor of International Economics at the Faculty of Political Science, University of Rome. I was overjoyed, having waited for that moment since 1964. During those six years I had held an *unpaid* position as a voluntary assistant (*assistente volontario*). At that time, paid teaching positions in Italian universities were so scarce that one had to hope for someone's death to open a new position.

At last, I had finally made it. My enthusiasm was even greater because holding a paid job allowed me finally to get married, which I promptly did. As soon as I returned from my honeymoon, I went to the business office at the University of Rome to cash my first paycheck. The employee looked at his records, asked me to repeat my name, and declared that I was not on the payroll. Seeing my obvious disappointment, he asked when I had been appointed, and grinned broadly at

Originally published in *Policy Review* 17, summer 1981, pp. 115–17, and reprinted with permission.

my answer. "Two months ago?" He could not believe my naiveté. He referred me to the Assistants' Office, to which I went immediately.

"Maybe it is just some additional small formality that will be quickly taken care of," I was thinking. The Assistants' Office was closed. A note on the door informed me that the office was open to the public only on "odd" days (Monday, Wednesday, and Friday) from 9 a.m. to 12:30 p.m. Slightly upset, I returned home.

The following morning at 8:30 I was at the Assistants' Office where a long line of people waited behind the closed door. Unlike Englishmen, I hate "to queue," but under the circumstances I was willing to stand in line for hours if necessary. Two hours later, when my turn came, I was finally able to explain my problem to a faceless bureaucrat, who listened somewhat impatiently. After I had finished, he gave me, in a didactic tone, what he obviously regarded as an elementary lecture on administrative procedure: "Your decree of appointment was sent to the Ministry of Public Education last week. There, it must be signed by the Minister, after the relevant office has checked its formal correctness. As soon as signed, it will be sent to the accounting office of the Ministry for classification. The accounting office of the Ministry will then send it to Corte dei Conti (similar to the General Accounting Office in the United States) for registration. Once registered, it will have to go to Direzione Generale del Tesoro (a branch of the Ministry of the Treasury), which will then send it to Banca d'Italia. In due time, Banca d'Italia will pay the University of Rome, which in turn will pay you."[1]

I felt tears come to my eyes, but managed to control myself and asked, "And in the meantime?" His voice lowered as he assumed the general attitude of a conspirator. "In the meantime, you may borrow up to 50 percent of your salary from the University. You know," he added, "we are not supposed to do this. It isn't 'normal procedure,' but we understand your problems. So, if you are interested, fill out these forms and give them to me. I'll try to have your loan ready for next month." Ironically, I had to thank him.

Frustratingly long, cashless months went by, and, as Christmas ap-

1. This is an abridged, much shorter version of the true procedure. I have reduced it to its essentials for lack of space.

proached, I decided to try to speed these bureaucratic procedures up. Having found out that my file was stuck at the Corte dei Conti, I went there. It was almost impossible to find a parking place in that area. So I "parked" on a sidewalk and ran upstairs. The office was closed. A note on the door announced that the office was open to the public only from 12 to 1 p.m. on "odd" days. Since it was 10 a.m., and I couldn't risk leaving my car on the sidewalk for two hours, I decided to come back another day. The following week I was there at 12 o'clock . . . only to discover a new sign on the door notifying the public that the office was open only from 9 a.m. to 10 a.m. on "even" days.

Finally, after several other unsuccessful attempts, I managed to see the relevant bureaucrat. "Is my file here?" I asked. He looked at his records, "Yes, it has been here for five months. Are you in a hurry?" I didn't know whether to laugh or cry, and barely succeeded in avoiding resort to violent means. But I did succeed in getting him to process my file that same day by filling out a form for "recommended" cases—a system he had devised to bring attention to files of persons who had some political clout. (He was unable to process all the files he was in charge of, and had to resort to some kind of rationing.)

My problems were far from over, but due to space I'm forced to limit myself. Finally, in August of the following year I was paid—eighteen months after my appointment! I did get all my back pay and could pay back the money the University of Rome had lent me.

You might think that this is an exceptional case. Well, not really. Still drawing from my personal experience, here is another example. In 1976 I passed the *concorso* and was appointed Full Professor, beginning May 1. The promotion also involved a pay raise. However, it was not until January 1979 that I finally began being paid as Full Professor—thirty-three months to "process" my file.

Bureaucratic slowness, however, is apparently at its best in the case of old age pensions. People who retire from a government job discover immediately that getting their monthly pension from the government is not as simple as they might have thought: It takes between three and five *years* to process the relevant file. Many Italians believe that this is an intentional policy on the part of the government, an effort to try to save money by betting that some of those entitled to an old age pension will die without heirs before receiving it. It is hard to accept this "conspiracy" explanation, because it attributes *intelligence* (even if of an evil kind) to the leviathan. It is much more credible to attribute these episodes to the natural, physiological working of the "visible tentacles" of statism.

Tales from the Public Sector: Red Tape all'Italiana

It has been observed that Italians tend to be rather secretive about their salaries. Whereas Americans are at times inclined to talk, often with pride, about their annual pay, Italians positively refrain from mentioning it. Banca d'Italia, Italy's central bank, recently announced two openings for blue-collar positions within its organization. One of the potential applicants wanted to know before applying what salary the job entailed. Since he was not able to get the information from the local branch of Banca d'Italia, he wrote to the central administrative office in Rome. The reply he got was that the pay was revealed only to those who already worked there.

The usually well-informed intellectuals maintain that the explanation for the loquacity of Americans and the secretiveness of Italians on the issue of their pay goes back to cultural factors: the Protestant ethic on the one hand, and Catholic culture on the other. Maybe so. I venture to suggest, however, that as far as Italian civil servants are concerned, another, simpler explanation might apply: They do not know what their pay actually is. Let me illustrate by drawing from my own experience.

I have always been puzzled by the amount of my salary as a university professor (in Italy, university professors are, I regret to say, state employees). It has never been a nice, round figure like, let us say, \$15,000 a year, or \$1,250 a month. On the contrary, the amount has always bordered on the use of decimals, and it has tended to fluctuate mysteriously. For example, in February of this year my paycheck

Originally published in *Policy Review* 26, fall 1983, p. 93, and reprinted with permission.

amounted to 1,484,965 lire (at the present exchange rate the last two digits—65 lire—are worth slightly more than 4.6 cents). I decided that it was incompatible with my faith in the rational pursuit of self-interest not to try to understand why my salary was what it was. I therefore asked a friend, the director of our university institute and an expert on the details of life in this great peninsular republic, to enlighten me.

"You are lucky," he said. "I have just been able to understand the issue myself. A group of theoretical mathematicians have just published a paper in a learned statistical journal dealing with the determination of university professors' salaries. It's quite simple, really." He took a sheet of paper full of figures from his wallet and turned on his pocket calculator.

New Math

That did not catch me unprepared: I had brought my calculator along and did not refrain from sporting it.

"You start from an annual salary of 24,125,220 lire," he said.

"Why?"

"Because that's the annual pay of a civil servant at the top of his career, and university professors have been equated to top civil servants."

"But that's not what I make," I observed.

"I know," he replied patiently. "You have to multiply that figure by 0.486."

"Why?"

"Because a professor at the beginning of his career is paid 48.6 percent of that salary. I know," he added, preventing me from interrupting, "I know you are not at the beginning. We must find your seniority coefficient. When were you appointed full professor?"

"In 1976."

He worked on his calculator for a few minutes and then announced, beaming: "Your seniority coefficient is 1.32. We have to multiply the previous result by 1.32."

The amount was still different from my paycheck.

"Now," he said, "we must multiply this figure by 1.122. I am not sure why, but I believe that it was a once-and-for-all increase of 12.2 percent they gave us a few years ago. The resulting figure must then be divided by 12 to get the monthly salary."

"It's still not right."

"Sure," he said acidly. "We have to multiply the outcome by 0.095. You know—the 9.5 percent fixed withholding."

At that point I gave up, so he continued undisturbed.

"Your basic salary is 1,309,609 lire. You are married and have two children, so we must add the 58,391 lire family allowance. Finally, there is the *contigenza* [a lump sum, equal for everybody, given as an indemnity against inflation]: 555,116 lire. Your monthly salary is 1,923,116," he concluded.

"No, it's not."

"That's because we must subtract the amount withheld: 436,151 lire."

"That takes us to 1,486,965 lire," I said. "Why is my salary 1,484,965 lire?"

"Do you have it credited to your bank?"

"Yes," I admitted.

"Then you must subtract 2,000 lire for the bank's commission, and you get to the figure you actually received. Quite simple," he added triumphantly.

Well, it is not as simple as that. In March my salary dropped to 1,334,965 lire (150,000 lire less than the previous month), but I have not made any further investigation. I just do not want to know. So please, never ask me how much I make as a university professor. I could not tell you.

Part 3

Going Underground

The Underground Economy

1. One way to measure the popularity of a given subject is provided by the number of names commonly attached to it. If this is the case, then a good indication of the popularity of the so-called underground economy is provided by the great variety of names by which it is designated. "Submerged," "underwater," "parallel," "irregular," "shadow," "unobserved," "undeclared," "subterranean," "unreported," "secret," "hidden," "informal," "black" (and its variations: "black market," "black labor," "black cash"), "cash economy," and so on, ad nauseam.

Not all of these labels are value-free. Indeed, most if not all of them possess some degree of "persuasive strength" and are vehicles of personal feelings, ways to express approval or censure, rather than ways to refer to the phenomenon. Although I am convinced that labels are important and that it would be eminently desirable to find an appropriate, neutral label for the underground economy, I am not going to try to find one myself and will keep using the term "underground" without any derogatory intention.

A somewhat related and more important problem is that of definition. Of the many and often quite different definitions that have been suggested, I would adopt the following two that are in fact almost identical. The first is Vito Tanzi's: "the underground economy . . . is GNP that, because of unreporting or underreporting, is not measured by official statistics."[1] The second is that of Barbara Shenfield, according to whom the underground economy is "that part of the economy

Lecture given at the Heritage Foundation, Washington, D.C., in 1980 or 1981.

1. V. Tanzi, "Underground Economy Built on Illicit Pursuits Is Growing Concern of Economic Policymakers," *IMF Survey*, February 4, 1980.

which is undeclared to governmental authorities and undisclosed in official statistics."[2]

2. Although interest in the underground economy is a relatively recent development, there are good reasons to believe that the phenomenon itself has always existed. It was a naive delusion to believe that income statistics could accurately record *all* income produced by the economy. Statisticians are often well aware of the limitations of their own trade, and it is, therefore, rather puzzling that the evidence of the existence of unrecorded income should receive so much attention today. Even more naive was the implicit belief that unrecorded income should be a negligible fraction of total income, that people, that is, would not find a way to hide part of their revenues from the tax collector. I tend, therefore, to agree with Mrs. Shenfield's view that we "may be partly influenced by the growth of attention to the phenomenon. We may see more of it because we look for more of it."

Maybe so. Yet there are good reasons to believe that, even though there has always been an underground economy, its size and extent have grown considerably in modern times. For the underground economy is really a form of escape from excessive government and from unbearable taxation. Therefore, a growth in the size of unrecorded income is to be expected when taxation and government grow.

Furthermore, it is surprising that the phenomenon is so widespread as to be almost universal, affecting in various degrees not only *all* Western countries but also most (if not all) Communist countries. Thus we read that in Germany "[t]he 1977 Report of the Deutsche Bundesbank observed that 'cash payment is unquestionably gaining ground again in some fields . . . of business activity where services are rendered without taxes . . . and (are) settled in cash.'"[3] "In France, too, tax evasion is so widespread that, according to economist Serge-Christophe Kolm, 'There is a majority to oppose strong detention, enforcement and penalty, since everyone sees clearly what he would lose in tax.'" "In Sweden . . . an unofficial estimate by the Council for the Prevention of Crime reckons that about 10 percent of the country's national prod-

2. B. Shenfield, unpublished MPS paper, 1980.

3. V. Tanzi, op. cit.

uct is now in the untaxed shadow economy."[4] The head of the United Kingdom's Inland Revenue Service, Sir William Pile, is widely quoted for having stated recently that "unrecorded income" in England may be as high as 7.5 percent of that country's GNP. And recognition of the existence of the underground economy has led to recent upward revisions of the national accounts data in a number of countries, including Italy, France, West Germany, Japan, and Sweden.

An interesting by-product of these revisions of income statistics is that they make the idea of "fine-tuning" highly improbable. When real GNP admittedly differs by as much as 10 percent from observed GNP—the exact percentage being unknown—it makes little sense to support an economic policy aimed at controlling the time pattern of income to the percentage point. The "natural" unreliability of income data—evidenced by the underground economy—makes the very idea of an interventionist economic policy of demand management rather quixotic.

3. I now turn to the question of the evidence for the existence of the underground economy. This is a fundamental question, for, if the underground economy is "hidden," how do we know of its existence? Before I go into the various indicators that have been used to support the underground economy hypothesis, let me stress that, in many cases, there is nothing hidden about the underground economy. A good example is provided by a headline on the front page of the major newspaper in Naples—*Il Mattino*—two years ago. As evidence that inflation was increasing, the headline read: "Price of contraband cigarettes up to 600 lire"! Those who have been in Naples know that there is nothing hidden about contraband, which is one of the oldest underground economy activities.

Conspicuous consumption has at times been used as an indicator of the existence of the underground economy. Thus a British journalist has recently attempted to find an answer to the following problem: "Since 1973, Italy ha[s] been subjected to as much foul economic medicine as Britain, but all the squeezes, freezes and billion-dollar

4. Richard Rose, "The Makings of a Do-It-Yourself Tax Revolt," *Public Opinion,* August–September 1980.

clampdowns applied here never managed to produce quite the degree of drabness and misery apparent in Britain. Italians continued to spend conspicuously." After having noted that "Italy leads the Common Market in imports of Rolls Royce cars and caviar, and it comes second to Britain in champagne drinking," and that Italians run "more cars per head of population than the British, the Belgians and the Dutch," the British commentator provides us with what he considers the ultimate form of conspicuous consumption, definitive evidence of "the lavishness of the Italian lifestyle": "Even the most obscure industrialist has little problem raising the odd million dollars to pay his kidnappers"! All of this leads Matthews to conclude that "it [is] hard to avoid the feeling that there [is] more wealth around than official statistics allow."[5]

Incidentally, Italian tax laws also consider conspicuous consumption an indicator of possible tax evasion. Thus Italians are required to report on their income tax forms the model of car they own, whether they own a boat, horse, airplane, a second home, and whether they employ servants. Also, in line with Matthews's ideas on conspicuous consumption, many kidnapped industrialists, after having paid their ransom and having been freed, find that their troubles are not finished: Their incomes are usually thoroughly investigated by the taxman!

Other indicators of the underground economy include expenditure in relation to income, and the demand for large banknotes. With regard to the first, at the micro-level, cross-section studies showing strata of the population for which expenditures exceed income do not necessarily imply that income is underreported. The result might be due to the use of current, rather than permanent, income—an aspect of the so-called "regression fallacy" exposed by Professor Friedman.[6] A different use of the income-expenditure approach to the underground economy is provided, at the macro-level, by the divergence in the measurement of national income based on the two concepts. When estimates of GNP based on income data prove to be significantly below those based on expenditure, statisticians are inclined to inter-

5. C. Matthews, "'Underground' Workers Keep Italian Economy Running," *International Herald Tribune,* February 5, 1979.

6. M. Friedman, *A Theory of the Consumption Function,* NBER, 1957.

pret the divergence as an indication of the existence (and size) of unreported income.[7] However, this method provides only an indirect, and not necessarily reliable, measure of the underground economy. If unreported income is spent on goods and services which are themselves produced by the underground economy, one could have a situation in which there is no divergence between income and expenditure measures of GNP while having an underground economy. Furthermore, the income-expenditure approach does not take into account transactions in the form of barter, and it is, therefore, likely to underestimate the size of the phenomenon. Finally, at the micro-level, as in the case of conspicuous consumption, the tendency for some people to live beyond their means must not be overlooked. As for the increased demand for large banknotes, there are other influences beside the underground economy; namely, inflation and, as far as the U.S. dollar is concerned, the use by foreigners of the American currency. This is apparently widespread, especially in South America.[8]

Another indicator of the existence of the underground economy is tax evasion. Indeed, the two terms are considered almost synonymous. However, as an indicator of the *size* of the underground economy, tax evasion is unreliable. First of all, estimates of the extent of tax evasion are often conjectural and seldom dependable. Second, and more important, even though tax evasion and the underground economy are undoubtedly connected, they do not necessarily coincide. In transactions involving more than one party, for instance, authorities might gather the necessary information from one party, even though the other party (or parties) fails to report it. Therefore, one can have instances of tax evasion that do not result in underreporting of income. Furthermore, national income figures are not necessarily based (exclusively) on tax data. Such is, for example, the case of national income accounts for Italy. As a result, tax evasion can at best be an indirect indicator of the existence of an underground economy, and one cannot rely on it to determine the size of the underground economy.

7. See M. O'Higgins, *Measuring the Hidden Economy,* The Outer Circle Policy Unit, London, July 1980.

8. M. Thurn, "The Underground Economy," MPS unpublished paper, 1980.

The most widely quoted official estimate of the size of the underground economy based on tax evasion is that of the United States Internal Revenue Service. In September 1979, the IRS published a study entitled *Estimates of Income Unreported on Individual Income Tax Returns.* The study, based on information from the IRS Taxpayer Compliance Measurement Program for the tax year 1973, adjusted to provide national figures and inflated to provide data for 1976, estimates unreported legal-source income in the United States in 1976 to have ranged from $75 billion to $100 billion. To this the IRS adds an estimate of unreported illegal-source income ranging from $25 billion to $35 billion. The resulting total of $100 billion to $135 billion—6 percent to 8 percent of legal GNP—should measure the size of the underground economy in the United States in 1976.[9] To the reasons stated above about the nonautomatic connection between tax evasion and size of the underground economy, one might add that estimating illegal-source income directly is, at best, highly conjectural.

More promising results seem to come out of the use of monetary statistics in trying to determine the size of the underground economy. Two approaches have been used in this respect. The first looks at the so-called currency ratio, the ratio of currency to demand deposits, and attributes any increase in the ratio to the demand for currency from the "cash" economy, to the need, that is, to finance underground-economy transactions. Estimates for the United States vary greatly depending on the kind of methodology used. Thus Professor Gutmann arrives at an estimate of $250 billion for 1979—a little over 10 percent of legal GNP. His method is quite simple: He assumes that from 1937 to 1941 there was no underground economy and that, therefore, the currency ratio then prevailing must be considered "normal." Any increase in the ratio since then must be attributed to the underground economy. All that is needed in order to estimate the size of the underground economy is to multiply the extra currency demanded by the ratio of legal GNP to legal money (excluding the extra currency). The result is then interpreted as an estimate of income produced by the underground economy.

9. For this and the following studies for the United States, see the excellent summary in V. Tanzi, op. cit.

Using a slightly different methodology, Vito Tanzi arrives at a very different estimate. According to Tanzi, in 1976 unreported income ranged from about $60 billion to $70 billion, a much lower estimate than Gutmann's. Tanzi stresses, however, that his estimate "does not include any criminal or other activities not brought into existence by taxes," and that it is limited to tax evasion and underground economy which result in extra currency use. "But—he adds—some tax evasion as well as some underground activities . . . may not result in additional use of currency. Therefore, it is possible that the estimates . . . may be biased downward."[10]

The second monetary approach to the underground economy looks at the aggregate demand for money, rather than at the currency ratio. The highest estimate obtained through this method is that of Professor Edgar L. Feige. He assumes that in 1939 there was no underground economy, and that, therefore, the ratio of total dollar transactions to GNP for that year is to be considered "normal." Assuming that the transaction velocity of money has remained constant since 1939, it is then possible to estimate the value of total transactions for a given year, and the corresponding level of GNP. The difference between this value of GNP and the official one measures the size of the underground economy. On the basis of these assumptions, Feige arrives at an estimate of $540 billion to $700 billion for 1978, or over 33 percent of GNP. Feige's methodology has been criticized on the ground that it would have generated negative estimates for the underground economy for each year between 1939 and 1972, and his estimates are generally believed to be too high.

Be that as it may, the wide discrepancies among the various estimates reflects the difference in the methodologies used, and it is far from clear that the various studies are measuring the same thing. Furthermore, that difference confirms that the underground economy is still firmly underground, and will hopefully remain impervious, defeating all attempts at an exact measurement of its size (which would be the first step toward its destruction).

10. V. Tanzi, "Underground Economy, Income Tax Evasion, and the Demand for Currency in the United States, 1929–76," IMF, unpublished paper, November 1979.

M_2 / Y (%)	1958–62	1963–67	1968–72	1973–77
Italy	64.4	73.6	85.8	95.7
U.S.A.	43.0	43.7	44.4	45.9
Great Britain	39.2	34.8	33.5	37.6
France	33.5	39.7	42.4	48.6
Germany	34.7	40.6	46.9	57.8

4. I now turn to Italy and its tremendously successful underground economy. The existence of an underground economy in Italy can be argued on several grounds.[11]

The first is related to the behavior of the demand for money as measured by official income statistics. The money/income ratio in Italy has been growing rapidly in the past decades, and its absolute value seems unusually high as compared to other countries. This ratio measures the amount of money—cash, demand deposits, and time deposits, in the M_2 definition—that the average Italian holds in relation to his income. Official figures suggest that in 1978 the average Italian held an amount of money roughly equivalent to one year's income. In a country that was going through its sixth consecutive year of double-digit inflation, this seemed rather hard to explain in terms of rational behavior. Furthermore, the ratio was exceptionally high in comparison with the same ratio in other countries (see Table).

A possible explanation for the peculiarity of the behavior of the money/income ratio in Italy is provided by the underground economy. Its existence would explain the very high value of the ratio for two sets of reasons. First of all, firms operating in the underground economy might not have access to the "legal" credit market. They might, therefore, be forced to hold large amounts of money both in the form of deposits and in cash.

Mention must be made at this point of the institutional differences that give the money/income ratio in Italy a distinct meaning in comparison to other countries. First of all, the Italian financial system dif-

11. See A. Martino, "Another Italian Economic Miracle?" *Policy Review*, forthcoming. [See pp. 177–95 in this volume.]

fers from that of most other countries in that Italian banks pay interest on demand as well as on time deposits. Checking accounts thus serve as a store of value to a greater extent than elsewhere.[12] The second, and more important, institutional difference is that in Italy checking accounts are secret. They can be inspected only in the case of a criminal investigation, and the inspection must be authorized by the court. Therefore, they provide a good hiding place for tax evaders. It is worth noting that when, a couple of years ago, rumors were circulated that the government was considering abolishing the secrecy of checking accounts and imposing a once-and-for-all tax on them, panicky members of Parliament withdrew some three million dollars from their checking accounts at the special Parliament bank in two hours!

The secrecy of checking accounts also means that the currency ratio —the ratio of currency to demand deposits—is not a meaningful indicator of the size of the underground economy in Italy. Given the secrecy of deposits, illegal activities do not necessarily require the use of currency but can be settled through checks. This is why the underground economy in Italy is not necessarily a "cash" economy. Finally, the fact that the money/income ratio is so much higher in Italy than in other countries doesn't necessarily mean that the underground economy in Italy is correspondingly bigger.

The existence of the underground economy also explains the very high value of the money/income ratio for a second, more obvious reason. If income produced by the underground economy is not recorded in the official income statistics, the observed ratio is much higher than the "true" one. That is, the amount of money the average Italian holds in relation to his income is smaller than that suggested by the official figures. The matter, of course, deserves very careful analysis. However, while the hypothesis that the money/income ratio is due to the existence of the underground economy strongly recommends itself, the value of the ratio could provide an indication of the size of the underground economy. If the conjecture is valid and if the existence of the underground economy is the only factor behind the difference between the ratio in Italy and that in the other countries (which is un-

12. J. M. Boughton, "Demand for Money in Major OECD Countries," *OECD Economic Outlook Occasional Studies,* OECD, December 1978.

likely), then statistically recorded income might fall short of true income by a very large fraction. It would certainly not be surprising if official income statistics were, say, 30 percent below the mark.

The second reason for the belief in the existence of a substantial underground economy in Italy was unintentionally supplied by Istituto Centrale di Statistica (ISTAT, the government statistical office). ISTAT's first reaction to the money/income hypothesis was to deny that error in the official income figures could exceed 5 percent at most—the actual percentage suggested being 0.35 percent! Less than a month later, however, in March 1979, ISTAT revised its income figures upward by almost 10 percent!

A third indirect indicator of the existence of an underground economy in Italy is tax evasion. Thus, in his very interesting article on tax evasion, Professor Richard Rose states:

> Historically, Italy has been the leader in non-payment of taxes and there is little doubt that it still is at the head of the pack. One unpublished OECD report estimates that tax evasion there is as high as 27 percent of total reported income. Upwards of one in six Italian workers engages in *lavoro nero* (black work), and the national statistical institute estimates that a majority of taxpayers evade payment of at least a portion of tax due.[13]

The preceding consideration leads Professor Rose to conclude that there is room for improved enforcement of tax laws in Italy, because "the level of tax evasion is so high and methods of tax collection have previously been backward or even archaic."

Even though I happen to belong to that unfortunate minority of Italians who, being on fixed income, find it impossible to evade taxes, I must confess that I am flattered by the recognition that Italy leads the world in tax evasion. I must also say, however, that I find Professor Rose's statement highly misleading and his conclusion completely wrong. The fact that Professor Rose fails to consider is that, despite the allegedly high level of tax evasion, Italians do not pay less for their government than is the case in other countries. Indeed, we pay more than most. According to the Minister of Finance, Franco Reviglio, the

13. R. Rose, op. cit., pp. 13–14.

ratio of total public-sector spending to gross national product—which is the only correct measure of the cost of government—has risen from 49.2 percent in 1976 to 55.8 percent in 1979.[14]

If Italians evade taxes more than other peoples, this is due—aside from the superior ingenuity of my countrymen—to the fact that our tax laws implicitly take tax evasion into account. In the 1950s, for example, Luigi Einaudi estimated that if taxpayers in certain income brackets had paid all their "due"—i.e., had they not practiced tax evasion—their taxes would have exceeded their income! Tax evasion, in other words, is for the average Italian an essential condition for survival: if the 27 percent of reported income represented by tax evasion, to which Professor Rose alludes, were added to the taxes already being paid, it would bring total "fiscal pressure" to the neighborhood of 65 to 70 percent (assuming that the government deficit would disappear). I doubt very much that Professor Rose would approve of taxation taking away 70 percent of the average taxpayer's income!

It must be added at this point that the distinguishing feature of the Italian tax system is its lack of transparency. Italians, that is, pay taxes without realizing it. This can be easily understood if one looks at the tax structure. Income-tax revenue amounted in 1978 to 11.4 percent of national income—a rather low figure, possibly reflecting substantial tax evasion. Most of the revenue from the income tax is paid in the form of withholding, and people are used to thinking of their income in terms of the net figure, without considering the amount their employer has had to turn over to the taxman. Indirect taxes amount to 11.3 percent of national income, and again people pay these taxes without realizing it. For instance, the price of gasoline is 750 lire a liter (roughly $3.20 per gallon), of which some 500 lire is sales tax: two thirds! Thus the owner of a gas station was telling me that he must be considered more a tax collector than a businessman! Most people are not aware of this, and they tend to attribute the exorbitant price of gas entirely to the greed of Arab sheiks and multinational oil companies. To income taxes and indirect taxes one must add social security taxes, amounting to 15.7 percent of national income. Again, people

14. F. Reviglio, *Il significato economico della rivalutazione dei conti nazionali,* unpublished paper, ISPE, June 1979.

are seldom aware of paying these taxes, as they are generally withheld by their employer. To the 38.4 percent of "explicit" taxes one must add the 17.2 percent of the hidden tax of government deficit, which very few people indeed perceive as a tax, tending rather to put the blame for inflation and unemployment on a variety of scapegoats ranging from labor unions to "capitalism."[15] The lack of transparency of the Italian tax system explains how a country of ingenious tax evaders can end up sacrificing 55.8 percent of its income (in 1979) to the greed of bureaucrats and politicians. In the light of all of this, I find Professor Rose's conclusion that there is room for "improved" enforcement of tax laws in Italy rather disturbing.

Finally, as for social security taxes which are in Italy the highest in the EEC and twice as high as in the United States, I find it hard to share Professor Rose's implicit conclusion that revenue from this source is high because people approve of the existing government programs to which it is destined. A much more likely explanation is that these taxes are almost impossible to evade, at least in the official economy. Needless to say, the very high level of social security taxes is one of the major forces behind the existence of the underground economy because it creates an incentive for collusion between employer and employee that benefits both of them.

Let us now return to tax evasion as an indicator of the existence of the underground economy. Thus far we have shown that the fact that Italians evade taxes doesn't imply that they do not pay taxes. To this we must now add that the fact that Italians pay taxes does not mean that they do not evade!

The list of tax evaders usually comprises mostly self-employed people. For some inscrutable reason, most studies put plumbers in the first place, but the list, of course, includes other professionals, such as lawyers, doctors, electricians, domestics, gardeners, storekeepers, cab drivers, salesmen, farmers, craftmen, and mechanics. One of the reasons for the diffusion of tax evasion is that, given the complexity of our tax laws, it is a lot easier to evade taxes than to pay them. Thus, despite the simplicity of my income, I have always resorted to a tax consultant

15. For the figures on fiscal pressure, see Istituto Centrale di Statistica, *I Conti degli Italiani,* Rome, 1979.

to help me fill out my income-tax form! Incidentally, he is very scrupulous and I suspect that I end up paying more than I should, but he has never given me the legally compulsory receipt for his honorarium!!

Other areas of tax evasion include real estate transactions (but these lead to underestimation of wealth rather than income) and foreign trade. In the case of international transactions, underinvoicing of exports and overinvoicing of imports is also a means to take money out of the country. A very interesting example of the ingenuity of people engaged in foreign trade unrelated to the underground economy is provided by the so-called *tondinisti,* the producers of steel rod, most of them from the area around Brescia. The *tondinisti* from Brescia were so efficient that their German, French, and English competitors were experiencing a loss in their market share. The latter resorted to the EEC for help against the "unfair competition" of the *tondinisti,* charging that they were practicing dumping. The EEC then set a minimum price that was well above that of the *tondinisti* and remunerative for the relatively less efficient German and French producers. The immediate result was that in Brescia the weight of one ton jumped from 1,000 to 1,200 kilos! But even more ingenious was the other device used by the *tondinisti* to circumvent the minimum price. In their contracts they included a deadline that was well ahead of the delivery date that had been agreed, with penalties for late delivery equal to the difference between the official EEC price and that mutually stipulated!

Another indicator of the existence of a substantial underground economy in Italy is provided by the labor market. According to official figures, the "activity rate"—the ratio of the labor force to total population—has been declining rapidly and is presently at a level that is generally considered exceptionally low. Several studies, independently conducted by various researchers using different methodologies, challenge the reliability of official figures and suggest that the "true" activity rate is much higher than the recorded one. In the area around Modena, for example, official statistics peg the activity rate at 34 percent, whereas a recent study gives 46 percent as the true figure. All of this work points in the direction of a substantial underground labor force: It is estimated that the underground economy employs no fewer than 6 million people.

For most of the underground labor force, obviously, tax evasion and unrecorded income are strictly related. In other cases, outright fraud is involved. It has been estimated, for example, that about one-half of the officially unemployed hold "unofficial" jobs, and the estimate has been confirmed by a Ministry of Labor survey whose results were made known in June of this year, according to which 57 percent of those listed as unemployed in Naples hold a stable job (while drawing unemployment benefits). Another area in which fraud and the underground economy go hand in hand is in the field of pensions. The number of people qualifying for an invalid's pension has swollen to an incredible 5,437,528—almost 10 percent of the total population! In 1979, 43 percent of those drawing a pension from INPS (the Italian equivalent of Social Security) were "disabled." Some of these are not included in the labor force even though they often work (as in the recent case of a professional photographer who was drawing a pension for the blind). The same is true for those on old age pensions.

To the "nonunemployed" and to the fake invalids, one must add youngsters who hold a stable job while being excluded from the formal labor force, women classified as housewives who take occasional or precarious jobs, and illegal foreign workers. In the case of foreign workers it is interesting to note that some of them come from the communist world. This so-called noninstitutional labor force constitutes the bulk of the underground labor force.

Underground activities performed by the noninstitutional labor force range from textiles and machinery to nuns embroidering fabric, housewives producing made-in-Italy jeans, and several thousand small businesses engaged in many types of production.

The success of the underground economy has led to an increase in the demand for leisure in the official economy that has taken the form of moonlighting and absenteeism. Not surprisingly, university professors are leading the field. It used to be said that the university professor had three advantages: July, August, and September. I regret to add that the amount of time devoted to the fulfillment of his duties at the university during the rest of the year is such as to leave ample room for other, more lucrative activities. I am usually ashamed to quote my salary to an American colleague because it is very low by American standards. An American academician would normally be unaware, however, that an Italian professor's salary is usually a tiny fraction of his total income. Professor Friedman claims that university professors all over the world tend to make the same income; what varies from country to country is the number of jobs that they must hold in order to make that income. There is little doubt that Italian professors confirm that law.

This extensive evidence from the labor market—together with that provided by monetary figures and tax evasion—make it safe to say that the underground economy in Italy produces between one-fourth and one-third of the country's national income.

5. I come now to the causes of the growth of the underground economy. It seems obvious that the underground economy is a form of escape from government, or, in Professor Rose's words, "a general retreat from politics" and a symptom of the "decline in respect for government." The fact is that government intervention in the economy has usually meant an increase in taxation and, therefore, an increase in the incentive to evade taxes. But that is not, unfortunately, the end of the story. Government intervention in my country and, to a lesser extent, in other countries as well, has also meant high social security costs, stifling regulations, reduced or nonexistent labor mobility, and absenteeism. If one adds labor union pressures, rapidly rising nominal wages, and strikes, one understands why a substantial fraction of the productive resources of the country has gone underground.

Let's not forget, however, that another cause for the existence of the underground economy is simply the inevitable degree of approximation of national income statistics. It was a naive delusion, stimulated by the Keynesian dream of fine-tuning the economy in order to smooth out any deviation from the desired trend, to believe that macroeconomic variables could be exactly quantified and measured. The complex reality of the interreaction of decisions made by millions of individuals in the marketplace is by its nature impervious to exact measurement. Let me add that this is not necessarily all bad. Indeed, our freedom might very well depend on the poor quality of statistics. What is exactly measured can be more easily confiscated or taxed, stolen or destroyed. The less politicians and bureaucrats know about national wealth, the better for all of us.

I now come to the consequences of the underground economy. Its existence obviously infuriates statists of all kinds because it provides evidence of their impotence to control and regulate human activities.[16] But even if one disregards the expected moralistic criticism of the interventionists, there still remains a substantial set of negative effects attributed to the existence of the underground economy.

The first kind of criticism focuses on the distortions introduced by the underground economy in the measurement of macroeconomic variables. It has been argued for example, that employment statistics become less meaningful as a result of the underground economy, because the unemployment rate becomes overstated. As we have seen, this is true in Italy on a very large scale. However, the overestimation of the unemployment rate does not per se pose any problem. In order to argue that this is a negative consequence of the existence of the underground economy, one would have to argue that because of the overstated unemployment rate the government engages in unnecessary "full employment" policies that result in economic instability. But even if this is so—and it is far from clear that the illusion can last for a long time—the negative effects come not from the underground economy itself but from the adoption of full employment policies that would presumably be ineffective and destabilizing even if the unemployment rate were correctly measured. I find it paradoxical that the underground economy is blamed for its greatest achievement: that of providing job opportunities to people who would not otherwise have any chance to make a living.

Other macroeconomic variables that become distorted because of the underground economy include, among others, the rate of growth of the economy. This is in fact higher than the recorded one if the underground economy grows faster than the "official" GNP. Again, I see no negative consequence in this. In order to argue that this is

16. It is interesting to note in this respect that "British trade unions . . . do not normally attack the undeclared economy as such, because they are aware of the liking for it of many of their members." (B. Shenfield, op. cit.) The same is true of the Italian trade unions and of the Italian left in general. They are vociferous in denouncing tax evasion and violations of labor laws, but singularly silent about the need to do something to cut the underground economy down to size. Their position on this issue is limited to vague generalizations about the shameful existence of "black labor" and tax evasion, but they have put forward no concrete proposal.

detrimental to society one would have to assume that the government will engage in expansionary policies because of the understated rate of growth. But experience suggests that expansionary policies seldom achieve the desired goal of promoting growth anyway, and the blame for the negative impact of such policies rests on the government and on the illusion that one can artificially promote economic growth. The existence of the underground economy has nothing to do with such delusion.

If one accepts the notion that stabilization policies of the Keynesian fine-tuning type are destabilizing anyway, the fact that the underestimation of the growth rate and the overestimation of the unemployment rate make them impossible should be considered as an advantage of the existence of the underground economy, and not as a negative consequence of it.[17]

Finally, the fact that the "size of the public sector, whether measured as a ratio of taxes or expenditure to GNP, is magnified" because of the underestimation of income, should definitely be considered one of the major advantages of the underground economy: it allows us to complain effectively about excessive government before it really reaches fatal levels!

A second kind of criticism is based on noneconomic considerations. Thus, for example, as previously mentioned, Professor Rose interprets the underground economy as a manifestation of decline in respect for government and a form of retreat from politics. He is also convinced that "Governments soon lose out as the spread of tax evasion costs them more and more money. And honest taxpayers lose, too, for those successful in disinvesting in government turn the tax system into

17. I, therefore, disagree with Professor Feige when he says that because of the underground economy "the extent and magnitude of these problems (inflation and unemployment) have been exaggerated in the official statistics and, because economic actors have responded to these false signals, we have seriously exacerbated our difficulties" (*The Washington Post,* September 21, 1980). Our difficulties have been exacerbated by the delusion that it was possible to eliminate even minor economic fluctuations by pursuing economic policies oriented toward short-run stability. The poor quality of statistics evidenced by the existence of the underground economy is only an additional reason against such measures, but it is certainly not the only one.

a means of redistributing income from the honest to the dishonest." Even assuming that tax evasion results in a loss of revenue for the government, it is far from clear that this should be considered detrimental to society. In order to argue that, one would also have to assume that a given amount of money is more socially beneficial if spent by the government than it is if spent by private individuals. Given the size of contemporary governments, this assumption is rather hard to swallow. Furthermore, it is not certain that the existence of the underground economy and related tax evasion inevitably result in a loss of government revenue. It might very well be argued that the existence of the underground economy increases the wealth of society as a whole and, therefore, raises the revenue that can be collected from the "official" economy. If the underground economy would simply cease to exist, society would be so much poorer that the tax base might very well be substantially smaller than it now is, and government revenue would accordingly be diminished.

Finally, as for the idea that tax evasion determines a redistribution of income from the honest to the dishonest, this is not necessarily the case. No tax evader collects all the benefits of his action. Almost always tax evasion also benefits those who do not evade. It does so indirectly, by promoting economic activities that would not otherwise exist, but it also does it directly. Take, for example, the case of restaurants, currently accused of being big tax evaders in Italy. Should tax evasion on the part of restaurant owners disappear overnight, as the Italian government hopes, who would be hurt? Is there any doubt that the increased honesty of restaurant owners would result in higher bills (and fewer meals) for their law-abiding customers? The owner of the restaurant does not evade for himself only, he does so also on behalf of, and for the advantage of, us, his customers.

Another criticism of the underground economy is that it has undermined respect for the law. Needless to say, this is a very serious criticism: When people start disobeying the law, they end up violating all laws, good and bad. However, I feel in complete agreement with Mrs. Shenfield on this point: "the truth is that it is Governments themselves which have undermined respect for law." And I am confident that the "ill effects of the undeclared economy on respect for law may not be permanent if the State abandons its own oppressive fiscal and interventionist policies and practices."[18]

Societies—Voltaire maintained—are like games: Without rules they do not exist. It is a paradox of our times that the increase in disrespect for the law has naturally followed the introduction of excessive numbers of rules and regulations. For any given society there is a maximum amount of legislation that can be easily enforced because everybody perceives the existing rules as "just" and essential for the survival of society. But once that maximum is overcome, and the production of legislation increases to the point that even the most law-abiding citizen finds it hard to know all the details of the existing and continuously changing legal rules, most people will simply give up and choose to ignore the law. The obvious cost for society is that even needed and useful laws will go unenforced. If this is the case, then the obvious solution is to reduce the number of legal restrictions placed on society to its essential minimum, so that enforcement no longer becomes impossible. Unless the quality of legislation is improved and its quantity is restricted, however, the degree of law abidance will continue to remain low.

Activities in the underground economy are not necessarily "criminal." Indeed, in Italy at least, criminal activities involve only a small fraction of total unreported income. Most of the activities in the underground economy would be perfectly legitimate in a less-interventionist framework. People have been forced underground by absurd legislation and confiscatory taxation. By violating the existing laws, moreover, they are undoubtedly rendering an important service to society. In the case of Italy, for example, the country would be much poorer and the unemployment problem intractable if the underground economy did not exist.

From this point of view, the underground economy confirms the relevance of Adam Smith's famous insight:

> The uniform, constant, and uninterrupted effort of every man to better his condition . . . is frequently powerful enough to maintain

18. B. Shenfield, op. cit.

the natural progress of things toward improvement, in spite both of the extravagance of government, and of the greatest errors of administration. Like the unknown principle of animal life, it frequently restores health and vigour to the constitution, in spite, not only of the disease, but of the absurd prescriptions of the doctor.

Another Italian Economic Miracle?

When the law interferes with people's pursuit of their own values, they will try to find a way around. They will evade the law, they will break the law, or they will leave the country.—Milton and Rose Friedman, Free to Choose *(New York: Harcourt Brace Jovanovich, 1980), p. 145.*

1. As is well known, economists have always concerned themselves with the analysis of the unintended effects of human action. Indeed, economics can be defined as the study of such unintended effects.[1] It is also known that politicians seldom pay attention to such secondary effects, rather concentrating on the immediate, intended consequences of their decisions. A good example of this contrast is provided by the wonderful story of a little town in Abruzzi that was plagued by a large number of vipers. The local politicians thought it wise to attempt to solve the problem by offering a reward for any viper killed. The unintended effect of their action was—as any economist could have easily predicted—an increase in the supply of vipers: Peasants started breeding vipers in their basements.

Originally published as "Measuring Italy's Underground Economy" in *Policy Review,* spring 1981, pp. 87–106, which was a revised version of a paper given at the Mont Pèlerin Society Meeting, Stanford, Calif., 1980.

The money/income hypothesis was first suggested to me by Professor Milton Friedman in June 1978. In reply to my concern over the high money/income ratio in Italy at that time, he mentioned that unreliability of income data might have been a possible explanation. In September of the same year, at the Hong Kong meeting of the Mont Pèlerin Society, similar doubts were suggested by Professor David Meiselman. I am also grateful to Ciro De Falco and Michael O'Connor of the U.S. Treasury office in Rome for statistical assistance.

1. In Italian, this can be summarized by a rather appropriate acronym: L.E.N.IN.—*leggi degli effetti non intenzionali.*

When it comes to finding a way around the law, the size of the unintended consequences of political decisions depends, of course, on many factors, not least the quantity and quality of legislation. But it also depends on cultural factors, such as the ingenuity of the people, their willingness and capacity to evade the law, the history of the country, etc. With this in mind, it is fair to say that Italy is second to no one. Its twenty-five centuries of history can be viewed as the struggle between the shrewdness of legislators and the ingenuity of the people in frustrating their efforts.

It is a testimony of the victory of the Italian people over their rulers that so many "new" laws are nothing more than the reinstatement of already-existing laws that have never been enforced. Their continuous defeat, however, has not prevented legislators from continuing in their efforts. Indeed, the flow of new legislation is such that it gives an unprecedented meaning to Jonathan Swift's famous remark: "If books and laws continue to increase as they have done for fifty years past, I am in concern for future ages, how any man will be learned, or any man a lawyer."

What follows is an account of the so-called underground economy in Italy, which I consider a masterpiece of my countrymen's ingenuity, a second Italian economic miracle which has saved the country from bankruptcy, and an example for the other "free" countries to follow.

2. In the second half of 1978 the Italian economy presented a puzzle to economic observers. The money supply had been consistently growing at the rate of 20 to 25 percent per year for almost three years. This was true for both the M_1 (currency plus demand deposits) and the M_2 (currency, demand deposits, and time deposits) aggregates. The rate of growth of M_1 had reached the 20 percent mark in the first quarter of 1976 and remained in the 20 to 25 percent range since then. The rate of growth of M_2 had been in the same range since the third quarter of 1975. The government deficit—the main source of money creation—had risen from 14,707 billion lire in 1976 (10.4 percent of national income) to 22,531 billion in 1977 (13.2 percent) and was expected to be in the neighborhood of 35,000 billion for fiscal 1978 (reaching an all-time high of 17.2 percent of national income). Yet the trade surplus was expected to be a record $3.5 billion, and even more puzzling was the fact that, despite the high rate of monetary growth, the rate

of inflation was going down, putting an unfair strain on the nervous systems of those of us who had unwisely predicted an acceleration of the inflationary process.

3. The short-term puzzle was coupled with a long-run paradox relating to the money/income ratio.[2] This ratio has been high in Italy (as compared to other industrialized countries), and it has shown the tendency to increase rather quickly over time (see Table 1). It is a known fact of monetary theory that the demand for money increases more than in proportion with income, so that an increase in the money/income ratio is to be expected.[3] However, while the rapid increase was hard to reconcile with the inflationary history of the country, the absolute value of the money/income ratio seemed unusually high.[4]

In Table 2 the average M_1 income ratio in the past four quinquennia in Italy is compared to the same ratio in the United States, Great

2. As is known, this is one way to measure the demand for money: "the real quantity of money can be expressed in terms of the number of weeks of aggregate transactions of the community, or aggregate net output of the community, to which it is equal." Milton Friedman, "A Theoretical Framework for Monetary Analysis," in R. J. Gordon, ed., *Milton Friedman's Monetary Framework* (Chicago: University of Chicago Press, 1974), p. 2.

3. "A 1 per cent increase in real income per capita has therefore, on the average, been associated with a 1.8 per cent increase in real cash balances per capita and hence with a 0.8 per cent *decrease* in income velocity." Milton Friedman, "The Demand for Money: Some Theoretical and Empirical Results," in *The Optimum Quantity of Money and Other Essays* (Chicago: Aldine, 1969), p. 113. Also, "Judged by the long-period evidence, money is in this respect a 'luxury' like durable consumer goods, rather than a 'necessity' like bread. A one per cent increase in real per capita income has on the average been associated with an increase in real per capita money holdings of about one and two-thirds per cent." Milton Friedman, "The Demand for Money," in *Dollars and Deficits* (Englewood Cliffs, N.J.: Prentice-Hall, 1968), p. 199.

4. The high money/income ratio led many of us to fear that, should people decide to decumulate cash balances, this might result in an autonomous inflationary potential. See Giannino Parravicini, "Il mercato monetario e finanziario e la spesa pubblica," *Bancaria,* nn. 5–6, 1977, and Antonio Martino, "Finanza inflazionistica e tasso d'interesse," *Rivista di politica economica,* nn. 8–9, 1977, reprinted in *Rivista di politica economica, Selected Papers,* no. 11, 1977, as "Inflationary Finance and 'the' Interest Rate."

TABLE 1

	M_1 / Y (%)	M_2 / Y (%)
1958	28.6	58.2
1959	30.7	62.5
1960	31.8	65.1
1961	32.8	66.8
1962	34.2	69.4
1963	34.9	69.9
1964	34.2	69.3
1965	36.1	72.9
1966	38.4	77.5
1967	38.8	78.4
1968	40.8	81.5
1969	42.7	83.0
1970	46.2	82.8
1971	50.6	87.5
1972	55.8	94.5
1973	56.7	95.2
1974	54.1	93.0
1975	51.5	97.5
1976	49.9	97.1
1977	49.9	96.1
1978	50.6	97.1

Sources: *International Financial Statistics*, IMF; Banca d'Italia; ISTAT. M_1 = Currency + Demand Deposits; $M_2 = M_1$ + Time Deposits; Y = Gross Domestic Product. M_1 and M_2 data are averages of stocks as of end of quarter for 1958–66; data for 1967–78 are monthly averages. All figures are based on the "old" GDP series.

Britain, France, and West Germany. As can be seen, the time pattern of the ratio in Italy differs from that of the other countries in that it increases steadily over the whole period. Even more significant, I believe, is the fact that the ratio is substantially higher in Italy than in the other countries and the difference tends to grow over time.

Similar conclusions can be arrived at by looking at the M_2/income

TABLE 2. M_1 / Y (%)

	1958–62	1963–67	1968–72	1973–77
Italy	31.6	36.4	47.2	52.4
U.S.A.	28.7	24.8	22.3	19.2
Great Britain	24.9	21.3	18.6	16.1
France	30.3	33.9	29.1	27.2
Germany	15.8	15.3	14.8	14.9

ratio (Table 3). Even here the ratio is substantially higher in Italy than in the other countries, and the gap grows bigger over time.

4. There are several possible explanations for the apparent paradox, and they are not mutually incompatible. The first one is the secular decline in income velocity mentioned above. This is true of the M_2 figures for all of the five countries considered, although to a different extent. The secular decline explains why the ratio is increasing, but it does not explain why it is so much higher in Italy than in the other countries, or why it increases at such a rapid rate.

A second possible factor might be an increase in the precautionary demand for money due to the general climate of uncertainty. This might explain why the ratio is high but not why it is rising, and it is doubtful that it has played a role for such a long period of time.

A third explanation is given by the lack of alternatives open to small savers. This has undoubtedly played a significant role in Italy. Indeed, time deposits might be the only option available to small savers because the stock market is negligible, and small savers might lack the kind of sophisticated financial knowledge required to look for other alternatives (such as taking the money out of the country, which, by the way, is illegal).[5] However, it is hard to believe that this factor alone

5. "[T]he Italian financial system differs institutionally from most of the others examined . . . in that Italian banks pay interest on demand as well as on time deposits. . . . Checking accounts thus serve as a store of value to a greater extent than elsewhere." J. M. Boughton, "Demand for Money in Major OECD Countries," *OECD Economic Outlook Occasional Studies,* OECD, December 1978, p. 39. Another factor that plays a role in making checking accounts an attrac-

TABLE 3. M_2 / Y (%)

	1958–62	1963–67	1968–72	1973–77
Italy	64.4	73.6	85.8	95.7
U.S.A.	43.0	43.7	44.4	45.9
Great Britain	39.2	34.8	33.5	37.6
France	33.5	39.7	42.4	48.6
Germany	34.7	40.6	46.9	57.8

can explain the growth of the ratio in times of high inflation. For if it is true that both demand deposits and time deposits pay interest, it is also true that nominal interest rates on all kinds of deposits have consistently been lower than the rate of inflation, so that real interest rates have been negative. Why didn't they try to avoid the inflation tax by increasing their spending (especially on consumer durables)? After all, this would have been a perfectly legal (albeit, therefore, less attractive) way of avoiding a tax.

A fourth possibility might be offered by some sort of "money illusion." People might have interpreted the high rates of inflation of the past few years as exceptional and come to the conclusion that negative real rates of interest were going to be temporary. This might have been true in the early stages of the inflationary process, but, after many years of double-digit inflation and negative real rates, money illusion must have been eroded.[6]

---

tive store of value is their secrecy. They can be inspected only in the case of a criminal investigation, thus providing a good hiding place for tax evaders.

6. Real interest rates on government bonds have thus been estimated:

1972	−0.64	1976	−12.35
1973	−5.76	1977	0.28
1974	−17.44	1978	1.94
1975	−0.42		

Where: real rate = nominal rate − rate of inflation of the following year. See Rainer Masera, *Disavanzo pubblico e vincolo del bilancio* (Milano: Edizioni di Comunità, 1979), p. 72. Nominal rates on deposits are generally lower than on government bonds. Therefore, real rates on deposits have been even more negative than the ones above.

All of the above, and undoubtedly other factors as well, might have played a role at one time or another. However, even if taken together, it is hard to believe that they can account for the fact that the average Italian holds almost one year's income in cash and keeps on adding to his money holdings even though these continue to deteriorate in real terms because of inflation. The "true" explanation might be a completely different one.

5. A possible explanation for the peculiarity of the Italian monetary figures and trends—which complements those mentioned above—might be given by the so-called underground sector of the Italian economy. Should there be such a sector, its existence might explain the behavior of the money/income ratio better than any other hypothesis.

Indeed, supposing there is such a sector, firms operating in it might not have access to the "legal" credit market. They might, therefore, be forced to hold large amounts of money both in the form of deposits and in cash.[7] This might make the money/income ratio higher than otherwise. The growth of the underground sector relative to the whole economic system could, however, explain why the money/income ratio has been increasing.

7. The secrecy of deposits (see note 5 above) makes them even more suitable to this task. This is why the ratio of currency to demand deposits, which has been used as an indicator of the size of the underground economy in other countries, would not be as meaningful in Italy. For, given the secrecy of deposits, illegal activities and tax evasion do not necessarily imply the use of currency but can be settled through checks. For a study of the ratio of currency to demand deposits (the "currency ratio") as an indicator of the size of the underground economy in the United States, see Vito Tanzi, "Underground Economy, Income Tax Evasion, and the Demand for Currency in the United States, 1929–1976," IMF unpublished paper, 1979. Also, about the "cash" economy in England, *Tax Avoision,* The Institute of Economic Affairs, Readings 22, 1979.

It could be argued that, since demand deposits can serve the same purpose as currency because of their secrecy, the ratio of M_1 to M_2 (the latter being made up of currency, demand deposits, and time deposits) could be used in place of the currency ratio. Now, the M_1/M_2 ratio in Italy has shown the same time pattern generally attributed to the ratio of currency to demand deposits—that is, it has been *falling* with economic development. However, there is a notable exception: In the quinquennium 1968–72 the ratio has been *increasing,* reaching a peak in 1973, and then resuming its downward trend. It might be that the exceptional behavior of the ratio during that time is somewhat connected to the

Still more important seems to be the obvious consideration that, if income produced by the underground economy is not recorded in income statistics, the "true" money/income ratio is lower than the recorded one. This might explain why the ratio is so much higher in Italy than elsewhere, and why it keeps on growing.

As should be obvious, all of this is strictly conjectural. Just as the few superficial remarks above on the demand for money do not amount to a statistical analysis, saying that the existence of the underground sector might explain things does not prove anything in any meaningful sense.

However, if the above conjecture is valid and if the existence of the underground economy is the only factor behind the difference between the ratio in Italy and that in the other countries, then statistically recorded income might fall short of "true" income by a very large fraction. It would not be surprising if official income statistics were, say, 30 percent below the mark.

6. The hypothesis above is based on the implicit assumption that monetary statistics are more reliable than income statistics. If something is wrong with the recorded ratio, that is, the acceptance of the hypothesis means putting the blame on the denominator (GNP) rather than on the numerator (M_2).

This assumption was confirmed by the reaction of the government statistical office (ISTAT: Central Institute of Statistics) to the money/income hypothesis. As a result of such a reaction, ISTAT unintentionally confirmed the unreliability of income statistics and the existence of a substantial underground economy.

---

underground economy (it was a period of labor unrest on a larger-than-usual scale, and of particularly foolish legislation). However, any hypothesis would require extensive statistical analysis.

M_1 / M_2	(%)
1953	68.20
1958	57.98
1963	57.04
1968	56.75
1973	66.57
1978	53.15

In November 1978 a brief summary of the hypothesis was published in a major national newspaper.[8] It was suggested that, as a "simplistic arithmetical exercise," paradoxically supposing that the true ratio had remained stable over time, the underground economy's contribution to national income in 1977 might have been "in the neighborhood of 40%," so that 28 percent of GNP was not recorded in the official income statistics. The article came out at a time when many people were talking about the underground economy, and, maybe because of enthusiasm, the "simplistic arithmetical exercise" was taken as a serious estimate.[9]

It followed that in February 1979, ISTAT set up a committee to study the reliability of income data and the problem of the underground economy (Commissione per la formazione e gli impieghi del reddito). On the occasion of its first meeting (February 22, 1979), ISTAT senior statisticians strongly criticized the money/income hypothesis on two grounds. First, it was argued that monetary statistics were not necessarily more reliable than income data. Second, an income of 30,000 to 60,000 billion lire could not conceivably pass unrecorded. The explanation given for the fact that the M_2/income ratio was so much higher in Italy than elsewhere was the one mentioned above about the lack of alternatives open to small savers and the high nominal rates on deposits. Finally, it was suggested that the statistical error in the official income figures was unlikely to exceed 700 billion

8. Antonio Martino, "L'economia clandestina ci ha salvato dal baratro," *Il Giornale Nuovo,* November 19, 1978.

9. Shortly after the appearance of the article, the authoritative Italian economic weekly *Il Mondo* published a survey of opinions on the size of the underground economy ("Il tesoro sommerso," *Il Mondo,* December 13, 1978), in which it quoted me as saying that income produced by the underground economy actually *was* in the neighborhood of 40 percent. In the same survey, several economists, industrialists, and government officials—using different methodologies—suggested widely different *estimates* of the size of the underground economy, ranging from 15 percent to 35 percent of national income. My "estimate," therefore, turned out to be the most extreme! ISTAT senior statisticians were also quoted in the same survey. For them, an error of 5 percent was conceivable, although unlikely, but "people who talk of 30–40 percent don't know what they are talking about."

lire, i.e., 0.35 percent! The arguments given by ISTAT in defense of official income statistics were very plausible.[10] However, it was hard to believe that the error was only in the order of one-third of 1 percent!

The skepticism was confirmed (and faith in the reliability of ISTAT figures shaken) when, the following month, March 1979, following increasing criticism of official figures, ISTAT decided to revise its GNP time series from 1975 onward. *Income figures were revised upward by almost 10%!* (See Table 4.)

A nice by-product of the decision was the possibility it offered to ridicule believers in "fine-tuning." Arguments going on at that time about the desirable size of the target rate of growth—the alternative positions differing by less than 1 percent—were made to look absurd by the official admission that income figures had been 10 percent underestimated.[11]

Moreover, the decision encouraged further speculation about the size of the underground economy[12] and lent credibility to the money/income hypothesis.[13]

> *The fact that six million persons are quietly working in defiance of the law amounts not only to a huge social rebellion but also to a new kind of conflict, one very different from the self-destructive kind in Britain. Faced with an untenable situation, huge numbers of Italians have decided to ignore rather than try to change the system.—C. Matthews, "'Underground' Workers Keep Italian Economy Running,"* International Herald Tribune, *February 5, 1979.*

7. The existence of a substantial underground economy helps explain a few puzzles relating to the labor market. The "activity rate"

10. Indeed, so much so that I decided not to publish a somewhat longer version of the money/income hypothesis that I had already completed. It was published the following month. See Antonio Martino, "Metamorfosi della ricchezza sommersa," *Alleanza,* March 1979, pp. 22–24.

11. Antonio Martino, "Quando scienza economica significa fumo negli occhi," *Il Giornale Nuovo,* April 22, 1979.

12. For example, see "Tirata a galla può esplodere," *Il Mondo,* April 20, 1979; Luigi Frey, "Dal lavoro nero alla misurazione del reddito 'sommerso,'" *Notiziario Ceres di economia del lavoro,* May 16, 1979; "E dall'economia sommersa emerge una sorpresa," *Il Mondo,* June 29, 1979.

13. Barbara Ellis, "Italy's prosperous anarchy," *Forbes,* April 2, 1979.

TABLE 4. *Gross National Product, Market Prices (Billions of lire)*

	Old figure	Revised figure	Percent difference
1975	115,072	125,378	+ 9.0
1976	143,849	156,657	+ 8.9
1977	172,988	189,978	+ 9.8
1978	201,000	220,743	+ 9.8

Source: F. Reviglio, "Il significato economico della revalutazione dei conti nazionali," unpublished paper, ISPE, June 1979.

—the ratio of the labor force to total population—has been declining rapidly and is presently at a level that is generally considered exceptionally low. According to ISTAT figures, in 1978 there were 21,730,000 Italians in the labor force out of a population of 55,806,000, or 38.9 percent. If one excludes the 1,571,000 unemployed, the activity rate falls to 36.1 percent.[14] ISTAT stresses that the decline of the activity rate is a historical process: In 1861 it was roughly 60 percent, and by the beginning of the century it had dropped to 50 percent. However, some economic observers believe that the decline in the activity rate cannot be interpreted as a "normal" continuation of a historical trend. They claim that the ratio of the labor force to total population has dropped from 44 percent at the end of the '50s to less than 34 percent in 1976 and that such a decline is much sharper than in any other industrialized country.[15]

According to ISTAT, several factors account for the decline in the activity rate. First there are demographic changes which have increased the percentage of total population made up of people older than sixty-five and younger than fourteen years of age. Then there have been migratory movements which have in the past contributed to the decline in the rate. The third, and more important, factor is the increase in the number of students who stay in school beyond compul-

14. See *I conti degli Italiani* (Rome: ISTAT, 1979), p. 5.

15. Bruno Contini, *Lo sviluppo di un'economia parallela* (Milan: Edizioni di Comunità, 1979), p. 15.

sory education and the increase in the number of years they remain in school. Another factor is the decline of agricultural employment which might have meant that some members of the family (especially women and children) have left the labor force. More specifically related to our point is the last factor: the "improvement" in social security benefits and their extension to still other groups in society has led many people to drop out of the "official" labor force, either by early retirement or by qualifying for a pension for the "invalid," i.e., disabled citizen. The number of these has swollen in recent years to an incredible 5,437,528, almost 10 percent of total population, in 1979. Of the 12,603,678 people who draw a pension from INPS (the Italian equivalent of Social Security), 43 percent are "disabled citizens."[16] Some of these people are not included in the labor force even though they often work (as in the recent case of a professional photographer who was drawing a pension for the blind), and the same is true for those on old-age pension.

A host of studies have pointed out in recent years the inadequacy of official figures of the activity rate. First, some observers have estimated that about one-half of the officially unemployed hold "unofficial" jobs (while drawing unemployment benefits). Second, roughly 1,400,000 youngsters between the ages of fourteen and twenty-nine hold "precarious" jobs while being officially considered students and, therefore, outside the labor force. Third, about 1,250,000 people above fifty years of age, while drawing a pension for old age, "unofficially" work. Fourth, almost 600,000 women between thirty and forty-nine years of age, while being classified as housewives and excluded from the labor force, hold occasional and precarious jobs. Finally, 235,000 minors between ten and fifteen years of age, although excluded by definition from the labor force, do work. This last figure, according to other sources, should be increased to 430,000.[17]

Another factor that plays a role in supporting the idea of an underground economy in the labor market is given by the presence of for-

16. See "Siamo un popolo di invalidi, almeno per l'INPS," *Il Giornale Nuovo,* March 29, 1980.

17. Luigi Frey, op. cit.

eign workers. These, for the most part, hold jobs that Italians consider menial or unpleasant, such as servants or miners. Significantly enough, some of them come from the communist world. Thus the old communist leader Giorgio Amendola recently cited the example of Polish miners employed in Sardegna (a region with a high rate of unemployment) as evidence that unemployment statistics are misleading.[18] Estimates of the number of foreign workers employed in Italy widely differ, for many of them enter the country illegally. However, their number should not be less than 500,000 and might well be close to 750,000.[19]

Considering these various factors, it is estimated that the underground economy employs around 6 million persons.[20]

8. To this so-called "noninstitutional" labor force one must add moonlighters. This phenomenon takes place on a grand scale in Italy and involves all categories. My favorite "Friedman's law" is thus undoubtedly confirmed. Professor Friedman has argued that university professors all over the world tend to have the same income; what varies from country to country is the number of jobs they must hold in order to make that income. Not all income from moonlighting is recorded, and it obviously adds to the underground economy. Moonlighting apparently involves 1,300,000 people.[21] However, estimates are highly unreliable, because of the often-present illegal element.

Examples of moonlighting could fill a whole book. The Rome Post Office, which employs 1,500 people to distribute the mail in the city, handles the same amount of correspondence handled by Romana Recapiti, a private delivery agency, which employs 300. Needless to say, Romana Recapiti is faster and more reliable than the Post Office. But the interesting thing is that most of the 300 people working for Ro-

18. Giorgio Amendola, "Interrogativi sul 'caso' Fiat," *Rinascita,* n. 43, November 9, 1979, pp. 13–15.

19. Giuseppe Alvaro, "La valutazione dell'economia sommersa: principali problemi statistici ed economici," I.S.P.E. unpublished paper, 1979.

20. The estimate of 6 million underground workers is that of Luigi Frey, *Tendenze dell'occupazione* (Rome: Ceres, 1978). This estimate is supported by a number of studies that show that the activity rate is in many cases 20 percent higher than the official one. See Bruno Contini, op. cit., and the bibliography.

21. Giuseppe Alvaro, op. cit.

mana Recapiti are moonlighting employees of the Post Office. Not surprisingly, the rate of absenteeism at the Post Office is in the neighborhood of 50 percent.

Indeed, absenteeism and moonlighting go hand in hand and represent a typical feature of contemporary Italy. It has been acutely observed that Italians are socialist in the morning and capitalist in the afternoon. What this means is that many bureaucrats work for the government in the morning and moonlight in the afternoon. They hold the government job because it entitles them to retirement schemes, health insurance, fringe benefits, and, of course, a salary, with very little (or no) work. Then, in the afternoon, they moonlight for some capitalist "underground" organization, where they make money and show their talents and efficiency, "unprotected" by labor unions or social benefits. This is particularly true of the bureaucracy of government ministries that has succeeded in maintaining the 8 a.m. to 2 p.m. working hours first introduced at the time of World War II. Of course, almost no one reports to work at 8 a.m., and most leave before 2 p.m. Thus ministries have been defined as buildings where those who are a bit late to work meet on the stairs those who leave work a bit early!

Absenteeism is typical of the "official" economy and is present in all sectors: public, semipublic, and private. It is the inevitable consequence of the legislation that has been introduced to "protect workers' rights." When I was teaching in Naples I was approached by someone who wanted to work as a research assistant. When I told him that no position was available and that, therefore, I could not pay him, he replied that he was willing to work for free since he already had a job. "How are you going to find the time to do research?" I asked him. He answered that he had plenty of time, because he was "exonerated from work," being a union leader.

A wonderful example of the effects of legislation on absenteeism and its effects on production is provided by the case of Alfasud, the semipublic automobile factory of the Alfa Romeo company. "When things are going well at the Alfasud car plant, only about one in five of its workers do not show up. Under such optimum conditions, car production may reach 520 units a day in a plant built to produce 1,000. . . . Last year it lost some $100m. Since it belongs to the state by way of Alfa Romeo and the Finmeccanica holding of Iri there is of course no talk of closing it down." The high rate of absenteeism at Alfasud should be blamed on "an anomalous system of penalties for absence. A worker who arrives half an hour late to the factory is docked part of his salary, whereas if he reports sick he is not penalized. But sick leave is only legitimate if it lasts for a minimum of three days. So a worker who misses a train connection is better off financially if he turns round and spends the next three days at home rather than going on and arriving late. The company is penalized doubly: first by the absence of the manpower, and second because the first three days of illness are not covered by the workers' social insurance, but are borne by the company itself."[22] What the author of the article fails to mention is that the connection between absenteeism and the underground economy is confirmed, in the case of Alfasud, by the sharp increase in the rate of absenteeism at harvest time. Many Alfasud employees "went to the assembly line . . . directly from farming"; they have retained their farms and take care of them by not reporting to work.

Absenteeism is, of course, much higher in the public than in the private sector. Newspapers have recently come out with the story of a street sweeper in Palermo who has totaled 1,278 days of absence in five years,[23] and that of an employee of the public transportation company in the same city who totaled 700 days of absence in 27 months.[24] Both of them claimed that they could not work because of "hypochondriasis"—a nervous disturbance because of which they were convinced that they were sick. It is far from clear that they will lose the legal case brought against them by their employers. Absenteeism is also present in the private sector, although to a smaller extent. And yet Fiat claims that in 1979 it lost the production of 300,000 cars because of absenteeism and strikes (both due to foolish legislation and connected to the underground economy).[25]

22. "Alfasud, Italy's well-intended industrial disaster," *The Economist,* March 10, 1979, p. 81.

23. "Controcorrente," *Il Giornale Nuovo,* January 6, 1980.

24. "Assente 700 giorni in 27 mesi di lavoro," *Il Giornale Nuovo,* February 5, 1980.

25. The effects of absenteeism and strikes on productivity are illustrated by

9. Absenteeism is not the only factor making labor costs in the "official" economy artificially high. Another element is social security contributions. In 1975, direct pay as a percentage of total labor costs in industry was 50 percent in Italy, as compared to 76 percent in the United Kingdom, 63 percent in West Germany, and 58 percent in France, Holland, and Belgium. However, social security contributions were highest in Italy: 28 percent, versus 12 percent in the United Kingdom, 18 percent in West Germany, 23 percent in Holland and Belgium, and 24 percent in France.[26] In some cases, social security contributions amount to more than 55 percent of total labor costs. The incentive this provides to both workers and employers to try to evade the social security tax by creating "underground" jobs needs no comment.

Another factor that plays a large negative role in the official economy is labor mobility. As an industrialist remarked: "Hire someone in your factory and it's like you're married. You can't fire him."[27] Besides the fact that in the official economy employers cannot make mistakes in the sense that it is almost impossible to fire someone, labor mobility is also greatly reduced in the sense that labor unions oppose overtime work,[28] and they even resist mobility within the same factory.

Finally, mention must be made of the high rate of increase in nominal wages that the unions succeed in obtaining in the official economy thanks to their monopoly power. The average annual increase in hourly earnings in manufacturing from 1965 to 1977 has been higher in Italy than in any other EEC country: 15.2 percent, as compared to 12.2 percent in France, 12.1 percent in Belgium, 12 percent in the United Kingdom, 10.9 percent in Holland, and 8.4 percent in West Germany.[29]

On top of all of this, there are strikes which are typical of the offi-

---

the fact that Alfa Romeo currently produces 7.2 cars per worker per year, and Fiat 11, as compared to Opel's 29 and Toyota's 43. Fiat claims that it can never use more than 65 percent of its productive capacity.

26. *Primo Rapporto CSC sull'Industria Italiana* (Rome: Confederazione Generale dell'Industria Italiana, 1978), p. 28.

27. See Barbara Ellis, op. cit.

28. For a fascinating story, see "No overtime please—we're Italian," *The Economist,* July 8, 1978.

29. "Europe's Rising Underground," *The Economist,* February 25, 1978.

cial economy (and absent in the underground economy) at a rate that has earned Italy the nickname of "strikeland."[30] In the face of absenteeism, high social security costs, reduced or nonexistent labor mobility, labor union pressures, rapidly rising nominal wages, and strikes on a large scale, it should not be surprising that firms in the official economy are not doing very well. A good example is given by Iri, the giant state holding, Europe's largest industrial employer, which has succeeded in accumulating debts for an incredible amount: 30,000 billion lire (some $34 billion).[31]

10. Mention must, also, be made of tax evasion and its relation to the underground economy. It is generally believed that Italians do not pay taxes, or that they pay less than is the case in other European countries. The statement is wrong: the ratio of total public-sector spending to Gross National Product—which is the only correct measure of the cost of government—has risen from 49.2 percent in 1976 to 55.8 percent in 1979.[32] However, it might conceivably be true that there is some correlation between the underground economy and tax evasion, and that if all income produced in the country were correctly recorded those percentages would be much smaller. It is an undeniable fact that Italians do not object to tax evasion on moral grounds (except, of course, when it is someone else who evades). For instance, my dentist was telling me that he was not going to take care of one of his patients anymore, "because—he said indignantly—she asked me to give her a receipt for her payment." The receipt, incidentally, is legally compulsory, and it is a criminal offense not to issue it! However, many people simply ignore the law; plumbers, doctors, lawyers, and other professionals seldom bother to issue the legally compulsory receipt.

30. For example, according to International Labor Office figures, the number of days of strike per 1,000 workers per year from 1963 to 1972 in the EEC countries has been Luxembourg = 0, Holland = 36, West Germany = 54, Denmark = 86, Belgium = 291, France = 325, Great Britain = 576, Ireland = 1,086, Italy = 1,481.

31. "Il 'buco' dell'Iri è di 24 mila miliardi," *Il Giornale Nuovo,* February 6, 1980; "Superano i 30 mila miliardi i debiti Iri," *Il Giornale Nuovo,* March 20, 1980.

32. Franco Reviglio, op. cit. The percentages above refer to the old GNP figures. They are reduced by some 5 percentage points if one refers to the new GNP figures.

Obviously, their income goes unrecorded and it adds to the size of the underground economy.[33]

It is a sad by-product of the discussions about the underground economy that the government is now engaged in an all-out war against tax evasion.[34]

11. I would like to conclude on an optimistic note and venture to predict that the efforts of legislators will keep on being frustrated by the ingenuity of my countrymen. For what has been argued in this paper is that lawlessness can be beneficial. Monetary figures and a great deal of evidence in other areas suggest that the underground economy in Italy produces anywhere between one-fourth and one-third of national income. Obviously, activities within the underground economy are often carried on by violating the law—income-tax evasion, evasion of social security contributions, violation of labor laws, and outright fraud (as in the case of pensions).[35] However, if they respected the law, most, if not all, of these activities would simply not exist, and the social cost of law abidance would be enormous. They are undeniably beneficial to society. However, they also entail a social cost, for when people start violating the law they end up violating all laws, good and bad. In order to find a solution, we should remember the words of Frederic Bastiat: "No society can exist unless the laws are respected to a certain degree. The safest way to make laws respected is to make them respectable. When law and morality contradict each other, the citizen has the cruel alternative of either losing his moral

33. The fact that professionals evade taxes is implicitly acknowledged by our tax laws. Income tax rates are higher for professionals than for people on fixed income, with the justification being that "professionals evade taxes."

34. One of the first measures introduced is that it is now compulsory for restaurants and hotels to give their customers a receipt, and even customers are fined if they leave the restaurant or the hotel without such a receipt. Several other measures are in the process of being introduced.

35. Of course, some of the activities in the underground economy not mentioned in this paper are of the "traditional" criminal type, such as prostitution, gambling, drug traffic, contraband, kidnapping (a growth industry at the moment), extortion, etc. Here the social benefits of violating the law are doubtful or absent. But it can be argued that their existence is part of the social cost of an excessive amount of bad legislation.

sense or losing his respect for the law."[36] Until the quality of legislation is improved and its quantity restricted, the best Italians can hope for is affluence from lawlessness.

APPENDIX

	Government Deficit (Billions of lire)	M_1 (Billions of lire)	M_2 (Billions of lire)	Consumer Prices (1970 = 100)
1970	−3,226	31,185	47,858	100.0
1971	−4,759	37,099	55,800	104.8
1972	−5,745	43,506	65,808	110.8
1973	−7,972	54,089	81,240	122.8
1974	−8,961	59,162	94,020	146.3
1975	−16,523	67,120	117,011	171.1
1976	−14,707	79,776	141,599	199.8
1977	−22,531	98,501	189,172	236.5
1978	−34,090	122,579	230,665	264.4
1979	−33,046	151,295	277,747	312.6

Sources: *International Financial Statistics*, IMF; Banca d'Italia; ISTAT. M_1 and M_2 are end-of-the-year figures.

36. Frederic Bastiat, *The Law* (1850) (Irvington-on-Hudson, New York: The Foundation for Economic Education, Inc., 1974), p. 12.

Part 4

Fantasies Collide with Reality

Was Keynes a Keynesian?

John Maynard Keynes has been the most influential economist of this century. Sir John Hicks has called the third quarter of this century "the age of Keynes,"[1] and the definition is very appropriate. In discussing Keynes's impact on the study of economics, Professor Hutt says: "Keynes' attempt to 'shake up' the economists somehow led a whole generation of students of economics to despise, rather than examine, the great tradition which constituted 'classical' economic science."[2]

My experience confirms the validity of that statement. A young Italian who approached the study of the "dismal science" in the first half of the 1960s would have been confronted with a reassuringly clear and simple picture of the history of economic thought. Economists, according to this picture, were divided into two groups: those *before* Keynes, variously labeled "classical" or "neoclassical," and those *after* Keynes, including Keynes himself. The economists of the first group belonged to the prehistoric era of economics—"Neanderthal men," according to Walter Heller—and their works perfectly suited Professor Stigler's definition of a "classic": A book is a classic if everybody talks about it and no one has read it. It was widely assumed that it was a net waste of precious time to try to ascertain what exactly they had said. They did not deserve such an honor.

They were, according to the generally accepted wisdom, completely remote from the reality of the modern world, irrational believers in perfect downward flexibility of wages and prices, stubborn supporters

Heritage Lecture, March 4, 1981.

1. J. Hicks, *The Crisis of Keynesian Economics,* Oxford, 1974, p. 1.

2. William H. Hutt, *The Keynesian Episode,* Liberty Fund, Inc., Indianapolis, 1979, p. 34.

of the view that the economic system always and inevitably operates under full employment equilibrium conditions, heartless and insensitive to the unemployment problem, faithful to the absurd notion that an increase in the quantity of money would lead to a proportional increase in prices, and a decrease to a proportional decrease, and so on *ad nauseam*. Finally, it was argued, it was due to their myopic insistence on the importance of old-fashioned orthodoxy that the world had suffered the horrors of the Great Depression, with its widespread unemployment, which the classical economists simply dismissed as "voluntary."

Those who believe that this is an unfair presentation of the way economics was taught in many Italian universities at that time need only glance through the books of Dudley Dillard, Alvin Hansen, and Joan Robinson, which had been published in Italian during those years for the benefit of the intellectual education of the new generations.[3]

At the other end of the economic spectrum was Keynesian theory, or rather, "the Keynesian revolution," with its modern approach to contemporary economic problems, promising indefinite economic growth under conditions of full employment and price stability. Fairness dictates, however, mentioning that even Keynes's own writings belonged to the classics in Stigler's sense, for the *Treatise on Money* was seldom mentioned, the *Tract on Monetary Reform* simply ignored, and the number of those who had actually read *The General Theory* was only marginally different from zero. Students anxious to learn the new gospel were referred not to Keynes's own writings—"too difficult for beginners"—but to the writings of the Keynesian economists.

I must confess that this unscholarly lack of interest in *The General Theory* on the part of some Italian Keynesians was not entirely unjustified. *The General Theory* is an exceedingly difficult book, poorly written and deadly boring. This opinion is widely shared by many distinguished economists, even some of those who are not unsympathetic to Keynesian economics. Thus Paul Samuelson has judged it "badly written," "poorly organized," "arrogant, bad-tempered, polemical"; Frank

3. D. Dillard, *Guida all'economica keynesiana,* ETAS-KOMPASS, 1964; A. H. Hansen, *Guida allo studio di Keynes,* Giannini, 1964; J. Robinson, *Teoria dell'occupazione,* Edizioni di Comunità, 1962, and ETAS-KOMPASS, 1966.

Knight maintained that its style was more "like the language of the soap-box reformer than that of an economist writing a theoretical tome for economists"; and Gottfried Haberler has argued that "the *General Theory* would have been much less influential . . . had Keynes written a scholarly, well-balanced treatise instead of providing an *ad hoc,* makeshift theory serving as underpinning for a combination of a policy tract, a passionate call for economic reforms, and an impassioned indictment of orthodoxy."[4]

Whether the lack of attention toward Keynes's own writings on the part of some Keynesians was justified or not, it leaves us with the question of whether Keynes belongs to the Keynesian group. Keynes himself was clearly not sure of it, for, according to Sir Austin Robinson, in Washington in 1944, "after he dined the night before with the Washington Keynesian economists (said): 'I was the only non-Keynesian there'."[5] Again, according to Lord Balogh, the Keynesian revolution was "never fully accepted by Keynes,"[6] and Joan Robinson has complained that Keynesians "sometimes had some trouble in getting Maynard to see what the point of his revolution really was."[7]

The question is made more difficult by the fact that it is far from clear who the "true" Keynesians are. Statements to the effect that "we are all Keynesians now" have been made by people holding quite different views on economic policy. Even President Nixon joined the crowd of the "all Keynesians now." It is hard, therefore, to separate those who deserve to be called Keynesian from those that Professor Hutchinson calls "pseudo-Keynesians," and Joan Robinson "bastard Keynesians" (possibly including Keynes among them). Indeed, the

4. P. A. Samuelson, "Lord Keynes and the General Theory," *Econometrica,* July 1946, p. 190; F. H. Knight, "Unemployment: And Mr. Keynes's Revolution in Economic Theory," *Canadian Journal of Economics and Political Science,* February 1937, pp. 101, 119; G. Haberler, "Sixteen Years Later," in R. Lekachman, ed., *Keynes' General Theory: Reports of Three Decades,* New York, St. Martin's Press, 1964, p. 294. These and similar statements are found in W. H. Hutt, op. cit., pp. 25ff.

5. A. Robinson, "A Comment," in T. W. Hutchinson, *Keynes v. the "Keynesians" . . . ?*, The Institute of Economic Affairs, London, 1977, p. 58.

6. See T. W. Hutchinson, op. cit., p. 34, n. 1.

7. J. Robinson, "What Has Become of the Keynesian Revolution?" in Milo Keynes, ed., *Essays on John Maynard Keynes,* Cambridge University Press, 1975, p. 125.

success of Keynesianism has been so widespread that Keynesians today range from communists—like Luigi Spaventa, a distinguished, Cambridge-educated Italian economist, who has been elected senator in the list of the Italian Communist Party—to some "supply-siders" who, perhaps unconsciously, often support a kind of Keynesian policy in reverse.

If Keynes were guilty, that is, of simplistically grouping together under the label of "classical" economists all those who had preceded him—thereby giving birth, in Dennis Robertson's words, to "some composite Aunt Sally of uncertain age"[8]—it would be no less simplistic to think of the Keynesians as a homogenous group accepting the same theoretical framework and identical policy conclusions. A choice must be made regarding the meaning to be attached to the label "Keynesian." Given the influence that they have had in my country, both in the academic profession and at the policy-making level, I consider "true" Keynesians those economists that Professor Hutchinson calls "pseudo-Keynesians"—namely, the late Sir Roy Harrod, Lord Kahn, and Mrs. Joan Robinson.

The importance of the question was Keynes a Keynesian? is stressed by the large number of substantial theoretical works devoted to an analysis of the economics of Keynes, as opposed to Keynesian economics, which have come out in recent times. Just to mention a few outstanding examples: the pioneering work of Axel Leijonhufvud, and that of Sir John Hicks and Don Patinkin.[9] In what follows, however, I shall not enter into the theoretical differences between Keynes and his followers, but I shall address myself to the more mundane problem of the general political differences and of those on economic policy matters.

A good example of the general political philosophy of the Keynesians and their attitude toward the free enterprise system has been recently

8. *Economic Journal,* September 1937, p. 436, as quoted by Lord Kahn, "A Comment," in T. W. Hutchinson, op. cit., p. 48.

9. A Leijonhufvud, *On Keynesian Economics and the Economics of Keynes,* Oxford University Press, 1968; D. Patinkin, *Keynes' Monetary Thought: A Study of Its Development,* Duke University Press, 1976; J. R. Hicks, *The Crisis in Keynesian Economics,* Basic Books, 1974.

provided by Mrs. Robinson in an article in the *Journal of Economic Literature.*[10] The first part of the article is devoted to an account of the history of economics based on a criticism of what Mrs. Robinson regards as the classical economists' motives. This is an old hobby of the most notorious of the "Keynesians of the left." In her book *Economic Philosophy,* for example, she comes out with the statement: "The hard-headed Classicals . . . were arguing against the narrow nationalism of Mercantilists in favour of a more far-sighted policy, but they were in favour of Free Trade because it was good for Great Britain, not because it was good for the world." In her opinion this is all that is needed to justify the view that the "very nature of economics is rooted in nationalism" and to question the scientific nature of the pure theory of international trade.[11]

The more interesting part of the article for our present purpose, however, is its conclusion, because it shows her views on capitalism and economic freedom. It is worthwhile to quote the whole relevant portion.

Says Mrs. Robinson:

> . . . the neoclassicists conceived the object of production to be provision for consumption. But consumption by whom, of what?
>
> The question was supposed to be settled by appeal to the individual's freedom of choice, but there are three very large objections to such a solution.
>
> The first arises from inequality of the distribution of purchasing power between individuals. The nature of accumulation under private enterprise necessarily generates inequality and is therefore condemned to meeting the trivial wants of a few before the urgent needs of the many.
>
> Secondly, many kinds of consumption that are chosen by some individuals generate disutility for others. The leading case is the spread of private motor cars—the higher the level of consumption, the more uncomfortable life becomes . . .

10. J. Robinson, "What Are the Questions?" *Journal of Economic Literature,* 1978.

11. J. Robinson, *Economic Philosophy,* C. A. Watts, 1962, chap. 6, pp. 126–27.

> Thirdly, to keep the show going, it is necessary continually to introduce new commodities and create new wants. In a competitive society, a growth of consumption does not guarantee a growth of satisfaction.
>
> These questions involve the whole political and social system of the capitalist world; they cannot be decided by economic theory, but it would be decent, at least, if the economists admitted that they do not have an answer to them. (p. 1337)

It is probably superfluous to do so, but before I go on to try to determine whether the values embodied in Mrs. Robinson's argument would have been shared by Keynes, I would like to spend a few words on the validity of Mrs. Robinson's thesis. Let us discuss each of the three questions in turn.

The first statement is simply wrong. Available evidence indicates, without a shade of doubt, that no system has satisfied "the urgent needs of the many" better than the private enterprise system. Secondly, historical evidence also indicates that "conspicuous consumption" has actually diminished under capitalism, in the sense that the gap between the consumption pattern of the wealthy and that of the poor has been greatly reduced. Most goods that are mass consumed today were the privilege of a few yesterday. The great advantage of capitalism is that it succeeds—thanks to its superior efficiency—in turning new products for the elite into mass-produced goods for the many. What upper-income people spend on their "trivial wants," therefore, is often an investment that society makes for the discovery of new products. Finally, it is an undeniable fact that the percentage of total spending that goes to "meeting the trivial wants of a few" in modern capitalist societies is negligible compared to that going to "the urgent needs" of the many.

The second statement contradicts the first and provides evidence to the effect that, even according to Mrs. Robinson, capitalism has proved to be a great equalizer. "The spread of private motor cars" is a good indicator of the fact that capitalism satisfies not only the urgent needs but also the trivial wants of the *many*. What Mrs. Robinson seems to be suggesting is that if "the others" did not have a private motor car, life would be easier for those who do. A rather undemocratic perspective.

The third objection to economic freedom is the most baffling. Mrs. Robinson seems to have derived it from J. K. Galbraith, and in her book *Economic Philosophy,* she explicitly quotes from *The Affluent Society* (chap. 6). The idea, in her own words, is that "[i]t is by no means obvious that goods which carry their own wants with them, through cunning advertisement, are a Good Thing. Surely we should be quite as well off without the goods and without the wants?" (ibid.)

As Professor Hayek has pointed out:

> The argument . . . starts from the assertion that a great part of the wants which are still unsatisfied in modern society are not wants which would be experienced spontaneously by the individual if left to himself, but are wants which are created by the process by which they are satisfied. It is then represented as self-evident that for this reason such wants cannot be urgent or important. This crucial conclusion appears to be a complete *non sequitur* and it would seem that with it the whole argument . . . collapses.
>
> The first part of the argument is of course perfectly true: we would not desire any of the amenities of civilization—or even of the most primitive culture—if we did not live in a society in which others provide them. The innate wants are probably confined to food, shelter, and sex. All the rest we learn to desire because we see others enjoying various things. To say that a desire is not important because it is not innate is to say that the whole cultural achievement of man is not important. . . .
>
> How complete a *non sequitur* Professor Galbraith's conclusion represents is seen most clearly if we apply the argument to any product of the arts, be it music, painting, or literature. . . . Surely an individual's want for literature is not original with himself in the sense that he would experience it if literature were not produced. Does this mean that the production of literature cannot be defended as satisfying a want because it is only the production which provokes the demand?[12]

12. F. A. Hayek, *Studies in Politics, Philosophy, and Economics,* pp. 313–15.

To this it might be added that the production of new wants is the most important of all wants. Most of the things we enjoy today did not exist in the Stone Age. Progress *is* the discovery of new wants.

Finally, the fact that capitalism "does not guarantee a growth of satisfaction" (because it creates new wants) must be considered as its greatest virtue. A satisfied society is a static, dead society; it is a society with no change, no progress, no hope. The greatest driving force for progress is the dissatisfaction produced by the continuous discovery of new wants.

In the light of these considerations, one can only agree with Professor Hayek's conclusion:

> It is not to be denied that there is some originality in this latest version of the old socialist argument. For over a hundred years we have been exhorted to embrace socialism because it would give us more goods. Since it has so lamentably failed to achieve this where it has been tried, we are now urged to adopt it because more goods after all are not important. (ibid., p. 317)

Let's now return to our original question: Did Keynes share this hatred of a free enterprise system? Would he approve of the pro-socialist bias of so many Keynesians? Judging from his writings, the answer must be an unqualified no. It is well known that he referred to the British Labor Party as a "class party," adding that "that class is not my class" and that in the class struggle he would always be on the side of the "educated bourgeoisie." Even more to the point, this is what he wrote in 1925:

> . . . the Labour Party will always be flanked by the Party of Catastrophe—Jacobins, Communists, Bolshevists, whatever you choose to call them. This is the party which hates or despises existing institutions and believes that great good will result merely from overthrowing them—or at least that to overthrow them is the necessary preliminary to any great good. This party can only flourish in an atmosphere of social oppression. . . . In Great Britain it is, in its extreme form, numerically very weak. Nevertheless its philosophy in a diluted form permeates . . . the whole Labour Party. However moderate its leaders may be at heart, the Labour Party will always de-

> pend for electoral success on making some slight appeal to the widespread passions and jealousies which find their full development in the Party of Catastrophe. I believe that this secret sympathy with the Policy of Catastrophe is the worm which gnaws at the seaworthiness of any constructive vessel which the Labour Party may launch. The passions of malignity, jealousy, hatred of those who have wealth and power (even in their own body) ill consort with ideals to build up a true Social Republic. Yet it is necessary for a successful Labour leader to be, or at least to appear, a little savage. It is not enough that he should love his fellow-men; he must hate them too.[13]

These words could hardly have been written by someone sympathetic to socialism and would certainly not be compatible with policy recommendations aiming at having the British economy modeled after the Eastern European model. But, someone might object, this was Keynes in 1925, and Keynes changed his mind quite frequently. Couldn't it be that the evolution of his ideas had gradually led him to socialism at a later stage of his life? Again, in my opinion the answer is no. All one needs to do is read the final chapter of the *General Theory*, where he says:

> But there . . . still remains a wide field for the exercise of private initiative and responsibility. Within this field the traditional advantages of individualism will still hold good.
>
> Let us stop for a moment to remind ourselves what these advantages are. They are partly advantages of efficiency—the advantages of decentralization and of the play of self-interest. The advantage to efficiency of the decentralization of decisions and of individual responsibility is even greater, perhaps, than the nineteenth century supposed; and the reaction against the appeal to self-interest may have gone too far. But, above all, individualism, if it can be purged of its defects and its abuses, is the best safeguard of personal liberty in the sense that, compared with any other system, it greatly widens the field for the exercise of personal choice. It is also the best safeguard of the variety of life, which emerges precisely from this extended field of personal choice, and the loss of which is the great-

13. J. M. Keynes, *Essays in Persuasion*, pp. 327–28.

> est of all the losses of the homogeneous or totalitarian state. For this variety preserves the traditions which embody the most secure and successful choices of former generations; it colours the present with the diversification of its fancy; and, being the hand-maid of experiment as well as of tradition and of fancy, it is the most powerful instrument to better the future.[14]

If one discounts some element of obscurity in this rather cryptic statement, a genuine passion for a system based on individual liberty and personal responsibility, as well as on freedom of choice, emerges. Certainly these words would not go along with the hatred for the individual's freedom of choice that Mrs. Robinson consistently shows in her writings.

Mrs. Robinson claims that on this issue Keynes was subject to alternating "moods." For example she writes:

> When Keynes (in his "moderately conservative" mood) maintained that, provided overall full employment is guaranteed "there is no objection to be raised against the classical analysis of the manner in which private self-interest will determine what in particular is produced," he had forgotten that in an earlier chapter he had written "There is no clear evidence from experience that the investment policy which is socially advantageous coincides with that which is most profitable."[15]

In my opinion, Mrs. Robinson's position does not mean that there was a prosocialist tendency in Keynes's personal preferences. It is true that he seems to have changed position quite often, so that there always is some degree of contradiction in his writings. However, I would maintain that, from the point of view of general political preference, he was personally as remote from socialism as possible.

The way I interpret Keynes's position is that his great concern was that of *saving* capitalism, not of destroying it. He was convinced that mass unemployment would in due time produce a radical political

14. J. M. Keynes, *The General Theory of Employment, Interest, and Money,* p. 380.

15. J. Robinson, op. cit., chap. 6. Both of Keynes's quotes are from the *General Theory.*

change and the destruction of our way of life. The irony is that, in attempting to provide us with a formula that would have prevented mass unemployment and thus saved capitalism, he ended up providing statists of various persuasions with a rationalization for government growth and for increasing degrees of socialism.

The position of the Keynesians of the left on this issue is diametrically opposed to that of Keynes. In Professor Hutchinson's words:

> It is important to emphasise the connection between inflation and government intervention in and regulation of the economy. Although Pseudo-Keynesian economists did not, of course, *want* inflation, some of them—*quite unlike Keynes*—wanted very much indeed its usual fruits and consequences in the form of wage- and price-controls, regulation of profits, widespread subsidisation, import-controls, etc., for which inflation provides a pretext. Some of the more extreme Pseudo-Keynesians were certainly strongly in favour of destroying the mixed economy and replacing it by a regime of "purposive direction" and "comprehensive planning." A permissive attitude to the money supply is well calculated to promote such objectives, and sophisticated defences for such permissiveness were devised.[16]

In other words, these latter Keynesians were part of what Keynes called the Party of Catastrophe, quite remote from his own political position. Their political views are very hard to understand, for, as Walter Eltis has pointed out:

> A notable feature of recent economic history is that the successful economies have not in general been those with a detailed network of government regulations and controls over wages, prices, trade and investment. On the contrary, they have been economies which have given the price mechanism great scope to allocate resources. It is, therefore, rather puzzling why so many Keynesians wish to run the British economy in an essentially East-European . . . way.[17]

16. T. W. Hutchinson, op. cit., p. 40.

17. W. Eltis, "The Keynesian Conventional Wisdom," *Lloyds Bank Review,* July 1977, p. 38.

I regret to add that it is this latter kind of Keynesianism that Cambridge-educated Italian economists have thought wise to import into my country, with the predictable economic results.

At this point, I would like to stress that the contrast between Keynes's general political preferences and the impact of Keynesian policy prescriptions on the working of Western economies is not due to the fact that Keynesians have "betrayed" or misinterpreted the message of the *General Theory*. On the contrary, I would maintain that the disruptive component of Keynesianism can be found in Keynes's own theory. In a sense it is true that, as Joan Robinson claims, Keynes was not fully aware of the implications of his theory.

In other words, Keynes *was* a Keynesian. He was a Keynesian *malgré soi*, unintentionally. The roots of Keynesianism lie in the *General Theory;* Keynesianism is perfectly consistent with Keynes's own views. It is Keynes's own child, even if an unwanted child. (No better case can be made for planned intellectual parenthood!)

As pointed out by Professor Hutchinson, the disruptive component of Keynesianism—the means through which Keynesians of the left have been trying to destroy the private enterprise system and to arrive at a system of "comprehensive planning"—is the inflationary bias. This is due to the fact that in Keynes's theory "money does not matter," or, as Sir John Hicks has pointed out, "there is nothing important that can be done with monetary policy," so that it is hardly surprising that the "view which emerges from *The General Theory* is more radical than 'full employment without inflation'; it is nothing less than the view that inflation does not matter."[18]

It is probably true that Keynes was not an inflationist and that the underestimation of the dangers of inflation in the *General Theory* was due to the circumstances of the time. It is also true that, as Professor Hutchinson has shown, by 1937 Keynes was already warning about the dangers of inflation at a time when unemployment was still in the neighborhood of 12 percent. Also, there is no reason to believe that Keynes had changed his mind on the issue of inflation from the time he wrote:

18. J. Hicks, *The Crisis in Keynesian Economics,* op. cit., p. 61.

> Lenin was certainly right. There is no subtler, no surer means of overturning the existing basis of Society than to debauch the currency. The process engages all the hidden forces of economic law on the side of destruction, and does it in a manner which not one man in a million is able to diagnose.[19]

There is no ambiguity here: Keynes was very well aware of the disruptive nature of inflation and of its incompatibility with the survival of the existing economic order. His articles in *The Times* show that in 1937 he was still convinced of that.[20]

But the fact that Keynes was not an inflationist at heart does not mean that when his followers were supporting inflationary policies they were misinterpreting the meaning of his theory. On the contrary, it can be convincingly argued that they were being faithful to Keynes's views on the role of money as they emerge from the *General Theory,* and were only carrying Keynes's position to its logical conclusion.

That the Keynesian theory is biased in favor of an inflationary policy, despite the fact that Keynes was not an inflationist at heart, can be shown by the following considerations:

1. The *General Theory* is based on the assumption of nominal wage rigidities and the resulting "trade-off" between inflation and unemployment. Remember Keynes's famous statement:

> . . . it is fortunate that the workers, though unconsciously, are instinctively more reasonable economists than the classical school, inasmuch as they resist reductions of money-wages, which are seldom or never of an all-round character, . . . whereas they do not resist reductions of real wages, which are associated with increases in aggregate employment and leave relative money-wages unchanged.[21]

This view inevitably leads to the idea that inflation (as long as it is unexpected) can play a beneficial role in bringing real wage rates back to their equilibrium level and restoring full employment. If full employment is the most urgent goal of economic policy, inflation loses

19. J. M. Keynes, *Essays in Persuasion,* op. cit., pp. 78–79.
20. See T. W. Hutchinson, op. cit.
21. J. M. Keynes, *The General Theory,* op. cit., p. 14.

its negative connotation and becomes an innocuous (if not desired) by-product of a full employment policy.

2. Even though, as Professor Hutchinson has shown, Keynes's 1937 articles for *The Times* show that Keynes was worried about inflation at a time of still high unemployment, they also show that he had a very peculiar idea of what inflation really is. Consider the following:

> [W]hat do we mean by 'inflation'? If we mean by the term a state of affairs which is dangerous and ought to be avoided . . . then we must not mean by it merely that prices and wages are rising. For a rising tendency of prices and wages inevitably . . . accompanies any revival of activity. . . . It is when increased demand is no longer capable of materially raising output and employment and mainly spends itself in raising prices that it is properly called inflation.[22]

This view that one cannot talk of inflation as long as price increases are accompanied by an increase in economic activity echoes the view expressed in the *General Theory* that increases in aggregate demand will result mostly in increased employment and output as long as there is unemployment, mostly (or exclusively) in inflation after full employment has been reached. It is entirely consistent with this view, therefore, to regard price increases as noninflationary as long as there is unused productive capacity. Inflation is regarded as a problem only *after* full employment has been achieved. Keynesianism is biased in favor of inflation because of Keynes's own interpretation of it.

3. Keynes's obsession with the short run was also doomed to result both in destabilizing macroeconomic policies and in an inflationary bias. His all-too-famous statement that "in the long run we are all dead" inevitably resulted in a myopic view of stabilization policies which stressed the immediate, direct consequences of expansionary actions and neglected their ultimate inflationary impact. The truth is that "we always live in the long run," i.e., whatever happens today is the consequence of policy decisions made sometime in the past. But Keynesian economists, following their master's emphasis on the short run, simply disregarded it.

22. J. M. Keynes, "Borrowing for Defense: Is It Inflation?" *The Times*, March 11, 1937, reprinted in T. W. Hutchinson, op. cit., pp. 74ff.

4. Keynes's view of the economy in simple macroeconomic terms tended to ignore the distortion of relative prices that inevitably accompanies a change in the price level. The disruptive effect of inflation on the working of the price system and on the allocation of resources was accordingly given little attention by Keynesian economists, who could not, therefore, understand the negative consequences of inflation.

5. Finally, the single most important feature of the *General Theory* is that it tends to attribute a very minor role to the quantity of money in the determination of aggregate spending. In Keynes's world, money affects aggregate demand if, and only if, it succeeds in lowering "the" interest rate, and if this, in turn, stimulates investment and discourages saving. The possibility that changes in the quantity of money may influence spending *directly* is not even considered, and this severely limits the Keynesians' ability to understand the nature and the origin of the inflationary process.

A very good example of this kind of Keynesian reasoning is provided by Joan Robinson's review of Costantino Bresciani-Turroni's classical book on the German hyperinflation.[23]

Mrs. Robinson criticizes Bresciani-Turroni's analysis of the German hyperinflation:

> The author assumes . . . that an increase in the quantity of money was the root cause of the inflation. But this view, is impossible to accept. An increase in the quantity of money no doubt has a tendency to raise prices, for it leads to a reduction in the rate of interest, which stimulates investment and discourages saving, and so leads to an increase in activity. But there is no evidence whatever that events in Germany followed this sequence.

What Mrs. Robinson seems to be saying is that since interest rates were not excessively low, the German hyperinflation was not produced by the fantastic growth in the quantity of money. We are not told what interest rate Mrs. Robinson has in mind, whether nominal or real.

23. C. Bresciani-Turroni, *The Economics of Inflation—A Study of Currency Depreciation in Post-War Germany, 1914–1923,* London, 1937; J. Robinson, "Review," *The Economic Journal,* 48, September 1938, pp. 507–13. What follows is a short version of a chapter in my monograph *Constraining Inflationary Government—A Lesson from Italy,* The Heritage Foundation, forthcoming.

Now, it is a fact of which we all are painfully aware today that *nominal* interest rates tend to increase during inflation, so that it is not surprising that the German hyperinflation was not marked by "excessively low interest rates." It would seem that Mrs. Robinson believes that money had nothing to do with the German hyperinflation. And yet, toward the end of her analysis, Mrs. Robinson substantially weakens her position by stating: "the quantity of money was important, not because it caused inflation, but because it allowed it to continue."

This last statement shows an astonishing misunderstanding of the nature of inflation. Had the quantity of money been kept under control, on Mrs. Robinson's own admission, inflation would not have continued. But to say that inflation would not have "continued" amounts to saying that there would have been no *inflation,* maybe just a once-and-for-all increase in the price level. This is the essence of the monetary theory of inflation: there cannot be *sustained* increases in the price level unless the quantity of money grows faster than output does. This does not mean that there cannot be occasional, isolated variations of the price level for a variety of reasons. There can be, but they will never develop into inflation unless the quantity of money is increased. A nonmonetary inflation is a logical impossibility.

In the light of all this, I think it is fair to say that, although inflation was not part of Keynes's intentions, and although he was very well aware of its dangerous nature, the misunderstanding of the phenomenon and the adoption of inflationary policies are perfectly consistent with his theory. The Keynesians simply applied his theory and carried it to its logical implications.

How is it that the work of an economist, committed to the protection of a free society and well aware of the threat to its survival posed by inflation, has ended up providing a rationalization for the economic policies of those who wish to destroy capitalism? Undoubtedly, theoretical weaknesses go a long way in answering this question. But there is a more fundamental reason that in my opinion accounts for the unintended consequences of Keynes's work, and it has to do with his personality.

Keynes has been an unusually lucky man. To begin with, he was born in the right country and at the right time. He was also fortunate enough to have two outstanding parents: His father, John Neville, was the author of an important book on economic methodology and a Cambridge don; his mother was the first woman to become mayor of that town. Keynes was educated at Eton—probably the best school in the world at that time—and at Cambridge, where he studied under Alfred Marshall, the greatest English economist of the time. Last but not least, he lived at a time when domestic help was still available, and this was no small fortune, for it is impossible to shine one's own shoes and write general theories at the same time!

His exceptional intellectual endowment and the outstanding environment he lived in convinced him of the tremendous power of ideas. His famous concluding remarks of the *General Theory* confirm this:

> [T]he ideas of economists and political philosophers, both when they are right and when they are wrong, are more powerful than is commonly understood. Indeed the world is ruled by little else. (p. 383)

This conviction was typical of his intellectual milieu. Alfred Marshall had written:

> Ideas whether those of art and science or those embodied in practical appliances are the most "real" of the gifts that each generation received from its predecessors. The world's material wealth would quickly be replaced if it were destroyed but the ideas by which it was made were retained.[24]

It was from this belief in the superiority of ideas that Keynes probably derived what John Burton has called "the elite's power of persuasion." This is a recurrent element of Keynes's personality. His collection of political writings is called *Essays in Persuasion.* Donald E. Moggridge tells us of Keynes's "almost desperate desire to influence policy,"[25] and Professor Hayek confirms that Keynes "was really su-

24. A. Marshall, *Principles of Economics,* 5th ed., MacMillan, London, 1907, p. 780.

25. J. Burton, "Keynes's Legacy to Great Britain: 'Folly in a Great Kingdom,'" in *The Consequences of Mr. Keynes,* The Institute of Economic Affairs, London, 1978, p. 49; D. E. Moggridge, *John Maynard Keynes,* New York, Penguin Books, 1976, p. 31.

premely confident of his powers of persuasion and believed that he could play on public opinion as a virtuoso plays on his instrument."[26]

Keynes did not like politicians: He had said of them that "they're awful," "their stupidity is inhuman," and called them "madmen in authority" and "lunatics." In this respect he was echoing Adam Smith's wisdom: ". . . that insidious and crafty animal, vulgarly called a statesman or politician." However, unlike Smith, Keynes believed that he could influence them and use their power to do good. In this perspective, his last conversation with Professor Hayek is illuminating. Hayek tells us:

> I had asked him whether he was not getting alarmed about the use to which some of his disciples were putting his theories. His reply was that these theories had been greatly needed in the 1930s, but if these theories should ever become harmful, I could be assured that he would quickly bring about a change in public opinion.[27]

In other words, Keynes was convinced that, thanks to the power of ideas and his own power to persuade, it was possible to achieve great results through government action. In the words of James Buchanan and Richard E. Wagner:

> [H]e operated under what his biographer called the "presuppositions of Harvey Road"—that governmental policy, and economic policy in particular, would be made by a relatively small group of wise and enlightened people.[28]

This belief translated itself into the idea that by manipulating the government budget it was possible to cure the inherent instability of a free enterprise system. The unintended result of this prescription

26. F. A. Hayek, *A Tiger by the Tail: The Keynesian Legacy of Inflation,* IEA, 1972, p. 103.

27. F. A. Hayek, ibid.

28. J. M. Buchanan and R. E. Wagner, "Democracy and Keynesian Constitutions: Political Biases and Economic Consequences," in *The Consequences,* op. cit., p. 16. According to Professor Hutchinson, "Basically the most serious weakness was political: that is, an over-optimism, perhaps even naiveté, regarding the possibility of enlightened management of the economy by popularly-elected governments." op. cit., pp. 8–9.

was—as we all well know—that of removing the budget constraint on government action, and this, in turn, had disastrous unintended consequences.

The growth of government in almost all Western nations in the third quarter of the twentieth century is to a very large extent due to the influence of Keynes's theory. As Buchanan and Wagner have remarked:

> Keynesian economics has turned the politicians loose; it has destroyed the effective constraint on politicians' ordinary appetites to spend and spend without the apparent necessity to tax.[29]

It is still too early to know whether Keynesianism will prove to be a disease "fatal for the survival of democracy"—as the authors maintain—but it is to be believed that Keynes would be horrified by the unintended effects of his theories.

The *General Theory* ends with the assertion: "At the present moment people are unusually expectant of a more fundamental diagnosis; more particularly ready to receive it; eager to try it out, if it should be even plausible." After forty-five years, the general disappointment caused by the appalling consequences of Keynesianism makes this statement even more appropriate today than it was then. It is to be hoped that future economic historians will refer to the last quarter of the twentieth century as "the age of Milton Friedman."

29. J. M. Buchanan and R. E. Wagner, ibid., p. 27.

The Modern Mask of Socialism

Definitions

The meaning of "socialism" has undergone a modification almost as radical as that suffered by its opposite—"liberalism"—in the United States, where "*as a supreme, if unintended, compliment, the enemies of the system of private enterprise have thought it wise to appropriate its label.*"[1] For the greatest part of the twentieth century, socialism has meant

> the abolition of private enterprise, of private ownership of the means of production, and the creation of a system of "planned economy" in which the entrepreneur working for profit is replaced by a central planning body.[2]

It can be argued that, whereas the change of meaning of liberalism is due to its success, the corresponding change in the meaning of socialism is due to its abysmal failure. Today, very few people who call themselves socialist seem prepared to advocate that kind of socialism. In fact, those ideas seem in danger of extinction, surviving only in North Korea, Vietnam, Cuba, and Harvard University.

I intend to deal with the process through which socialism has

The Sir Ronald Trotter Lecture, New Zealand Business Roundtable, Wellington, New Zealand, October 1998, pp. 5–32.

1. "[Economic Liberalism is] *the theory that the best way of promoting economic development and general welfare is to remove fetters from the private-enterprise economy and to leave it alone. . . . the term has acquired a different—in fact almost the opposite—meaning . . . : as a supreme, if unintended, compliment, the enemies of the system of private enterprise have thought it wise to appropriate its label.*" Joseph A. Schumpeter, *History of Economic Analysis,* New York, 1954, p. 394.

2. F. A. Hayek, *The Road to Serfdom* (1944), a book dedicated to "The Socialists of All Parties," Routledge & Kegan Paul, London, 1962, p. 24.

changed its meaning, and try to answer the question of what it exactly means to be a "socialist" today.

The Century of the State

The century that's coming to its end has been the century of the state, a century of dictators, the century of Hitler and Stalin, as well as the century of arbitrary government, and of unprecedented intrusion of politics into our daily lives—a Fascist century. It has produced the largest increase in the size of government in the history of mankind. Just to mention a single, but very significant, indicator, in 1900 the ratio of government spending to GDP in Italy was 10 percent, in the 1950s 30 percent, and it is now roughly 60 percent. Similar considerations apply to most countries.

In this sense, a prophecy has been confirmed. In the entry "Fascism" in the *Enciclopedia Italiana,* signed by Benito Mussolini,[3] one reads:

> If the 19th century has been the century of the individual (for liberalism means individualism), it may be conjectured that this is the century of the State . . . that this is the century of authority, a Fascist century.

From the point of view of the role of government in society, during the interwar years there was little to choose between the right and the left: The right was prepared to do in the name of the nation what the left wanted to do in the name of the class, but their programs were very similar.[4] Which confirms the basic theme of Hayek's *Road to Serfdom* that "*the rise of Fascism and Nazism was not a reaction against the social-*

3. But apparently written by philosopher Giovanni Gentile.

4. Take the following statement: *We are socialists, we are enemies of today's capitalistic economic system for the exploitation of the economically weak, with its unfair salaries, with its unseemly evaluation of a human being according to wealth and property instead of responsibility and performance, and we are all determined to destroy this system under all conditions.* Adolf Hitler, May 1, 1927. Quoted by John Toland, *Adolf Hitler,* New York, 1977, p. 306.

ist trends of the preceding period, but a necessary outcome of those tendencies. (p. 3)[5]

Pessimism

In other words, the "socialist consensus" common to both the extreme right and the socialist left in the interwar years left very little room for the liberal views which had been typical of the nineteenth century. It's not surprising, therefore, that in the 1940s and after liberals of all parties were pessimistic about the future of a liberal order—socialism seemed to be winning.[6]

A notable example of the widespread pessimism about the future of liberty after the war is offered by the foremost non-Marxist prophet of doom, Joseph A. Schumpeter, who in 1942 wrote: "*Can capitalism survive? No. I do not think it can. . . . [T]he actual and prospective performance of the capitalist system is such . . . that its very success undermines the social institutions which protect it, and 'inevitably' creates conditions in which it will not be able to live and which strongly point to socialism as the heir apparent.*"[7]

5. Hayek adds: "*It was the prevalence of socialist views and not Prussianism that Germany had in common with Italy and Russia*" (p. 7). Ivor Thomas, in a book apparently intended to explain why he left that (Labour) party, comes to the conclusion that "*from the point of view of fundamental human liberties there is little to choose between communism, socialism, and national socialism. They are all examples of the collectivist or totalitarian state . . . in its essentials not only is completed socialism the same as communism but it hardly differs from fascism*" (pp. 241–42). *The Socialist Tragedy,* Latimer House, London, 1949, quoted by F. A. Hayek, *Studies in Philosophy, Politics, and Economics* (1967), Simon and Schuster, New York, 1969, p. 227. Of course, Hayek's thesis is as hotly denied today by many socialists as it was when it first appeared more than fifty years ago. However, it is also true that most socialists today disassociate themselves from communism and its history.

6. This was the subject of a paper I presented to the Mont Pèlerin Society Regional Meeting held in Christchurch, New Zealand, in November 1989. It has been published under the title "Are We Winning?" CIS Occasional Papers 29, St. Leonards, Australia, 1990, pp. 1–11 ("*Foreword,*" M. James). [See pp. 318–28 in this volume.]

7. Joseph A. Schumpeter, *Capitalism, Socialism and Democracy,* Third edition, Harper Torchbooks, The University Library, Harper & Row, New York, 1950, p. 61. By socialism Schumpeter meant a society where "*the control over means of production and over production itself is vested with a central authority—or [where] the eco-*

The pessimism has continued to flourish until recently. However, even though until recently pessimists have outnumbered optimists, opinions about the future of a liberal order have always differed widely.

Optimism

At the beginning of the 1970s things started to change. As Milton Friedman put it twenty-five years ago:

> There are faint stirrings and hopeful signs. Even some of the intellectuals who were most strongly drawn to the New Deal in the thirties are rethinking their positions, dabbling just a little with free-market principles. They're moving slowly and taking each step as though they were exploring a virgin continent. But it's not dangerous. Some of us have lived here quite comfortably all along.[8]

At about the same time, David Friedman was even more blunt than his father:

> Socialism, as a coherent ideology, is dead and is not likely to be revived . . . Yet many people . . . call themselves socialists. "Socialism" has become a word with positive connotation and no content.[9]

By the end of the 1970s, thanks to the election of Margaret Thatcher in 1979, and of Ronald Reagan in 1980, and to the success of their liberal policies, pessimism gradually subsided and a new mood started to take hold. More and more people started to express dissatisfaction

---

nomic affairs of society belong to the public and not to the private sphere." And in 1949 he commented on the birth of the Mont Pèlerin Society with a somewhat dismissive remark. After having listed a series of socialist principles, which, as a result of the "disintegration of capitalist society," were being "*taken for granted by the business class . . . and by the large number of economists who feel themselves to be opposed to [100 percent] socialism,*" he added: "*I believe that there is a mountain in Switzerland on which congresses of economists have been held which express disapproval of all or most of these things [e.g., socialist policies]. But these anathemata have not even provoked attack*" (*op. cit.*, pp. 415–25).

8. *Playboy* interview, February 1973, reprinted in *There's No Such Thing as a Free Lunch,* Open Court, LaSalle, Ill., 1975, pp. 1–38. The quote is on p. 38.

9. David Friedman, *The Machinery of Freedom, Guide to a Radical Capitalism,* Harper Colophon Books, 1973, p. 129.

with the old socialist prescriptions and indicate a preference for market mechanisms. Socialists of the old school became fewer and fewer. As a result, liberals began to hope for the future of a liberal order. A notable precursor of the change and a conspicuous exception to the prevailing climate of pessimism was Arthur Seldon, cofounder of the Institute of Economic Affairs in London. In a letter to *The Times* on August 6, 1980, he went as far as to predict: "*China will go capitalist. Soviet Russia will not survive the century. Labour* as we know it *will never rule again. Socialism is an irrelevance*" (emphasis added). At that time, this view was regarded as preposterous, an eccentric example of English witticism. Ten years later it seemed prophetic, if not obvious. Today, many people would consider it slightly too optimistic.

Socialism's Evolution

But let's go back to the evolution of socialism. The original, and unifying, political platform of socialists fifty years ago included nationalization, central planning, high and rapidly rising levels of public spending and taxation, highly progressive if not confiscatory income-tax rates, exchange controls, wage and price controls, etc. By the end of the 1960s, many of these policy prescriptions had been abandoned, and a second kind of socialism became prevalent. Its political program was exemplified by that of the English Labour party (and to some extent also by that of the Tories!), and it consisted of a combination of Keynesianism, deficit spending, wage and price controls (incomes policy, as it was called in England), the Phillips curve (the idea that you could reduce unemployment by increasing inflation), and so on.

The "monetarist" revolution and the appalling results of the economic policies in the 1970s (especially in England, where they resulted in the "British disease")[10] took care of discrediting most of the program of "second generation socialists."

10. See Samuel Brittan and Peter Lilley, *The Delusion of Incomes Policy,* Temple Smith, London, 1977; and Samuel Brittan, "How British Is the British Disease?" *The Journal of Law & Economics* 21, no. 2, October 1978, pp. 245–68.

The End of Keynes

The most important part of the change in socialist orthodoxy beginning in the 1970s was in the field of macroeconomic policy, and it had to do with the abandonment of Keynesianism.[11] In a Keynesian world, price stability was not necessarily desirable. Most Keynesians were convinced that inflation was the unavoidable price of economic growth, that there was a stable trade-off between inflation and unemployment,[12] that it was possible to reduce interest rates through monetary expansion, and that the time horizon for monetary policy decisions had to be dictated by the needs of short-term stabilization policies. All of these views have succumbed to the empirical evidence and the theoretical analyses of the last thirty years.

There is no evidence that economic growth inevitably involves price inflation. On the contrary, there are good reasons to believe that monetary instability hinders long-term projects and makes economic growth more difficult, as evidenced by the experience of a number of Latin American countries.

The idea of a stable trade-off between inflation and unemployment is thoroughly discredited: An unexpected acceleration of inflation may temporarily reduce unemployment below its "natural rate," but this effect is short-lived. Only an accelerating inflation could keep unemployment below its natural rate, but even that unappetizing possibility is dubious.[13]

11. I have dealt with many of these issues in my previous incarnation as a monetary economist. See, for example, "Budget Deficits and Constitutional Constraints," *Cato Journal* 8, no. 3, pp. 695–711; "La fine della discrezionalità nel governo dell'economia," Prolusione, Giornata LUISS, December 18, 1992, LUISS, 1993, pp. 32–65, reprinted, with modifications, in *Notiziario,* Università degli Studi di Torino, anno undicesimo, no. 1, January–February 1995, pp. 2–13; "Monetary and Fiscal Rules, Past Successes and Future Prospects," in *Policy* 14, no. 1, pp. 3–9.

12. J. Tobin and L. Ross, "Living with Inflation," *New York Review of Books,* May 1971; J. Tobin and L. Ross, "A Reply to Gordon Tullock," *Journal of Money, Credit and Banking,* May 1972; J. Tobin, "Inflation and Unemployment," *American Economic Review,* March 1972; J. Tobin, "More on Inflation," *Journal of Money, Credit and Banking,* November 1973.

13. M. Friedman, "The Role of Monetary Policy," *The American Economic Review*

Manipulation of monetary aggregates can influence interest rates only temporarily: As soon as inflationary expectations catch up with reality, the Keynesian "liquidity effect" is replaced by the "Fisher effect," which will more than offset the initial impact of the unexpected change in monetary policy.[14] Nominal interest rates tend to be higher, not lower, when monetary policy is loose.

As for stabilization policies, it is now largely (though certainly not unanimously) agreed that our insufficient knowledge, unreliable short-run macroeconomic forecasts, and variable time lags in the impact of monetary policy decisions make it likely that policies aimed at stabilizing the short run may end up being procyclical rather than anticyclical.[15] Attempts at "fine-tuning" the economy often result in additional, avoidable instability.[16]

58, no. 1, March 1968; M. Friedman, *Unemployment* versus *Inflation? An Evaluation of Phillips Curve,* London: The Institute of Economic Affairs, Occasional Paper 44, 1975; M. Friedman, *Inflation and Unemployment: The New Dimension of Politics—The 1976 Alfred Nobel Memorial Lecture,* London: The Institute of Economic Affairs, Occasional Papers 51, 1977; Gordon Tullock, "Can You Fool All People All the Time?" *Journal of Money, Credit and Banking,* May 1972; Gordon Tullock, "Inflation and Unemployment: The Discussion Continued," *Journal of Money, Credit and Banking,* August 1973; Michael D. Bordo and Anna J. Schwartz, "The Importance of Stable Money: Theory and Evidence," *Cato Journal* 3, pp. 63–82, reprinted with modifications in Dorn and Schwartz, 1987: 53–72.

14. Daniel L. Thornton, "The Effects of Monetary Policy on Short-Term Interest Rates," *The Federal Reserve Bank of St. Louis Review,* May–June 1988, pp. 53ff.

15. Milton Friedman, "Commodity-Reserve Currency," *Journal of Political Economy,* 59 (June 1951a): 203–32; reprinted in Friedman, 1953, pp. 204–50; Milton Friedman, "Les effets d'une politique de plein emploi sur la stabilité économique: Analyse formelle," *Economie appliquée,* July–December 1951b, reprinted under the title "The Effects of a Full-Employment Policy on Economic Stability: A Formal Analysis," in Friedman, 1953, pp. 441ff.; Milton Friedman, *Essays in Positive Economics,* Chicago: University of Chicago Press, 1953; Milton Friedman, "The Optimum Quantity of Money," in *The Optimum Quantity of Money and Other Essays,* Chicago: Aldine, 1969; Milton Friedman, *Capitalism and Freedom* (1962), Chicago: University of Chicago Press, 1965; Gottfried Haberler, *Economic Growth and Stability. An Analysis of Economic Change and Policies.* Los Angeles, Nash Publishing, 1974; Christina D. Romer, "Is the Stabilization of the Postwar Economy a Figment of the Data?" *The American Economic Review,* June 1986, pp. 314ff.; Allan H. Meltzer, "Is Monetarism Dead?" *National Review,* November 4, 1991, 30–32.

16. "*Monetarists . . . favor stable policy rules that reduce variability and uncertainty*

Finally, budget deficits were regarded as the ultimate propellant of economic growth when, under the influence of the "Keynesian revolution," most economists believed that high employment and stability could be achieved through appropriate manipulations of the budget. In recent times, however, we have witnessed a reversal in the profession's conventional wisdom. Deficits are now being blamed for a lot of different economic problems: inflation, unemployment, slow growth, the stock market crash, high interest rates, balance of payments difficulties, instability of exchange rates and a variety of other troubles.

While some of these criticisms are dubious or definitely unfounded,[17] it is increasingly recognized that, whereas deficit-financed increases in public spending change the structure of total spending, by transferring funds from the private to the public sector, their long-run impact on the level of aggregate demand may very well be negligible in most cases. The "rediscovery" of the importance of financial prudence and the end of the deficit-spending strategy have had a very important impact on the growth of public spending, because budget deficits make government growth easier. The possibility of running a deficit allows politicians to hide the cost of government from those who bear it. It is harder to increase the size of government when spending must be financed with an increase in explicit taxation. Another component of the political platform of second-generation socialists has been abandoned. The birth of today's socialism—socialism of the third generation—can be traced to the failure of Keynesianism.

---

for private decision-makers. They argue that government serves the economy best by enhancing stability and acting predictably, not by trying to engineer carefully timed changes in policy actions which are frequently destabilizing." Meltzer, 1991, p. 31.

17. For an assessment of the issue, see K. Alec Chrystal and Daniel L. Thornton, "The Macroeconomic Effects of Deficit Spending: A Review," *The Federal Reserve Bank of St. Louis Review* 70, no. 6, 1988, especially their conclusion: "*The once-prevalent Keynesian approach . . . has come under attack. Increasingly, both theoretical innovations and empirical evidence suggest that modern economies are not well characterized by the Keynesian view. Support for the National Rate Hypothesis, which argues that deficit spending has no effect on equilibrium level of output and employment in the long run has grown. . . . [A]n effective use of deficit spending . . . imposes information requirements on policymakers that are unlikely to be attained.*"

The Market Comes to the Rescue of the Market

The evolution of socialism and the wave of optimism about the future of liberalism was also fueled by dramatic changes in the historical arrangements of the world. Established powers were wiped out, the "evil empire" collapsed, dictators nearly disappeared from Earth, and—as a consequence?—the intellectual climate changed drastically.

One of the main factors in the historical changes which have marked the 1980s and the beginning of the 1990s was the liberalization of the international movement of goods, services, and capital,[18] which resulted in a "filter mechanism" (in Nozick's jargon),[19] "filtering out" undesirable arrangements: Governments that mismanaged their countries were penalized by the outflow of capital. The importance of capital movements in forcing governments to adopt wise policies cannot be overemphasized. High-inflation countries, high-deficit countries, countries with unreliable legal frameworks, or excessively punitive to private productive investments were forced by capital movements to mend their ways. The market, i.e., the greater degree of international openness, has promoted promarket, liberal policies and, by so doing, it has contributed to undermine the socialist consensus.

However, "*the view that governments today stand helpless before the gale of market forces is a gross exaggeration,*" as evidenced by the "*best and simplest measure of a government's involvement in the economy . . . public spending. In rich industrial countries, this has followed a persistently upward trend since the latter part of the 19th century.*"[20]

In any case, there can be such a thing as excessive optimism. At the beginning of the 1990s, many people thought that we had come to a radical change of the political paradigm, so that the principles of a free society were going to rule unchallenged everywhere, and social-

18. "*Rarely has free trade seemed so fashionable. In December 1993, when the Uruguay round of GATT talks ended, 100-odd countries promised to cut tariffs, dismantle non-tariff barriers to trade and liberalise trade in services. As if that were not enough to be going on with, scarcely a week passes without some politician, somewhere, mooting a new effort to make trade, as he sees it, freer still.*" *The Economist,* September 16, 1995, p. 27.

19. Robert Nozick, *Anarchy, State, and Utopia,* Basic Books, New York 1974.

20. *The Economist,* December 6, 1997, p. 90.

ism *as we knew it* had come to an end.[21] The events of the 1980s had convinced many observers that the struggle was over: Capitalism had won.[22]

Pessimism Again

We soon learned better: in the past two to four years we have witnessed a revival of socialism, especially in Europe. Of the fifteen countries that are members of the European Union, thirteen have governments that can be called "socialist"—the latest being Germany, where Helmut Kohl was ousted as I was writing this paper. Furthermore, Japan and the "Asian tigers" are undergoing a serious crisis, which some people blame on capitalism, and the Russian Federation has seen the return of a communist-controlled government. The original optimism is now ridiculed, and a new pessimistic trend is under way.

A notable example of this pessimistic mood was recently provided by Rupert Murdoch in an article in *National Review,*[23] in which he compared some statements made at the beginning of the 1990s with a similar one made by a Cambridge historian in 1913: "*The struggle of reason against authority has ended in what appears to be a decisive and permanent victory for liberty.*"[24] We all know what happened after 1913. Couldn't it be that the sensational changes of the 1980s, which had prompted some to predict the "End of History," the final triumph of liberty over

21. "*The past few months have shattered the pattern of the previous 45 years. Most importantly, the failed god of the command economy has been finally laid to rest. Eastern Europe had already been freed from this superstition by the removal of the occupying army that had imposed it. The liberation of the Russians and the other peoples of the ex-Soviet Union can now seriously begin. And many other countries have started to remove their intellectual army of occupation, the widespread belief that Marx was right at least about economics.*" *The Economist,* September 28, 1991, p. 21.

22. The optimistic trend had reached a climax in 1989, leading, for example, a noted American conservative to declare that "*1989 was the most significant year in the most important decade since World War II.*" Edwin J. Feulner Jr., *Conservatism in a New Age,* The Heritage Foundation, 1990.

23. R. Murdoch, "Reinventing Socialism," *National Review,* September 1, 1997, pp. 38–40.

24. J. B. Bury, *The History of the Freedom of Thought,* as quoted by Murdoch.

socialism, were just a transient interruption in the erosion of our liberties?[25]

A Temporary Lapse in an Otherwise Inexorable Process?[26]

In other words, have we mistaken a temporary lapse in the historical process toward socialism for a radical change of direction?[27] I don't think so. From the point of view of the ideological confrontation, I am convinced that we live in one of the happiest times in the contemporary history of mankind. It seems to me that never before has the case for freedom been more thoroughly analyzed and better understood.

I realize that this is a strong statement. There is an inevitable distortion on our perspectives produced by chronological selection. Few people who are great thinkers in the eyes of their contemporaries stand the test of time and are still considered great by future generations. As a result, we are often led to believe that there are more great scholars among our contemporaries than there were in the past. However, even if we allow for this distortion, it still seems true to me that a very large number of the great liberal thinkers of all times belong to this century. Furthermore, even though ideas always have parents, in the sense that their origin can be traced back to past achievements, the case for freedom as presented by today's thinkers is more consistently

25. Of course, there are innumerable counter-examples to Murdoch's quote. Marxists have been forecasting the imminent demise of capitalism for a century and a half. Even a widely respected economist like John Maynard Keynes was not immune from gloomy prophecies about the future of capitalism: "*We are today in the middle of the greatest economic catastrophe of the modern world . . . the view is held in Moscow that this is the last, the culminating crisis of capitalism and that the existing order of society will not survive it.*" 1931, as quoted in "On the Edge," *The Economist*, September 5, 1998, p. 17.

26. What follows is taken from my paper "Ideas and the Future of Liberty," in *Libertarians and Liberalism, Essays in Honour of Gerard Radnitzky*, Hardy Boullion, ed., Avebury Series in Philosophy, Avebury, 1996, pp. 288–97.

27. To put it differently, are contemporary events confirming Schumpeter's warning? "*The transformation of social orders into one another is an incessant process but, in itself, a very slow one. To an observer who studies a moderate span of 'quiet' time, it may well seem as if the social framework he beholds did not change at all. Moreover, the process often suffers setbacks which, considered by themselves, may suggest to him the presence of an opposite tendency.*" J. A. Schumpeter, *op. cit.*, p. 419.

argued and better supported than ever before. Finally, more people are aware of the importance of freedom today than at any other time in the past fifty years. Of course, this is true only in the realm of ideas. The same does not necessarily hold as far as actual policies are concerned.

Socialism's New Mask

While defining today's socialism is nearly impossible, there are certain policy prescriptions which are common to many if not most socialist parties. Their common denominator is given by the fact that contemporary socialists have come to tolerate the market system because of its superior efficiency, but they do not accept the implications of an order based on individual liberty.[28] Their position, in other words, is based on a distrust of the spontaneous order, on a bias against a society arranged as much as possible on individual choices.[29] Let's look at a few examples.[30]

28. According to Hayek, "*socialism is a species of collectivism,*" its essential feature being "*a central direction of all economic activity according to a single plan, laying down how the resources of society should be 'consciously directed' to serve particular ends in a definite way*" (p. 26). This he contrasts with the "*liberal argument based on the conviction that where effective competition can be created, it is a better way of guiding individual efforts than any other. . . . Economic liberalism . . . regards competition as superior . . . because it is the only method by which our activities can be adjusted to each other without coercive or arbitrary intervention of authority*" (p. 27). It must be noted that Hayek regards the competitive order as superior to central planning not only because it is more efficient in the production of goods and services, and in the promotion of the general welfare, but especially because it is compatible with individual liberty and the absence of coercion. This is an especially important argument because, while most people, even on the left, today are willing to concede that a market economy is more efficient than a centrally planned one, many of them miss the main point, i.e., that a market order allows greater scope to individual liberty than any alternative arrangement. F. A. Hayek, *The Road to Serfdom,* op. cit.

29. The renewed popularity of socialist parties in recent months owes much to the crisis in financial markets, which many people have blamed on "excessive" market freedom. "*[T]he biggest risk now to the world economy may lie not so much in a deep depression, which could be averted. It is that there may be a wholesale retreat from free markets. Any such retreat would damage longer-term growth prospects . . . for decades to come.*" "On the Edge," *The Economist,* September 5, 1998, p. 19.

30. A good example of the negative impact of the recent financial crisis on the

Regulation

The first is the great reliance on a huge and ever-increasing body of regulation. Regulation is for today's socialists what public ownership of the means of production and central planning were for them half a century ago. As pointed out by Murdoch:

> No one talks about nationalizing industries any more. But then no one *has* to nationalize industries—because the extraordinary growth of regulation has given effective control of them to the government without its having to assume the hassle of ownership. Socialism has effectively reinvented itself. We can call it "Neosocialism." And it's right here.[31]

Regulation is one of the areas which identify today's socialism: While all socialists and most liberals agree that some amount of regulation may be necessary, the difference between the two is given by the socialists' high propensity to give government the power to control the economy through regulation. In this, as in other areas (like taxation, environmental protection, public spending, etc.), the difference between socialists and liberals is quantitative. A liberal can claim with Paracelsus that "*All things are poison and none without poison. Only the dose determines that a thing is no poison*" (Dosis sola facit venenum).

A good example is given by labor-market regulation, especially in Europe. What many European countries have in common is that their governments engage in job-destroying interferences in labor markets to an extent that is unknown in the United States. For example, legislation aimed at the lofty ideal of protecting the "weaker party" in labor contracts has made it extremely costly to fire a worker. Since hiring

---

prospects of liberalism is given by the diminished popularity of the privatization of public pension schemes. It is argued that the volatility of stock prices makes private pension schemes too risky, and that existing pay-as-you-go government plans should be preserved rather than replaced by private arrangements. This argument is clearly flawed: "*The* average *annual real return on stocks has been 7 per cent since 1926—i.e., over a period that includes the Great Depression, not just a measly market correction. There is no twenty-year period in American history in which stocks have fallen.*" *National Review*, September 28, 1998, p. 9.

31. *Op. cit.*, p. 39.

decisions are made under uncertainty, the fact that employers are not allowed to make mistakes has made them very cautious in hiring, reluctant to take risks. This has produced two unintentional results: On the one hand total employment, though possibly more stable than it would otherwise have been, is also smaller. On the other hand, unemployment tends to last longer: For example, nearly half of the unemployed in Europe stay in that condition for more than twelve months, compared with only 11 percent in the United States. The percentage is 70 percent in Italy—a record among industrialized countries.[32]

Another main cause of unemployment is the tax on jobs, the so-called "wedge"—the difference between labor costs and take-home pay.[33] Since the tax falls on all kinds of employment, its job-destroying consequences are felt at the macro level: Total employment is smaller than otherwise.[34] (Of course, this is true only in the "official" economy, not in the "underground" or "informal" economy, where the tax on jobs is evaded.) The wedge in Italy exceeds 50 percent of the labor cost: For every $1,000 given to the worker, the employer pays

32. Also, legislation "protecting" female workers has made hiring women more expensive than hiring men—as a result, not surprisingly, the female unemployment rate is almost twice as high as its male counterpart. In Italy, the noble desire to treat all citizens equally has inspired legislation which imposes the same treatment, in terms of wage rates and other benefits, in the South as in the North. This was supposed to "protect" Southern workers from the humiliation of receiving a lower salary than their Northern colleagues. Obviously, as could have easily been predicted, unemployment in the poorer regions of the South is much higher than in the North. If one could legislate prosperity, poverty would have ended centuries ago—poorer regions do not become prosperous at the whim of legislators. A wage rate that's appropriate for a wealthy area is prohibitive for a poor one. And it's hard to believe that unemployed Southerners feel relieved by the knowledge that if they had a job it would be as remunerative as it is in the North.

33. What matters for employers is total labor costs, inclusive of the nonsalary component, whereas it's the net salary that matters for the worker. As a result of this wedge, equilibrium in each microlabor market is reached at a level of employment smaller than it would otherwise be: The demand for and supply of labor are equalized at a point to the left of that which would have prevailed in the absence of the "tax on jobs."

34. See Anthony de Jasay, "How to Stifle Employment by 'Social Protection,'" *The Wall Street Journal Europe,* March 20–21, 1998.

a tax that's greater than $1,000. Not surprisingly, this results in fewer jobs.

The propensity of socialists of all parties to regulate labor markets, often with disastrous results, is exemplified by the French and Italian left's proposal to legislate a mandatory thirty-five-hour week. The stated aim of the proposal is that of increasing employment; its actual consequence is likely to be an increase in unemployment.

Most socialists in Europe are still fearful of the impact of technical change and increased productivity on employment, which brings to mind

> a story that a western businessman told me a few years ago. He had recently been touring China, where he came upon a team of nearly a hundred workers building an earthen dam with shovels. The businessman lamented that with an earth-moving machine, a single worker could create the dam in an afternoon. The curious response from the local official was, "Yes, but think of all the unemployment that would create." "Oh," said the businessman, "I thought you were building a dam. If it's jobs you want to create, then take away their shovels and give them spoons!"[35]

Tax Harmonization in Europe

Regulation is very fashionable in the European Union. It is here that socialists of all parties and of all countries have found an effective way to increase centralized control over our lives. For example, under the innocent label of "tax harmonization," the EU is in the process of introducing a tax cartel, which would severely limit capital movements within the Union and prevent tax competition.[36]

One of the arguments favored by proponents of tax harmonization in Europe runs as follows: Since capital is more mobile than labor, it is harder to tax it. As a result, taxation on labor is growing more rapidly than on capital. To remedy this distortion, EU countries must agree

35. Jerry Jordan, "Jobs Creation and Government Policy," unpublished paper, November 30, 1996.

36. What follows draws from my piece for *The Wall Street Journal Europe,* July 29, 1998.

on a common tax policy on capital. This seemingly plausible thesis is full of fallacies. First, its supporters seem convinced that if EU governments could increase taxation on capital, they would reduce taxation on labor. The possibility that an increased taxation on capital would result in an overall increase in taxation is not even considered. Yet it should be obvious that total spending is not fixed—its total size depends on the size of government revenue, and it is possible, indeed probable, that if revenue is enlarged because of tax harmonization this will result in an increase in spending rather than in a reduction in other forms of taxation. The second fallacy is even worse: The argument assumes that there is such a thing as the "right" tax policy, independent from the distinctive characteristics of the country. It further assumes that this right policy can easily be known to tax "experts" and that, if adopted, it will suit all European countries well. This is nonsense. Each EU country has different peculiarities, and a tax policy that is appropriate for a given EU country is totally inappropriate for another possessing different traits. Why should, say, a country with a low capital/labor ratio be prevented from trying to remedy its handicap by enticing the inflow of foreign capital with a friendly tax policy? Why should the same tax policy apply to countries that have very different endowments of productive factors? Furthermore, capital mobility is not restricted to the EU area. Should EU countries agree to a common tax policy, the likely outcome is likely to be an outflow of capital toward non-EU countries practicing a less oppressive form of taxation. But the main fallacy is the rejection of fiscal competition among EU countries, which is by far the most effective way on the one hand to contain excessive taxation, while on the other allowing for the kind of continuous "trial and error" method aimed at correcting the limitations of existing tax arrangements. This is to some extent the method used in countries like Switzerland and the United States, which for centuries have had a federal government. Why shouldn't Europe, which does not even have a federal government, follow a different course?

Examples of absurd EU regulations could fill several volumes. They include, among other things, the definition of a sausage, the specification of the size of bananas, rules governing the export of duck eggs, and the like. In some instances these result in embarrassment, as in the case of the Italian Minister of Health who, in enforcing a EU directive, indicated as optimal size for condoms one slightly bigger than the European standard, which, understandably, prompted many people to ask on the basis of what kind of evidence the minister thought Italians needed some extra leeway.

Environmentalism, etc.

Another area where neosocialists and liberals differ is environmentalism.[37] As in the case of regulation, they both agree that some amount of environmental protection is necessary. The difference between the two is in the amount of environmental protection deemed desirable and in the ways to achieve it—socialists rely on governmental coercion, liberals on market mechanisms. The threat of socialist environmentalism is subtle and deadly; its plausibility makes it acceptable even to reasonable believers in freedom; its appeal to the uninformed is enormous; the half-baked scientific assertions used to justify all kinds of government intervention for the sake of the environment require extensive information on the part of those who wish to criticize them.[38] Potentially, environmentalism poses a risk for the

37. George Orwell's view is as relevant today as it was in 1937: "*One sometimes gets the impression that the mere words 'Socialism' and 'Communism' draw towards them with magnetic force every fruit-juice drinker, nudist, sandal-wearer, sex-maniac, Quaker, 'Nature Cure' quack, pacifist, and feminist in England.*" George Orwell, 1937, as quoted in *Contentions,* April 1990, p. 1. The words *socialism* and *communism* may be on their way out, but the people mentioned by Orwell continue to stick together, usually on the left of the political spectrum.

38. And the problem is made worse by the widespread practice of environmentalists trying "*to influence both public and governments by the deliberate suppression of anything that might suggest that the bases of their proposals are less than certain.*" Peter D. Finch, "The Lalonde Doctrine in Action: The Campaign Against Passive Smoking," The Center for Independent Studies, *Policy,* Winter 1990, pp. 22–25; the quote is on page 25. Though Finch refers to a different problem, the deliberate simplification of complex scientific issues in order to scare the public and prompt government into action is one of environmentalists' favorite tactics. In other words, "*Greens and other activists treat environmental issues as though they are certain events, ignoring the scientific evidence that casts doubt even on the existence of these problems.*" Richard L. Stroup, "The Green Movement: Its Origin, Goals and Rele-

future of liberty as serious as that posed by wholesale socialism in the past.[39]

Under the same heading as the environment, I should add another unusual threat which comes from the enormous variety of "small" restrictions to our personal freedoms that are continuously being introduced in the name of safety, health, and other lofty ideals. Each one of them, taken by itself, seems trivial. Taken together, they amount to a wholesale attack on our independence.

The purpose of the law has been distorted, so that now the state, instead "*of protecting, as far as possible, every member of the society from the injustice or oppression of every other member of it,*"[40] tries to protect individuals *from themselves,* destroying the very concept of personal responsibility in the process.[41]

---

vance for a Liberal Society," in the same issue of *Policy,* pp. 57–63. According to Stroup, this attitude "*is true of the scientific literature on the greenhouse effect . . . , stratospheric ozone . . . , and acid precipitation . . . , and the epidemiological evidence on the large and well-known . . . hazardous waste sites such as Love Canal.*" The quote is from page 59.

39. In my view "reasonable" environmentalism is far more dangerous than "ecoterrorism." The latter, however, performs the crucial function of making the former look acceptable. On ecoterrorism, see "Ecoterrorism: The Dangerous Fringe of the Environmental Movement," *Backgrounder,* no. 764, The Heritage Foundation, April 12, 1990. This is true even of related areas of public policy. Think, for example, of the "animal rights" movement: The more ardent supporters of "liberation zoology" will probably be frustrated in their demands, but the more moderate position of those who advocate restrictions on the laboratory use of animals or on hunting is likely to succeed. See Charles Oliver, "Liberation Zoology," *Reason,* June 1990, pp. 22–27. And both are probably paving the way to the more radical position of "liberation botany," which will fight for the protection of "vegetable rights."

The consequences of environmental restrictions on economic activity can be harmful. In Sicily, for example, the regional government has created a natural park of some 85,000 hectares, where the construction or modification of roads and buildings are prohibited, industrial activity is not allowed, and restrictions are imposed on tourism and agriculture. Not surprisingly, the unemployment rate in the area reaches 50 percent.

40. Adam Smith, *The Wealth of Nations* (1776), The Modern Library, New York, 1937, p. 651.

41. What is frightening is that this kind of tyranny is often enforced by the

The welfare state—"public" health care in particular—has gradually instilled the notion that we do not own our health. The results of this view are schizophrenic. On the one hand, the increase in life expectancy becomes the cause of national anxiety, since an aging population imposes costs "on society."[42]

On the other hand, the most common line of argument is the opposite: Since "the government" pays for our medical care, we are not free to live our lives in a manner that is deemed unhealthy by the authorities. The standard argument about the paraphernalia of restrictions on activities considered unhealthy is that people who engage in them are more likely to get sick and "impose a cost on society." As a result, what is deemed dangerous or unhealthy is banned, and what is considered healthy or otherwise beneficial is made compulsory: speed limits; compulsory helmets for motorcyclists; compulsory seat belts; restrictions

---

public even before it becomes the object of government policy. As pointed out by *The Economist,* the phenomenon is particularly acute in America, where there is "*an odd combination of ducking responsibility and telling everyone else what to do. . . . A conformist tyranny of the majority, an intolerance of any eccentricity, is creeping into America, the west coast in particular. . . . As Americans get even richer, they seem to grow more risk-averse, so that they become paranoid about hazardous waste in their district, obsessed with their cholesterol levels, and ready to spend large premiums for organic vegetables. It being a free world, they are welcome to do so, even if the risks from hazardous waste are exaggerated, or the risks from natural carcinogens in organic vegetables greater than from pesticides. But must they become killjoys in the process? Being bossed by faddish doctors is something people have come to expect. But neighbours and friends (and advertisers) have no need to be ruthlessly disapproving of the fellow who prefers cream and an early coronary to self-absorption in a costly gym building muscles he will never need.*" "America's Decadent Puritans," *The Economist,* July 28, 1990, pp. 11–12.

42. A good example was given by a recent *Washington Post* article explaining that "*smokers 'save' the Social Security system hundreds of billions of dollars. Certainly this does not mean that decreased smoking would not be socially beneficial. In fact, it is probably one of the most cost-effective ways of increasing average longevity. It does indicate, however, that if people alter their behavior in a manner which extends life expectancy, then this must be recognized by our national retirement program.*" "*Not smoking could be hazardous to pension system. Medicare, social security may be pinched if anti-tobacco campaign succeeds, report says,*" *The Washington Post.* Or, in the words of a health economist: "*Prevention of disease is obviously something we should strive for. But it's not going to be cheap. We will have to pay for those who survive.*" Both quotes are taken from Florence King, "I'd Rather Smoke Than Kiss," *National Review,* July 9, 1990, pp. 32–36.

on the sale of pornographic material, on the consumption of drugs, alcohol, tobacco,[43] and so on. We are heading toward a society where dangerous sports will not be permitted, pedestrians will be required to have a license, obesity will be illegal and what we are allowed to eat will be determined by the National Dieting Board! At this point, the patriotic citizen does not know what to do: If he lives dangerously, he imperils the financial future of the public health system, whereas if he decides to live a long, healthy life, it's Social Security that's in trouble.

The war on smoking has been carried a bit too far: "*[I]n Colorado, on the eve of being executed for rape and murder, Mr. Gary Lee Davis made his last request: a smoke. Is that too much to ask? It is in Colorado, where death row is a smoke-free facility. Request denied.*"[44]

Examples of the attempts to regulate our lives could fill several volumes. Their absurdity should not make us forget the danger they pose to our liberty. Whatever it is that we intend to do, we should be well advised to follow Lawrence Peter's advice: "*do it now! There may be a law against it tomorrow.*"

Conclusion

These are no longer times of ideological confrontation; the differences between liberals and socialists today are smaller than in the past. This is because socialism is an empty shell—the label continues to be used, but its content has been lost, possibly forever. However, while socialism is dead, statism is not. We have freed ourselves from the danger of wholesale socialism, but we are still facing the continuous erosion of our liberties in a piecemeal fashion.

This is a mixed blessing. On the one hand, once the socialists abandoned the holistic model of a centrally planned society, rational discussion became possible.[45] The focus of political debate has shifted

43. We have forgotten Ludwig von Mises's wisdom: "*everyone should abstain by his own impulse from enjoyments harmful to his organism.*" *Socialism* (1932) Liberty Fund, Inc., Indianapolis, 1979, p. 207, n. As for smokers, we should support Lord Harris's F.O.R.E.S.T. (Freedom Organization for the Right to Enjoy Smoking Tobacco).

44. *National Review,* November 10, 1997.

45. Socialists, in other words, have abandoned what Karl R. Popper called

from the general architecture of society to the desirability of specific policy proposals. This in and of itself is an epochal change, making ideological confrontation more amenable to rational discourse. On the other hand, the piecemeal aggression against our liberties is subtler and harder to combat. Many of the new socialists' proposals may appear sensible, and careful scrutiny is required to show their negative consequences. However, let's not forget that, as Karl R. Popper has taught us,

> we shall always have to live in an imperfect society. This is so not only because even very good people are very imperfect; nor is it because, obviously, we often make mistakes because we do not know enough. Even more important than either of these reasons is the fact that there always exist irresolvable clashes of values . . . There can be no human society without conflict: such a society would be a society not of friends but of ants.[46]

What this means is that there is no such thing as *victory* (or defeat, for that matter), a state of affairs which, once attained, will forever be maintained. The struggle for freedom is a "natural," inescapable component of life. We can successfully meet the challenges of our time and score a temporary "victory," but new problems will soon come up, as new ways of hindering our personal liberties are discovered or old ones are resurrected.[47]

"holistic" or "utopian" social engineering and have adopted a more piecemeal approach to social problems. "*The characteristic approach of the piecemeal engineer is this. Even though he may perhaps cherish some ideals which concern society as a whole . . . he does not believe in the method of redesigning it as a whole. Whatever his ends, he tries to achieve them by small adjustments and readjustments which can be continually improved upon. . . . Holistic or Utopian social engineering as opposed to piecemeal social engineering, is never of a 'private' but always of a 'public' character. It aims at remodeling the 'whole of society' in accordance with a definite plan or blueprint; . . . and at extending the power of the State . . . until the State becomes nearly identical with society.*" Karl R. Popper, *The Poverty of Historicism* (1957), Routledge & Kegan Paul, London, 1974, pp. 66–67.

46. Karl Popper, *Unended Quest* (1974), Open Court, La Salle, Ill., 1976, p. 116.

47. On the other hand, there is no permanent victory for the other side either. That's why I don't agree with Murdoch when he says that "*capitalism has not triumphed. Neosocialism is triumphing.*"

Part 5

Money and Europe

Toward Monetary Stability?

Our problem is that of defining an adequate monetary system based on simple rules and of finding the way toward such a system. We cannot seek merely to return to some arrangement of the past. The monetary problem was never solved in the past.—*Henry C. Simons, 1936*

The Change in Rhetoric

The most significant change in the field of monetary matters in the past few years has been the increased recognition of the importance of monetary stability on the part of Western governments and the economic profession. That monetary stability should be regarded as an important goal of policy is a big change from the not-so-distant past, when the overwhelming majority of government officials and fashionable economists believed that the appropriate goal was to achieve a degree of monetary *instability* that was most conducive to high employment and economic growth.

It is an open question whether the change must be credited to the impact of the "Counter-Revolution in Monetary Theory" or to the brutal lessons of the reality of the great inflation of the 1970s. The fact remains that, at least for the time being, monetary stability has been restored to its place as a high-priority goal. Unfortunately, however, such a change might be a necessary condition for an improved performance of the monetary system, but it is far from being a sufficient condition.

In some countries, the change in the consideration of the importance of monetary stability has been accompanied by a significant reduction of the rate of inflation. This is true, for example, in England

Originally published in *International Background* 12, no. 3, 1984, pp. 75–83. Also presented at the Mont Pèlerin Society Regional Meeting, Paris, France, February 29–March 3, 1984, and reprinted with permission.

and in the United States. In other countries, inflation has been reduced somewhat, but it still remains unacceptably high, despite the change in the priority of policy goals. Italy is a good example of this second kind of monetary performance. Still other countries continue to experience unbelievably high rates of inflation.

It would be excessively optimistic, however, to conclude that the countries where the change in rhetoric has been accompanied by a reduction in the rate of inflation have achieved the kind of monetary policy system that can guarantee monetary stability for a long period of time. As far as the United States is concerned, one need only refer to Professor Milton Friedman's view, according to which,

> unfortunately, the damage has now been done, and there is no easy, or for that matter, difficult way out. Continuation of present levels of monetary growth promises disaster. A sharp reduction in monetary growth would mean reduced nominal GNP growth next year. Combined with the delayed impact on inflation of the recent monetary explosion, the result would be recession . . . There is no middle course that at this point will avoid both higher inflation and at least a decided slowing, if not premature termination, of the expansion.[1]

And, as for monetary policy in England under Mrs. Thatcher's rule, it is Michael Parkin's view that

> United Kingdom monetary policy has been through a savage deflation similar in kind though different in magnitude to its very many predecessors. Policy is now embarked upon a renewed reflation. This too is similar in kind though as yet of unknown magnitude to its many predecessors. It can be predicted with great confidence that some, if not all the gains in fighting inflation that have been bought at such high price will be dissipated in this process.[2]

1. "Why a Surge of U.S. Inflation Is Likely Next Year," *The Wall Street Journal,* September 5, 1983.

2. "Monetarism: Any Verdict Yet? The United Kingdom 1979–83," Paper presented at the Mont Pèlerin Society 1983 Regional Meeting, Vancouver, August 28–September 1, 1983.

The Italian Case

If the change in rhetoric in the United States and in the United Kingdom has not resulted in a significant change in performance, it has not been without consequences. The increased importance attached to the goal of monetary stability in those countries has convinced many people that the monetary authorities were pursuing "monetarist" policies, when in fact, as shown by Professor Friedman's and Michael Parkin's analyses quoted above, they were not. The perception of those policies as monetarist and their poor performance will undoubtedly work in the direction of giving "monetarism" a bad name. This is a very unfortunate development, because a correct public understanding of the role of money in the economy is essential for the attainment of a stable monetary system and because monetarism already enjoyed a bad reputation. In the words of the late Harry G. Johnson, for example,

> in the United Kingdom, . . . such contemporarily illiterate monetary policy amateurs as Nicholas Kaldor and J. R. Hicks use the term "monetarism" to describe any and all views at variance with their own view of British policy problems. (In Britain, in fact, the majority view bases itself on the axiom "monetarism" = Milton Friedman = "The Treasury View" = utter nonsense; in the same circles, incidentally, the corollary is "Keynesianism" = incomes policy).[3]

Or, as stressed by Samuel Brittan:

> The campaign of vilification has been so successful that many educated citizens believe the principal tenet of "monetarism" to be support for Latin American dictatorships employing torture. Those of a more charitable disposition suppose it to be a label for hardships deliberately imposed on peoples by governments to punish them for laziness or poor productivity.[4]

3. "Comment on Mayer on Monetarism," in Thomas Mayer, *The Structure of Monetarism,* W. W. Norton, New York and London, 1978, p. 126.

4. *How to End the "Monetarist" Controversy,* The Institute of Economic Affairs, London, 1981, p. 11.

In the light of the above considerations, the change in rhetoric unaccompanied by a change in performance must be viewed as a negative development. However, the performance of monetary policy in countries, like Italy, where the rhetoric has remained bad, should help to redress the balance of public opinion *in favor* of monetarism. The fervently "antimonetarist" policies of Banca d'Italia (Italy's Central Bank) can hardly be considered a successful alternative to a monetarist stabilization policy. Let me illustrate.[5]

It has been argued—and extensive empirical evidence seems to support such a conclusion—that "the impact of a change in the rate of money growth shows up *initially and temporarily* on output and employment."[6] Empirical evidence seems to suggest that such has been the case for the Italian economy in the first years of the present decade. Historically, there has been a very high correlation between the rate of growth of M_1 (currency plus demand deposits) and the rate of growth of spending and prices in Italy.[7] Now, if one looks at the rate of M_1 growth in the last seven years, the picture that emerges is very clear. From the second quarter of 1976 to the second quarter of 1980 M_1 grew at an annual rate of more than 20 percent (22.2 percent). A remarkable feature of these seventeen quarters of monetary expansion has been its relative steadiness: On a monthly basis, the annual rate of growth of M_1 has ranged from 18.9 percent (March 1977) to 26.2 percent (November 1979), with very little variability. It is, therefore, fairly safe to assume that such a steady rate of monetary growth had been incorporated into the decision-making process and become part of the prevailing expectations of economic actors.

In May 1980, however, the trend has been reversed and the rate of M_1 growth started to decline from the high level that had prevailed in the previous four years to a much lower (and more reasonable) level. The decline in the rate continued gradually throughout 1980

5. What follows is taken from my paper "Government Growth, Hidden Taxation, and Economic Decline," forthcoming.

6. D. S. Batten and C. C. Stone, "Are Monetarists an Endangered Species?" *Federal Reserve Bank of St. Louis Review,* May 1983.

7. See, for example, A. Martino, *Monetarismo?* Il Mulino, no. 280, 1982, pp. 180ff.

and 1981, reaching a minimum of 8.4 percent in the second quarter of 1982. (In March of that year the annual rate of growth of M_1 was 7.2 percent). Even though the decline was fairly gradual, its size was substantial: In the second quarter of 1982 the rate of M_1 growth was slightly more than 40 percent of what it had been two years before. The almost two years of monetary restraint can then, conceivably, be held responsible for the stagnation of real growth in 1981 and 1982 (as well as 1983, according to provisional figures).

If this explanation is correct, it follows that the ongoing stagnation is, at least in part, the "price" we are paying for an anti-inflationary monetary policy, and it is a price we are paying in vain because beginning in March 1982 the rate of M_1 growth has started to accelerate again, so that by the fourth quarter of 1982 it had gone up to 16.5 percent. In the first six months of 1983, the rate of growth of M_1 has averaged 15.6 percent. Rather than curing our inflation, monetary policy has just produced an avoidable worsening of the recession. It would have been worth to pay such a temporary price to get rid of the inflation (after eleven consecutive years of double-digit inflation), but that would have required a continuation of the policy of monetary restraint. Since that policy seems to have been abandoned, inflation will continue with the price of the cure having been paid in vain.[8] At present, inflation is running at the rate of 15 percent per year, with no real growth in output (indeed, the final figures for 1983 might even show a slight decline in real GDP).

Why Do Central Banks Misbehave?

In practice, we have relied almost wholly on authorities. . . . Relying so largely on the discretion of authorities in so important an area of policy is highly objectionable on political grounds in a free society. Experience has demonstrated that it has also had unfortunate monetary consequences. . . . The role of the monetary authorities is to provide a stable monetary background . . . Yet the vagueness of their responsibilities and the wide range of their discretion has left them no means other than "wisdom" and personal perspective of withstanding contemporaneous pressures and has denied them the bulwark that clearly assigned responsibilities and definite rules would have provided.—Milton Friedman, 1960

8. Monetary figures are based on Banca d'Italia, Supplemento al Bollettino, Conti Finanziari, various issues.

The problem now becomes: Why has the performance of monetary policy been disappointing, even in countries that have adopted an admirable monetarist rhetoric? There are several possible answers to this question, and one need not assume that central bankers are of necessity evil and/or incompetent. The first possible answer is that, despite the monetarist rhetoric, monetary authorities, consciously or unconsciously, still rely on the old Keynesian orthodoxy. For example, according to Professor Friedman:

> If the question, "Are you now or have you ever been a monetarist?" were put to the seven members of the Federal Reserve Board, not a single one would say yes. . . . (T)he Federal Reserve has always opposed the use of monetary targets; it has always claimed that it could not in fact control effectively the quantity of money.[9]

Other examples could be found: In his otherwise admirable Annual Report (*Relazione*), delivered on May 31, 1983, the Governor of Banca d'Italia lists a variety of "inflationary factors." Nowhere is the possibility that inflation has been the result of the rapid growth in monetary aggregates explicitly considered. Yet another example is provided by a collection of essays by academic economists, including representatives of Banca d'Italia, on inflation that was published two years ago: *The quantity of money is not even mentioned anywhere in the whole book.*[10]

A more convincing argument in favor of the thesis that the monetary theory of inflation is still largely ignored by central bankers is the indirect one based on their choice of intermediate targets of monetary policy. Such is, for example, the case of Banca d'Italia, which uses total domestic credit as an intermediate target, rather than monetary aggregates.[11] Such a choice proves the "antimonetarist" bias of the Italian

9. "What Could Reasonably Have Been Expected from Monetarism: The United States," Paper presented to the Mont Pèlerin Society Regional Meeting, Vancouver, August 28–September 1, 1983.

10. CNEL, *Inflazione e scala mobile,* Rome, 1981.

11. Total domestic credit is defined as "the sum of loans (both in lire and in foreign currency) to the private sector by banks and special credit institutions, of bonds issued by enterprises and of domestically financed public-sector borrowing requirement." See A. Penati and G. Tullio, "Total Domestic Credit as an Intermediate Target of Monetary Policy in Italy," in F. Spinelli and G. Tullio, ed.,

Central Bank: An essential item of monetarist policy is the "*acceptance of a monetary aggregate by the monetary authorities as their primary target*" (M. Friedman, *op. cit.;* emphasis added).

Incidentally, Banca d'Italia's decision to attempt to control total domestic credit (CTI), rather than monetary aggregates, is not based on empirical evidence showing that such a credit aggregate is an intermediate target of monetary policy preferable to the quantity of money. On the contrary, recent studies conclude that

> no evidence was found suggesting a stable relationship between CTI and the final targets of monetary policy. By contrast, the relationships between monetary aggregates, nominal income, and the exchange rate were found to have greater stability. Furthermore, aside from stability considerations, it appears that movements in CTI account for a smaller fraction of the cyclical variability of nominal income than that accounted for by monetary aggregates. In addition, movements in CTI contain very little information on long-run movements of nominal GDP. . . . (T)he tests cast doubts on the validity of CTI as an intermediate target of monetary policy and reinforce the impression that the transmission mechanism of monetary impulses underlying the CTI model does not adequately explain some important features of the Italian economy in the 1970s.[12]

The choice of total domestic credit as an intermediate target of monetary policy is particularly difficult to understand in a country like Italy, where the empirical evidence confirms the monetary theory of inflation in its crudest and most simplistic form: The time pattern of the consumer price index mirrors that of M_1 with a fixed two-year lag.[13]

As mentioned earlier, even monetary authorities that formally accept monetarist principles are far from following monetarist policy prescriptions. This is true of the United States, where the Fed's procedures have recently prompted Allan Meltzer to say:

Monetary Policy, Fiscal Policy and Economic Activity: The Italian Experience, Gower, 1983, which provides a brilliant analysis of the consequences of such a choice.

12. A. Penati and G. Tullio, op. cit., pp. 58–60.

13. See A. Martino, "Monetarismo?" op. cit., p. 197. The correlation coefficient is 0.994.

> The Federal Reserve should not have been permitted to pursue the kinds of policies that it has for as long as it has. The Fed produces too much variability in money growth. It produces, on average, too much money growth. . . . The Fed's procedure currently is to estimate interest rates . . . to set the interest rate and accept the money growth that results.[14]

The phenomenon is epidemic among central bankers. Indeed, I could not mention the case of *one* contemporary monetary policy approved of by monetarist economists. This leaves us with a puzzling question: If the case for a monetarist monetary policy is firmly established both on theoretical and on empirical grounds, why aren't central bankers behaving accordingly? Barring the possibility that they are evil and/or incompetent by profession, why do they refuse to adopt the best monetary procedures available? Isn't there a strong incentive for them to do so, thereby gaining immortal fame? Clearly, a better explanation of the behavior of monetary authorities is required.

The Institutional Framework

I have identified as the central problem the behaviour of the Bank of England. This is not to say that the Bank of England is populated by evil people. It is simply that the institutional incentives and constraints that impinge upon those operating monetary policy are not compatible with the goals of achieving firm and predictable monetary behaviour. Better monetary performance cannot be delivered by better monetary management. It is not a managerial problem. It is a problem that can only be tackled by a fundamental redesign of the institutions that deliver monetary policy.—Michael Parkin, 1983

Should the central bankers' disregard for monetarist policy prescriptions be due to genuine ignorance, the problem would take care of itself in due time, when younger and better-educated generations will replace the present one. There is a great deal to be said in favor of such an optimistic perspective. However, I fear that the problem is largely of a different nature, so that a more fundamental solution is required. In particular, I am convinced that monetary instability is only a symptom of a much deeper problem which might be conveniently labeled the "government push." Let me illustrate by drawing from my

14. *Towards a Stable Monetary Policy, Monetarism vs the Gold Standard,* The Heritage Foundation, Washington, D.C., 1982, pp. 5–6.

country's experience. I believe that the conclusions that can be drawn from Italy's experience have general significance.[15]

It is generally recognized that the structure of political incentives in a democracy is biased in favor of government growth because of three asymmetries in the perception of costs and benefits of public spending. First of all, the political process tends to favor decisions that result in benefits for a small group of beneficiaries and whose cost is spread over a large number of taxpayers. The second asymmetry results from the fact that the political process tends to favor decisions based on *visible* benefits and *invisible* costs. The visibility of benefits guarantees the support for the proposal by the potential beneficiaries, while the invisibility of costs neutralizes the opposition of those who will bear them. Finally, the political process favors decisions that result in an *immediate* gain (even if small) whose cost (even if large) is paid in the distant *future.* This last asymmetry is particularly acute in Italy because, given the high instability of the executive (the average life expectancy of Italian governments is less than a year), the time horizon of political decision makers tends to be very short. Governments generally tend to favor spending decisions that confer an immediate gain to some group in society, even if the future cost of the decision is substantial, because in all likelyhood it will be borne by another government.

If the above analysis is correct, we would expect government to show a tendency to finance spending by a device that (a) spreads costs over a large number of taxpayers; (b) hides these costs from those who bear them; (c) produces immediate benefits at the expense of high (if not disastrous) consequences in the future. Such a device exists, and it is called a deficit. Its time pattern confirms the preceding analysis beyond any doubt.

As Table 1 clearly shows, the government deficit has been growing rapidly since 1960, both as a percentage of total public-sector spending and as a percentage of GDP. In 1960, for every million lire of public spending, 950,000 lire came from explicit taxes of one kind or another; in 1982, for every million lire of public spending, only 715,000

15. For a more detailed analysis of what follows, see A. Martino, *Constraining Inflationary Government,* The Heritage Foundation, Washington, D.C., 1982.

TABLE 1. *Government Deficit as a Percentage of*

	Government Spending	GDP
1960–64	5.7%	2.1%
1965–69	9.7%	3.8%
1970–74	18.4%	7.5%
1975–79	25.3%	12.2%
1980	21.9%	11.0%
1981	25.7%	13.4%
1982	28.5%	15.4%

Sources: International Monetary Fund, *International Financial Statistics*, 1983; Banca d'Italia.

lire were paid for by explicit taxes—the rest was "financed" by the deficit. As a percentage of GDP, the deficit increased more than threefold from 1960 to 1970; and it again increased more than three times from 1970 to 1982. (It is worth noting that from 1960 to 1982 nominal GDP has increased more than twentyfold). Furthermore, all declines in the absolute size of the deficit (in 1961, 1967, 1969, 1976, and 1979) were invariably followed by sharp increases that more than offset the decline and confirmed the rapidly growing trend. In nominal terms the deficit was 190 times higher in 1982 than 1960.

As for the effects of the rapid growth of the deficit on monetary policy, with the (temporary?) exception of the May 1980–March 1982 period, the rate of monetary growth seems to have been heavily conditioned by the need to finance growing government deficits. The average annual rate of growth of M_1 has gone from 13.7 percent in 1960–64 to 14.7 percent in 1965–69, to 19.5 percent in 1970–74, to 20.8 percent in 1975–79. It has then followed the pattern mentioned earlier.

These figures suggest that there is a causal link going from the deficit to the average annual rate of growth of M_1. It is far from clear whether the rapid growth in public-sector deficit has made inflationary monetary policy unavoidable. The gradual deceleration in the rate of M_1 growth in the May 1980–March 1982 period took place in the face of a growing deficit, and this seems to suggest that a stable monetary policy might have been pursued despite the growth in public sector's financial irresponsibility. If such were the case, it might also be argued that the inflationary policy has been the cause rather than the consequence of the government's fiscal irresponsibility.

That an anti-inflationary monetary policy is possible, even in the face of rapidly growing government deficits, has been argued, with specific reference to Italy, by David Laidler.

> The implementation of a policy of gradually reducing the rate of monetary expansion involves certain technical problems, but here too, we do not believe that these are by any means insurmountable. If it is to be able to control the money supply, the Bank of Italy must obviously be relieved of any obligation to automatically buy public sector debt. The removal of this obligation is necessary, though it is not a sufficient condition for monetary growth targets to be met. The fact that it is now being removed makes this a particularly opportune time to adopt monetary targets. However, if the Bank attempts to stabilize interest rates at levels below those that the market finds acceptable, it will inevitably find itself acting as a residual buyer of public debt and will be unable to control the behavior of its own cash liabilities. Thus, to make a commitment to monetary targets, the Bank must at the same time abandon any commitment that it might have for treating interest rates as policy targets in their own right.[16]

It is still too early to know whether David Laidler's admirable advice to the Banca d'Italia will be followed or not. I am afraid, however, that it will not. Admittedly on the basis of real political difficulties and faulty economic logic, Italy's Central Bank is likely to stick to its inadequate intermediate target, with the not-so-hidden belief that, by so doing, it can keep interest rates below the level they would otherwise attain. In his Annual Report (*Relazione*) mentioned above, the governor of Banca d'Italia justified the choice of total domestic credit as an intermediate target of monetary policy on the ground that

16. "The Role of Money in Controlling Inflation: An Elementary Exposition," in F. Spinelli and G. Tullio, ed., op. cit., p. 11.

the huge government deficit had reduced the availability of credit to private productive investment, and that it was his duty to "restore" the availability of credit through monetary expansion. As mentioned before, little attention was paid to the inflationary consequences of such a procedure, and inflation was blamed on a variety of ad hoc factors.

In other words, the governor's argument can be stated as implying that if Banca d'Italia refused to buy public-sector debt (and create money in the process), the attempt to sell it to the market would result in a substantial increase in interest rates and the "crowding out" of private productive investment. Such an argument, therefore, implies that debt monetization can (permanently?) keep interest rates below the level that would otherwise prevail. This notion, once so popular in the Keynesian literature, is now thoroughly discredited. Expansionary monetary policy tends to *raise* nominal rates of interest, rather than lower them. It may be that a sudden shift to a restrictive monetary policy raises nominal interest rates, but this does not mean that debt monetization can keep them at a "low" level for an indefinite period of time. It would seem as if Banca d'Italia's monetary procedures were due to its refusal to abandon old fashioned Keynesianism.

As stated previously, it is true that Keynesianism is still alive and well at Banca d'Italia. However, it is not clear why an institution endowed with a large research department, with no shortage of overpaid economists, and with an enormous and very modern library, should continue to ignore recent and not-so-recent developments in monetary theory. If Keynesianism is the problem, why are they still Keynesian?

Another possible explanation runs as follows:

> Higher government spending provokes taxpayer resistance. Taxpayer resistance encourages government to finance spending by monetary creation, thereby increasing monetary growth and hence inflation, which, as a by-product very welcome to legislators, raises effective tax rates without legislation.[17]

17. M. Friedman, "Response to Questionnaire on Monetary Policy," Appendices to the minutes of evidence taken before the Treasury and Civil Service Committee, London, June 1980, pp. 55–56.

Such an explanation, however, implies that monetary policy decisions are made by the government, or that the central bank is not independent. Such is not the case in Italy, where Banca d'Italia's independence is, at least formally, guaranteed.

My favorite explanation is slightly different. I believe that it was Napoleon who said that the true cause of the French revolution was vanity, liberty just being a pretext. Similarly, Keynesianism is just a pretext; the true cause of Banca d'Italia's monetary performance must be found in the fact that it is a great deal simpler, from a political point of view, to foot the bill of the government's financial irresponsibility than it would be to adopt a policy of monetary restraint. The refusal to buy public-sector debt would put Banca d'Italia on the wrong side of the government, as it would eventually force it to reduce spending or increase taxes. The increase in interest rates would expose monetary authorities to the criticism of labor unions and businessmen alike, not to mention the very powerful leftist press. It is true that the policy of debt monetization results in inflation, but, as long as the monetary theory of inflation is scorned or ignored, no one will blame it on the central bank. It is also true, and monetary authorities must be aware of it, that such a policy cannot last forever. However, so far it has allowed the central bank to avoid a confrontation with the government.

In other words, I believe that the choice of an inflationary policy is due to the size of the public-sector deficit and to "social selective incentives," to use Mancur Olson's expression,[18] that have convinced Banca d'Italia to yield to political pressures and give up its institutional duty to preserve monetary stability. Courage is, after all, a very scarce commodity. Such a policy of surrender was explicitly rationalized almost ten years ago by the governor of the time with these words:

> We have asked, and still ask ourselves the question if Banca d'Italia could have refused or could still refuse to finance the deficit of the public sector by refraining from using the faculty given by the law to buy State securities. The refusal would make it impossible for the State to pay salaries to the civil servants of the military order, of

18. *The Rise and Decline of Nations,* Yale University Press, New Haven and London, 1982, pp. 24ff.

> the judiciary order, of the civil order, and pensions to citizens in general. It would look like an act of monetary policy, but would in fact be a seditious act that would be followed by the paralysis of the institutions.[19]

The governor gave no reason why public spending simply *had to be* financed by printing money. The consequences of that decision can be easily summarized: Public-sector deficit equaled 8.1 percent of GDP in 1974, and it has now reached, as previously mentioned, 15.4 percent of GDP. By interpreting debt monetization as inevitable, Banca d'Italia not only gave up its institutional duty, it also encouraged financial irresponsibility on the part of the government. Had monetary authorities refused to buy public-sector debt, it is highly doubtful that the government deficit could have reached its present size.

A Monetary Constitution?

If the above analysis is correct, the poor performance of monetary policies in Western democracies is due to a combination of factors. These include the survival of the Keynesian interpretation of monetary policy as aimed at controlling interest rates and the resulting refusal to control monetary aggregates instead. However, the ultimate cause of our present state of monetary disorder must be found in an institutional framework that allows monetary policy to be used to finance government growth. Contrary to what has been suggested,[20] even independent central banks can be persuaded that it is in their political interest to pursue inflationary policies.

The solution must then be found in changing the institutions that deliver monetary policy, in moving from the present arrangement based on "authorities" to one based on "rules," in adopting, that is, a

19. *Relazione del Governatore della Banca d'Italia sull'esercizio 1973,* Rome, 1974, p. 30 (my translation). See A. Martino, "Inflation and Its Causes in a 'Mixed' Economy: The Italian Case," in *Anti-Inflationary Policies: East-West,* CESES, Milan, 1974, pp. 327ff.

20. See, for example, T. Bethell, "Has the Dragon Been Slain?" *Reason,* August 1983, p. 46: "the new market sophistication exacts good behavior from the Fed. Therefore we may expect a period of monetary stability."

monetary constitution. As is well known, a number of proposals have been made that would take monetary policy decisions away from the arbitrariness of central banks and trust it to some set of impartial rules. Some of the proposals are of dubious validity. I personally doubt, for example, that a true gold standard is feasible today.[21] Other proposals, while representing fascinating theoretical exercises, are highly unlikely to be seriously considered as practical solutions. Such is, in my opinion, the case of the denationalization of money or of competing currencies.[22] I do not mean to say that the arrangements proposed would not be *desirable.* However, these proposals do not solve the problem of how to convince politicians to accept them and are, therefore, highly unlikely to ever come about. The same can be said of the idea of making it financially rewarding for central bankers to pursue a stable monetary policy by tying their salaries to the rate of monetary growth so that excessive expansion would result in a decrease of their salary.[23]

The problem, in my opinion, arises from the fact that money is of necessity a government monopoly, or, in the words of Aaron Director, "a suitable monetary framework cannot be provided by competition . . . it constitutes one of the requisite legal institutions."[24] In my view, by far the most desirable and achievable rule is the Friedmanian one of a constant rate of growth of the money supply. Such a proposal is well known, and it needs no further comment.

What chances are there of such a rule being adopted (in performance, not just in rhetoric)? I do not believe that this or any other monetary rule can be effectively adopted, unless we solve the basic underlying problem of a fiscal constitution. I entirely agree with Henry C. Simons's view that "An enterprise system cannot function effectively in

21. The classical analysis of this problem is Milton Friedman's famous essay "Real and Pseudo Gold Standards," *The Journal of Law and Economics,* October 1961.

22. F. A. Hayek, *Choice in Currency,* Occasional Paper 48, Institute of Economic Affairs, London, 1976; and *Denationalisation of Money,* Hobart Paper Special 70, Institute of Economic Affairs, London, 1976.

23. M. Reynolds, "Incentive vs. Bad Money: Let's Try Indexing Salaries of the Board of Governors," *Pathfinder,* July–August 1981.

24. "The Parity of the Economic Market Place," *The Journal of Law and Economics,* October 1964.

the face of extreme uncertainty as to the action of monetary authorities or, for that matter, as to monetary legislation."[25] However, I also believe that the opposite is true, that we cannot have monetary stability in countries that have abandoned the "enterprise system" and engaged in democratic statism and arbitrary government. As long as government remains unconstrained, as long as budget deficits are possible, the temptation to finance public spending by resorting to money creation will prove to be irresistible.

This, in my opinion, is the real problem: Monetary instability is just a symptom of a deeper disease. All proposals to deal with the symptom without tackling the roots of the problem will, sooner or later, prove to fail. History tells us that this is a very long story indeed: For centuries, governments have mismanaged their currencies in order to finance their expenditures. Only if we succeed in achieving an effective set of constraints on government and a fiscal constitution can we hope to have a stable monetary environment.[26]

25. "Rules Versus Authorities in Monetary Policy," *The Journal of Political Economy* 44 (1936), 1–30.

26. See *La Costituzione fiscale e monetaria, Vincoli alla finanza inflazionistica,* CREA, Rome, 1983.

Nationalism, Money, and Europe

The Nation-State

The idea of Europe is under attack these days, and often for good reasons. As a liberal, however, I find it disturbing that the legitimate criticism of the dirigiste excesses of the EEC should provide an excuse for resurrecting an old enemy of individual freedom: national sovereignty.

For a believer in a free society, the nation is a largely arbitrary, historically determined unit, or, as Professor Friedman puts it:

> To the free man, the country is the collection of individuals who compose it, not something over and above them. He is proud of a common heritage and loyal to common traditions. But he regards government as a means, an instrumentality, neither a grantor of favors and gifts, nor a master or god to be blindly worshiped and served.[1]

Furthermore, we would be well advised to remember the restrictions on personal liberties, the bloody atrocities, and the wars that have been inflicted on the peoples of Europe by the worship of the nation-state. The history of no country is immune to the shameful consequences of nationalism, and I doubt that believers in a free society could share the idea that "*nations whose nationalism is destroyed are subject to ruin.*" It comes from the Libyan leader, Colonel Muammar Qaddafi.

In order to avoid misunderstandings, let me make it clear that I re-

Presented at the National Review Institute Italy Conference, "Does the Nation State Exist? Immigration and Regionalism," October 23–25, 1992, unpublished.

1. Milton Friedman, *Capitalism and Freedom,* 1962, Phoenix Books, The University of Chicago Press, 1965, pp. 1–2.

gard a centralized European government, endowed with the powers that national governments possess today, as far more dangerous to individual liberties than national sovereignty. However, the possibility of such a European leviathan coming into existence is nil, and we should stop using it as a rhetorical device.

Are There European "Public Goods"?

The European nation-state is also largely obsolete as a political decision-making unit: It is both too large and too small. It is too large to accommodate variety within its borders, and it is too small to deal with global issues. There are genuine European "public goods," common goals that cannot be effectively pursued at a national level. Let me briefly deal with two of them: the single market and monetary unification.

The most important goal of European institutions and the justification for their existence is the creation and protection of a single market for goods, productive factors, and services. The benefits of a unified market are generally considered unambiguous: By common consent, a unified market is regarded as a genuine "*European public good*": It cannot be provided at the national level. European institutions' major task, therefore, is that of preventing the introduction of restrictions to market freedom. These would very likely come about if entrenched national interests were allowed to obtain them by their national governments, as history unambiguously confirms.[2] Even if we limit ourselves to relatively recent times, the record of national sovereignty is appalling: In "*liberal*" England, twenty-five years ago restrictions on foreign exchange were such that Britons were allowed to take out of their country no more than £50. And let's not forget that the American Founding Fathers were so convinced of the "*public good*" na-

2. This is also James M. Buchanan's view: "*Separate governmental units . . . cannot be trusted to maintain the openness of internal markets. . . . To achieve and to maintain genuine economic integration over the whole territories described by Western Europe . . . a constitutional structure must be put into place that will, at the same time, insure the freedom of markets and insure against the concentration of coercive political authority in a central supranational government.*" See "The Constitutional Moment of the 1990s," Preliminary draft prepared for lecture in Rome, October 1991.

ture of free trade that they deemed it necessary to enshrine the "*commerce clause*" into the American Constitution.

This in no way should be interpreted as a justification for all the things that have been done in Brussels, but, in criticizing the dirigiste excesses of the EEC, we should not lose sight of the reasons for the existence of an European framework.

Furthermore, the EEC is not as costly as many people think: The total cost of all European institutions for the year 1992 is slightly more than U.S. $47 billions, or $145 for every citizen of the twelve European countries. The Italian government alone spends that much every seven weeks. Also, the costs of the European bureaucracy are substantially smaller than those of national ones: only 5 percent of that total.

The least defensible part of the EEC activities is the Common Agricultural Policy. However, the Community is certainly not the worst offender in that respect: In the EEC, "*farm subsidies are, on average, equivalent to 49% of the value of farm output. In EFTA countries subsidies average 68% of farm output and in Switzerland as much as 80%.*"[3] No one, as far as I know, has ever argued that the Swiss cantons or the American states should aim at dismantling the federal structure of Switzerland and the United States just because the agricultural policies of those countries are indefensible. Rather than using the EEC's dirigisme as evidence of the superiority of national sovereignty, which is a historically incorrect conclusion, we should aim at making the European institutions work in the direction of freedom for our own advantage and for the benefit of both the newly liberated countries of Eastern Europe and of the entire world.

Is Money a European "Public Good"?

Would Europe benefit from a common currency? If, for the moment, we ignore both the difficulties of achieving that result and the preoccupations with the conduct of monetary policy after the establishment of a common currency, the answer is positive: Europe and the world would benefit a great deal from a common European currency.

For example, a common European currency could provide an alter-

3. *The Economist,* October 17, 1992, p. 73.

native to the U.S. dollar as an instrument of international liquidity. The "national" currency of such a large market could achieve the same degree of acceptability presently enjoyed by the dollar. The competition between the two major international currencies would result in some kind of "Gresham's law" in reverse, because the more stable currency would be preferred in international transactions. The overall stability of the international monetary system would increase.

In particular, Europe would benefit in that it would be able to use its own currency, rather than the U.S. dollar, as a reserve asset.[4] Needless to say this would not be a minor advantage, and, by itself, might in fact be as important as (if not more important than) the saving in transactions costs. The United States would also benefit to the extent that a monetary system based on two currencies would make the external value of the dollar less volatile.

Inside Europe, a common currency would eliminate balance-of-payments problems, making the adjustment process smooth and automatic. There would be no balance-of-payments problems between, say, England and France because both countries would be using the same currency. National economic policies would, therefore, be relieved of one of their present worries.[5]

With a common European currency, provincial considerations would play no role in monetary decisions, which would aim at overall stability rather than respond to "local" pressures. As a result, for example, there would be only one rate of inflation rather than twelve. This is a very important consideration indeed: I know of no economist willing to argue that a proliferation of *regional* currencies within

4. If Europe had a common currency, there would be one central bank rather than twelve. This, in and of itself, might result in a considerable saving if the European central bank would cost less than the present twelve national central banks (this is, however, not clear, considering the rather lavish way eurocrats tend to treat themselves.) Even more important, the dollar reserves presently used by the national central banks would become unnecessary and, if the common currency were allowed to float freely in international markets, the European central bank's reserve requirement would be very small.

5. Also, scarce resources presently dissipated in the collection, analysis, and discussion of intra-European balance-of-payments statistics could be diverted to more productive uses.

a given country would increase overall monetary stability on a *national* level.[6]

A common currency would make the liberalization of capital movements within Europe automatic and irreversible, with all the known advantages in terms of personal liberty and economic efficiency. It would be as difficult to restrict capital movements in an area using the same currency as it is within a given country.

These advantages, however, apply to a common currency, not to a system of pegged exchange rates like the one envisioned in Maastricht for the transition period. Identifying monetary unification with fixed exchange rates[7] is an old mistake: It was the basic assumption of the Werner plan of 1970, of the 1972 "snake," and of whatever is left of the present European Monetary System. It is the idea that "*irrevocably fixed exchange rates between national currencies*" and "*coordination of policy between separate national authorities*" are necessary (and sufficient?) first steps toward monetary union. Once fixed exchange rates are attained, eurocrats maintain, monetary unification will be completed.[8]

6. It is in the light of this argument that one should read *The Economist*'s point: "*simply ask whether America would be better off with separate currencies for each of its states*" (op. cit.). Strangely enough, the only problem that the authoritative publication sees in having the United States use fifty different currencies is that of the cost of converting one into another!

7. "*The adoption of* a single currency, *while not strictly necessary for the creation of a monetary union, might be seen—for economic as well as psychological and political reasons—as a natural and desirable further development of the monetary union.*" Delors Report, April 1989, p. 10.

Strangely enough, this identification of monetary union with a system of fixed exchange rates is explicitly accepted even by *The Economist:* "*A fully fixed system would eliminate the bands within which the currencies are allowed to fluctuate. Monetary union would then go one step further by adopting a single currency.*" *The Economist,* op. cit., p. 18.

8. The belief that fixed rates are (a) almost indistinguishable from monetary union, and (b) a necessary step toward that goal is unacceptable. In the words of Professor Milton Friedman:

> The basic fact is that a unified currency and a system of freely floating exchange rates are members of the same species even though superficially they appear very different. Both are free market mechanisms for interregional or international payments. Both permit exchange rates to move freely. Both exclude any administrative or political intermediary in payments between resi-

As the recent turmoil in foreign exchange markets confirms, the belief that fixed rates are (a) almost indistinguishable from monetary union, and (b) a necessary step toward that goal is unacceptable. We can either aim at a common currency for Europe or allow exchange rates to perform the adjustment process. A priori, a common European currency would represent a superior monetary arrangement. For, while the smoothness of the adjustment process and the elimination of balance-of-payments problems could also be achieved by a system of freely floating exchange rates among European national currencies, all the other advantages can be attained only by a single currency for Europe.

Rules vs. Discretion in Monetary Policy

However, the reasons that make us worry about monetary management by national central bankers are even more valid when referred to a single currency for Europe. Monetary mismanagement on a national level can be a disaster; on a European level it would be a catastrophe of unbearable proportions.[9]

The problem arises because, with the end of the gold standard, money, in addition to its traditional functions, has become an instrument of discretionary policy to an extent that was inconceivable be-

---

dents of different areas. Either is consistent with free trade between areas, or with a lessening of trade restrictions.

On the other hand, national currencies linked by pegged exchange rates, whether or not through the mechanism of gold, and a system of variable exchange rates, controlled and manipulated by governmental bodies, either through an adjustable peg or day-to-day market operations, are also members of the same species. Both are interventionist standards. Neither, in my opinion, is consistent with a permanent lessening of barriers to international trade, but only with oscillating barriers as nations shift from surplus to deficit." Friedman, 1968, pp. 271–72.

9. "*In a monetary union the design of the central authority is crucial. It must be the anchor against inflation that gold was in the gold standard and the D-mark is in the present EMS. An EMU under a badly run European central bank would be much worse than the EMS under the well-run Bundesbank. In setting up the new central bank a balance would have to be struck between accountability and independence.*" "From A to EMU," *The Economist,* June 24, 1989, p. 20.

fore. Discretionary manipulation of monetary aggregates on the part of "independent" central banks can produce procyclical rather than anticyclical consequences. Instead of achieving a higher degree of stability, monetary policy becomes an autonomous source of instability.

In any case, the outcome of discretionary monetary policy in terms of increased economic instability, already harmful at the national level, would be disastrous at the European level. It's hardly surprising, therefore, that so many people consider that risk unacceptable, and oppose a common currency for Europe altogether.

My view is that a common European currency may be desirable or undesirable (feasible or unfeasible) depending on the kind of monetary constitution (or lack of it) that will be adopted.[10] If we could establish a set of rules making discretionary manipulation of monetary aggregates impossible, a common currency for Europe would represent a superior arrangement compared to what we now have. If, on the other hand, money continues to be used as an instrument of (discretionary) *policy,* monetary unification would be dangerous and it is unlikely to be achieved.

If Europe does not get a common currency, it will not reap its great advantages and monetary policy will continue to be in the hands of "independent" central bankers. Money will remain exposed to the temptations of politicians to use it as a way to purchase consent; monetary stability will exist only if governments consider it in their own self interest.

A Third Option?

It would seem that we are left with only two options: either a common currency for Europe, replacing existing national currencies, or a system of national currencies linked by flexible rates of exchange. This last one is at the moment the most likely, but the fact that it appears inevitable does not make it ideal. As a confirmed supporter of flexible exchange rates, let me stress that at this time in Europe freely

10. By monetary constitution I mean a regime "*in which the discretion of the policymaking authorities is constrained, at least in the short run.*" Leijonhufvud, 1987, p. 130.

floating rates are not immune from grave defects. First of all, it is unlikely that national central banks will refrain from intervening in the foreign exchange market, with the resulting temptation of competitive devaluations. Should this occur, the ensuing monetary disorder would impede the orderly working of the market. Secondly, and more important, if central banks continue to interfere in the determination of exchange rates, the resulting disequilibria in the balance of payments could provide a nearly irresistible temptation to restrict capital movements and resurrect exchange controls, as has already happened in Spain. It would be a severe blow to the ideal of Europe united in freedom. Finally, and most important, the events of the past few weeks have shown that European nation-states have become too small in relation to the size of global financial flows to be viable currency areas. Every day foreign exchange transactions in the world exceed U.S. $1,000 billions—more than the total reserves of all IMF countries. Flexible exchange rates among national European currencies, though undoubtedly superior to pegged ones, would be exposed to wild fluctuations in a world of such large foreign exchange transactions.

It may well be that there is, after all, a third possibility (other than flexible rates or the replacement of existing national currencies). What I have in mind is the well-known proposal of a parallel European currency circulating alongside national ones, thereby offering Europeans a choice in currency. This would result in an implicit monetary constitution, which might offer an adequate guarantee of monetary stability.

On the other hand, should we reach the conclusion that even this is, for whatever reason, impossible today, and that there is no such thing as a foolproof monetary constitution, we should base our opposition to a common European currency on these arguments. Considering the dismal record of monetary mismanagement at the national level, national monetary sovereignty is a very poor ideal indeed.

An Appendix: Competing Currencies

Many liberal critics of European monetary unification support currency competition. Different monetary instruments would be offered by (private?) competitive suppliers, and, if the rates at which they exchanged for one another were flexible and continuously determined by the market, a virtuous circle would be established which would lead to the elimination of the less stable currencies in favor of the more stable ones.

Choice in currency is an important component of freedom in general and a desirable feature of a truly free society. However, I believe that there are various reasons, aside from political feasibility, which make (private?) competitive currencies unsuited as a monetary constitution for Europe.

The first, and possibly most important, function of money is to be a unit of account, allowing prices to be expressed in a single measuring unit. The simplification money introduces in economic calculations is enormous. Money prices transmit information and allow markets to perform their function of information retrieval systems. As such, money resembles language: It conveys information. As in the case of language—most people are proficient in only one language—we tend to think in terms of *one* unit of account. Whenever we are abroad, in a country using a different currency, we experience, at least at the beginning, a marked difficulty in understanding the meaning of prices expressed in the foreign currency. This is to say that it would be costly to think in terms of two or more currencies all the time, especially if—as required by the logic of competition—their exchange rate would vary continuously.[11] People are much better off with one yardstick, one unit of measurement—in fact that's the very reason why they have a unit of measurement in the first place. Converting all the time from meters and centimeters to feet and inches gets to be annoying, useless, and time consuming. In all likelihood, therefore, most people would prefer thinking in terms of only one currency, and competition between currencies would be severely limited.

Secondly, according to the logic of competing currencies, competition favors the most stable one, thereby creating an incentive for the money-suppliers to make sure their currency is not rejected because of its instability. Yet stability does not seem to be the only cri-

11. "*If the money issued by different banks competed freely in the market, the result would be either the emergence of a private monopoly or oligopoly of money creation, or the circulation, side by side, of several kinds of money with fluctuating exchange rates between them. Either one of these outcomes would be intolerable. The immediate result would be to bring the government back into the business of money creation.*" Haberler, 1987, p. 80.

terion for success in currency competition: The U.S. dollar is not the most stable currency in the world, yet most international transactions are conducted in dollars. Other factors play a role in the competition of currencies. One is the well-known one of the size of the domestic market. Like language, whose usefulness increases with the number of people speaking it, the importance of a given currency increases with the number of people using it. Its acceptability tends to be self-reinforcing: the greater the number of people who already use it, the more likely it is that it will become acceptable to others, largely without regard to its past performance. The Swiss franc may be more stable than the U.S. dollar, but the fact that the number of people using the Swiss franc is smaller makes people prefer to use the dollar. In short, currency competition is likely to be imperfect and unlikely to act as a filter mechanism in favor of the most stable currency.

Finally, as in the case of language, in the choice and use of money there is a considerable amount of inertia: People don't ask themselves which is the most effective language for communicating with others, they just pick up the language spoken in the area where they grow up. And, once they have learned it, they continue to use it without even asking themselves whether it is the most convincing language available. This is because in most cases the cost of learning a superior language (whatever that means) outweighs the benefits. At least in the short run (as measured in decades, if not centuries), therefore, people stick to the language they already know. The same is true of money: The dollar may be a monetary instrument superior to the Italian lira, but when I am in the United States I always translate prices from dollars into lire to understand their *real* meaning. Currency competition is more a notion for theoretical economists that a realistic proposal for monetary reform.

European Monetary Union: A Fatal Mistake?

Foreword

As a rule, we all like to be liked. Understandably, we seek the sympathy of our audience. Alfred Marshall did not accept the rule, and he wrote:

> Students of social sciences must fear popular approval, evil is with them when all men speak well of them. . . . It is almost impossible for a student to be a true patriot and to have the reputation of being one at the same time.[1]

I tend to agree with Alfred Marshall. My views on EMU have earned me general criticism in Italy, where I have been accused of all kinds of transgressions: of being anti-European, eurosceptic, and Anglophile—the ultimate insult.

The reason for all these reprimands is that I do not share the general enthusiasm for EMU. I believe that while a *common* European currency—one that is introduced in a noncoercive way—might be desirable, a *single* currency, compulsorily imposed on an unconvinced population, is not. Let me try to illustrate, by looking separately at the three components of the Maastricht plan: the single currency, the set of fiscal rules, and the lack of rules of monetary conduct.

Originally prepared for the European Research Group, London, July 3, 1998, and reprinted with permission.

1. Quoted in A. C. Pigou, *Economics in Practice,* London, 1935, pp. 10–11.

Advantages of a Common Currency

Let's start with the single currency.[2] To begin with, I wish to stress that it's not true that a single market is unachievable without monetary unification. It is perfectly possible to have one without the other: Commonwealth countries had a common currency without economic integration; Canada and the United States have economic integration without a common currency. At present, we have a single European market without a European currency.[3]

But would Europe benefit from a common currency? If, for the moment, we ignore the preoccupations with the conduct of monetary policy after the establishment of a common currency, the answer is positive: Europe and the world would probably benefit from a common European currency.

Interestingly enough, most commentators seem convinced that the only advantage of a common currency for Europe would be that of reducing uncertainty in foreign exchange markets. I do not wish to deny the importance of reduced uncertainty in foreign exchange markets and of a saving in transactions costs, but it seems reductive to see no other advantage in a common currency for Europe: Exchange rate uncertainty has not prevented international trade from growing (in fact it has grown faster under flexible than under fixed rates), and, as for transactions costs, tourism does not seem to have suffered much from them.

International stability. A common European currency could provide

2. I have dealt with this issue on various occasions. See, for example, "A Monetary Constitution for Europe?" *Cato Journal* 10, no. 2, fall 1990, pp. 519–33; reprinted in *Reshaping Europe in the Twenty-First Century,* Patrick Robertson, ed., Macmillan, London, 1992, pp. 97–118; also, with modifications, under the title "Europe's Monetary Future," *Studia Diplomatica* 47, no. 6, 1994, Institut Royal des Relations Internationales, Bruxelles, pp. 15–28; and in *Bangladesh Institute of International and Strategic Studies Journal* 16, no. 1, January 1995, pp. 45–68; again reprinted, with further modifications, under the title "The Future of Europe," *The Heritage Lectures* 521, The Heritage Foundation, 1995.

3. Also, it's dubious, to say the least, that claiming that there is a "fundamental link" between political and monetary union would bring us closer to a common currency for Europe. As maintained by Karl Lamers, "Compelling Case for Monetary Union," *Financial Times,* November 7, 1994, p. 16.

an alternative to the U.S. dollar as an instrument of international liquidity. The "national" currency of such a large market could achieve the same degree of acceptability presently enjoyed by the dollar. The competition between the two major international currencies would result in some kind of "Gresham's law" in reverse, because the more stable currency would be preferred in international transactions. The overall stability of the international monetary system would increase.

In particular, Europe would benefit in that it would be able to use its own currency, rather than the U.S. dollar, as a reserve asset.[4] The United States would also benefit to the extent that a monetary system based on two currencies would make the external value of the dollar less volatile.

Balance-of-payments equilibrium. Inside Europe, a common currency would eliminate balance-of-payments problems, making the "adjustment process" smooth and automatic. There would be no balance-of-payments problems between, say, Germany and France, because both countries would be using the same currency. National economic policies would, therefore, be relieved of one of their present worries.

Freedom and efficiency. A common currency would make the liberalization of capital movements within Europe automatic and irreversible, with all the known advantages in terms of personal liberty and economic efficiency. It would be as difficult to restrict capital movements in an area using the same currency as it is within a given country. The overall efficiency of the single market would be enhanced.

These are not necessarily *all* of the benefits from a common currency for Europe, but it seems to me that they are possibly more important than the advantage of reduced uncertainty in foreign exchanges and of savings in transactions costs.

However, these advantages would be attained only if two conditions are met: that the common currency is general, i.e., that it does not divide the single European market; and that it is stable. The euro does not meet either of these conditions: It has already resulted in the ex-

4. If Europe had a common currency, there would be one central bank rather than twelve. Even more important, the dollar reserves presently used by the national central banks would become unnecessary and, if the common currency were allowed to float freely in international markets, the European Central Bank's reserve requirement would be very small.

clusion (voluntary or involuntary) of four of the fifteen countries, and it is far from certain that it is going to be stable.

Discretion vs. Rules

In the field of money and public budgets, the liberal view, which stresses the need for impartial rules and constraints on the discretionary powers of government, is contrasted by the Keynesian one, which views money and the public budget as instruments of short-run discretionary policy.[5]

For the better part of the last fifty years, the Keynesian view has been prevalent: Only the accurate manipulations of monetary aggregates and especially of the public budget by the authorities in charge of economic policy could prevent the instability, the cyclical fluctuations, and the crises that were typical of a capitalist system. It was up to economic policy—the enlightened action of government officials—to remedy the deficiencies of a market economy, prevent stagnation, recession, and mass unemployment.

Today, the traditional liberal wisdom is vindicated: A growing number of economists supports the need to take monetary policy decisions away from the discretion of monetary authorities and entrust money to a monetary constitution, a set of impartial rules aimed at providing that framework of stability without which markets cannot efficiently operate. Similar considerations apply to fiscal policy: A decreasing number of economists today believe that full employment, price stability, and economic growth can be achieved by the expert manipulation of budget deficits, while more and more economists of all persuasions have finally come to accept the need for a fiscal constitution, a set of rules making it impossible for governments to borrow their countries into bankruptcy.

The Keynesian ideas that inflation was the unavoidable price of eco-

5. What follows draws on my paper "Monetary and Fiscal Policy vs. Monetary and Fiscal Rules," in K. R. Leube, A. M. Petroni, and J. S. Sadowsky (a cura di), *An Austrian in France, Un Autrichien en France,* Festschrift in honour of Jacques Garello, La Rosa Editrice, Turin, 1997, pp. 311–37; reprinted, with modifications, under the title "Monetary and Fiscal Rules, Past Successes and Future Prospects," in *Policy* 14, no. 1, Autumn 1998, pp. 3–9.

nomic growth, that there was a stable trade-off between inflation and unemployment, that it was possible to reduce interest rates through monetary expansion, and that the time horizon for monetary policy decisions had to be dictated by the needs of short-term stabilization policies have all succumbed to the empirical evidence and the theoretical analyses of the last thirty years.

There is no evidence that economic growth inevitably involves price inflation. On the contrary, there are good reasons to believe that monetary instability hinders long-term projects and makes economic growth more difficult, as evidenced by the experience of a number of Latin American countries.

The idea of a stable trade-off between inflation and unemployment is thoroughly discredited: An unexpected acceleration of inflation may temporarily reduce unemployment below its "natural rate," but this effect is short-lived. Only an accelerating inflation could keep unemployment below its natural rate, but even that unappetizing possibility is dubious.[6]

Manipulation of monetary aggregates can influence interest rates only temporarily: As soon as inflationary expectations catch up with reality, the Keynesian "liquidity effect" is replaced by the "Fisher effect," which will more than offset the initial impact of the unexpected change in monetary policy.[7] Nominal interest rates tend to be higher, not lower, when monetary policy is loose.

As for stabilization policies, it is now largely (though certainly not unanimously) agreed that our insufficient knowledge, unreliable short-

6. Milton Friedman, "The Role of Monetary Policy," *The American Economic Review* 58, no. 1, March 1968; *Unemployment* versus *Inflation? An Evaluation of Phillips Curve,* London, The Institute of Economic Affairs, Occasional Paper 44, 1975; *Inflation and Unemployment: The New Dimension of Politics—The 1976 Alfred Nobel Memorial Lecture,* London, The Institute of Economic Affairs, Occasional Papers 51, 1977; Gordon Tullock, "Can You Fool All the People All the Time?" *Journal of Money, Credit and Banking,* May 1972; "Inflation and Unemployment: The Discussion Continued," *Journal of Money, Credit and Banking,* August 1973; Michael D. Bordo and Anna J. Schwartz, "The Importance of Stable Money: Theory and Evidence," *Cato Journal* 3, spring 1983, pp. 63–82, reprinted with modifications in Dorn and Schwartz, 1987, pp. 53–72.

7. Daniel L. Thornton, "The Effects of Monetary Policy on Short-Term Interest Rates," *The Federal Reserve Bank of St. Louis Review,* May–June 1988, pp. 53ff.

run macroeconomic forecasts, and variable time lags in the impact of monetary policy decisions make it likely that policies aimed at stabilizing the short run may end up being procyclical rather than anticyclical. Attempts at "fine-tuning" the economy often result in additional, avoidable instability.[8]

In a sense, EMU can be viewed as a recognition of the liberal position in favor of monetary and fiscal rules: Discretionary monetary policy will be replaced by a firm commitment to price stability on the part of an independent European Central Bank. Debt monetization, by far the single most important cause of price inflation in this and previous centuries, will become impossible. The Treaty explicitly forbids the European Central Bank to come to a defaulter's rescue, i.e., to monetize any country's borrowing.

Not only will member countries be unable to finance government spending through inflation, they will also be bound by a "stability pact" to keep their deficit at less than 3 percent of GDP. Except under unusual recessionary circumstances, violators would face automatic or semiautomatic and massive fines.[9] Should the process succeed, discretionary fiscal policy on the part of national governments would dis-

8. "*Monetarists . . . favor stable policy rules that reduce variability and uncertainty for private decision-makers. They argue that government serves the economy best by enhancing stability and acting predictably, not by trying to engineer carefully timed changes in policy actions which are frequently destabilizing.*" Allan Meltzer, "Is Monetarism Dead?" *National Review,* November 4, 1991, pp. 30–32. See also Milton Friedman, "Commodity-Reserve Currency," *Journal of Political Economy,* 54, June 1951a, 203–32; reprinted in *Essays in Positive Economics,* Chicago, The University of Chicago Press, 1953, pp. 204–50; "Les effets d'une politique de plein emploi sur la stabilité économique: Analyse formelle," *Economie appliquée,* July–December, 1951b, reprinted under the title "The Effects of a Full-Employment Policy on Economic Stability: A Formal Analysis," in *Essays in Positive Economics,* Chicago, The University of Chicago Press, 1953, pp. 441ff.; *Capitalism and Freedom* (1962), Chicago, The University of Chicago Press, 1965; "The Optimum Quantity of Money," in *The Optimum Quantity of Money and Other Essays,* Chicago, Aldine, 1969; Gottfried Haberler, *Economic Growth and Stability. An Analysis of Economic Change and Policies.* Nash Publishing, Los Angeles, 1974; Christina D. Romer, "Is the Stabilization of the Postwar Economy a Figment of the Data?" *The American Economic Review,* June 1986, pp. 314ff.

9. *See* "EMU, And What Alice Found There," *The Economist,* December 14, 1996.

appear. Finally, the adoption of a single European currency would mean the end of arbitrary manipulations of the exchange rate—"exchange rate policy," as it was called, would vanish. In its intentions at least, the Maastricht world is one of strict and impartial rules, a living monument to the liberal wisdom.

This being said, it is surprising that some liberals question not the workability of the plan, but the desirability of its goals—as if restraining arbitrary government in the fields of money and public budgets were incompatible with their ideals. Criticism of EMU—on the part not of die-hard Keynesians, but of well-known advocates of a liberal order—has stressed that constraints on the size of the budget deficit would deprive European countries of much needed automatic fiscal stabilizers. Still others have mourned the end of national stabilization policies, which would condemn our countries to otherwise avoidable instability. Nor have these eccentricities been the privilege of a few lunatics.[10] The same arguments have been used by American economists, which is surprising. None of them, as far as I know, has ever advocated that each state in the United States should have its own currency, be free to run large budget deficits, be allowed to monetize its debt, and manipulate the exchange rate in its dealings with the other forty-nine states!

It could be argued that it is not acceptable to compare the United States, a politically united and economically homogeneous country, with the European Union, a collection of different and heterogeneous sovereign states. However, if the discretionary manipulation of money and public budgets is considered harmful, even sovereign and independent countries could only benefit from the adoption of fiscal and monetary rules that would put an end to the follies of the past.

The Maastricht plan of monetary unification deserves criticism, but it seems to me ironic that we should criticize it because it puts an end to the political manipulation of money, deficits, and exchange rates. It may be argued, however, that the Maastricht constraints are too much of a good thing, that countries with very different economic circum-

10. The eccentrics are thus defined by *The Economist:* "Britain's minds-of-oak Eurosceptics, who think EMU, however conceived, is a foreign plot to enslave them." See "The Wrong Design," *The Economist,* December 14, 1996, p. 13.

stances need diverse monetary policies. (Which brings to mind one of the innumerable Titanic stories: "Leaning against a bar on the Titanic after disaster had struck, John Jacob Astor is supposed to have said, 'I asked for ice, but this is ridiculous.'")

The fiscal constraints of EMU must be criticized not because they are undesirable—in my view they are a necessary component of a liberal order—but because they are clearly ineffective. This is amply evidenced by the "creative accounting" gimmickry used by many countries to achieve the required deficit-to-GDP ratio of 3 percent, and by the immediate abandonment of fiscal prudence by some countries, notably Italy, as soon as they were included in the euro-eleven club.

Also, it is undeniable that fiscal convergence is neither a necessary nor a sufficient condition for monetary unification. The most indebted country in the European Union (Belgium) and the least indebted (Luxembourg) have had the same currency for a very long time. Many countries in the world have similar financial conditions and keep having different currencies.

Which brings us to the main point of my argument: The real goal of those constraints was that of reassuring markets that the new currency was going to be reliable. As shown by opinion polls, this goal has not been accomplished: A substantial percentage of European public opinion is very skeptical of the euro. Their skepticism is entirely justified, because, as I shall mention later, EMU offers no credible monetary constitution, no effective constraints on the discretionary powers of the European Central Bank.

The Risk of Rejection

Even if we assume that the advantages are real and important, they are not likely to be achieved by the Maastricht strategy, which furthermore implies very serious risks. Let me illustrate.

The basic flaw in the game plan is that the euro is a *fiduciary* currency, which is introduced *coercively*. In other words, the value of the euro depends on the trust it commands on the part of those who will be asked to use it. Since the new currency will be imposed on both those who trust it and those who don't, there is the clear danger of a rejection—as opinion surveys amply suggest.

Let me illustrate. Money resembles language: It conveys information. As in the case of language—most people are proficient in only one language—we tend to think in terms of *one* unit of account, ours.[11] Whenever we are abroad in a country using a different currency, we experience, at least at the beginning, a marked difficulty in understanding the meaning of prices expressed in the foreign currency. People are much better off with one yardstick, one unit of measurement—in fact, that's the very reason why they have a unit of measurement in the first place. As you well know, converting all the time from feet and inches to meters and centimeters gets to be annoying, useless, and time consuming. In all likelihood, therefore, most people would prefer to continue thinking in terms of the currency they've always used. What I mean is that, as in the case of language, in the use of money there is a considerable amount of inertia:[12] People don't ask themselves which is the most effective language for communicating with others, they just pick up the language spoken in the area where they grow up. And, once they have learned it, they continue to use it without even asking themselves if it is the most convincing language available. This is because in most cases the cost of learning a superior language (whatever that means) outweighs the benefits. At least in the short run (as measured in decades, if not centuries), therefore, people stick to the language they already know. The same is true of money: Almost forty years after the monetary reform in France, many people still think in terms of the old franc rather than the new one.

Things, of course, would be made considerably worse if there were doubts about the stability and reliability of the new currency. Let's suppose, for example, that German savers, not trusting the euro, decide to take their savings into a currency they know and trust (say, the Swiss franc, the British pound, or the U.S. dollar). The potential "flight from the euro" would likely result in an increase in interest rates, with disastrous consequences for countries like Italy that base their hopes of fiscal balance on a reduction of interest rates. The resulting increase in budget deficits would present a dilemma for European

11. Phillip Cagan, "Competitive Monies: Some Unanswered Questions," *Cato Journal* 5, no. 3, winter 1986, 943–47.

12. See Bordo and Schwartz, *op. cit.*, 1987.

policy makers: They could either increase taxation, thereby making the recession worse, or they could agree to abandon the stability pact, thereby making it possible to regress to the old fiscal folly. Considering the political climate in continental Europe, with a prevalence of socialist governments, it is likely, if not probable, that the initial excess of fiscal orthodoxy will quickly leave room to old-fashioned budgetary extravagance.

Instability and Conflict

Even without a potential flight from the euro, the inauguration of EMU seems to possess all the ingredients for a major recession: At least at the beginning, monetary policy will have to be restrictive, in order to make the new currency accepted by markets; fiscal policy of the Keynesian type will be almost impossible if the stability pact holds; labor markets in continental Europe are notoriously more rigid than elsewhere; and, finally, if the euro is accepted, it might appreciate in relation to other currencies. I know of no economist who would deny that those circumstances can result in a serious slowdown, if not an extensive contraction in economic activity and employment.

Also, European countries have very different growth rates, wage dynamics, labor-market flexibility, and productive structures: To think that a "one-size-fits-all" monetary policy can accommodate these differences is naive. More likely, there will be sharp differences of opinion as to which kind of monetary policy is best under the circumstances: Economists in different countries may suggest very different courses of action. It would be very surprising if these differences do not translate themselves into political conflict. Even if one does not go as far as Martin Feldstein, who predicts that the single currency will result in open confrontation,[13] there is no doubt that, contrary to what is maintained by supporters of EMU, its introduction is likely to make the participating countries less rather than more united. These conflicts would be especially acute in the case of "asymmetric shocks" that af-

13. Martin Feldstein, "EMU and International Conflict," *Foreign Affairs,* November–December 1997, pp. 60–73.

fect the eleven countries in different ways, requiring diverse responses in each of them.[14]

The ECB's Accountability and the Need for Rules

Monetary union in Europe is capable of being good, bad or indifferent. All depends on precisely how it is done. "European Monetary Union," The Economist, *June 24, 1989*

At the bottom of these problems lies the very unsatisfactory institutional arrangements regarding the European Central Bank (ECB). To say that the ECB is "independent" presumably means that it does not have to yield to pressures coming from national governments. However, this does not guarantee that in fact the ECB will resist the demands of national governments. Also, those demands are likely to be contradictory—one country asking for a more expansionary and another for a more prudent course of action. It's not inconceivable that the "weight" of the country will play a role in the ECB's decision on which kind of policy to adopt. In other words, it is misleading to say that the eleven countries are surrendering their monetary sovereignty "to Europe"—they are in fact surrendering it to the most influential country in the group.[15]

Furthermore, the more important question concerns not the ECB's independence, but its accountability. Considering the enormous powers bestowed on it, it is astonishing that ECB's officials are responsible only to God for their behavior.

The preoccupations with the issue of monetary sovereignty are entirely justified: Money matters and, as Milton Friedman has often repeated, it is too important to be left to central bankers. The reasons that make us worry about monetary management by national central bankers are even more valid when referred to a single currency for Europe. Monetary mismanagement on a national level can be a dis-

14. See, for example, Josef Joffe, "The Euro: A Huge, Dangerous Gamble for Europe," *Herald Tribune,* May 2–3, 1998.

15. The institutional problem in the EU is not limited to the ECB. There is a general, and undesirable, tendency toward centralization. See Roland Vaubel, *The Centralization of Western Europe,* IEA Hobart Paper 127, London, 1995.

aster; On a European level it would be a catastrophe of unbearable proportions.[16]

The problem arises because, with the end of the gold standard, money, in addition to its traditional functions, has become an instrument of discretionary policy to an extent that was inconceivable before. As previously mentioned, discretionary manipulation of monetary aggregates on the part of independent central banks can produce procyclical rather than anticyclical consequences. Instead of achieving a higher degree of stability, monetary policy becomes an autonomous source of instability.[17]

16. *In a monetary union the design of the central authority is crucial. It must be the anchor against inflation that gold was in the gold standard and the D-mark is in the present EMS. An EMU under a badly run European central bank would be much worse than the EMS under the well-run Bundesbank. In setting up the new central bank a balance would have to be struck between accountability and independence.* "From A to EMU," *The Economist,* June 24, 1989, p. 20.

17. It is not enough, in other words, to say that empirical evidence does not support the view that stabilization policies have in fact had a stabilizing effect on the economy (Romer, 1986); the problem is that empirical evidence suggests that they may have had a *de*stabilizing effect. According to Friedman:

> Anna Schwartz and I have examined the cyclical behavior of the quantity of money in the United States for the whole period since 1867. Throughout that period monetary growth has risen and fallen not with but before economic activity. The cyclical peak of monetary growth regularly precedes the cyclical peak of economic activity by an interval that varies a great deal, but on average is something like six to nine months; the cyclical trough of monetary growth regularly precedes the cyclical trough of economic activity by an average interval of roughly the same length. Moreover, sizable monetary accelerations and decelerations tend to be followed by sizable expansions and contractions in economic activity; modest accelerations and decelerations, by modest expansions and contractions. . . . The evidence is clear: variability in the rate of monetary growth is associated with variability in economic growth. High monetary variability accompanies high economic variability, and vice versa. . . . The Federal Reserve has sought to use monetary policy to stabilize the economy—that is, to vary monetary growth in order to offset forces introducing disturbances into the economy. Had it succeeded, high monetary variability would have been associated with low economic variability, not with high economic variability. The correlations between the moving standard deviations that we have calculated would have been negative or zero, rather than systematically positive. The implication is again that monetary variability

This in no way implies incompetence on the part of the monetary authorities: Even the most competent central banker does not possess all the knowledge that would be required to make a discretionary anticyclical monetary policy succeed. Information about the working of our macroeconomic systems are inadequate; short-term predictions are seldom sufficiently reliable; decisions may be untimely, and lags in the effects of monetary changes are largely unknown in advance.[18]

In any case, the outcome of discretionary monetary policy in terms of increased economic instability, already harmful at the national level, would be disastrous at the European level. A common currency for Europe would be desirable if its adoption meant an end of discretionary short-term policy. Should European nations agree on some kind of monetary constitution, making discretionary manipulation of monetary aggregates impossible, a common currency for Europe would greatly increase overall stability both in Europe and in the world. One could think of a rule fixing the rate of growth of some monetary aggregate to a predetermined level and mandating its continuation for an extended period of time (say, three to five years).

The adoption of a monetary rule would be highly desirable per se if it would eliminate the variability of monetary growth, with its accompanying economic instability and uncertainty. It would also be the solution for the creation of a common currency for Europe. All

---

has been a source of economic variability, not an offset.—Milton Friedman, "Monetary Policy for the 1980s," in *To Promote Prosperity, U.S. Domestic Policy in the Mid-1980s,* ed. John Moore, Hoover Institution, Stanford University, 1984, pp. 33–34.

18. "A common criticism of policymaking is that economists and policymakers do not know enough about how the economy functions to have a model that describes accurately the behavior of macroeconomic variables like real GNP and the price level. In this case, it has been argued that policy action based on a flawed or incomplete model might cause more harm than good." Michael D. Bradley and Dennis W. Jansen, "Understanding Nominal GNP Targeting," *The Federal Reserve Bank of St. Louis Review,* 71, no. 6, November–December 1989, p. 37. As a result, "one cannot be confident that relaxing . . . constraints on discretionary policymaking will bring a net social benefit." Leijonhufvud, 1987, p. 131.

the justified worries about the surrender of national monetary sovereignty to a (politically irresponsible) European Central Bank would lose meaning if money were entrusted to predetermined (and agreed-upon) rigid rules rather than to the whim of policy makers possessing discretionary power. Furthermore, if the chosen rule were credible, it would reassure markets and eliminate the risk of rejection. In any case, if monetary rules are necessary at the national level, they are essential at the European level.[19]

Choice Rather than Coercion

By far the most effective method to prevent the risk of rejection and to automatically guarantee the ECB's responsible conduct would be to introduce the common currency in a noncoercive way. In other words, Europe should give up the idea of having a *single* currency abruptly replacing national moneys, and opt for a *common* currency competing with national currencies. Suppose the European Union decided to create its own currency, and allowed all member countries to choose whether to replace their national currency with the European one or to allow their citizens to use one or the other, as they think best. Most large countries would probably choose the latter solution, and a monetary constitution, based on currency competition, would rule. The different monetary instruments would compete against each other, and, if the rates at which they exchanged for one another were flexible and continuously determined by the market, a virtuous circle would be established by a "Gresham's law" in reverse, which would lead to the elimination of the less-stable currencies in favor of the more-stable ones.

A common—unlike a single—currency could be introduced in a

19. Moreover, the argument against binding rules that they are "undemocratic" because they prevent "*elected officials from responding as best they can to the wishes of the electorate*" obviously does not apply to the case of Europe. See Axel Leijonhufvud, "Constitutional Constraints on the Monetary Powers of Government," in *The Search for Stable Money, Essays on Monetary Reform,* James A. Dorn and Anna J. Schwartz, eds., University of Chicago Press, Chicago and London, 1987, pp. 129–43, for a criticism of such an argument.

noncoercive, voluntary way: There would be no risk of rejection. The action of the ECB would be effectively constrained by competition. The common currency would gain acceptance only if it proved to be stable and reliable. There would be no conflict over the choice of monetary policy goals. The single market would not disintegrate. This—a variation on the English "hard ecu" proposal—should have been the way to go. As things stand today, there is the real danger of monetary instability, followed by the disintegration of Europe.[20]

Conclusion

In the words of a German commentator, "the euro is more than a gamble. Living with the straitjacket of economic sovereignty forgone, Europe must part with its cherished statist and corporatist traditions; it must unleash the market and allow wage flexibility and geographic mobility to carry the brunt of adjustment."[21] However, that's not what a socialist-dominated Europe is likely to do. Many supporters of EMU on the left of the political spectrum would agree with Milton Friedman: "money can be a potent tool for controlling and shaping the economy. Its potency . . . is exemplified . . . by the extent to which control over money has always been a potent means of exacting taxes from the populace at large, very often without the explicit agreement of the legislature."[22] For them, EMU is one step in the direction of a more rigidly controlled economy; they are unlikely to accept greater reliance on market discipline in return for the advantages of a common currency.

20. For an early analysis of a voluntary, common currency scheme, see Roland Vaubel, *Choice in European Monetary Union,* The Institute of Economic Affairs, Occasional Paper 55, London, January 1979. Also, by the same author, "Currency Competition versus Governmental Money Monopolies," in *Cato Journal,* winter 1986, pp. 927–42.

21. J. Joffe, *op. cit.*

22. M. Friedman, "Should There Be an Independent Monetary Authority?" in *In Search of a Monetary Constitution,* Leland B. Yeager, ed., Harvard University Press, Cambridge, Mass., 1962, reprinted in *Dollars and Deficits, Inflation, Monetary Policy and the Balance of Payments,* Prentice-Hall, Englewood Cliffs, 1968, p. 174.

For these reasons, I dare criticize EMU in a country, like Italy, where 80 percent of public opinion and 90 percent of the establishment are passionately in favor of it. I don't mind the insults,[23] and take comfort in the words of Cardinal Suenens: "if one turns a light on in the dark, one is likely to get mosquitoes"!

23. For example, my views have been dismissed as "totally senseless" by Alain Minc, *Corriere della sera,* December 5, 1994; I have been accused of having destroyed the international credibility of the lira by Massimo Riva, *L'Espresso,* March 24, 1995; Romano Prodi, our present prime minister, has graciously called me "the only anti-European Italian," *Corriere della sera,* May 4, 1995; the leader of the former Communist party, Massimo D'Alema, and the minister of Defense, Beniamino Andreatta, have accused me of anti-Europeanism, *La Stampa,* December 6, 1995; and even conservative commentators seem convinced that my criticism of EMU explains the center-right defeat in the 1996 political elections.

A Monetary Constitution for Ex-Communist Countries

1. The Case for a Monetary Constitution

The importance of monetary stability derives from the significant independent influence of monetary change on the subsequent course of economic activity. If money did not matter at all or were of only secondary importance in affecting the flow of spending, income, and prices, monetary stability would be of little relevance. —*Bordo and Schwartz, 1983*

After the interlude of the Keynesian revolution, monetary stability has been restored to its status as an important policy goal (Dorn, 1987). The experience of the 1970s and 1980s and the theoretical works that have accompanied it have helped dispose of most Keynesian ideas on money and monetary policy. From the point of view of its importance, price stability has reacquired the position it held in pre-Keynesian times, when it was believed that a stable purchasing power of money was a necessary precondition for a free and prosperous economy.

In a Keynesian world, price stability is not necessarily desirable. Most Keynesians were convinced that inflation was the unavoidable price of economic growth, that there was a stable trade-off between inflation and unemployment, that it was possible to reduce interest rates through monetary expansion, and that the time horizon for monetary policy decisions had to be dictated by the needs of short-term stabilization policies. All of these views have succumbed to the empirical evidence and the theoretical analyses of the last twenty years.

There is no evidence that economic growth inevitably involves price inflation. On the contrary, there are good reasons to believe that

Originally published in *Cato Journal* 12, no. 3, winter 1993, pp. 533–55, and reprinted with permission.

monetary instability hinders long-term projects and makes economic growth more difficult, as evidenced by the experience of a number of Latin American countries.

The idea of a stable trade-off between inflation and unemployment is thoroughly discredited: An unexpected acceleration of inflation may temporarily reduce unemployment below its natural rate, but this effect is short-lived. Only an accelerating inflation could keep unemployment below its natural rate, but even that unappetizing possibility is dubious (Friedman, 1968, 1975, 1977; Bordo and Schwartz, 1983).

Manipulation of monetary aggregates can influence interest rates only temporarily: As soon as inflationary expectations catch up with reality, the Keynesian "liquidity effect" is replaced by the "Fisher effect," which will more than offset the initial impact of the unexpected change in monetary policy (Thornton, 1988). Nominal interest rates tend to be higher, not lower, when monetary policy is loose.

As for stabilization policies, it is now largely (though certainly not unanimously) agreed that our insufficient knowledge, unreliable short-run macroeconomic forecasts, and variable time lags in the impact of monetary policy decisions make it likely that policies aimed at stabilizing the short run may end up being procyclical rather than anticyclical. Attempts at "fine-tuning" the economy often result in additional, avoidable instability (Friedman, 1951a, 1953, 1965, 1969; Haberler, 1974; Meltzer, 1991).[1]

For these reasons, the old pre-Keynesian wisdom that monetary stability is a necessary (though by no means sufficient) condition for economic progress has again acquired widespread popularity. Price stability may not be a cure-all, but, while there is no long-lasting benefit to be gained from the instability of the price level, this may in itself be the cause of serious economic problems.

In other words, the post-Keynesian "counterrevolution" has resulted in the abandonment of money as an instrument of (discretion-

1. "Monetarists . . . favor stable policy rules that reduce variability and uncertainty for private decision makers. They argue that government serves the economy best by enhancing stability and acting predictably, not by trying to engineer carefully timed changes in policy actions which are frequently destabilizing." H. A. Meltzer, 1991, p. 31.

ary) policy, limiting its role to its three traditional functions as unit of account, medium of exchange, and store of value or "temporary abode of purchasing power," to use Milton Friedman's felicitous expression.

I mention these well-known facts because if monetary stability were not desirable, if discretionary (and erratic) monetary policy were advantageous, the whole subject of a monetary constitution would lose its meaning. It can be argued that monetary stability is even more important for a country in transition from central planning to the market. In such a country, the amount of long-term investment projects is unusually large: Infrastructures need to be built, obsolete plants and equipment need to be replaced by economically viable ones, the remains of the follies of planning must be removed to make room for the new structures (Jordan, 1991; Hanks and Schuler, 1991). Building a market economy from scratch requires confidence in the future and long-term investment plans; both need a stable money. All the more so since the reconstruction will inevitably need the participation of foreign investors, who are certainly not encouraged by countries with dismal records of monetary performance.

The lesson for policymakers in ex-communist countries is simple enough: Money must be regarded as an integral part of the institutional framework—monetary stability being one of the rules of the game—and not as an instrument of policy. The transition involves transferring from the arbitrary decisions of authorities to the market the most fundamental task of any economic system: that of directing resources to their most productive uses. However, for the price system to perform that task satisfactorily, prices must not send wrong signals; that is, inflationary "static" must not interfere with the working of prices. That's why price stability, always a precious commodity, is of paramount importance for the transition process of ex-communist countries.

Finally, it is not enough for prices to be stable; their stability must also be regarded as long lasting, not as a transient and accidental phenomenon. When people plan for the distant future, the expected behavior of prices matters more than past behavior (Leijonhufvud, 1987). The argument for price stability, in other words, must be complemented with the case for the *credibility* of a policy of stability. It's not enough that prices are stable, they must also be expected to remain stable. It is here that the need for a monetary constitution comes in. *The monetary constitution must not be designed for the transition, must not be intended to last only for a limited time, but it must explicitly aim at guaranteeing price stability for an indefinite duration.* There is no need, in other words, for special monetary arrangements aimed at easing up the transition process and destined to be replaced by other rules once the transition is completed. The commitment to monetary stability must be intended and interpreted to be a permanent one, so as to encourage long-term projects and earn the confidence of domestic and foreign investors.

1.1 THE TRANSITION

That a monetary arrangement guaranteeing price stability for the indefinite future should be the ultimate aim of reformers in ex-communist countries can be more easily agreed upon than what the transitional path to stability should be. It has been argued that a disinflationary policy adopted before the privatization of the economy has been completed could have serious drawbacks and be doomed to fail. If a monetary squeeze replaces present inflationary tendencies, the effect on the reallocation of resources may not be as successful as it would be in a market economy. In a country where resources are privately owned and markets are allowed to operate, the slowdown induced by a monetary squeeze is likely to be temporary and its effects to be compensated by efficiency gains as resources are more rationally allocated. In a still collectivized economy, it can be argued that such a reallocation of resources is unlikely to take place, so that the monetary squeeze will affect "most the smaller and more privatized entities . . . rather than the politically protected large state owned enterprises" (Walters, 1991, p. 41). Rather than diverting resources toward more productive uses, the disinflation would hurt the small productive units and discourage new initiatives. Furthermore, "the squeeze devastates the SOE's (state owned enterprises) profits and since much of central government revenue is derived from the surpluses, there is a catastrophic fall in government revenue, which . . . will induce monetary expansion to fill the gaps . . . which in turn generates a new wave of inflation" (Walters, ibid.).

Such an analysis is probably too catastrophic. Taken literally, it would appear to suggest that an inflationary monetary policy, by inflating the SOE's profits and hence the government revenue, would be . . . a precondition for a reduction in the government deficit and a slower rate of monetary expansion. In order to bring the inflation down, one must first conduct an inflationary policy! Aside from this paradox, the fact remains that if the economy is not privatized there is no transition. As long as there is no market, the problem is that of defining the ideal monetary policy *for a command economy*. Furthermore, even assuming that the pessimistic evaluation is justified, what is the alternative? The continuation of the old inflationary policy would not make the transition simpler, it would solve no problem, and it would add difficulties of its own making to an already tragic situation. This is why in what follows I shall assume that we are talking about countries that are really moving from plan to market, where privatization is being achieved on a large scale, new markets are continuously coming into existence, and prices are freed from administrative control. If, on the other hand, aside from market-talk, nothing is being done in the real economy to allow the price system to work, markets to be formed, and private property to be securely established, monetary arrangements become secondary: there are no monetary gimmicks which can make a semiparalyzed, near-command economy prosperous and successful.

I shall not, therefore, make any distinction between monetary arrangements for the initial stages of the transition and those for the final steps. My point is that discretionary monetary policy is seldom useful and often harmful, and this is true in a market economy, in an economy in transition from plan to market, and even in a planned economy. What we have learned in the past twenty years is that manipulating monetary aggregates on a daily or weekly basis will solve no problem and it might add to the overall instability of the economy. From an a priori point of view the ideal rate of inflation may not be zero,[2] but nobody has suggested a better number yet.

2. "Proposals for monetary reform usually assume that the public prefers a noninflationary rate of monetary growth. This may be true, but it has not been demonstrated. Nor has it been shown that the rate of inflation that maximizes wealth, or the utility of wealth and private consumption, is identically zero." H. A. Meltzer, 1983, 1987, p. 204.

2. *What Kind of Monetary Constitution?*

The argument in favor of a monetary constitution in general[3] and for the ex-communist countries in particular leaves us with the problem of choosing the specific set of rules to be adopted. Now, it is indeed more important to agree on the need for rigid rules that to agree on the particular rule to adopt (Buchanan, 1983).[4] However, as long as supporters of monetary constitutions widely disagree on what kind of rules must replace the present discretionary conduct of monetary policy, they are unlikely to make theirs a convincing case. I shall, therefore, look at some of the monetary constitutions that have been (tried or) proposed and attempt to single out their advantages and drawbacks, in the effort of finding out an arrangement suitable for the ex-communist countries.

2.1 GOLD

The oldest form of monetary constitution is the gold standard, which can still count on many advocates.[5]

Supporters of gold believe that a gold-backed currency would severely limit the discretion of monetary authorities and the power of

3. "An enterprise system cannot function effectively in the face of extreme uncertainty as to the action of monetary authorities." H. C. Simons, 1936. Also: "Unless we can get an effective change in monetary regimes, we cannot expect our politicians or our central bankers to resolve the incipient stagflation dilemma. Until and unless we begin to take the long-term perspective in our private and in our public capacities, including the adoption of new and binding constitutional constraints on the fiscal and monetary powers of government, we are doomed to remain mired in the muck of modern politics." J. M. Buchanan, 1983.

4. The "debate-discussion (on monetary reform) is prematurely joined when we start referring to the advantages and disadvantages of this or that rule, this or that regime . . . But, prior to this discussion, we should try to attain consensus on the need for 'some' alternative regime that will embody greater predictability than the unconstrained monetary authority that describes that which now exists" (p. 124).

5. For a vigorous debate on the pros and cons of a return to gold, see, for example, A. H. Meltzer and A. Reynolds, 1982.

government to debauch the currency for political purposes.[6] On the other hand, critics of the gold standard maintain that historically its performance was not as good as its supporters claim.[7]

The trouble with gold, as emphasized by Friedman's classical work (1951b, 1961), is that there is an enormous difference between a 100 percent gold standard, a "real" gold standard in which gold is used as money, and a "pseudo" gold standard, in which money is linked to gold through governmental fixing of its price.[8] Furthermore, if a 100 percent gold standard is destined to evolve into a fractional reserve system (Meiselman, 1983), then it is fair to conclude that the monetary arrangement which would result from adopting the gold anchor would be exposed to the kind of monetary instability which has been typical of fractional reserve systems, with bank panics and the like (Cagan, 1987).

However, the historical evidence on the performance of gold is mixed and far from conclusive. For example, Italian history from 1845 to 1915 seems to support the case for gold. The gold standard was the ruling monetary system from the beginning of "Risorgimento"—the process by which Italy became unified and the preunitarian states were dissolved—until World War I erupted. Those were years of great transformations, comparable in scope, even though not in direction, to what is going on in the ex-communist countries. It may be more than a historical curiosity to see how this early type of monetary constitution performed.

6. "Gold convertibility served a purpose. If we are to re-establish some kind of rule, it has to be one that is credible, that people will believe. It has to be one that is difficult to violate. And . . . that has to be a gold standard of some sort." A. Reynolds, 1982.

7. "Countries had price stability even though they violated the gold standard rules frequently. Some countries didn't have price stability even though they stayed on the gold standard. . . . A guarantee of what? A guarantee of the price of gold. That's all that's guaranteed by the gold standard. . . . Efficient at what? Efficient at telling us about the price of gold. I don't believe the gold standard solves the problems of modern economy adequately." A. H. Meltzer, 1982.

8. Friedman regards only a real gold standard "as constituting an improvement rather than a deterioration in our monetary arrangements." M. Friedman, 1984.

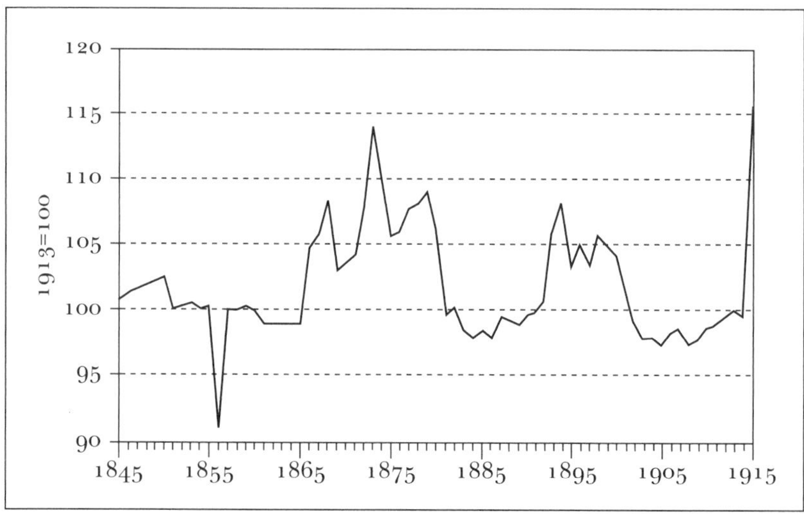

FIGURE 1. *Italy: The Price of Gold, 1845–1915*
Source: Banca d'Italia

From 1845 to 1915, the nominal price of gold was not perfectly stable, but it fluctuated year in and year out, periods of stability being followed by sharp decreases or increases (see Figure 1). Moreover, the *real* price of gold fluctuated along a declining trend until the unification was completed (1871), and it continued to swing along a fairly stable trend until the start of World War I (see Figure 2). During those 70 years, consumer prices were not stable: the unification was accompanied by inflation, followed by deflation, then stability, and finally moderate inflation in the first decade and a half of the twentieth century (see Figure 3).

However, if one looks at the gold-standard years in a historical perspective, there is no question that in terms of price stability those were years of unrivaled success (Figure 4). If the yardstick by which one measures the success of a monetary standard is price-level stability, the gold-standard period, on the basis of this circumstantial evidence, was superior to any other time in Italy's history.[9] One can question whether

9. For a comprehensive analysis of Italy's monetary history see F. Spinelli and M. Fratianni, 1991.

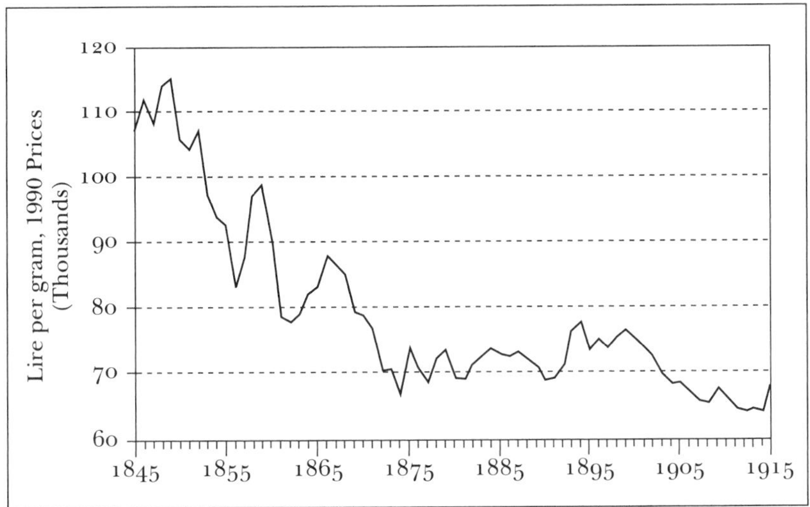

FIGURE 2. *Italy: Real Price of Gold, 1845–1915*
Source: Banca d'Italia

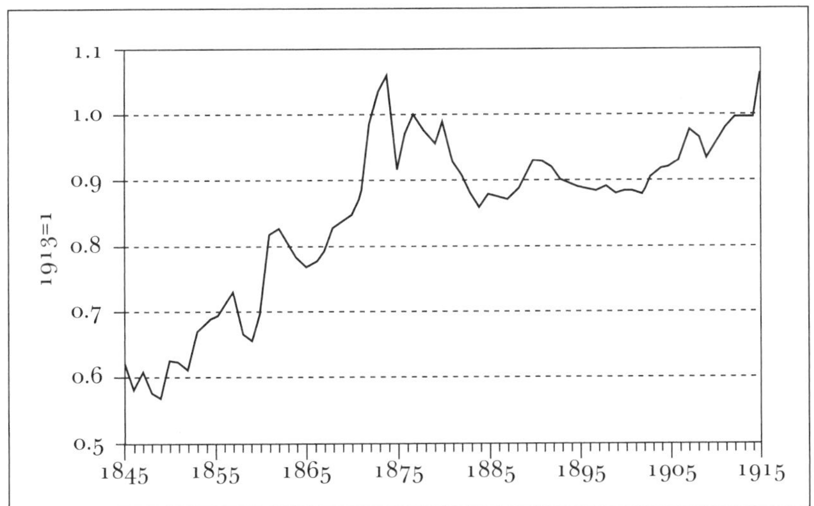

FIGURE 3. *Italy: Consumer Price Index, 1845–1915*
Source: ISTAT, Banca d'Italia

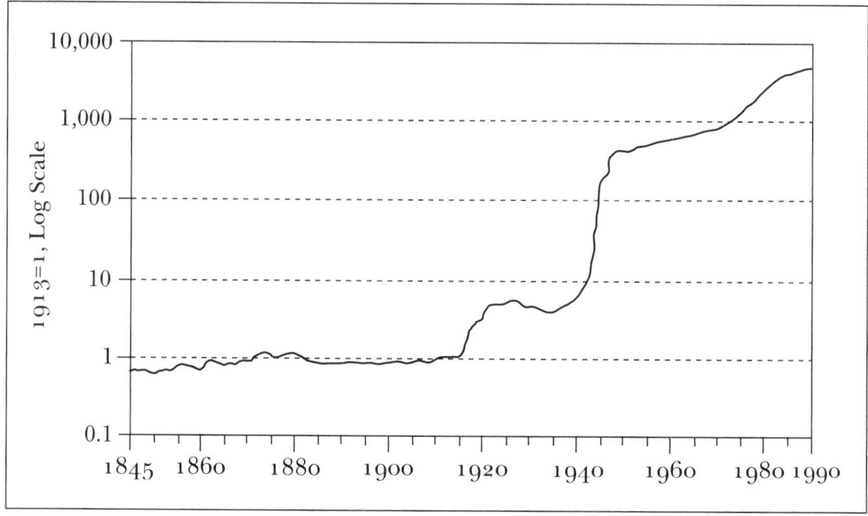

FIGURE 4. *Italy: Consumer Price Index, 1845–1990*
Source: ISTAT, Banca d'Italia

this outcome is entirely attributable to the gold anchor or not, but it is a fact that those were the most stable in the past 145 years of Italian history.

The obvious answer to the apparent contradiction in the evaluation of the performance of gold is that it is better to have some kind of monetary constitution limiting the discretionary powers of monetary authorities, no matter how imperfect, than to have no constitution at all. The gold standard was far from perfect, and it is doubtful whether it could provide us with an answer to today's problems, but it has proven, at least in the case of Italy, to be better than a purely discretionary regime.[10]

10. Almost all academic economists are convinced that the gold standard does not provide an answer to today's problems. See, for example, G. Haberler, 1974. "The gold standard broke down with the outbreak of the war in 1914. It was superficially restored in the early 1920s but was definitely swept away and abandoned in the Great Depression. There is now no chance that it will be resurrected" (p. 162).

2.2 CURRENCY COMPETITION

Following a famous proposal by Friedrich A. Hayek (1976), a more radical kind of monetary reform has received considerable attention: the privatization of money. Different monetary instruments would be offered by competitive suppliers, and, if the rates at which they exchanged for one another were flexible and continuously determined by the market, a virtuous circle would be established by a "Gresham's law" in reverse, which would lead to the elimination of the less-stable currencies in favor of the more-stable ones.

It is beyond the scope of this paper to go into the details of the various proposals.[11] I shall limit myself to looking at competing currencies as a monetary constitution which could be adopted by ex-communist countries. Let me make it clear that I am convinced that choice in currency is an important component of freedom in general and a desirable feature of a truly free society (Friedman, 1991). However, I believe that there are various reasons, aside from political feasibility, which make private competitive currencies unsuited as a monetary constitution for ex-communist countries.

The first, and possibly most important, function of money is to be a unit of account, allowing prices to be expressed in a single measuring unit. The simplification money introduces in economic calculations is enormous.[12] Money prices transmit information (Friedman, 1984b) and allow markets to perform their function of information-retrieval systems (Hayek, 1945). As such, money resembles language: It conveys information. As in the case of language—most people are proficient in only one language—we tend to think in terms of one unit of account (Cagan, 1986). Whenever we are abroad in a country using a different currency, we experience, at least at the beginning, a marked difficulty in understanding the meaning of prices expressed in the foreign currency. This is to say that it would be costly to think in terms of two or

11. For an excellent presentation of the argument for competing currencies, see R. Vaubel, 1986.

12. Instead of having n prices for n commodities, without money the number of prices would be $T = 0.5\ n(n-1)$. In a world of 1,000 commodities, instead of 1,000 money prices there would be 499,500 "real" prices. R. A. Mundell, 1968, pp. 45–46.

more currencies all the time, especially if—as required by the logic of competition—their exchange rate would vary continuously.[13] People are much better off with one yardstick, one unit of measurement—in fact, that's the very reason why they have a unit of measurement in the first place. Converting all the time from meters and centimeters to feet and inches gets to be annoying, useless, and time consuming. In all likelihood, therefore, most people would prefer thinking in terms of only one currency, and competition between currencies would be severely limited. On a priori grounds, this objection would seem to carry particular weight in countries where people have very limited experience with the working of prices and markets.

Secondly, according to the logic of competing currencies, competition favors the most stable one, thereby creating an incentive for the money suppliers to make sure their currency is not rejected because of its instability. Yet stability does not seem to be the only criterion for success in currency competition: the U.S. dollar is not the most stable currency in the world, yet most international transactions are conducted in dollars. Other factors play a role in the competition of currencies. One is the well-known one of the size of the domestic market. Like language, whose usefulness increases with the number of people speaking it, the importance of a given currency increases with the number of people using it. Its acceptability tends to be self-reinforcing: The greater the number of people who already use it, the more likely it is that it will become acceptable to others, largely without regard to its past performance. The Swiss franc may be more stable than the U.S. dollar, but the fact that the number of people using the Swiss franc is smaller makes people prefer to use the dollar. In short, currency competition is likely to be imperfect and unlikely to act as a filter mechanism in favor of the most stable currency.

Finally, as in the case of language, in the choice and use of money there is a considerable amount of inertia (Bordo and Schwartz, 1987):

13. "If the money issued by different banks competed freely in the market, the result would be either the emergence of a private monopoly or oligopoly of money creation, or the circulation, side by side, of several kinds of money with fluctuating exchange rates between them. Either one of these outcomes would be intolerable. The immediate result would be to bring the government back into the business of money creation." G. Haberler, 1987, p. 80.

People don't ask themselves which is the most effective language for communicating with others, they just pick up the language spoken in the area where they grow up. And, once they have learned it, they continue to use it without even asking themselves whether it is the most convincing language available. This is because in most cases the cost of learning a superior language (whatever that means) outweighs the benefits. At least in the short run (as measured in decades, if not centuries), therefore, people stick to the language they already know. The same is true of money: The dollar may be a monetary instrument superior to the Italian lira, but when I am in the United States I always translate prices from dollars into lire to understand their real meaning. Currency competition is more a notion for theoretical economists that a realistic proposal for monetary reform, especially in countries where monetary sophistication is limited.

2.3 A MONETARY GROWTH RULE

The third kind of monetary constitution is the well-known one of a constant monetary growth rule (Friedman 1959, 1969).[14]

The logic of this proposal is well known and it need not be repeated here. In one form or another it is accepted by nearly all monetarists.

I am still convinced that Friedman's monetary rule would offer a superior monetary arrangement in most circumstances. However, we must acknowledge the fact that (at least in a legislated form) it has never really been tried and that, in Friedman's own words, even in the United States "the Fed has been unable or unwilling to achieve such a target, even when it sets it itself, and that it has been able to plead inability and thereby avoid accountability" (1984). This poses a major

14. See also: "Proponents of stable monetary policy have studied the quality of specific rules. If central banks would concentrate on keeping the money supply on the path they have committed themselves to they would provide a public good: price level stability. Such a predictable policy would, as empirical evidence shows, contribute to a stable development of overall demand, a result which has not been achieved by the discretionary policies actually pursued in industrial countries. It would eliminate a great deal of the price variations on financial markets about which many observers complain so much." E. Langfeldt, J. Scheide, and P. Trapp, 1989, p. 40. I have argued that a monetary growth rule would be the ideal arrangement for Europe should the EEC adopt a common currency. A. Martino, 1990.

problem to supporters of this type of monetary constitution: If even the monetary authorities of the country where the case for Friedman's rule is known best (the United States) have been unable or unwilling to enforce it, what likelihood is there that it might be given a chance in countries where its significance is less understood and appreciated?[15]

The unpleasant conclusion of the previous considerations is that, for one reason or another, none of the major types of monetary constitutions that have so far been proposed appears immune to criticism. The gold standard would have the advantage of simplicity and credibility, but in its fractional version it would be exposed to crisis, it would not necessarily guarantee economic stability, and it would not be self-enforcing: Monetary authorities might decide to go off gold whenever they deemed it necessary.[16] A monetary constitution based on competing currencies has the enormous advantage of not being dependent on

15. Friedman himself has been forced to acknowledge: "I remain persuaded that a monetary rule that leads to a predictable long-run path of a specified monetary aggregate is a highly desirable goal superior either to discretionary control of the quantity of money by a set of monetary authorities or to a commodity standard. However, I am no longer so optimistic as I once was that it can be effected by either persuading the monetary authorities to follow it or legislating its adoption" (1984).

16. In the case of gold there is an additional difficulty. While a gold-backed currency would be ideal in terms of its credibility for countries that are beginning to try to come out of the communist mess, and despite the enormous mining potentialities of the C.I.S. (formerly U.S.S.R.), golden reserves, according to the latest figures, are not adequate. "Soviet gold stocks, previously estimated by the CIA to be worth between $25 billion to $30 billion, have fallen to only $2.7 billion according to a September 27 statement by Grigory Yavlinsky, the Soviet Union's chief economic policymaker. Gold reserves declined by nearly 700 tonnes in 1989 and 1990. Gorbachev's government apparently sold gold worth more than $25 billion over the past three years. Only about 240 tons of Soviet gold reserves now remain according to Yavlinsky. *Izvestia* disputed this claim on October 3, however, citing sources in the Soviet gold-extracting organizations who put the reserves at over 300 tons. Market value: over $2.5 billion" (The Heritage Foundation, *U.S.S.R. Monitor,* October 1991). Also, the "former Soviet Union . . . has reserves of only 240 tonnes, a tenth of what most western analysts had long reckoned it had" (*The Economist,* January 11, 1992, p. 65). Therefore, a gold standard must be ruled out, or, as one of its supporters, Robert Mundell, reluctantly concludes: "Gold can no longer be the solution" (1991).

the goodwill of authorities for its existence: It is self-enforcing. However, it's doubtful that it would work, and even more doubtful that it could be an appropriate solution for countries that lack sophisticated knowledge of prices and markets. The monetary growth rule would be ideal . . . if authorities would allow it to work, but the empirical evidence available so far suggests that, even if formally adopted, it would not be carried out. It would seem that monetary economists have no workable rule to prescribe. We agree on the need for a monetary constitution, but we haven't devised one that's likely to be (a) appropriate for ex-communist countries, (b) acceptable to its rulers, and (c) likely to deliver monetary stability.[17]

3. A Modest Proposal

The answer to those who demand answers is that there are no answers.
—Harold Adams Innis, quoted by Johnson 1975, p. xii

The problems faced by ex-communist countries in their attempt to go from a centrally planned to a market economy are enormous.[18] To

17. After the first draft of this paper was written, I came across a very interesting proposal by S. H. Hanke and K. Schuler (1991b, 1992). The currency board plan they support is extremely elegant in its simplicity, but it leaves two questions unanswered. First of all, aside from all the well-known objections to fixed exchange rates, how are we to find out which exchange rate between the foreign reserve currency and the domestic currency is "appropriate" (1991b, p. 23)? A short period of floating would allow us to single out the rate appropriate for present circumstances, but how do we know whether the same rate would be appropriate in the future, given the tremendous changes that are likely to take place? Second, the "real" money supply now in circulation in ex-communist countries, notably the former U.S.S.R., is as small as the authors claim for the obvious reason that those countries are undergoing very rapid inflation. If, accepting the authors' proposal (1991b, p. 25), we'd move from the present arrangement to the one proposed, freezing the "real" money supply at its present low level, the inevitable outcome would a dramatic, disastrous deflation and depression.

18. The size of the ex-communist countries' difficulties has generated a great number of jokes. One of them: "There are two ways to solve the crisis of the Soviet economy. The realistic way is to have people from outer space come straighten out the mess. The fantastic way is for the Soviet people to sort it out on their own" (quoted by E. H. Methvin, 1990).

a large extent, they are also unprecedented, so that the literature on how to go from plan to market is virtually nonexistent.[19] Furthermore, each of the former communist countries is different from all others because of its history, culture, degree of economic performance, etc. The idea of a general prescription for success valid for all countries is, therefore, quixotic at best. And, as for a monetary constitution, it's hard to believe that countries in a state of institutional disarray may succeed where our "free" countries have egregiously failed for so long, despite the determined efforts of monetary economists and public-choice theorists. Finally, as I have tried to show, economic theory does not offer a foolproof recipe for monetary stability, one that is definitely going to be accepted by the relevant authorities, sure to be implemented once accepted, and certain to deliver monetary stability if implemented.

Yet before succumbing to defeatism, it's worth remembering that there are no irreversible historical processes and that there is no reason why the ex-communist countries could not succeed where others have failed. In fact, if it is true that they are today in a precarious, if not desperate, economic predicament, it is also true that for them the stakes are higher than they would be for any of our "free" countries. We can endure a moderate amount of instability; in their case mone-

19. John G. Greenwood (1990) lists five preconditions (he calls them "fragile foundations") for a successful economy, that should be adopted by ex-communist countries: A. the rule of law, B. a relatively incorrupt bureaucracy and independent judiciary, C. predominantly private ownership of property, D. free market prices, and E. a stable monetary system. Meltzer (1991): "To work efficiently, the market requires institutions and structure. Private property, accounting and legal systems, and a monetary framework must be put in place." However, he acknowledges that "Economic theory does not provide a blueprint for the transition from socialism to a market economy" (p. 276). To the above preconditions, Niskanen (1991) adds the "cultural attitudes" that are essential for the proper functioning of a market economy. There is little doubt that all of these are necessary (though it's doubtful that they are sufficient) ingredients for the transition. One moment's reflection on their extraordinary scope and importance will make one wonder if the ex-communist countries' chances of success are as good as we all hope. Nutter's 1969 "classical" analysis of the differences in the organization of a communist (as contrasted to a free) society gives a vivid illustration of the breadth of the transformation.

tary instability might frustrate their aspirations of prosperity and their hopes for freedom.

What follows has neither ambition of precision nor claim of originality: Most of the reflections that follow are well known, and they are all of questionable validity. But I feel entitled to take refuge in Harold Adams Innis' observation quoted above.

3.1 SOME PRECONDITIONS: PRIVATIZATION

As previously mentioned, a monetary constitution's main purpose is that of allowing the price system to work effectively in allocating resources and in facilitating long-term investment decisions. It is a device for reducing uncertainty and favoring the risk-taking choices that are essential to economic progress. However, in order for the price system to work, people must respond to the incentives that are implicit in price changes. This poses no problem on the demand side: Buyers are likely to economize on items affected by a price increase, and vice versa. But as long as production is in the hands of "public" entities, it is far from certain that price signals will produce the necessary reaction on the supply side. In other words, for the price system to work, supply must be decentralized and the economy must be privatized. Extensive privatization of the economy is far more important than stability for the success of the transformation. And it's doubtful that ex-communist countries would be interested in the stability offered by a stagnating economy. As long as the size of government remains overbearing, there is little hope for prosperity and economic growth.

3.2 A FISCAL CONSTITUTION

The second fundamental precondition for a successful monetary constitution concerns again the size of government: the level of spending, taxation, and the deficit. It is generally recognized that fiscal and monetary rules are strictly connected (Meltzer, 1987, 1991; Jordan, 1991). This is fairly obvious: monetary instability is often the result of budget deficits, inflation being instrumental to the financing of government spending. Of the two main causes of instability—mistakes in the conduct of monetary policy and "*artless budget deficits,*" as Machlup used to call them—the second has always been prevalent, and it seems to be the more relevant for the ex-communist countries' quandary.

Here again the experience of our "free" countries is not particularly encouraging: Despite the declared best intentions of governments, spending, taxation, and borrowing have continued to grow unrestrained in many countries. The explanation of the contrast between the good intentions and the appalling results is simple: The growth of government is not a managerial problem; it cannot be solved by changing the managers. It is a problem of rules: Without an effective set of constitutional constraints, political incentives will always and everywhere result in the uninterrupted growth of spending and taxation (Martino, 1989, 1990).[20]

It is absolutely indispensable, therefore, that the monetary constitution be accompanied by a fiscal constitution, limiting government spending and taxation and mandating a balanced budget. On this last issue, I must make clear that I am aware that an annually balanced budget is not necessarily the best prescription from a stabilization point of view. A policy that would balance the budget over the cycle would be superior. However, the experience of several countries suggests that the growth of government spending is facilitated by the possibility of running a deficit. Furthermore, once the limitation of an annually balanced budget is removed, there are powerful incentives that push in the direction of increasing deficits. Such, for example, has been the experience of Italy since 1961 (Martino 1989, 1991).

In some cases, it might be difficult to achieve a balanced budget in a relatively short time. Also, the attempt could be very costly from a political point of view.[21] For example, the consolidated budget deficit of the republics of the new Commonwealth of Independent States is estimated—at the moment of this writing—to run in excess of 20 percent of GNP (Sachs, 1991). It would be nearly impossible to eliminate

20. "There will be no escape from the protectionist-mercantilist regime that now threatens to be characteristic of the postsocialist politics in both Western and Eastern countries so long as we allow the ordinary or natural outcomes of majoritarian democratic processes to operate without adequate constitutional constraints" J. M. Buchanan, 1989, p. 8.

21. An interesting historical illustration of the political cost of pursuing a determined policy of balancing the budget is offered by Italy from the unification to 1876. See A. Martino, 1991.

a deficit of that size overnight. What the fiscal constitution could and should mandate is an obligatory *tendency* toward a balanced budget: All new or greater expenses should be financed exclusively out of tax revenue or by the reduction of other expenditures (Martino, 1982). In any case, debt monetization should be forbidden: The government should be prohibited from borrowing from the central bank.

3.3 FEDERALISM AND REVERSE REVENUE SHARING

A budget balanced on an annual basis would be desirable only insofar as it would be implemented at a "low" level of government spending: The Swedish prescription of a nearly-balanced budget with spending in excess of 60 percent of GNP is not what I would recommend as a model for the ex-communist countries.[22] A mandatory balanced budget combined with a tax-limitation provision could be an effective way to achieve a ceiling on government spending (Milton and Rose Friedman, 1979).

The constitutional solution should also address the problem of the relationship between the various levels of government. Federalism, which is today advocated as the appropriate solution for the peaceful coexistence of different geographical, ethnical, or linguistic groups within the same country, also offers an indication for a constitutional solution to the problem of taxation. What I have in mind is a system of "reverse revenue sharing" as suggested by Dwight Lee (1985). Under such an arrangement, all taxing authority would reside in the local units of government (at the level that best suits the history of the country), and each local unit would be required to give the central government some proportion of the tax revenue it raises, with this proportion being uniform over all local units of government.

The advantages of such an arrangement would be numerous (Lee, 1985). First of all, it would establish some kind of fiscal competition among the different local governments, because excessively oppressive local tax systems would drive taxpayers away toward more-favorable tax environments. No local unit would therefore abuse its taxing au-

22. For an excellent analysis of Sweden's present predicament, see P. Stein and I. Dörfer, 1991.

thority and an automatic constraint on taxation would become effective. Furthermore, if the proportion of tax revenue to be given to the center is, say, 50 percent, for every dollar the local unit spent it would have to extract two dollars from its citizens in taxes. Obviously, the local units should also be subject to a balanced-budget constraint. The combination of a balanced budget at both central and local level and of the automatic constraint on taxation produced by reverse revenue sharing would result in a powerful disincentive to the growth of total government spending, and one that would need no policing to be enforced.

Apart from the fiscal constitution, the decentralization of government seems to offer the kind of flexible structure needed to accommodate regional diversities within the country. Federalism also allows policy competition and experimentation: The debate on public policy problems can then leave the abstract and dogmatic domain of ideological confrontation and be based on the more pragmatic and potentially fruitful approach of comparing the concrete results of the various policy solutions. Since there is ample room for legitimate disagreement on what the "ideal" tax structure should be, the experimentation made possible by federalism and fiscal competition could provide the "discovery procedure" needed to arrive at a more meaningful understanding of the problem and of its possible solutions. Federalism could also offer a healthy check on total government power and on its tendency to grow over time: It is no accident that federal structures, like Switzerland or the United States, have often been more successful in containing the growth of government than nonfederal ones. Finally, the ideals of federalism can be betrayed and corrupted, witness present tendencies in the United States or the growth of eurodirigisme in the EEC. There clearly is the additional task of devising constitutional constraints on the central powers in federal structures to prevent them from evolving into the kind of centralized leviathan they were supposed to replace. While reverse revenue sharing would represent a first important step in the right direction, more needs to be done. This last problem, while strictly connected with that of a monetary-fiscal constitution, obviously lies outside the scope of this paper.

3.4 A FALSE PROBLEM: THE MONETARY OVERHANG

One of the monetary problems of the transition that has received considerable attention is that of the so-called overhang, the idea that citizens of ex-communist countries are (were) holding more cash than they really want(ed) because there is (was) nothing they can (could) spend it on (Walters, 1991; Sachs, 1991). The existence of this large amount of unspent (unspendable) cash balances in the hands of the public has led to speculation on how to prevent it from creating an inflationary bubble: Should the government mop up these balances with a large issue of bonds, use them as the counterpart in the privatization program, or inflate them away? A conceivable solution could have been offered by monetary reform, a change in the monetary unit, the conversion of the excess supply of the old currency into the new currency at a noninflationary rate. In short, the solution to the monetary overhang should have received high priority in the transition to a stable monetary system.

There are good reasons to believe that the problem will disappear with the liberalization of prices: Once goods become available, there is no reason to suppose that people will be holding more cash than they really want. If prices are liberalized, the overhang will wither away. Discussion of a monetary constitution for the ex-communist countries can proceed as if the overhang never existed.

3.5 SHOULD THE EXISTING CURRENCY BE REPLACED BY A NEW ONE?

An important question is whether the introduction of a monetary constitution should be accompanied by the adoption of a new monetary unit. On the one hand, it could be argued that changing the currency would make it evident that authorities were seriously committed to a policy of monetary stability. On the other, what has been said before about the inertia in the use of money on the part of most people would suggest the opposite conclusion: A change in the monetary unit might add to the general climate of uncertainty and make matters worse. There is no general answer to this question, and in most cases the problem is already solving itself. In those countries where the transition is well under way without hyperinflation there is no need to change the currency. On the other hand, if the countries of the new Commonwealth of Independent States do not succeed in avoiding hyperinflation—and at the moment of this writing it does not seem likely that they will succeed[23]—by the time they decide on a new monetary constitution it is probable that the old currency will have become worthless and will need to be replaced by a new one.[24]

3.6 THE ISOLATED COUNTRY CASE

Ex-communist countries, as previously mentioned, are not a homogeneous lot. The "ideal" monetary constitution, therefore, will be different depending on the country's characteristics. For a country that has avoided hyperinflation in the initial stages of the transition and wants to retain total independence and national monetary sovereignty, the adoption of a fiscal constitution of the kind outlined above plus a monetary growth rule should take care of most of the problems.[25]

23. "The Soviet central bank's presses are disgorging rubles at full capacity 24 hours a day. According to official Soviet statistics, 3.6 times more rubles have been printed this year than last year. Money supply rose 44 percent in the first six months of this year, igniting an inflation soaring at 3 percent a week." The Heritage Foundation, *U.S.S.R. Monitor,* October 1991.

24. Gordon Tullock (1991) has suggested that ex-communist countries "should start with two currencies—the one which they now have, and which is inflating and which should be managed in such a way that it continues inflating at whatever the rate it has right now, and a new one which would be held stable. All existing contracts would be in terms of the currency in which they were made, i.e., the existing currency, and people would be free to make future contracts in either one. I would assume that this system would lead rather quickly to the extinction of the existing currency and the substitution of the new one. No one should get particularly hurt provided the monetary authorities can guarantee both stability for the new currency and that the old currency will inflate at its historic rate."

25. Two crucial aspects of the monetary growth rule that I have not dealt with here are: (a) what should be the precise numerical value of the rate of growth of the money supply, and (b) which monetary aggregate should be chosen for targeting. The reason for the omission is fairly obvious: The choice of the monetary aggregate depends on the institutional framework of the country in question. A particular aggregate might be suitable in one country and totally meaningless in another. No monetary theorist I know has ever claimed that there is only one monetary aggregate meaningful for all countries. In general, the monetary base

If the country is "large" enough to afford it, flexible exchange rates should also provide the solution for its international monetary relations (Friedman, 1950, 1953). Full convertibility and freedom of foreign exchange markets would also guarantee a modicum of currency competition: If they so choose, people would be allowed to hold foreign exchange (or gold) as a more reliable store of value than nominal assets denominated in the country's currency. Distrust of the stability of the national currency would lead people to take refuge in foreign currencies (and/or gold) and give the authorities a signal of their incipient failure.

If, on the other hand, the country is too "small" to afford a flexible-rate regime, it could peg its currency to that of a larger country. However, historical evidence on this arrangement is contradictory: It seems to have worked well in the case of Hong Kong, but it contributed to the Chilean recession in the early 1980s. The moral of the story is that in some circumstances a "small" open economy cannot afford complete monetary sovereignty and may be forced to give up the use of its own currency.

3.7 THE COMMONWEALTH OF INDEPENDENT STATES

Most of the countries in what used to be the Soviet Union (U.S.S.R.) are presently (January 1992) engaged in the formation of what is known as the Commonwealth of Independent States (CIS). Though the future of this association of autonomous republics is at the moment uncertain, it would seem that, if successful, it might develop into a kind of confederacy, with some central power in charge of the production of a few genuine "public goods" (like common foreign defense and the control of nuclear armaments) and total independence for the "confederate" republics in all other areas. Assuming that the initiative is successful, it would provide a framework for a monetary constitu-

---

is now the favorite choice of many monetarists, but even that preference is not absolute. As for the rate of growth, its precise numerical value has always been considered by proponents of a monetary growth rule as less important than the fact that it is maintained for a long period of time with little or no variability. A "'steady' and known rate of increase in the quantity of money is more important than the precise numerical value of the rate of increase." M. Friedman, 1969, p. 48.

tion different in one respect from the one outlined above for a single isolated country.

The ongoing debate on whether each republic should be allowed to have its own currency or remain within the ruble area, i.e., continue to use the Russian currency, could be solved by having the CIS adopt a "dual-currency system." The CIS as such would continue to use the ruble, and each republic would be allowed to have its own currency provided it accepted the rules suggested above for a fiscal constitution and constant monetary growth. This arrangement could play an important role in the enforcement of the individual republics' monetary constitution.

As previously mentioned, experience suggests that formal acceptance of a monetary growth rule does not automatically guarantee its implementation. This poses the problem of policing the enforcement of the rule. One could think of the introduction of a structure of incentives and disincentives aimed at making sure that monetary authorities do not, intentionally or unintentionally, depart from the target rate of growth of the money supply. The central bankers' salaries could be tied to their performance in implementing the monetary rule, they could be fired if they fail, etc.[26]

However, these arrangements are elaborate, and they can always be circumvented by an implicit agreement between political and monetary authorities. When, let us say, it is in the interest of the government to follow a path of monetary expansion in excess of what the rule dictates, it is not difficult to envision a connivance between the government and the central bank aimed at violating the rule. In other words, ideally there should be an *automatic* mechanism guaranteeing the enforcement of the rule. It is here, I believe, that the very valuable idea of competing currencies could be applied to the concept of a monetary constitution.

Under a dual-currency system, the CIS's own currency would compete with the individual republics' national currencies in a fashion similar to that which has been suggested for a parallel European currency (Vaubel, 1979). Each republic's currency would be freely convertible in the CIS's currency. Whenever inflationary expectations for

26. Something along these lines has been done in New Zealand.

a single republic's currency would increase, people would convert the national currency into the CIS's. The CIS would then demand the conversion of its excess holdings of the republic's currency into rubles from the republic's monetary authorities, which would be forced to revert to a less-inflationary policy. A mechanism of competition between currencies would thus be established, and it would act as an automatic mechanism of enforcement of the individual republics' monetary rule. The confederate currency would not only provide an alternative to "national" currencies, it would also act as a check on the inflationary propensities of republican governments. Finally, all national currencies should be freely convertible: Foreign exchange markets should be completely private, and anybody should be allowed to buy or sell foreign exchange at market prices. This again would reinforce the filter mechanism outlined above, increasing the range of alternatives to national money holdings and extending the competition among currencies.

4. Conclusion

The suggestions made above are merely an exercise in intellectual speculation and, as previously mentioned, have neither ambition of precision nor claim of originality. In the field of monetary policy more than in that of theory, we must never forget the idiosyncratic nature of most of our recommendations. Institutional factors are extremely important, and they should be taken into account whenever one engages in the unrewarding game of suggesting policy rules. One thing we know for sure: If the ex-communist countries really intend to complete their transition from communist planning to market freedom, they'll need a currency that's capable of performing its traditional functions adequately (Hanke and Schuler, 1991). We also know that if we entrust the stability of the currency to the discretionary power of monetary authorities, money could become an autonomous, potent source of instability. Hence, the superiority of rules. Which specific type of rule to adopt is in this respect less important than accepting the need for monetary rules. Ultimately, the choice of the constitutional setting can only be made in the light of the peculiarities of the relevant country.

REFERENCES

Bordo, M. D., and A. J. Schwartz, 1983. "The Importance of Stable Money: Theory and Evidence," *Cato Journal* 3, pp. 63–82, reprinted with revisions in Dorn and Schwartz, 1987, pp. 53–72.

Buchanan, J. M., 1983. "Comment, Constitutional Strategy and the Monetary Regime," *Cato Journal* 3, pp. 143–46, reprinted with added title and revisions in Dorn and Schwartz, 1987, pp. 119–27.

———, 1989. *Socialism Is Dead but Leviathan Lives On. The John Bonython Lectures,* CIS Occasional Papers 30.

Cagan, P., 1986. "Competitive Monies: Some Unanswered Questions," *Cato Journal* 5, no. 3, pp. 943–47.

———, 1987. "A Compensated Dollar: Better or More Likely than Gold?" in Dorn and Schwartz, *The Search for Stable Money, Essays on Monetary Reform,* pp. 261–77.

Dorn, J. A., 1987. "The Search for Stable Money: A Historical Perspective," in Dorn and Schwartz, *The Search for Stable Money, Essays on Monetary Reform,* pp. 1–28.

Dorn, J. A., and A. J. Schwartz, 1987. *The Search for Stable Money, Essays on Monetary Reform,* University of Chicago Press, Chicago and London.

Friedman, M., 1950. "The Case for Flexible Exchange Rates," reprinted in Friedman, *Essays in Positive Economics,* 1953, pp. 157–203.

———, 1951a. "Commodity-Reserve Currency," *Journal of Political Economy* 59, pp. 203–32, reprinted in Friedman, *Essays in Positive Economics,* 1953, pp. 205–50.

———, 1951b. "Less effets d'une politique de plein emploi sur la stabilité économique: Analyse formelle," *Economie appliquée,* reprinted under the title "The Effects of a Full-Employment Policy on Economic Stability: A Formal Analysis," in Friedman, *Essays in Positive Economics,* 1953, pp. 441ff.

———, 1953. *Essays in Positive Economics,* University of Chicago Press.

———, 1959. *A Program for Monetary Stability,* Fordham University Press, New York.

———, 1961. "Real and Pseudo Gold Standards," *The Journal of Law and Economics* 6, pp. 66–79.

———, 1962. *Capitalism and Freedom,* University of Chicago Press, 1965.

———, 1968. "The Role of Monetary Policy," *American Economic Review* 58, no. 1.

———, 1969. "The Optimum Quantity of Money," in *The Optimum Quantity of Money and Other Essays,* Aldine, Chicago.

———, 1975. *Unemployment "Versus" Inflation? An Evaluation of Phillips Curve,* The Institute of Economic Affairs, Occasional Paper 44, London.

———, 1977. *Inflation and Unemployment: The New Dimension of Politics—The 1976 Alfred Nobel Memorial Lecture,* The Institute of Economic Affairs, Occasional Papers 51, London.

———, 1984a. "Monetary Policy: Tactics Versus Strategy," excerpted with new title in Dorn and Schwartz, *The Search for Stable Money, Essays on Monetary Reform,* 1987, pp. 381–82.

———, 1984b. *Market or Plan?* CRCE, Occasional Paper 1, London.

———, 1991. "Free to Choose, Among Currencies Too," *The Wall Street Journal* 19 December.

Friedman, M., and R. Friedman, 1980. *Free to Choose, A Personal Statement,* Harcourt Brace Jovanovich, New York.

Greenwood, J. G., 1990. "The Preconditions for Economic Recovery in Eastern Europe," *G.T. Management (Asia) Limited.*

Haberler, G., 1974. *Economic Growth and Stability. An Analysis of Economic Change and Policies.* Nash Publishing, Los Angeles.

———, 1983. "Money, Markets, and Stability," *Cato Journal* 3, pp. 83–91, reprinted with new title in Dorn and Schwartz, *The Search for Stable Money, Essays on Monetary Reform,* 1987, pp. 73–80.

Hanke, S. H., and K. Schuler, 1991a. "Ruble Reform: A Lesson from Keynes," *Cato Journal* 10 (winter), pp. 655–66.

———, 1991b. "Currency Boards for Eastern Europe," *The Heritage Lectures* 355, The Heritage Foundation.

———, 1992. "Currency Convertibility: A Self-Help Blueprint for the Commonwealth of Independent States," *Foreign Policy Briefing,* Cato Institute 22.

Hayek, F. A., 1945. "The Use of Knowledge in Society," *American Economic Review* 35.

———, 1976. Denationalisation of Money, Hobart Paper Special 70, Institute of Economic Affairs, London.

Johnson, Harry G., 1975. *On Economics and Society,* University of Chicago Press, Chicago.

Jordan, J. L., 1991. "Fiscal and Monetary Policies During the Transition from Socialism to Capitalism," Paper presented to the Mont Pèlerin Society Regional Meeting, Prague.

Langfeldt, E., J. Scheide, and J. Trapp, 1989. "The Case for Money Supply Rules," *Geld und Währung/Monetary Affairs* 5, no. 2, pp. 30–47.

Lee, D. R., 1985. "Reverse Revenue Sharing: A Modest Proposal," *Public Choice* 45, pp. 279–89.

Leijonhufvud, A., 1987. "Constitutional Constraints on the Monetary Powers of Government," in Dorn and Schwartz, *The Search for Stable Money, Essays on Monetary Reform,* 1987, pp. 129–43.

Martino, A., 1982. *Constraining Inflationary Government,* The Heritage Foundation, Washington, D.C.

———, 1989. "Budget Deficits and Constitutional Constraints," *Cato Journal* 8, no. 3, pp. 695–711.

———, 1990. "A Monetary Constitution for Europe?" *Cato Journal* 10, no. 2, pp. 519–33.

———, 1991. "Le conseguenze non intenzionali della teoria keynesiana," *Quaderni di Metodologia delle Scienze Sociali,* LUISS, pp. 3–15.

Meiselman, D. I., 1987. "Is Gold the Answer?" in Dorn and Schwartz, *The Search for Stable Money, Essays on Monetary Reform,* 1987, pp. 257–60.

Meltzer, A. H., 1983. "Monetary Reform in an Uncertain Environment," *Cato Journal* 3, pp. 93–112, reprinted in Dorn and Schwartz, *The Search for Stable Money, Essays on Monetary Reform,* 1987, pp. 201–20.

———, 1991a. "Prices and Wages in Transitions to a Market Economy," Paper presented to the Mont Pèlerin Society Regional Meeting, Prague.

———, 1991b. "Is Monetarism Dead?" *National Review* 4, pp. 30–32.

Meltzer, A. H., and A. Reynolds, 1982. *Towards a Stable Monetary Policy, Monetarism vs. the Gold Standard, A Debate Between Allan Meltzer and Alan Reynolds,* The Heritage Foundation and The Institute for Research on the Economics of Taxation, Washington, D.C.

Mundell, R. A., 1968. *Man "and" Economics,* McGraw-Hill, New York.

———, 1991. "L'oro non basta," *Know How URSS* 1, no. 4.

Niskanen, William A., 1991. "The 'Soft Infrastructure' of a Market Economy," Paper presented at the Mont Pèlerin Society Regional Meeting, Prague.

Nutter, G. W., 1969. *The Strange World of Ivan Ivanov,* World Publishing Company, New York and Cleveland.

Sachs, J., 1991. "Goodwill Is Not Enough," *The Economist* 21, pp. 109–12.

Simons, H. C., 1936. "Rules Versus Authorities in Monetary Policy," *The Journal of Political Economy* 44, pp. 1–30, reprinted in F. A. Lutz and L. W. Mints, eds., *Readings in Monetary Theory,* 1951, R. D. Irwin, Homewood, Ill., pp. 337–68.

Spinelli, F., and M. Fratianni, 1991. *Storia monetaria d'Italia,* Arnoldo Mondadori Editore, Milan.

Stein, P., and I. Dorfer, 1991. *The Death Knell of Social Democracy: Sweden's Dream Turns Sour,* Institute for European Defence and Strategic Studies, London.

Thornton, D. L., 1988. "The Effects of Monetary Policy on Short-Term Interest Rates," *The Federal Reserve Bank of St. Louis Review,* pp. 53ff.

Tullock, G., 1991. "The Monetary Policy of Henry Simons," unpublished paper.

Vaubel, R., 1979. *Choice in European Monetary Union,* The Institute of Economic Affairs, Occasional Paper 55, London.

———, 1986. "Competing Currencies: The Case for Free Entry," *Cato Journal* 5, pp. 927–42, reprinted in Dorn and Schwartz, *The Search for Stable Money, Essays on Monetary Reform,* 1987, pp. 281–96.

Walters, A., 1991. "Monetary and Fiscal Policy and Aid in the Transition," Paper presented to the Mont Pèlerin Society Regional Meeting, Prague.

Part 6

The Future of Freedom

A Comment on "Nineteen Eighty-four: A False Alarm?" by Paul Johnson

In the past months, George Orwell's book has been widely analyzed, and all comments have inevitably centered on the question: Was his prediction confirmed, or was it falsified by contemporary evidence? I believe the question is essentially meaningless and completely misses the message of Orwell's work. *Nineteen Eighty-four* is not an exercise in scientific prediction. It is a political *prophecy*. Now, the purpose of prophecy is not that of describing the inevitable outcome of "the Inexorable Laws of Historical Destiny," to use Karl Popper's very appropriate expression. When the outcome is inevitable, prophecy is essentially useless: A priori knowledge of an unavoidable catastrophe serves no useful function. It is simply an exercise in masochism: "He who foresees calamities suffers them twice over."

The purpose of the kind of political prophecy expressed by *Nineteen Eighty-four* must be found precisely in the fact that the outcome Orwell describes is not inevitable. It can be avoided if people are aware of the impending danger. The prophecy, then, is a warning designed to alert people to the threat facing them if certain tendencies are allowed to continue. If Orwell's totalitarian nightmare has not, at least thus far, materialized, this is largely due to the fact that people in the Western world have been aware of the danger, even if to an insufficient extent. We can still prevent the realization of the totalitarian prophecy, and Orwell has shown us how: by making people aware of the existence of the threat.

Presented at the Mont Pèlerin Society Meeting, Cambridge, England, September 3, 1984.

Paul Johnson's argument is that Orwell was essentially a moralist, and that he "was certainly right to associate moral relativism with the totalitarian state." Even though the author of *Modern Times* makes a very convincing argument in favor of the notion that moral relativism and moral decadence are the roots of all evils and the essence of the totalitarian danger as denounced by Orwell, I am not sure that I agree with him. In fact, his paper reminded me, especially when he talks of the decay of Iver's train station, of the wisdom of G. B. Shaw's idea that "an Englishman thinks he is moral when he is only uncomfortable."

Johnson believes that totalitarianism is a system of moral relativism and quotes Lenin's "revolutionary conscience" and Hitler's "higher morality of the party" as two examples. I find it difficult to follow this kind of reasoning. It seems to me that the essence of totalitarianism is precisely the opposite. All totalitarian systems are based on the premise that *theirs* is the only valid morality, that their system of values and beliefs has *absolute* validity. It is because Hitler and Stalin believed that they were *absolutely* right and *moral* that they did what they did. It was not their moral relativism that produced their crimes; it was their moral absolutism that did it. Had they entertained doubts about the validity or the morality of their system of values, it is unlikely that they would have done what they've done. And the intolerance produced by moral absolutism is also evident when the system of morality is assumed to be derived directly from God's authority: Khomeini is no moral relativist. In fact, historical evidence amply supports F. W. Nietzsche's view that "morality is the best of all devices for leading mankind by the nose."

It may be, however, that Johnson's view refers to something else. If we define morality as that set of rules that makes it possible for different individual liberties to coexist, then it is true that totalitarianism violates basic individual rights—life, liberty, and property—and it is, therefore, immoral. But this is not new, and it has always been the main reason for opposing totalitarianism. However, what does this have to do with moral relativism? The violation of individual rights, the crimes of the various totalitarian regimes have never been the product of uncertainty about what is right and what is wrong. On the contrary, they have always resulted from an unlimited faith in the superior morality of some system of beliefs. As John Locke has taught us: "[T]he great enemy of tolerance is the tendency of men to be dogmatic in their beliefs, and their dogmatism, in turn, rests on the assumption that the knowledge to which those beliefs pretend is absolutely certain."

What is required here is a sharp distinction between moral *rules* and "moral" mores. Moral rules are derived from the old liberal principle that the only acceptable limitation to my freedom is provided by someone else's freedom. These rules are indeed universal. No society could survive for a long time or function effectively if it allowed its members to kill each other, steal from each other, injure each other, etc. (Even these rules, however, are not absolute. "Thou shall not kill," for example, does not apply to soldiers in time of war, and "thou shall not steal" is ignored in the field of taxation.) The particular kind of enforcement of these rules varies with time and from country to country, but they have always and everywhere existed in one form or another. And, as previously mentioned, it is true that totalitarian regimes are marked by large-scale violations of these moral rules. It is worth mentioning, however, that even totalitarians refrain from making violations of moral rules an explicitly accepted principle, and carry out their crimes often in secrecy, while the explicit laws of the country uphold the very principles they are violating.

"Moral" mores, on the other hand, have no absolute significance and seldom last for a long time. I see nothing wrong, for example, in the fact that today unmarried couples can openly obtain a room in a hotel. On the contrary, the removal of a meaningless and unjustifiable constraint on personal liberty must be welcomed. That restriction had nothing to do with morality proper; it was not part, as Johnson seems to believe, of a moral code. And there are still many unnecessary limitations on personal freedom imposed by tradition and custom that we should wish to have removed. It is, therefore, essential that we separate morality proper—that must be preserved and upheld if a liberal society is to survive—from the pseudomorality of "moral" mores that is often inimical to individual freedom and can be dispensed with.

Nineteen Eighty-four is a great book that has been, often intentionally, misunderstood. A good example of this misunderstanding is provided by the editor of a famous Catholic magazine who, in a radio interview in January, declared that Orwell was wrong . . . because it isn't true that "war is peace"! The truth, said the noted Catholic intellectual, is that "*peace* is peace." Amen.

Another misunderstanding of Orwell's book is to be found in *L'Unità,* the Italian Communist Party newspaper, which has devoted a lengthy set of articles to *Nineteen Eighty-four.*[1] One of the themes of the articles was that Orwell was wrong . . . in being afraid of electronics!

The Soviets go even further: "an article in *Pravda* of May 30, 1983, cites [*Nineteen Eighty-four*] as denouncing the . . . United States of America!"[2] And Soviet publicists have been "extolling the novel as a devastating indictment of 'bourgeois democracy' where 'the poisonous roots of anti-humanism, all-devouring militarism and oppression have today thrust up truly monstrous shoots.'"[3] Such an interpretation, however, makes it difficult to understand the banning of *Nineteen Eighty-four* in the Soviet Union. Why should Soviet citizens be prevented from being enlightened about the true nature of democratic capitalism? There is no doubt that both the peculiar misinterpretation of the book by the Soviets, and the fact that it is banned in the Soviet Union, are compliments to the greatness of Orwell's work. They also provide us with a clue for a correct interpretation of Orwell's message.

It is true that Orwell's book, as in the case of most literary masterpieces, has general validity. But it is also undeniable that what he had in mind was not totalitarianism *in general;* his analysis specifically refers to *Communist* totalitarianism. *Nineteen Eighty-four* is an anticommunist book. This explains why the Soviets are afraid of it, and why so many fellow travelers are busy trying to distort its meaning.

Orwell does not criticize *Soviet* Communism; he does not distinguish, as is so fashionable nowadays among pseudointellectuals, between Stalinism, which is supposed to be bad, and Communism, which is supposed to be not so bad. He is showing that by its very nature Communism is always totalitarian. It is a brutal oligarchy based on lie.

1. *L'Unità,* suppl. no. 298, December 18, 1983. It is interesting to note that this thick, twenty-page supplement was published well ahead of the beginning of the year. The Italian Communist Party wanted to be sure that *their* interpretation of the book was the first to come out. Another compliment to Orwell!

2. Alain Besançon, "Orwell in Our Time," *Survey,* spring 1984, p. 195.

3. Carl Gershman, "The Problem of Totalitarianism," *Survey,* op. cit., p. 198.

> The essence of oligarchical rule is not father-to-son inheritance, but the persistence of a certain world-view and a certain way of life, imposed by the dead upon the living. A ruling group is a ruling group so long as it can nominate its successors. The Party is not concerned with perpetuating its blood but with perpetuating itself. *Who* wields power is not important, provided that the hierarchical structure remains always the same. (p. 173)

And,

> Oceanic society rests ultimately on the belief that Big Brother is omnipotent and that the Party is infallible. But since in reality Big Brother is not omnipotent and the Party is not infallible, there is need for an unwearying, moment-to-moment flexibility in the treatment of facts. The key word here is *blackwhite*. . . . Applied to a Party member, it means a loyal willingness to say that black is white when Party discipline demands this. But it means also the ability to *believe* that black is white, and more, to *know* that black is white, and to forget that one has ever believed the contrary. (p. 175)[4]

In the special issue of *L'Unità* mentioned above, Enrico Berlinguer, leader of the Italian Communist Party, is asked what his reaction to the book had been. His reply: "I read it in 1950, as soon as the Italian translation came out. My reaction then was probably strongly influenced by the anticommunist and antisoviet interpretation that the book received during the cold war. At that time, some people saw in Orwell's description of the State a metaphor of the Soviet Union. This is no longer true."

Should Berlinguer's evaluation be true, we would have reasons to worry. For the only protection against the totalitarian threat is a correct perception of its existence and of its nature. The moment people no longer see Orwell's nightmare for what it is—a description of communism at work—that threat, which is even more formidable today that it was in 1949, will become real and imminent even for us, lucky citizens of the corrupt West.

4. George Orwell, *Nineteen Eighty-four,* New American Library, 1961.

Are We Winning?[1]

1. Who Are "We"?

From the point of view of this paper, the soul-searching question of trying to spell out the differences between freedom fighters is largely irrelevant. In our case, I believe that Aristotle's wisdom applies: "Things differ in what they have in common." "Conservatives," "libertarians," and "classical liberals" are likely to differ on many issues, but in our epoch their differences are unlikely to be as important as the values they share.

This was Hayek's opinion at the time of the first meeting of the Mont Pèlerin Society in 1947, when he remarked that his goal was that of putting together "a group of people who are in agreement on fundamentals, and among whom certain basic conceptions are not questioned at every step."

His evaluation of the number of such people was pessimistic: "the number of those who in any one country agree on what seems to me the basic liberal principles (is) small," especially if compared with the "very big" task it faced.[2]

The effectiveness of the Society in its infancy is illustrated by a remark Schumpeter made in 1949. After having listed a series of socialist principles, which, as a result of the "disintegration of capitalist so-

Presented at the Mont Pèlerin Regional Meeting, Christchurch, New Zealand, November 27, 1989.

1. Given the profession's unexciting record in forecasting, I shall abstain from making any kind of prediction, and obey Sam Goldwyn's advice: "*Never prophesy, particularly about the future.*" My aim is modest: I just want to determine whether we've made any progress in the confrontation with our opponents both at the intellectual and at the public policy level.

2. F. A. Hayek, "Opening Address to a Conference at Mont Pèlerin," *Studies in Philosophy, Politics and Economics,* 1967, Simon and Schuster, 1969, pp. 148–59.

ciety," were being "taken for granted by the business class . . . and by the large number of economists who feel themselves to be opposed to (one hundred per cent) socialism," he added: "I believe that there is a mountain in Switzerland on which congresses of economists have been held which express disapproval of all or most of these things (e.g. socialist policies). But these anathemata have not even provoked attack."[3]

We have come down from that mountain, but have we made any progress since then?

2. *Pessimists, Optimists, and Others*

On the question of freedom's future, opinions have always differed widely. Schumpeter himself was, as we all know, very pessimistic. At the time of the foundation of the Society, he wrote: "Can capitalism survive? No. I do not think it can. . . . (T)he actual and prospective performance of the capitalist system is such . . . that its very success undermines the social institutions which protect it, and "inevitably" creates conditions in which it will not be able to live and which strongly point to socialism as the heir apparent."[4]

The pessimism has continued to flourish until recently. For example, I remember that at the MPS meeting in Hillsdale in 1975, a prominent member of our Society was convinced that England would become a dictatorship in five years. Though many on the British left would probably say that his prediction was confirmed, most of us would conclude that this kind of pessimism proved to be excessive: Today, while socialism appears destined to fade away, capitalism is alive, and there seems to be a widespread revival of faith in the free enterprise system.

Indeed, in political rhetoric we have many reasons for being at least moderately optimistic in our evaluation of current trends. Political rhetoric has been changing fast in many countries, including, for example, the People's Republic of Italy. Twenty-five years ago, at the time

3. Joseph A. Schumpeter, "The March into Socialism," 1949, reprinted in *Capitalism, Socialism and Democracy,* Third edition, Harper Torchbooks, Harper & Row, New York, 1950, pp. 415–25.

4. J. A. Schumpeter, *Capitalism, Socialism and Democracy,* op. cit., p. 61.

of the 1963 general political elections, statism was the consensus of the overwhelming majority of politicians of almost all political parties. Those of us who dared to challenge the prevailing wisdom—based on deficit spending, national economic planning, nationalization, and direct government intervention—were labeled reactionaries and simply ignored by the new mandarins.[5]

The spectacular growth of government of the last twenty-five years, however, seems to have disappointed its promoters. On July 12, 1987, the leftist weekly *L'Espresso* published a debate between Claudio Martelli, deputy leader of the Italian Socialist Party, and Achille Occhetto, then deputy leader (now leader) of the Italian Communist Party. During the debate, Martelli said: "It's simple: both in the East and in the West we see the crisis of a philosophy that's been common to both social democrats and communists: statism." To which Occhetto replied: "I agree with you more than you do! . . . Statism, as you say, is the true burden of which both social democrats and communists must get rid." (Occhetto is presently trying to convince his party to change its name.)

Similar statements are being made by political leaders of different parties almost everywhere, and a comparable change can be observed both in the academic world and in public opinion. Isn't it tempting to conclude that we've been winning?

3. *The Time Horizon*

In answering that question, we must first of all be aware of the danger of historicism and be skeptical of what Karl Popper sarcastically calls the belief in the "Inexorable Laws of Historical Destiny." Our question, however, does not necessarily entail a fatalistic attitude toward history. It's a very important question, and, if we can specify its meaning exactly, it deserves to be asked.

The first problem is that of specifying the time interval under observation: Over which time span are we making our comparison? This is a universal problem. In the words of a scientist: "When people ask me whether the climate is getting warmer or colder, I generally answer

5. See my article "The Leaning Tower of Statism," *Reason,* February 1989, p. 46. [See pp. 65–67 in this volume.]

'yes.' It all depends on over what time scale we average. If the time scale is a few months, then the answer in the spring would of course be 'warmer' and in the fall 'colder.'"[6] The intellectual climate is now more favorable to the cause of freedom than it was twenty-five years ago, but does this mean that it is more favorable than it was, let us say, ten, fifty, or one hundred years ago?

What I mean is that there is the danger of mistaking a temporary lapse in the historical process for a radical change of direction. Schumpeter was well aware of this when he warned: "The transformation of social orders into one another is an incessant process but, in itself, a very slow one. To an observer who studies a moderate span of 'quiet' time, it may well seem as if the social framework he beholds did not change at all. Moreover, the process often suffers setbacks which, considered by themselves, may suggest to him the presence of an opposite tendency" (Schumpeter, 1949, p. 419).

4. Ideological Victory

Let me stress that at this point I am concerned with the intellectual climate, not with actual policy. We are all painfully aware that drastic changes in rhetoric do not necessarily translate themselves into changes in policy. It is important, therefore, to separate the two and maybe ask ourselves under what conditions a change in the intellectual climate results in a change in policy.

From the perspective of the ideological confrontation, I am convinced that we live in one of the happiest times in the contemporary history of mankind. It seems to me that never before has the case for freedom been more thoroughly analyzed and better understood.

I realize that this is a strong statement. There is an inevitable distortion on our perspectives produced by chronological selection. Few people who are great thinkers in the eyes of their contemporaries stand the test of time and are still considered great by future generations. As a result, we are often led to believe that there are more great scholars among our contemporaries than there were in the past. How-

6. S. Fred Singer, "My Adventures in the Ozone Layer," *National Review,* June 30, 1989, p. 36.

ever, even if we allow for this distortion, it seems still true to me that a very large number of the great liberal thinkers of all times belong to this century. Furthermore, even though ideas always have parents, in the sense that their origin can be traced back to past achievements, the case for freedom as presented by today's thinkers is more consistently argued and better supported than ever before. Finally, more people are aware of the importance of freedom on a theoretical level today than at any other time in the past fifty or one hundred years.

Let me illustrate. I think we all agree that the gravest threat to freedom comes from government; private threats are easier to deal with.[7] The growth of government and the resulting danger to freedom have two major sources. The first is the pressure coming from interest groups trying to secure political rents or to be sheltered from competition. This threat is more formidable because, as Adam Smith pointed out,[8] the collusion of private and political interests is favored by the structure of political incentives.

The second source of government growth has been socialism and its faith in the benevolence of government, what Frank Knight called "the essential content of socialism," which he thus defined: "It is imagined that the state, i.e. the government, conceived in the abstract as a benevolent and all-powerful agency—essentially as God rather than realistically as a group of politicians—could order economic affairs

7. This was Adam Smith's view: "*The capricious ambition of kings and ministers has not, during the present and the preceding century, been more fatal to the repose of Europe, than the impertinent jealousy of merchants and manufacturers. The violence and injustice of the rulers of mankind is an ancient evil, for which, I am afraid, the nature of human affairs can scarce admit a remedy. But the mean rapacity, the monopolizing spirit of merchants and manufacturers . . . may very easily be prevented from disturbing the tranquility of any body but themselves.*" *The Wealth of Nations* (1776), The Modern Library, New York, 1937, p. 460.

8. "*The member of parliament who supports every proposal for strengthening this monopoly, is sure to acquire not only the reputation of understanding trade, but great popularity and influence with an order of men whose numbers and wealth render them of great importance. If he opposes them, on the contrary, and still more if he has authority to be able to thwart them, neither the most acknowledged probity, nor the highest rank, nor the greatest public services, can protect him from the most infamous abuse and detraction, from personal insults, nor sometimes from real danger, arising from the insolent outrage of furious and disappointed monopolists.*" Smith, 1776, p. 438.

rightly without generating new evils or incurring serious social costs; that humanity would with approximate unanimity approve and like the result; that no other serious problems would remain; and, finally, that everybody—or nearly everybody, apart, perhaps, from a few criminally recalcitrants—would 'live happily ever after.'"[9]

At the intellectual level, both of these sources of government growth have been subject to extensive critical scrutiny, and the underlying interplay of interests has been exposed. As a result, it's much more difficult today to enlarge the scope of government in the name of the "public good." We now have extensive empirical evidence that regulation often ends up serving the interests of the regulated producers, thus providing a good illustration of Adam Smith's view on the "mean rapacity and monopolizing spirit" of merchants and manufacturers.

Even more important, we have seen a dramatic shift of opinion away from the myth of the benevolent government in the past two decades. That shift has largely resulted from viewing government as a group of politicians rather than as a mythical, abstract entity. The sobering effect of the economics of politics on the intellectual climate has somewhat tempered the mystique of government as the problem solver, leading Jim Buchanan to conclude: "I can be very pessimistic when I look at many aspects of our current economic policy and as I contemplate post-Reagan political economy. But I am optimistic when I compare the discussion and dialogue in the 1980s with that which might have taken place in the 1960s or even the late 1970s. Ideas do indeed have consequences, the fatal conceit has been exposed, and the romantic notion will not return. Camelot will not return."[10]

The economics of politics and the economics of regulation are only two examples of our intellectual victories. Liberalism has faced the challenge of Marxism, Fascism, "Welfarism," and Keynesianism, and it has won: Except for a few desperate, hopeless fanatics, no one believes in central planning, nationalization, wage and price controls or

9. Frank H. Knight, "Socialism: The Nature of the Problem," *Ethics* 50, 1940, pp. 253–89, reprinted in *Freedom and Reform, Essays in Economics and Social Philosophy* (1947), Liberty Fund, Indianapolis, 1982, pp. 154–93. The quote is from p. 159.

10. J. M. Buchanan, "Camelot Will Not Return," *Reason*, January 1989, p. 37.

incomes policy, deficit spending, inflationary growth, protectionism, the superiority of public health care, and all the assorted paraphernalia of excuses for bigger government that were so overwhelmingly popular only a generation ago.

5. *Are Economists to Be Credited with the Change?*

An interesting question arises at this point: Must the intellectual change be credited to the work of prominent liberal thinkers in general, and economists in particular, or has it been the product of circumstances? As far as economists are concerned, George Stigler has always been convinced that, as a profession, they are not terribly relevant.

In a 1959 paper,[11] he asserted that "Economists are subject to the coercion of the ruling ideologies of their times," which would suggest that their output has little, if any, impact in shaping those ideologies. But, he adds: "I believe that the economics profession has been basically more conservative than the educated classes generally" (pp. 54–55). However, he has often repeated that "economists exert a minor and scarcely detectable influence on the societies in which they live" (p. 63), and "(t)he main lesson I draw from our experience as preachers is that we are well received in the measure that we preach what the society wishes to hear" (p. 13).[12]

On this point I tend to agree with Keynes: The views of economists are probably less important than he thought, but, as his own influence confirms, they are far from having a minor impact on society. Probably, a compromise between the two positions can be found in the view that economists influence society only when circumstances are "right," when their theories are not in sharp contrast with the organized interests of powerful pressure groups.

As far as our question is concerned, there is no doubt that the popularity of liberal ideas has been reinforced by the failure of statism and the desire to find an alternative. But it's equally true that without

11. G. J. Stigler, "The Politics of Political Economists," *The Quarterly Journal of Economics* 73, November 1959, reprinted in *Essays in the History of Economics,* University of Chicago Press, 1965, pp. 51–65.

12. G. J. Stigler, *The Economist as Preacher,* Basil Blackwell, Oxford, 1982.

the revolutionary contribution of liberal thinkers, both the analysis of "government failure" and the alternative to its problems would not have existed.

6. Public Policy Defeat?

That, however, is the intellectual part of the story. In terms of actual policy, things are totally different. While the rhetoric has changed dramatically, policies have not changed much. No one advocates a socialist system, but when it comes to policy, the organized action of pressure groups inevitably leads to more government intervention.

Nowadays we all seem to favor market discipline and competition in general—that is, for everybody else—but when it comes to our own interests we do not refrain from trying to use the democratic political process to extract political or monopolistic rents. We demand economy and efficiency from the suppliers of the goods and services we buy, but we like to have as high a pay as possible and we don't mind being sheltered from competition in what we produce. To some extent we are all guilty of this kind of schizophrenic behavior: I am normally very vocal in my opposition to the growth of government spending, but don't count on me to oppose increased spending on university professors' salaries! The same is true, for example, in the field of trade restrictions: people who support free international trade in principle—that is, for everybody else—often argue that their industry is a special case deserving some kind of protection.

It may very well be that we devote more energy to promote our interests as beneficiaries of political favors than we do to promote increased reliance on market processes for society in general. This is simply a variation on an old theme: We like high prices for the product we sell, and low prices for the products we buy. But our interest as producers of some good or service is greater than our interest as consumers of goods and services produced by others, and, as a result, we spend more efforts to keep the price of our product high than we do to keep other prices low. Or we devote more resources to increase government intervention on our own behalf than we do to reduce government intervention in favor of others. This can explain why, if we compare the size of government's interference in our lives today—in our times of great liberal rhetoric—with what it was twenty-five or even fifteen years ago, we must conclude that in most countries we are much worse off now than we were then.[13] Regardless of what measure one chooses, government has grown very rapidly in the past quarter century, and this is true, although to a different extent, of almost all Western countries.

It may very well be that what we are witnessing is an illustration of the Friedmans' cycle, the view that "a major change in social and economic policy is preceded by a shift in intellectual opinion . . . At first it will have little effect on social and economic policy. After a lag, sometimes of decades, an intellectual tide taken at its flood will spread at first gradually, then more rapidly, to the public at large and through the public's pressures on government will affect the course of economic, social, and political policy. As the tide in events reaches its flood, the intellectual tide starts to ebb" (pp. 455–56).[14] In a recent interview, however, Milton Friedman has explained that "it takes a long time. And I emphasize that the reversal in the climate of opinion is one thing; the reversal of policies is a very different matter. The real change in the intellectual climate didn't start until the late forties or early fifties. So you really don't expect it to be fully implemented until something like the year 2000" (p. 7).[15]

13. If one looks at Italy, for example, where, as previously mentioned, the change in rhetoric has been substantial, there is no doubt that statists of all parties have had a go at it: from 1960 to 1988, government spending has increased 75 times in nominal terms, 525 percent in real terms, and it has gone from less than one-third of gross domestic product (32.7 percent) to well over one-half (53.1 percent). Despite the fact that revenue has increased by leaps and bounds, the deficit has exploded: from 382 billion lire in 1960 to 124,000 billions in 1988, i.e., from 1.4 percent to 11.5 percent of GDP. In real terms total public debt outstanding has gone from US$82.3 billion in 1960 to almost US$740 billion in 1988. Similar conclusions can be reached with respect to all possible indicators of individual freedom.

14. Milton and Rose Friedman, "The Tide in the Affairs of Men," in *Thinking About America, The United States in the 1990s,* Annelise Anderson and Dennis L. Bark, eds., Hoover Institution, Stanford University, 1988, pp. 455–68.

15. "An Interview with Milton Friedman," by Peter Brimelow, in *Fraser Forum,* July 1989, pp. 4–20.

Maybe so. I often tend to agree with Professor Friedman, and I certainly hope that he is right on this issue. But how do we know that this is the case? Couldn't the present intellectual climate, as Schumpeter would say, be one of those "setbacks which, considered by themselves, may suggest . . . the presence of an opposite tendency"? Couldn't the present climate favorable to freedom be a temporary exception in history's course?

The obvious answer to these questions, of course, is that we do not know. There are no "inexorable laws of historical destiny," no deterministic trends in either intellectual climate or policy. There is no such thing as victory (or defeat for that matter), a state of affairs which, once attained, will forever be maintained. The struggle for freedom is a "natural," inescapable component of life. We can successfully meet the challenges of our time and score a temporary "victory," but new problems will soon come up, as new ways of hindering our personal liberties are discovered or old ones are resurrected.

The disappointing change in policy, furthermore, is to a large extent due to the limitations of our intellectual successes. For example, we haven't produced a workable, realistic plan or blueprint for dismantling the existing statist structure. The few instances in which there has been success in demolishing the socialist framework are remarkable in that there was (and there still is) no previous, generally accepted formula for neutralizing the entrenched interests which resist any change in the status quo.

Our present, moderate successes are especially vulnerable in that they have generally consisted in a change of policy *within a given, unchanged set of rules,* rather than in a constitutional change of rules. Constitutional arrangements are not eternal, but, if correctly devised, they certainly possess greater durability than do policy changes within given rules. Again, this is one of our intellectual weaknesses. For example, we all agree on the desirability of replacing discretionary policy with a monetary constitution. However, when it comes to the specific type of monetary constitution, our opinions widely differ: Some favor a fixed monetary rule, others want a gold standard, or competing currencies, or a variety of different remedies, and the same is true of a fiscal constitution. The wide discrepancy of views in our camp reduces the likelihood of significant success. That's why we have no a priori reason for being complacent, satisfied with the present state of affairs. *We are not winning.*

7. Moderately Optimistic Conclusion

I would like to end, however, on a moderately optimistic conclusion. First of all, if it is true that we are not winning in the sense that we don't have generally accepted (acceptable) constitutional solutions for the major problems of our times, it is also true that *they are losing:* The statist recipes once so popular are totally discredited so that our opponents don't know what to suggest.

But there is another reason for being optimistic. Like Churchill at the time of World War II, we can base our confidence in the future on their mistakes. The cumulative effect of decades of socialism has produced a state of near-bankruptcy which makes further expansions of government interference almost impossible. Statism is both intellectual and financially bankrupt: It has a past, albeit an inglorious one, but it has no future.[16] Under these circumstances, it is difficult to imagine any further growth in the size of government.

Maybe the change of rhetoric is not to be credited to our intellectual victories, being only a reflection of the simple arithmetic of government bankruptcy. In any case, if present trends continue, instead of capitalism being killed by its success, as Schumpeter maintained, we shall see socialism destroyed by its failures. Definitely, these are glorious days for us reactionaries!

16. Take Italy, for example. Interest payments on government debt amount to 16 percent of total public-sector spending, or 76 percent of net borrowing, i.e., 62 percent of total income tax revenue. Taxation on labor income in all its forms has reached unbearable proportions: Net take-home pay is only 54.8 percent of labor costs, and the tax protest front now includes organized business and labor. All of this while the failure of government is underscored by the tremendous success of private delivery of mail, private health insurance, private police protection, private schools, etc.

Liberalism in the Coming Decade: The Role of the Mont Pèlerin Society

The Mont Pèlerin Society meets again in Munich after 20 years —the 46th time it has met in the 43 years of its life.[1] The Society has grown: 39 people from 10 countries attended the first meeting in 1947; the present membership totals 488 members from 39 countries.[2] In the midst of great historical changes, a reflection on the role of our Society in today's world seems appropriate.

Presented at the Mont Pèlerin Society Meeting, Munich, Germany, September 1990.

1. There have been twenty-eight General Meetings since the MPS's foundation: Mont Pèlerin, 1947; Seelisberg, 1949; Blomendaal, 1950; Beauvallon, 1951; Seelisberg, 1953; Venice, 1954; Berlin, 1956; St. Moritz, 1957; Princeton, 1958; Oxford, 1959; Kassel, 1960; Turin, 1961; Knokke, 1962; Semmering, 1964; Stresa, 1965; Vichy, 1967; Aviemore, 1968; Munich, 1970; Montreux, 1972; Brussels, 1974; St. Andrews, 1976; Hong Kong, 1978; Stanford, 1980; Berlin, 1982; Cambridge, 1984; St. Vincent, 1986; Tokyo/Kyoto, 1988; Munich, 1990.

Regional and other meetings have been held in Tokyo, 1966; Caracas, 1969; Rockford, 1971; Salzburg, 1973; Guatemala City, Guatemala, 1973; Hillsdale, 1975; Paris, 1976; Brussels, 1977; Madrid, 1979; Stockholm, 1981; Viña del Mar, 1981; Vancouver, 1983; Paris, 1984; Sydney, 1985; Indianapolis, 1987; Taipei, 1988; Christchurch, 1989; Antigua, Guatemala, 1990.

See R. Max Hartwell, "The Re-emergence of Liberalism? The Role of the Mont Pèlerin Society," paper presented at the Mont Pèlerin Society meeting, Sydney, 1985.

2. According to the list published in the latest issue of our *Membership Directory* (not the most reliable publication), in 1989, out of a total of 488 members, 226 (46 percent) were from the United States, 151 (31 percent) from 16 European countries, and only the remaining 111 (23 percent) came from 22 countries of

According to the Society's historian, "*The common objective of those who met in Mont Pèlerin in 1947 was undoubtedly to halt and reverse current political, social, economic and intellectual trends towards socialism, and to ensure the revival of liberalism.*"[3]

In the light of recent history, it would be tempting to conclude that those trends have in fact been reversed, liberalism has been revived, and the Society has achieved its purpose. While the differences between the world in 1947 and today are undeniable, it is far from clear that our mission has been completed. It seems to me that liberty is still facing gigantic obstacles on both sides of the collapsed Iron Curtain and in the rest of the world. Let me mention just a few which might be on the agenda of our meetings in the next ten years.

A. The Collapse of Communism

The memorable events of the past several months in what are now called the ECCs (Ex-Communist Countries) have stimulated the hopes of freedom fighters all over the world, leading, for example, a noted American conservative[4] to declare that "*1989 was the most significant year in the most important decade since World War II.*" There is no doubt that the events of 1989 provide conclusive evidence of the collapse of communism both as a viable form of economic organization and as a political system, because it has been proven beyond any doubt that it was inefficient and it was not based on the consent of the governed. This is hardly new for the members of the Mont Pèlerin Society, but it is certainly pleasant to see one's political views so clearly confirmed.

History's pace of change in the past months has been so rapid that even our wildest hopes have not been able to keep up with it.[5] Yet a word of caution is probably needed. In many ECCs the demand for po-

---

the rest of the world. Nearly 60 percent of the Society membership comes from English-speaking countries (292 members, 59.8 percent).

3. R. Max Hartwell, "The Re-emergence of Liberalism? The Role of the Mont Pèlerin Society," op. cit.

4. Edwin J. Feulner Jr., "Conservatism in a New Age," The Heritage Foundation, 1990.

5. As far as I know, the only person who has repeatedly predicted the collapse of communist regimes before the end of the century has been Arthur Seldon.

litical freedom has translated itself into free (or quasi-free) elections resulting in the defeat of the formerly ruling communist party. This is undoubtedly a desirable change per se, but to those of us who believe in freedom the real question is whether the introduction of elements of political democracy in some Eastern European countries will start a process leading to the liberalization of those societies. In other words, will the change from totalitarian rule to electoral democracy widen the range of free choices open to individuals in their everyday lives, or will it just be a cosmetic change which will leave nearly everything else unchanged?

There is no doubt that, as a political decision-making mechanism, democracy is superior to its alternatives. But for a liberal, electoral democracy is not the only issue. He agrees with Herbert Spencer: "*the real issue is whether the lives of citizens are more interfered with than they were; not the nature of the agency which interferes with them.*"[6]

Or, as Professor Friedman has recently remarked:

> The unprecedented political upheavals that believers in human freedom have welcomed with so much joy can be the prelude to comparable economic miracles, but that is far from inevitable. They can equally be the prelude to a continuation of collectivism under a different set of rulers. Everything depends on the political will of the people, the economic understanding of their leaders, and the ability of those leaders to persuade the public to support the radical measures that are necessary.[7]

The first symptoms are not necessarily encouraging: In many cases, the paralysis of action has prompted extravagance of language but no

6. "*. . . these multitudinous restraining acts are not defensible on the ground that they proceed from a popularly-chosen body; for that the authority of a popularly-chosen body is no more to be regarded as an unlimited authority than the authority of a monarch; . . . as true Liberalism in the past disputed the assumption of a monarch's unlimited authority, so true Liberalism in the present will dispute the assumption of unlimited parliamentary authority.*" Herbert Spencer, *The Man versus the State* (1884), The Thinker's Library 78, Watts and Co., London, 1940, pp. 17–18.

7. "*The transition to freedom cannot be accomplished overnight. The formerly totalitarian societies have developed institutions, public attitudes, and vested interests that are wholly antithetical to the rapid creation of the basic economic requisites for freedom and prosperity.*" Milton Friedman, "Four Steps to Freedom," *National Review,* May 14, 1990, p. 33.

appreciable change. At the moment, Eastern European countries do not seem to have yet embarked on a process of radical reform promising to transform them into workable free market economies.[8] In many cases, this has been due to the fact that, as pointed out by James M. Buchanan, both in the East and in the West "*Th[e] loss of faith in politics, in socialism broadly defined, has not . . . been accompanied by any demonstrable renewal or reconversion to a faith in markets.*"[9]

As for the "economic understanding" of communist leaders, in an article entitled "Pricing in USSR Between Supply and Demand," Anatolij Derjabin recommended a radical reform of retail prices, lamenting for example that the price of milk was proportional to its *fat* content rather than to its *protein* content, "*as in most other countries*"![10]

After so many decades of planning mythology, the misunderstanding of the market is hardly surprising. But what I fear is happening is that the superior prosperity of market economies has generated the delusion that all that is needed in order to promote economic growth is the imitation of some of the *external* features of our economies, while leaving everything else unchanged. A good example is given by the notion that the dismal performance of communist economies is due to bad management. This is wrong: Management is not the problem. Market economies are not efficient because by chance they have been endowed with superior managers. They have better managers *because* they are efficient: It is the market that provides the filter mechanism required to make sure that only managers making the correct decisions survive and prosper. *Superior management is the consequence of market efficiency, not its cause.*

8. "*(E)very other country in Eastern Europe still faces the hard slog of establishing tax regimes, contract law, capital markets, environmental and safety regulations and employment rules. Dismantling and selling state-owned monopolies is an immense hurdle which no government has yet attempted to leap. . . . Nor are ECCs yet much of a low-cost manufacturing site. With no real market prices, there is no way to calculate the real cost of Eastern European labor or capital. Accounting systems are a fantasy, profits purely notional, productivity levels a mystery.*" "Don't Rush In," *The Economist,* June 16, 1990, pp. 18–19.

9. James M. Buchanan, *Socialism Is Dead but Leviathan Lives On,* The John Bonython Lectures, CIS Occasional Papers 30.

10. Anatolij Derjabin, "I prezzi URSS tra domanda e offerta," *Intermedia Journal,* October 31, 1987, p. 21.

I have often compared the attitude of some Eastern European reformers to the "cargo cult."[11] After World War II, the inhabitants of some Pacific Islands, having seen Western soldiers create an expanse of land and a strange tower, their effort being rewarded by the arrival of large metallic birds carrying all kinds of precious commodities, started to imitate them. They built fake landing strips and control towers, hoping that a cornucopia of goods would fall on them from the sky. The same is true of much market-talk going on in Eastern Europe these days: the idea that prosperity can simply be achieved by extolling the virtues of "market socialism" and "structural transformation" (whatever these words mean), in the absence of private property rights, freedom of contract, free trade, and a functioning price system.[12]

It would be grossly unfair, however, to generalize the imperfect understanding of the free market system shown by some leaders in Eastern Europe and ignore the existence of a surprisingly large number of dedicated freedom fighters who have continued to cultivate liberal ideas, often with substantial sacrifices and large personal costs.[13] Some of them are here with us. They remind us of a new and important goal for our Society: that of providing a forum for debating the innumerable problems posed by the transition from socialism to capitalism. That is a very difficult task: There is no magic formula, no "model" for the transformation of a planned economy into a competitive one.

We have nothing to teach them: Our record in dismantling the innumerable bits of piecemeal socialism that have proliferated in our

11. Antonio Martino, "Il Culto del Cargo," *Il Giornale,* December 28, 1989, p. 14.

12. For a devastating criticism of the notion of market socialism, see Anthony de Jasay, "Market Socialism: A Scrutiny, 'This Square Circle,'" The Institute of Economic Affairs, Occasional Paper 84, London, 1990.

13. See, for example, "No Third Way Out, Creating a Capitalist Czechoslovakia," Vaclav Klaus interviewed by John Fund, *Reason,* June 1990, pp. 28–31. It appears from Klaus's answers to the interviewer, however, that the problems facing Czechoslovakia are enormous and that there is no general consent that a market solution is required. The same seems to be true to a different extent in all ECCs, so that a pessimistic evaluation of the likelihood of the transformation of these countries into market economies is not without justification.

own countries over the decades is not sensational. Rather, we have a lot to learn from them: We could sharpen our understanding of the nature of the problem by discussing the difficulties encountered by our friends in Eastern Europe. In return, we can provide them with the kind of invaluable encouragement that the Society has supplied to many of us. Finally, we should not underestimate the informative content of our meetings, which seems particularly important in this respect. It's still true today, I believe, what Max Hartwell has said about the Mont Pèlerin Society in the past:

> Since the members formed part of an international information network for the circulation of liberal ideas, what they learned at society meetings was important, for it was at the meetings that the latest liberal ideas were presented and discussed. This is not to say that all delivered papers were important, and that all discussion was profitable, nor that all members benefited from the education that meetings provided. Attendance at meetings, nevertheless, could provide participants with a real opportunity for a comprehensive encounter with the theory, practice and problems of liberalism.[14]

The debate on liberal ideas in an international forum is more necessary to our friends from the East than it is to us. This task alone would be sufficient to fill the program of our meetings in the next decade.

B. Is Freedom Winning?

If the problems faced by Eastern European countries are numerous, serious, and unprecedented, the state of liberty in our "free" countries is not immune to new and formidable predicaments. The reason is simple and very well known: *While socialism is dead, statism is not.* We have, for the moment at least, freed ourselves from the danger of wholesale socialism, but we are still facing the continuous erosion of our liberties in a piecemeal fashion. And since a free country is one in which there is no particular individual to blame for the existing tyranny, we can only reproach ourselves for what is happening.

Capitalism's current problems, according to *The Economist,* are three:

14. R. Max Hartwell, op. cit., pp. 22–23.

the environment; the interplay of pressure groups resulting in the increase in government spending, taxing, and borrowing; and the growth of an "underclass" mostly due to the failure of public schools.[15]

The new wave of statism is first of all based on environmentalism.[16] The threat of environmentalism is subtle and deadly; its plausibility makes it acceptable even to reasonable believers in freedom; its appeal to the uninformed is enormous; the half-baked scientific assertions used to justify all kinds of government intervention for the sake of the environment require extensive information on the part of those who wish to criticize them. And the problem is made worse by the widespread practice of environmentalists trying "*to influence both public and governments by the deliberate suppression of anything that might suggest that*

15. First, the environment: "*The environmental challenge for mankind is not to stop pollution by stopping growth. . . . But, there are environmental problems . . . which do affect society and do reduce man's individual pleasure in growing richer.*" Second, there is the action of pressure groups whose "*basic purpose is to grab money from governments.*" This pressure results in the rapid growth of government spending and "*to pay the bills, a society has to accept either more government borrowing . . . or higher taxes . . . Whatever the outcome, an economy's productive potential is usually weakened. . . . Push this process too far and the true genius of capitalism—its ability to satisfy the material wants of most people most of the time—is gradually stifled. Yet depressingly few of today's governments grasp that truth.*" Finally, there is the growth of an "underclass," which is largely due to the "*failure of schools.*"

The paper, however, starts with the obvious acknowledgment that "[capitalism's] *basic western version has produced one huge success: in material terms, it works well for most of the people most of the time. They go out into the marketplace and, at the end of almost every year, they end up richer than they were. . . . Every day billions of private decisions are made, by individuals and by firms, to buy, sell, save, store, invest, scrap. Each of those decisions links in to others, the whole lot being sorted out by the invisible hand . . . (T)hat unseen hand has orchestrated a staggering increase in prosperity—and in life itself. . . . The rough-and-tumble of the capitalist marketplace is the surest and quickest way of lifting most of a country's population out of poverty.*" "Capitalism's visible hand," *The Economist,* May 19, 1990, pp. 13–14.

16. George Orwell's view is as relevant today as it was in 1937: "*One sometimes gets the impression that the mere words 'Socialism' and 'Communism' draw towards them with magnetic force every fruit-juice drinker, nudist, sandal-wearer, sex-maniac, Quaker, 'Nature Cure' quack, pacifist, and feminist in England.*" George Orwell, 1937, as quoted in *Contentions,* April 1990, p. 1. The words "Socialism" and "Communism" may be on their way out, but the people mentioned by Orwell continue to stick together, usually on the left of the political spectrum.

the bases of their proposals are less than certain."[17] Potentially, environmentalism poses a risk for the future of liberty as serious as that posed by wholesale socialism in the past.[18]

Extensive work has been done by believers in freedom to show alternative, free market solutions to environmental problems. To face this new challenge to a liberal order what is needed is more research of an interdisciplinary kind, based on the collaboration of scientists and economists. Again, this should be a high priority for the Mont Pèlerin Society in the near future.

Under the same heading as the environment, I should add another unusual threat which comes from the enormous variety of "small" restrictions to our personal freedoms that are continuously being introduced in the name of safety, health, and other lofty ideals. Each one of them, taken by itself, seems trivial. Taken together, they amount to a wholesale attack on our independence.

17. Peter D. Finch, "The Lalonde Doctrine in Action: The Campaign Against Passive Smoking," The Center for Independent Studies, *Policy,* winter 1990, pp. 22–25; the quote is on page 25. Though Finch refers to a different problem, the deliberate simplification of complex scientific issues in order to scare the public and prompt government into action is one of the environmentalists' favorite tactics. In other words, "*Greens and other activists treat environmental issues as though they are certain events, ignoring the scientific evidence that casts doubt even on the existence of these problems.*" Richard L. Stroup, "The Green Movement: Its Origin, Goals and Relevance for a Liberal Society," in the same issue of *Policy,* pp. 57–63. According to Stroup, this attitude "*is true of the scientific literature on the greenhouse effect . . . , stratospheric ozone . . . , and acid precipitation . . . , and the epidemiological evidence on the large and well-known . . . hazardous waste sites such as Love Canal.*" The quote is from page 59.

18. In my view "reasonable" environmentalism is far more dangerous than "ecoterrorism." The latter, however, performs the crucial function of making the former look acceptable. On ecoterrorism, see "Ecoterrorism: The Dangerous Fringe of the Environmental Movement," *Backgrounder* 764, The Heritage Foundation, April 12, 1990. This is true even of related areas of public policy. Think, for example, of the animal rights movement: The more ardent supporters of "liberation zoology" will probably be frustrated in their demands, but the more moderate position of those who advocate restrictions on the laboratory use of animals or on hunting is likely to succeed. See Charles Oliver, "Liberation Zoology," *Reason,* June 1990, pp. 22–27. And both are probably paving the way to the more radical position of "liberation botany," which will fight for the protection of "vegetable rights."

The purpose of the law has been distorted, so that now the state, instead "*of protecting, as far as possible, every member of the society from the injustice or oppression of every other member of it,*"[19] tries to protect individuals *from themselves,* destroying the very concept of personal responsibility in the process.

The welfare state—"public" health care in particular—has gradually instilled the notion that we do not own our health. The results of this view are schizophrenic. On the one hand, the increase in life expectancy becomes the cause of national anxiety, since an aging population imposes costs "on society." A good example was given by a recent *Washington Post* article explaining that "*smokers 'save' the Social Security system hundreds of billions of dollars. Certainly this does not mean that decreased smoking would not be socially beneficial. In fact, it is probably one of the most cost-effective ways of increasing average longevity. It does indicate, however, that if people alter their behavior in a manner which extends life expectancy, then this must be recognized by our national retirement program.*"[20] At this point, the patriotic citizen does not know what to do: If he lives dangerously, he imperils the financial future of the public health system, whereas if he decides to live a long, healthy life, it's Social Security that's in trouble.

On the other hand, the most common line of argument is the opposite: Since "the government" pays for our medical care, we are not free to live our lives in a manner that is deemed unhealthy by the authorities. The standard argument about the paraphernalia of restrictions on activities considered unhealthy is that people who engage in them are more likely to get sick and "impose a cost on society." As a result, what is deemed dangerous or unhealthy is banned, what is considered healthy or otherwise beneficial is made compulsory: speed limits; compulsory helmets for motorcyclists; compulsory seat belts; restrictions

19. Adam Smith, *The Wealth of Nations* (1776), Modern Library, New York, 1937, p. 651.

20. "*Not smoking could be hazardous to pension system. Medicare, social security may be pinched if anti-tobacco campaign succeeds, report says,*" *The Washington Post.* Or, in the words of a health economist: "*Prevention of disease is obviously something we should strive for. But it's not going to be cheap. We will have to pay for those who survive.*" Both quotes are taken from Florence King, "I'd Rather Smoke Than Kiss," *National Review,* July 9, 1990, pp. 32–36.

on the sale of pornographic material, on the consumption of drugs, alcohol, tobacco;[21] and so on. We are heading toward a society where dangerous sports will not be permitted, pedestrians will be required to have a license, obesity will be illegal, and what we are allowed to eat will be determined by the National Dieting Board!

If you think that this is ridiculous, exaggerated, or paradoxical, think for example of the EEC toy regulations. As pointed out by Digby Anderson,[22]

> The contemporary obsession with safety, especially safety for children, has found its true bureaucratic home in the EEC. . . . Committees have now recommended the statutory minimum dimensions of marbles based on the average width of toddlers' throats so that the Community shall protect its young from swallowing them. Or perhaps it is so that they *will* be able to swallow them rather than get them stuck: it's not clear. . . . The pea in a whistle may be governed by regulation as to its toxicity lest someone tread on a whistle, the pea escape, be picked up and chewed by a child desperately looking for a pre-EEC-ban-style marble. I'm unsure, [Anderson concludes,] about whether such peas will have to be the size of tennis balls (for marble-ish reasons) and how huge post-1990 whistles will have to be to incorporate them.

Examples of the absurd pretense to intrude into our privacy and regulate our lives could fill several volumes. Their absurdity should not make us forget the danger they pose to our liberty. Think of the bill signed by representatives of all political parties in Italy that, if approved, would have forbidden television on Saturday for the lofty purpose of forcing people to spend more time talking to their families. And what should we make of a society where a citizen who is considered old and mature enough to pay taxes, enter into a labor contract, get married, drive a car, contribute to determine the political future of his country by voting, or risk his life in its defense is not considered

21. We smokers should probably get together and support Lord Harris's idea of establishing F.O.R.E.S.T. (Freedom Organization for the Right to Enjoy Smoking Tobacco).

22. Digby Anderson, "Games that the Eurocrats play . . ." *Sunday Telegraph,* October 2, 1988.

old or responsible enough to go to a bar and drink a beer? Yet this is what is happening in the "*land of the free and the home of the brave.*"

Whatever it is that we intend to do, we should be well advised to follow Lawrence Peter's advice: "*do it now! There may be a law against it tomorrow.*"

I know that on some of these issues there is disagreement between our conservative and libertarian members, but it seems to me that this is an additional reason for devoting part of our agenda to a debate on them, which could help clarify matters and give us a better understanding of the differences between us. In any case, I believe it is more important to ask today the question that Spencer asked more than a century ago: "*in past times Liberalism habitually stood for individual freedom* versus *State-coercion. . . . How is it that . . . Liberalism has to an increasing extent adopted the policy of dictating the actions of citizens, and, by consequence, diminishing the range throughout which their actions remain free?*"[23]

The last set of problems involves both new and old challenges to a liberal order. Liberals have advocated for years the introduction of choice in education as a way to impose the discipline of competition on inefficient public school systems.[24] We have not made much progress in this area, despite the production of a substantial body of theoretical work, so that it seems appropriate to analyze the reasons for our failure and indicate a way to overcome the political and bureaucratic obstructions which so far have prevented experimentation.[25] However, the "growth of an underclass" is not the result of the failure of public schools only, but it is the most visible symptom of the failure of the entire welfare state apparatus. While freedom fighters have consistently criticized welfare statism, we are still divided on the alternatives that have so far been proposed, e.g., the negative income tax. Finally, we

23. Herbert Spencer, *The Man versus the State* (1884), op. cit., p. 5.

24. For example, this was the subject of my paper at the 1981 MPS meeting in Viña del Mar, Chile: "'Free' Education or Educational Freedom?"

25. Yet, there are signs that the tide might be changing. The "liberal" left is apparently beginning to see the light. See John Chubb and Terry Moe, *Politics, Market and America's Schools,* The Brookings Institution, 1990. According to the review "Schoolyard perestroyka," *The Economist,* June 16, 1990, the authors advocate choice in schools, and blame the problems of America's educational system on its bureaucracy.

cannot hope to dismantle the existing welfare state machine unless we can suggest a plausible alternative. Liberal welfare alternatives should be a high priority for our Society.

C. Government Growth and the Future of Liberty

By far, however, the most pressing set of problems plaguing contemporary capitalism is our old companion of almost all meetings: the growth of government spending, taxation, and borrowing. In most countries, the tendencies of the past have continued undisturbed, despite the dramatic change in political rhetoric. In my own country, the 1980s have witnessed repeated pronouncements on the part of all governments on the need to contain spending, taxation, and borrowing. The results have been disappointing, to say the least: From 1980 to 1989 public-sector spending has increased from 43.5 percent to 54 percent of GDP, public-sector revenue has gone from 35 percent to 43.3 percent, net borrowing from 8.5 percent to 10.7 percent, public debt outstanding has more than doubled in real terms, reaching the astronomical figure of roughly U.S. $900 billion. If the trends that have prevailed in the 1980s were allowed to continue through the 1990s, in the year 2000 public spending in Italy would absorb 75 percent of Gross Domestic Product, while explicit taxation would amount to 60 percent. It would be the end of our freedom and prosperity.

The explanation of the contrast between the good intentions and the appalling results is simple: The growth of government is not a managerial problem, it cannot be solved by changing the managers. It is a problem of rules: Without an effective set of constitutional constraints, political incentives will always and everywhere result in the uninterrupted growth of spending and taxation. In the words of James Buchanan: "*There will be no escape from the protectionist-mercantilist regime that now threatens to be characteristic of the post-socialist politics in both Western and Eastern countries so long as we allow the ordinary or natural outcomes of majoritarian democratic processes to operate without adequate constitutional constraints.*"[26] That's why I believe that a discussion on a fiscal and monetary constitution should continue to be a high priority in

26. James M. Buchanan, op. cit., p. 8.

our agenda. All the more so since there still is no consensus within the Society on the most effective way to constrain government.

The constitutional solution must address the problem of the relationship between the various levels of government. Federalism, which is the subject of this meeting's opening session, is today advocated as the appropriate solution for the peaceful coexistence of different geographical, ethnical, or linguistic groups within the same country. Whether in South Africa[27] or Canada,[28] the U.S.S.R. or China, the EEC or nation-states like Italy, Spain, or even the U.K., the decentralization of government seems to offer the kind of flexible structure needed to accommodate regional diversities within the country. Federalism also allows *policy competition* and experimentation: The debate on public policy problems can then leave the abstract and dogmatic domain of ideological confrontation and be based on the more pragmatic and potentially fruitful approach of comparing the concrete results of the various policy solutions.

But federalism could also offer a healthy check on total government power and on its tendency to grow over time: It is no accident that federal structures, like Switzerland or the United States, have often been more successful in containing the growth of government than nonfederal ones.[29]

Finally, the ideals of federalism can be betrayed and corrupted, witness the EEC's experience and the growth of *euro-dirigisme.* We clearly face the additional task of devising constitutional constraints on the central power in federal structures to prevent them from evolving into the kind of centralized leviathan they were supposed to replace.

27. Leon Louw and Frances Kendall, *South Africa: The Solution,* Amagi Publications, Bisho, Ciskei, 1986.

28. Peter Brimelow, "Mon Dieu! Montreal!" *National Review,* June 25, 1990, pp. 22–23.

29. An interesting proposal, which seems well worth investigating, is that of "reverse revenue sharing," according to which "*all taxing authority will reside in the states*" and "*(e)ach state will be required to give the central government some proportion of the tax revenue it raises.*" If adopted, this scheme would result in fiscal competition among local taxing authorities, thereby providing an automatic check on the taxing propensities of government. See Dwight R. Lee, "Reverse Revenue Sharing: A Modest Proposal," *Public Choice* 45, 1985, pp. 279–89.

On the economic front, an important facet of our times seems to be the potential shortage of savings. Keynes's prediction that "*as a rule . . . a greater proportion of income [is] saved as real income increases*"[30] has been falsified by the evidence. In many countries, like my own, the savings ratio has been steadily declining with the increase in real income. Such a tendency is obviously reinforced by demographic trends. Should it continue, it would constrain our growth potential. Demography and related issues like immigration, which have not always been prominent in the program of our meetings, deserve more careful scrutiny. It is to be hoped that we'll remedy this omission in the near future.

D. The Durability of Ideas

It is an important question for us whether ideas make a difference.[31] It seems to me that liberal ideas may not prevail in practice at the time of their conception, but they are more durable than their socialist counterparts.

Keynes's notorious view that in the long run we are all dead was wrong. We always *live* in the long run. Today is the last day of a long run which started sometime in the distant past. Yet, in a sense, he was right: he *is* dead. Forty-four years after his demise, Keynes *is* dead both physically and intellectually: Very little is left of his intellectual legacy. This is so because "*the ideas of economists and political philosophers . . . are more powerful than is commonly understood*" *only when they are right,* when they are in accordance with logic and evidence.

The ideas of great liberal thinkers have lasted much longer.[32] It is

30. J. M. Keynes, *The General Theory of Employment, Interest, and Money* (1936), Harcourt, Brace & World, New York, 1964, p. 97.

31. I have dealt with this issue elsewhere: "Are We Winning?" Address to the Pacific Regional Meeting of the Mont Pèlerin Society, Christchurch, November 1989, Center for Independent Studies Occasional Papers 29, pp. 27–30. [See pp. 318–28 in this volume.]

32. John Locke's philosophy is still relevant today, 286 years after his death; we derive inspiration from David Hume's writings 214 years after his decease; Adam Smith is alive and well in this two-hundredth anniversary of his death; and, 186 years after his departure, the philosophy of Immanuel Kant is still rele-

because of the durability of the liberal tradition, which has survived the dark years of the socialist consensus, that we can enjoy the excitement of our times. The events of 1989 confirm beyond any doubt the view that "*the force of ideas, propelled by the pressure of events, is clearly no respecter of geography or ideology or party label.*"[33] The consequences, however, of the intellectual legacy of socialism will continue to exist long after their intellectual roots have fallen into disrepute.[34] We face, therefore, the urgent task of showing how the intellectual change can be translated into a change in public policy.

We live in an exciting but complex world. Few of us would disagree with the comment of Alphonso X, "the learned" King of Castile (1252–84), a medieval patron of astronomy, who is quoted as saying: "*If the Lord Almighty had consulted me before embarking on the Creation, I would have recommended something simpler.*"[35]

The problems confronting us are numerous and intricate. Those that I have mentioned are only some of the many difficulties confronting the future of liberty in today's world. By themselves, they could fill our Society's agenda for the next decade. But that agenda will *always* be full, for the obvious reason that we shall never win. We cannot win not because of any intrinsic weakness in our philosophy, but because individual liberty is destined to be continuously challenged. Furthermore, our duty is to be ahead of our times, to offer a perspective on desirable future developments. We are doomed to be constantly ahead of politics.

---

vant for those very few who can understand it. On the other hand, only 107 years have elapsed since Karl Marx's death, and the number of Marxists, once enormous and growing, has declined so rapidly that it looks as if the only Marxists left reside in Albania and on American campuses. Keynesianism is no more successful.

33. Milton and Rose D. Friedman, "The 'Tide in the Affairs of Men,'" *Economic Impact* 66, 1989, pp. 74–79.

34. See my article "What Do Marx, Mussolini and Keynes Have in Common?" *The Wall Street Journal Europe,* December 27, 1983.

35. Quoted by Jessica T. Mathews, "Global Climate Changes . . . ," *Issues in Science and Technology,* Spring 1987, p. 58. A slightly different version of the same quote is that used by Dean Acheson as the epigram for his book; see *American Purpose,* 3, no. 7, September 1989, p. 49.

For 43 years the Mont Pèlerin Society has performed an invaluable role as a "clearinghouse" of liberal ideas. Since the threats to freedom are not, and will never be, in scarce supply, it is to be believed that the MPS will continue to be an indispensable source of inspiration to freedom fighters all over the world.

Index

absenteeism, 58, 170, 190–92
accountability, xii; European Central Bank (ECB), 277–79
Acheson, Dean, 343n35
administration. *See* red tape
Albania, 343n32
Alfasud and Alfa Romeo, 57, 190–91, 191–92n25
Alphonso X, king of Castile, 343
Alvaro, Giuseppe, 189n19, 189n21
Amato, Giuliano, 66
Amato government, 134
Amendola, Giorgio, 189
American Economic Review, 223n13, 224n15, 271n6, 272n8
American Purpose, 343n35
anarchy, 54, 62–63
Anderson, Annelise, 326n14
Anderson, Digby, 338
Andreatta, Beniamino, 282n23
animal rights movement, 336n17
Aristotle, 318
asymmetric shocks in different countries, risk of introduction of common European currency producing, 276–77
asymmetries in perception of costs and benefits of public spending, 39–41, 42–43, 96–98, 119–23, 249

Backgrounder, 336n17
"balanced budget norm," abandonment of, 122–23
Balogh, Lord, 201
Banca d'Italia, 152, 244, 246–47, 251–53
Bangladesh Institute of International and Strategic Studies Journal, 268n2
Bark, Dennis L., 326n14
Bastiat, Frederic, 125, 194–95
Batten, D. S., 244n6
Belgium, 56, 192, 193n30
Bennett, J. T., 17n6
Bensançon, Alain, 316n2
Benso, Camillo, Conti di Cavour, 51–52
Berlinguer, Enrico, 317
Berlin Wall, collapse of, xvi
Berlusconi governments, xi, 134
Bethell, T., 254n20
black market. *See* underground economy
Block, W., 104n1
bonds, governmental, 111, 182n6
Bordo, Michael D., 224n13, 271n6, 275n12, 283, 284, 294
BOT (Buono Ordinario del Tesoro), 111
Boughton, J. M., 165n12, 181n5
bracket creep (fiscal drag), 11–12, 25, 118–19
Bradley, Michael D., 279n18
Bresciani-Turroni, Constantino, 213
Brimelow, Peter, 326n15, 341n28
Britain. *See* United Kingdom
"British disease," 222
Brittan, Samuel, 143n9, 222n10, 242

Brookings Institution, 339n25

Buchanan, James M.: asymmetries in perception of costs and benefits of public spending, 42–43, 97, 121–22; classical liberalism, 323, 332, 340; deficits, 123; education, ix, xiv, 44–77n9; fiscal constitution, need for, 128; Keynes and Keynesianism, 216, 217; monetary constitution for ECCs, 288, 300n20; public goods, concept of, 258n2; "socialism is dead, but leviathan lives on," xiv; taxation and government spending, 42–43, 44–45

budget. *See* taxation and government spending

Buono Ordinario del Tesoro (BOT), 111

bureaucracy. *See* red tape

Burke, Edmund, 14

Burton, John, 215

Bury, J. B., 227n24

Bush (George H. W.) administration, 42

Cagan, Phillip, 275n11, 289

Canada, 34, 93, 105, 268, 341

capitalism and free enterprise: Keynesian views regarding, 202–9, 228n25; statist problems faced by, 334–40; statist *vs.* capitalist exploitation, 52, 127; twentieth-century pessimism and optimism regarding, 220–22, 226–29, 319–20

cargo cults, Eastern European reformers compared to, 333

cash economy, underground economy not necessarily operating as, 164–65

Catholic schools in Italy, 70, 87–88

Cato Institute, 129

Cato Journal, 28, 223n11, 224n13, 268n2, 271n6, 275n11, 281n20, 283

Cavour, Camillo Benso, Conti di, 51–52

Cazzola, Giuliano, 130n1, 130n4, 131n9, 131n11

CENSIS, 67

central banks: common European currency issues, 260n4, 269n4, 277–80; European Central Bank (ECB), 260n4, 277–79, 281; monetary policy and behavior of, 245–48, 254–55

Centrale del latte, Rome, 57

Centro Richerche Economiche Applicate (CREA), 84n1

charts. *See* tables, charts, and figures

checking accounts in Italy, role of, 165, 181–82n5

child labor and underground labor market, 170, 188

China, x, 232, 341

choice in education, 339–40

Christian Democratic Party, 13

Christianity and cult of poverty, 138–39

Chrystal, K. Alec, 225n17

Chubb, John, 339n25

CIS (Commonwealth of Independent States), 300, 304, 305–7

classical liberalism, ix–x, 318–44; change in meaning of, 218; defined, 218n1; economists' responsibility for move towards, 324–25; environmentalism, 234; historical perspective on apparent triumph of, 320–21; intellectual climate and policy change, relationship between, 321–24, 325–27, 342–44; Keynesian critique of, 199–200, 202, 203; Martino's, ix, xi; Mont Pèlerin

Society, future role of, 329–44; socialism and liberalism, quantitative difference between, 230; twentieth-century waves of pessimism and optimism regarding, 220–22, 226–29, 319–20; world events strengthening, x, xvi, 318–28
collective bargaining. *See* unions
command economy, monetary policy for, 287
commerce clause, U.S. constitution, 258–59
Common Agricultural Policy, EU, 259
common European currency, xv, 257–82; asymmetric shocks in different countries, risk of producing, 276–77; benefits and advantages of, 259–61, 268–70; competition in currencies, advantages of, 264–66, 281; deficit-to-GDP ratio of no more than 3%, 272, 274; discretion *vs.* rules in monetary policy (constitutional needs), 262–63, 270–74, 277–80; European Central Bank (ECB), 260n4, 277–79, 281; fixed *vs.* flexible exchange rates, 261–62, 263–64; Martino's unease regarding, 267; nation-state, concept of, 257–58; parallel European and national currencies, 263–64, 280–81, 306; popular rejection, risks of, 274–76; recessionary risks, 276–77; U.S. dollar, as alternative to, 259–60
Commonwealth of Independent States (CIS), 300, 304, 305–7
communism: collapse of, 330–34; ex-communist countries (ECCs), 330–34 (*see also* monetary constitution for ex-communist countries); Orwell's *Nineteen Eighty-four,* 316–17; statist policy, 52, 66, 320
Communist Party: Keynesians as members of, 202; pension reform, opposition to, 134; statist policy, move away from, 66; taxation and government spending, position on, 13
commutative justice, 146
competition in currencies, advantages of: common European currency, 264–66, 281; monetary constitution for ECCs, 293–95
compulsory education: financing, 74–77; problems with concept of, 69, 70–74
Confederazione Generale dell'Industria Italiana, 192n26
conspicuous consumption: free enterprise and, 203–4; underground economy, as indicator of, 159–60
constant monetary growth rule, 295–97, 304–5n25, 306
constitutional issues: commerce clause, U.S. constitution, 258–59; deficit constraints, 29, 43–46, 123; educational vouchers, 84–85; fiscal constitution, need for, 128; monetary policy, discretion *vs.* rules, 254–56, 262–63, 270–74, 277–80; monetary policy, ECCs (*see* monetary constitution for ex-communist countries); tax issues not submissible to public referendum, 117
consumer price index: gold standard, 290–92; quantity theory of money, 55
Contini, Bruno, 187n15
Corriere della sera, 282n23
corruption and statist policy, 59

Cosciani, C., 16n3
Craxi, Bettano, 83
CREA (Centro Richerche Economiche Applicate), 84n1
credit market, underground economy's lack of access to, 164, 183
criminal activities, underground economy and, 175, 194
CTI (total domestic credit), 246–47
Cuba, socialism in, 218
cult of poverty, 137–39
currency: large banknotes, demand for, 160, 161; money/income ratio, 164–66, 179–86; underground economy and currency ratio, 162–63, 165, 178–79. *See also* common European currency; monetary policy
currency competition, advantages of: common European currency, 264–66, 281; monetary constitution for ECCs, 293–95
currency exchange rates, fixed *vs.* flexible: common European currency, 261–62, 263–64; monetary constitution for ECCs, 305
Czechoslovakia, 333n13

D'Alema, Massimo, 282n23
debt, public. *See* public debt
decentralization of government, 302, 341. *See also* Federalism
deficits, xi–xii; asymmetries in perception of costs and benefits of public spending, 39–41, 42–43, 96–98, 119–23, 249; "balanced budget norm," abandonment of, 122–23; common European currency requiring 3% deficit-to-GDP ratio, 272, 274; constitutional constraints on, 29, 43–46, 123; engines of economic growth, viewed as, 28, 122–23, 225; freedom and taxation, 109–10, 124–25; "Friedman effect," 28–29, 42–43; government spending, as percentage of, 19, 34, 38, 250, 328n16; government spending financed by, 19–20, 25; government spending, relationship to, 35–43; increase in Italian deficit, 1961–1987, 33–36; interrupted *vs.* constant growth, 41–42; Keynesian views on, 28, 122–23, 225; marginal propensity for public-sector spending, 31–33; monetary constitution for ECCs, 299–301; monetary policy, 37, 248–54; percentage of GDP, expressed as, 3, 8, 19, 34, 35, 37, 44, 54, 94, 95, 109–10, 122, 123, 250, 254, 326n13; percentage of GNP, expressed as, 3, 300; problems created by, xiv–xv, 28–29; reduction of deficit *vs.* leaving it as is, 26–27; savings levels, 25–26; statist policy and fiscal irresponsibility, 54–55; tax and tax revenue increases, effect of, 3–6, 8; total public debt outstanding, 36–37; U.S. and Italian deficits compared, 33–35; welfare state, financial crisis caused by, 94–95; world expansion of, 1980's, ix. *See also* public debt
defined contribution and defined benefit pension systems, 132–33
Del Colle, E., 17, 23
Delors Report, 261n7
De Martino, Francesco, 57, 65
democracy, liberty more important than, 64
demographics, 129–31, 342
Denmark, strikes in, 56, 193n30

Derjabin, Anatolij, 332
Deutsche Bundesbank, 158
difference principle, 143–44
Dillard, Dudley, 200
Dini government, 134, 135
diplomas, legal value of, 85
Director, Aaron, 255
disabled or invalid pensions, 131–32, 170, 188
disposable income levels, 21–27
Disraeli, Benjamin, 68
distributist policy: effects of, 59–60, 61–62; freedom and taxation, 125–26; social justice, 139–46; tax evasion viewed as redistribution of income from honest to dishonest, 173–74; wastefulness of, 79
dogmatism and tolerance, 315
Dörfer, I., 301n22
Dorn, James A., 280n19, 283

Eastern Europe, collapse of Communism in, 330–34
ECB (European Central Bank), 260n4, 277–79, 281
ECCs (ex-communist countries), 330–34. *See also* monetary constitution for ex-communist countries
Economia Internazionale, 120n12
Economic Affairs, 83, 87n4, 88, 120n12
economic growth: deficits as engines of, 28, 122–23, 225; implications of, 22–25; inflation, relationship to, 270–71, 283–84; Italy and U.S. compared, 54; monetary stability policies, effect of, 244–45; preconditions for successful economy, 298n19; underground economy, consequences of, 172–73
Economic Journal, 15n1, 202n8, 213n23
Economie appliquée, 224n15, 272n8
Economist: capitalism, current problems of, 334–35; common European currency, 259n3, 261n6–7, 262n9, 272n9, 273n10, 278n16; Communism, collapse of, 332n8; educational choice, 339n25; gold standard and Soviet Union, 296n16; monetary policy, 262n9; pensions, 129, 130n1, 131n10, 132n12, 133n15, 134n16; socialism, 226n18, 226n20, 227n21, 228n26, 229n29, 235–236n41; taxation and government spending, 22n11, 29, 52; underground economy, 191n22, 192n28–29
economists: responsibility for move towards classical liberalism, 324–25; unintended effects, concern with, 91
ecoterrorism, 235n39, 336n17
education: Catholic schools in Italy, 70, 87–88; compulsory education, 69, 70–74; financing compulsory education, 74–77; financing noncompulsory higher education, 77–81; freedom threatened by government indoctrination, 68–82; kindergarten program, 99–100; merit criterion, 79; private provision of "public" services, 60; public educational failures and growth of underclass, 335, 339–40; public goods, education as, 68–70, 88; requiring *vs.* providing, 102
education vouchers: arguments against, 84–88; arguments in favor of, 88–89; financing compulsory education, 76–77; financing noncompulsory higher education, 81; socialist acceptance of, 83–89; welfare state, 102–3
EEC. *See* European Economic Community

efficiency problems: public financing of compulsory education, 76; public financing of noncompulsory higher education, 80–81; statist policies, 57–58
Einaudi, Luigi, 167
Ellis, Barbara, 186n13, 192n27
Eltis, Walter, 209
emigration of Jews to Israel, Soviet tax on, 77–78
EMU (European Monetary Union). *See* common European currency
England. *See* United Kingdom
environmentalism, 234–35, 335–36
envy, social justice as rationalization of, 137–39
Erasmus, 130n3
L'Espresso, 66, 282n23, 320
European Central Bank (ECB), 260n4, 277–79, 281
European Economic Community (EEC)/European Union (EU): absurd regulations promulgated by, 233–34, 338; Common Agricultural Policy, 259; cost of, 259; Federalism, 233, 341; labor market regulation, 230–31; nation-state, concept of, 257–58; pensions as percentage of GDP, 131; public goods, European, 258–62; tax harmonization, 232–34; underground economy, 169, 192, 193. *See also* common European currency
European Group, 267
evasion of taxes. *See* tax evasion
"evil empire," collapse of, 226
exchange rates, fixed *vs.* flexible: common European currency, 261–62, 263–64; monetary constitution for ECCs, 305
ex-communist countries (ECCs), 330–34. *See also* monetary constitution for ex-communist countries
expenditure in relation to income as indicator of underground economy, 160–61
expenditures, governmental. *See* taxation and government spending

Falcucci, Franca, 85
Fascism, x, 52, 57, 219, 323
Federalism, 233, 259, 301–2, 341
Federal Reserve Bank of St. Louis Review, 119n10, 224n14, 225n17, 271n7, 279n18
Federal Reserve Board, 246, 247–48
Feige, Edgar L., 163, 173n17
Feldstein, Martin, 276
Feulner, Edwin J., Jr., 227n22, 330n4
Fiat, 191, 191–92n25
figures. *See* tables, charts, and figures
"filter mechanism," 226, 332
financial crisis caused by welfare state, 92–95
Financial Times, 268n3
financing deficits through government spending, 19–20, 25
financing education: compulsory education, 74–77; noncompulsory higher education, 77–81
financing government spending, means of, 115–17
Finch, Peter D., 234n38, 336n17
Finer, S. E., 120n13
Finland, 46
Finmeccanica, 191
fiscal constitution. *See* constitutional issues; monetary constitution
fiscal drag (bracket creep), 11–12, 25, 118–19
Fisher effect, 224, 271, 284
fixed incomes, 16, 166
fixed *vs.* flexible exchange rates: common European currency,

261–62, 263–64; monetary constitution for ECCs, 305
Forbes, 186n13
forced labor, taxes on earnings as, 53, 104, 127
Foreign Affairs, 276n13
foreign trade as means of tax evasion, 169
foreign workers, 170, 188–89
Forte, Francesco, 88
France: deficit, 34; direct pay as percentage of total labor costs, 192; GDP, tax revenue as percentage of, 93, 94, 105; increase in nominal wages, 192; money/income ratios compared, 180, 181; steel rod *(tondinisti)* producers, 169; strikes, 56, 193n30; tax revenue as percentage of GDP, 30–31; underground economy, 158, 159; workweek, 232
Fraser Forum, 326n15
Fratianni, M., 17n5, 290n9
freedom and liberty, xv–xvii; capitalism and free enterprise, Keynesian views regarding, 202–9; Cavour on statism *vs.,* 51–52; democracy, liberty more important than, 64; education and government indoctrination, 68–82; environmentalism, problems raised by, 234–35, 335–36; equality's compatibility with, 146; exact measurement of macroeconomic variables, effects of, 171; government growth as threat to, 46, 322–24, 325–27, 340–42; intellectual climate and policy change, relationship between, 321–24, 325–27, 342–44; modern socialism's toleration of market system without acceptance of individual liberty, 229; Mont Pèlerin Society, future role of, 329–44; Orwell's *Nineteen Eighty-four,* 313–17; regulatory excesses, threats posed by, 175, 230–37, 334–39; safety and health regulations, threats posed by, 235–37, 336–39; social justice's compatibility with, 146–47; statist controls in "free" countries, effects of, 51–52, 63–64, 334–40; twentieth-century pessimism and optimism regarding, 220–22, 226–29, 319–20. *See also* taxation, liberty, and the welfare state
free enterprise. *See* capitalism and free enterprise
Frey, Luigi, 186n12, 189n20
Friedland, C., 120n13
Friedman, David, 221
Friedman, Milton: asymmetries in perception of costs and benefits of public spending, 39n2, 40n3; central banks, 277; collapse of communism, comments on, 331; common European currency, 261–62n8, 271n8, 277; constant monetary growth rule, 295–96, 304–5n25; currency competition, 293; demand for money, measuring, 179n2–3; education, 69–70, 75, 84n1; flexible exchange rates, 305; freedom and taxation, connection between, 9; gold standard, 255n21, 289; government spending slowed by deficit concerns ("Friedman effect"), 28–29, 42–43; inflation and unemployment, relationship between, 222, 223–24n13, 284; influence of, 217; intellectual climate and policy change, relationship between, 326, 343n33; invisible taxation, 16–17, 53;

Friedman, Milton (*continued*)
Martino's study under, x; monetary policy, 242, 243, 245–47, 252n17, 255, 271n6, 277, 278–79n17, 281n22, 284, 285, 301; Mont Pèlerin Society founded by, xi; nation-state, concept of, 257; optimism about future of capitalism, 221; political *vs.* market systems, 63; regression fallacy, 160; stabilization policies, 224n15; university professors, income of, 171, 189
Friedman, Rose, 40n3, 75n8, 301, 326, 343n33
Fund, John, 333n13

G7 (Group of 7), 30, 34, 35, 93, 94
Galbraith, J. K., 205
Garello, Jacques, 270n5
GDP. *See* Gross Domestic Product
General Theory. *See* Keynes, John Maynard, and Keynesianism
general theory of government growth, 38–42, 95, 119–20
Gentile, Giovanni, 219n3
George III, 27
Germany: deficit, 34; direct pay as percentage of total labor costs, 192; GDP, tax revenue as percentage of, 93, 105; hyperinflation, 213–14; increase in nominal wages, 192; money/income ratios compared, 180, 181; steel rod *(tondinisti)* producers, 169; strikes, 56, 193n30; underground economy, 158, 159
Gershman, Carl, 316n3
Il Giornale, 88n6, 333n11
Il Giornale Nuovo, 191n23–24, 193n21
GNP. *See* Gross National Product
gold standard, 255, 278, 288–92, 296
Goldwyn, Sam, 318n1
Gordon, R. J., 179n2
Gordon, S., 140n6
government: budget and spending (*see* taxation and government spending); decentralization and Federalism, 341; freedom, government growth as threat to, 46, 322–24, 325–27, 340–42; involvement and controls, xiii; monetary stability, institutional threats to, 248–54; moonlighting and absenteeism in public sector jobs, 190, 191; need for, 54, 62–63; short-term life government expectancy and long-term goals, 41; statism as destructive of, 62–63; statist controls in "free" countries, effects of, 334–40; underground economy and size of public sector, 173; underground economy as escape from, 171. *See also* headings at public; law and legislation
government bonds, 111, 182n6
government growth: asymmetries in perception of costs and benefits of public spending, 39–41, 42–43, 96–98, 119–23, 249; freedom and liberty, as threat to, 46, 322–24, 325–27, 340–42; general theory of, 38–42, 95, 119–20. *See also* taxation and government spending
Great Britain. *See* United Kingdom
Greenwood, John G., 298n19
Gresham's law, 269
Gross Domestic Product (GDP): common European currency requiring 3% deficit-to-GDP ratio, 272, 274; deficit as percentage of, 3, 8, 19, 34, 35, 37, 44, 54, 94, 95, 109–10, 122, 123, 250, 254, 326n13; economic growth, implications of, 22–23; government

spending as percentage of, 5, 8, 13, 17, 25, 29–30, 34, 37, 92, 105, 107–8, 115, 124, 128, 340; monetary policy, 245, 247; money/income ratio and underground economy in Italy, 180; OECD country pensions as percentage of, 131, 133; OECD country public spending levels as percentage of, 124; OECD country tax revenue as percentage of, 93, 94; pensions as percentage of, 131, 133; private GDP *vs.* public spending, 8; public debt as ratio of, 36–37, 110–12, 128; revision of figures upward, 10, 31; savings levels and, 26, 135; Taiwan's economic growth, 90; tax revenue as percentage of, 4–5, 8, 29, 30–31, 32, 93–94, 105–7, 114, 128; welfare state and social spending, 98, 99, 105, 107–8, 131
Gross National Product (GNP): deficit as percentage of, 3, 300; government spending as percentage of, 193, 301; ratio of public debt to, 55; underground economy as unmeasured portion of, 157, 159, 160–63, 172, 173, 187
Group of 7 (G7), 30, 34, 35, 93, 94
growth, economic. *See* economic growth
growth, governmental. *See* government growth; taxation and government spending
Gutmann, Professor, 162

Haberler, Gottfried, 201, 224n15, 265n11, 272n8, 284, 292n10, 294n13
Hanks, S. H., 285, 297, 307
Hansen, Alvin, 200
Harris, Lord, 76, 236n43, 338n21
Harrod, Sir Roy, 202
Hartwell, Max, 329n1, 330n3, 334
Hayek, Friedrich A.: currency competition, 293; education, 69–70, 73–74, 79; Keynesianism, 205, 206, 215–16; monetary policy, 255n22; Mont Pèlerin Society, founding of, xi, 318; socialism, 218n2, 219–20, 229n28; social justice, 146
health and safety regulations, threats to freedom posed by, 235–37, 336–39
health care, 66, 67, 100, 103, 105–6
Heller, Walter, 199
Heritage Lectures, 136, 199, 268n2
Hicks, Sir John R., 199, 202, 210, 243
Hitler, Adolph, 64, 219, 219n4, 314
"holistic social engineering," 137
Holland, 56, 192, 193n30
Hume, David, xvi, 62, 342n32
Hutchinson, T. W., 201, 202, 209, 210, 216n28
Hutt, William H., 199
hyperinflation: CIS, 304; Germany, 213–14
hypochondriasis, 191

ideology and policy change, relationship between, 321–24, 325–27, 342–44
illustrations. *See* tables, charts, and figures
IMF (International Monetary Fund), deficit as defined by, 33
immigration, 342
Imprimis, 59
income levels: disposable income, 21–27; distributist policy, effects of, 59–60, 61–62; expenditure in relation to income as indicator of underground economy, 160–61; increase in nominal wages, 56, 192;

income levels (*continued*)
"money illusion" (increase in nominal per capita income), 21–25; money/income ratio in Italy and existence of underground economy, 164–66; salaries, attempts to determine, 152–54
indoctrination via education, fears of, 68–82. *See also* education
inefficiency: public financing of compulsory education, 76; public financing of noncompulsory higher education, 80–81; statist policies, 57–58
inflation, xi, xiv; economic growth, relationship to, 270–71, 283–84; German hyperinflation, 213–14; hyperinflation, CIS, 304; hyperinflation, Germany, 213–14; interest rates, 213–14, 224, 271, 284; invisibility of certain taxation, effect on, 25; Keynes and Keynesianism, 209, 210–14, 223–24, 270–71, 283; large banknotes, demand for, 161; monetary constitution for ex-communist countries (ECCs), transitional period, 286–87; monetary policy and "government push," 248–54; monetary policy, effects of, 241–42, 245, 270–71; "money illusion" eroded by, 22; money/income ratio, 182; money supply and underground economy, 178–79; per capita cost of government, 17; savings levels, 25; slumpflation (inflation-cum-recession), 26–27; tax rates and, 12; unemployment and, 211–12, 222, 271, 284; world increase in, 1980's, ix
Innis, Harold Adams, 297, 299
Institute of Economic Affairs, 222
Instituto Centrale di Statistica (ISTAT), 19n8, 166, 168n15, 184–86, 187, 195
intellectual climate and policy change, relationship between, 321–24, 325–27, 342–44
interest: Keynesian view of inflation, 213–14, 224, 271, 284; monetary policy, 253, 271; money/income ratio, 182; public debt payments, 112, 128
International Background, 241
International Herald Tribune, 186
International Labor Office, 193n30
International Monetary Fund (IMF), deficit as defined by, 33
invalid or disability pensions, 170, 188
invisible taxation, 16–20, 25, 41, 53, 115–17, 125, 167–68
Ireland, strikes in, 56, 193n30
IRI, 57, 191, 193
Issues in Science and Technology, 343n35
Italian General Confederation of Labor, 13
Izvestia, 296n16

Jansen, Dennis W., 279n18
Japan, 34, 93, 105, 159
Jasay, Anthony de, 45, 231n34, 333n12
Jews emigrating to Israel, Soviet Union's tax on, 77–78
Joffe, Josef, 277n14, 281n21
Johnson, Harry G., 144–45, 243, 297
Johnson, M. H., 17n6
Johnson, Paul, 313–17
Jordan, Jerry, 232n35
Jordan, J. L., 285
Journal of Law and Economics, 222n10, 255n23
Journal of Money, Credit and Banking, 223n12, 224n13, 271n6

Journal of Political Economy, 140n6, 224n15, 256n25, 272n8

Kahn, Lord, 202
Kaldor, Nicholas, 243
Kant, Immanuel, 342n32
Kendall, Frances, 341n27
Keynes, John Maynard, and Keynesianism, ix, xiii–xiv, xvi, 199–217; abandonment of, 223–25, 323, 342; alternating moods and opinions, Keynes subject to, 207, 208; biographical information about Keynes, 214–16; capitalism and free enterprise, views regarding, 202–9, 228n25; constitutional constraints on deficits, effect of Keynesian revolution on, 44–45; deficits as engines of economic growth, 28, 122–23, 225; economists, influence of, 324; Fisher effect, 224, 271, 284; inflation, 209, 210–14, 223–24, 270–71, 283; influence of, 199–201, 214–17; "in the long run we are all dead," 212, 342; Keynesianism of Keynes, 210; liquidity effect, 224, 271, 284; marginal propensity for public-sector spending, 32; monetary policy, 246, 252–54, 270, 283–85; politicians, Keynes' dislike of, 216; pseudo-Keynesians or bastard Keynesians, 201, 202; savings levels, 26, 342; socialism and Keynesianism, xiii, 206–10, 222, 223–25; stabilization policies, 171, 173, 216–17, 223–25; wide-ranging nature of "Keynesian" economic theory, 201–2
kidnappings, 160, 194n34
kindergarten program, 99–100
King, Florence, 236n42, 337n20
Klaus, Vaclav, 333n13
Klein, Lawrence R., 90
Knight, Frank, 200–201, 322–23
Kogan, Norman, 84n
Kolm, Serge-Christophe, 158

Labini, Sylos, 83
labor costs: regulation of labor market increasing, 231–32; taxation increasing, 133–34; underground economy *vs.* official economy, 192–93
labor market and underground economy: absenteeism, 170, 190–92; activity rate and noninstitutional labor force, 169–71, 186–89; costs of labor in official economy, 192–93; foreign workers, 170, 188–89; moonlighting, 170, 189–90; taxation, role of, 133–34
labor market regulation, 230–32
labor mobility, 192
labor, taxes on earnings as forced form of, 53, 104, 127
labor unions. *See* unions
Labour Party, United Kingdom, 206–7, 222
Laidler, David, 251
Lamers, Karl, 268n3
Langfeldt, E., 295n14
Lao-tze, 90
Latin America's use of American currency, 161
Lau, Lawrence J., 90n1
law and legislation: beneficial nature of "lawless" underground economy, 194–95; distortion of purpose, 235, 337; regulatory burdens, effect of, 175, 230–37, 334–39; respect for, underground economy viewed as undermining, 174–76,

law and legislation (*continued*) 194–95; unintended consequences of, 177–78
Lee, Dwight R., 301, 341n29
legal value of diplomas, 85
Leijonhufvud, Axel, 202, 263n10, 280n19, 285
leisure demands created by underground economy, 170–71
Lekachmen, R., 201n4
Lenin, 58, 177n1, 211
Leube, K. R., 270n5
Liberal Party: Italian "economic miracle," role in, 54; taxation and government spending, position on, 13
liberal principles. *See* classical liberalism
liberty. *See* freedom and liberty
Libya, 257
Lilley, Peter, 143n9, 222n10
liquidity effect, 224, 271, 284
Locke, John, xvi, 314, 342n32
Louis XVI, 27
Louw, Leonard, 341n27
LUISS, 223n11
Luxembourg, strikes in, 56, 193n30

majority and minority rights, 63–64
managerial efficiency as product of market efficiency, 332
marginal propensity for public-sector spending, 31–33
market *vs.* political systems, 63–64
Marshall, Alfred, 215, 267
Martelli, Claudio, 66, 83–84, 88, 320
Martino, Antonio, about, ix–xi
Martino, Antonio, references to other writings of: collapse of Communism, 333n11; common European currency, 268n2, 270n5; education, 84n1, 88n5–7, 339n24; monetary constitutions for ECCs, 300–301; monetary policy, 120n12, 244n5, 244n7, 247n13, 249n15, 254n19, 270n5; socialism, 220n6, 223n11, 228n26, 343n34; social justice, 140n6; statism, 320n5, 342n31; taxation and government spending, 18n7, 39n1, 113n6–7, 114n8, 115n9, 120n12; taxation and individual liberty, 111n5, 113n6–7, 114n8, 115n9, 120n12, 123n15; underground economy, 164n11, 179n4, 185n8, 186n10–11; welfare state, 91n2
Marx, Karl, and Marxism: socialism and classical liberalism, evolution of, xvi, 227n21, 228n25, 323, 342n32; social justice, concept of, 138; statist *vs.* capitalist exploitation, 52, 127
Masera, Rainer, 182n6
Mathews, Jessica T., 343n35
Matthews, C., 160, 186
Il Mattino (Naples), 159
Meiselman, D. I., 289
Meltzer, Allan H., 224–25n15–16, 247–48, 272n8, 284, 287n2, 288n5, 289n7, 299
merit criterion in education, 79
Methvin, E. H., 297n18
Miglo, G., 88n5
milk: Centrale del latte, Rome, 57; Soviet discussion of pricing on fat *vs.* protein content, 332
Mill, John Stuart, 61, 69, 74, 102
Minc, Alain, 282n23
minority and majority rights, 63–64
Mirfin, D., 120n13
Mises, Ludwig von, 71, 127n21, 236n43
Moe, Terry, 339n25
Moggridge, Donald E., 215
Mondale, Walter, 3

Il Mondo, 185n9, 186n12
"monetarism," 222, 243–44
monetary constitution for ex-communist countries (ECCs), 283–310; CIS, 305–7; competition in currencies, advantages of, 293–95; constant monetary growth rule, 295–97, 304–5n25, 306; deficit controls, 299–301; Federalism, 301–2; gold standard, 288–92, 296; individual countries, specific needs of, 304–5; Martino's proposals for, 297–307; overhang (excess cash supply), false problem of, 303; parallel currencies, 306–7; privatization, 298; problems faced, 297–98; replacement of existing monetary units, 303–4, 305; reverse revenue sharing, 301–2; taxation and government spending, limits on, 299–301; transitional period, 285–87; types of monetary constitutions, 288–97
monetary constitution, need for (discretion *vs.* rules), 254–56, 262–63, 270–74, 277–80
monetary policy, xiv–xv, 241–309; central bank behavior, 245–48, 254–55; competition in currencies (*see* competition in currencies, advantages of); constant monetary growth rule, 295–97, 304–5n25, 306; constitution, ECCs (*see* monetary constitution for ex-communist countries); constitution, need for (discretion *vs.* rules), 254–56, 262–63, 270–74, 277–80; deficits, 37, 248–54; denationalization of competing currencies, 255; economic growth and, 244–45; European public good, money as, 259–62; government's institutional framework, problems arising from, 248–54; inflation, effect on, 241–42, 245, 270–71; interest rates, 253, 271; Italy, 242, 243–45, 248–54; Keynesian interpretation of, 246, 252–54, 270, 283–85; public debt, 37; quantity theory of money, 55; United Kingdom and United States, 241–42. *See also* common European currency
monetary statistics and underground economy: aggregate demand for money, 163, 178, 179n2; currency ratio, 162–63, 165, 178–79; large banknotes, demand for, 160, 161; monetary statistics used to derive size of, 162–63; money/income ratio, 164–66, 179–86; reliability of monetary statistics, 166, 184–86
monetary unification. *See* common European currency
"money illusion," 21–25, 183
Mont Pèlerin Society: founding of, xi, 318; future role of, 329–44; Martino's involvement in, xi; meetings of, 329n1; members of, 329; objectives of, 330; papers presented at, xi, 68, 177, 220n6, 241, 242n2, 246n9, 313, 329, 342n31; Schumpeter's comments on, 221n7, 318–19
moonlighting, 170, 189–90
Moore, John, 279n17
moral questions: moral relativism, 314–15; regulatory threats to concept of personal responsibility, 235–37, 336–39; statist policy, 53–54, 60–62; tax system, 125–27
Mundell, Robert A., 293n12, 296n16
Murdoch, Rupert, 227, 230, 238n47
Murero, Claudio, 130n5
Mussolini, Benito, 219

Naples, 159, 190
Napoleon, 253
national income, measuring, xiii
nationalization, 57, 230
National Review, 224n15, 227, 230n30–31, 236n42, 237n44, 272n8, 331n7, 337n20
Nazism, 52, 219–20, 220n5
"neoclassical" or "classical" economists, 199–200, 202, 203. *See also* classical liberalism
Neosocialism, 230
Netherlands, 56, 192, 193n30
new wants, importance of, 205–6
New Zealand, xi, 218, 220n6, 306n26
Nietzsche, F. W., 139, 314
Nineteen Eighty-four (Orwell), xv–xvi, 313–17
Niskanen, William A., 298n19
Nixon, Richard, 201
Nock, Albert J., 64
nominal *vs.* real income, 21–25, 27
noninstitutional labor force, 170, 186–89
North Korea, socialism in, 218
Notiziario, 223n11
Nozick, Robert, 1–4, 53, 126–27, 139–40, 144–45, 147, 226
Nutter, G. W., 298n19

Occhetto, Achille, 66, 320
OECD. *See* Organization for Economic Cooperation and Development (OECD) and OECD countries
O'Higgins, M., 161n7
Oliver, Charles, 336n17
Olson, Mancur, 253
Organization for Economic Cooperation and Development (OECD) and OECD countries: currency demands, 165n12, 181n5; pensions as percentage of GDP, 131, 133; public spending levels, 29, 92, 124; tax evasion, 16, 113–14; tax levels in OECD countries, 30; tax revenue as percentage of GDP, 93, 94
Orwell, George, xv–xvi, 234n37, 313–17, 335n16
overhang (excess cash supply) in ECCs, false problem of, 303
overtime, union resistance to, 192

Palladino, Giovanni, 130n1, 130n7, 133n13
Panorama, 130n1
Paracelsus, 230
parallel European common and national currencies, 263–64, 280–81, 306–7
Pareto, Vilfredo, 15, 39, 120
Parkin, Michael, 242, 243, 248
Parravicini, Giannino, 179n4
"Party of Catastrophe," 206–7, 209
Pathfinder, 255n23
Patinkin, Don, 202
patrimonial obligations, imposition of, 11–12
Peleggi, G., 31, 93
Penati, A., 246n11, 247n12
pensions, 129–35; defined contribution and defined benefit systems, 132–33; demographic threat to "pay-as-you-go" systems, 129–31; disability pensions, 131–32, 170, 188; GDP, as percentage of, 131, 133; increasing generosity of, 131–33; privatized, 134–35, 229–30n30; retirement age, reduction in, 132; underground economy, 170, 188; unsustainability of current system coupled with impossibility of reform, 133–34; voucher system, 103
personal responsibility: regulatory

threats to concept of, 235–37, 336–39; statism threatening concept of, 60–62
Peter, Lawrence, 237, 339
Petroni, A. M., 270n5
Phillips curve, 222, 223–24n13, 271n6
Pigou, A. C., 267n1
Pile, Sir William, 159
Playboy interview with Milton Friedman, 63, 221
Policy, 223n11, 234n38, 270n5, 336n17
policy change and ideology, relationship between, 321–24, 325–27, 342–44
Policy Review, 15, 16n2, 17n4, 53, 91n2, 114n8, 148, 152, 157, 164n11
political bargaining power: financing noncompulsory higher education, 79; income levels and, 59; unions, 56
political parties: tax reform, positions on, 13–14. *See also* specific parties
political *vs.* market systems, 63–64
politicians and bureaucrats as true beneficiaries of welfare state, 98–101
Popper, Sir Karl R., 137, 141, 146, 237–38n45, 238, 313
Post Office, 58, 189–90
poverty, cult of, 137–39
Pravda, 316
private enterprise. *See* capitalism and free enterprise
private provision of "public" services, 9; socialism and classical socialism, evolution of, 328n16; statist policy, 60, 62, 67; taxation and liberty, 105–6; welfare state, intentions *vs.* results of, 90–91
privatization: monetary constitution for ex-communist countries (ECCs), 298; public pension schemes, 134–35, 229–30n30
Prodi, Romano, 134, 282n23
PSI. *See* Socialist Party
public choice perspective, ix, xii
public debt: freedom and taxation, 110–12; GDP, as ratio of, 36–37, 110–12, 128; interest payments on, 112, 128; monetary policy, 252–53; pensions, 133; statism, 54–55, 67; taxation and government spending, 36–37, 39, 40. *See also* deficits
public goods: CIS, 305; concept of, 258–59; education as, 68–70, 88; European, 258–62; government spending on, 40
Public Opinion, 105n2
public school. *See* education
public sector firms: moonlighting and absenteeism in, 190, 191; statist management issues, 56–58; underground economy and size of, 173
public services, xii; health care, 66, 67, 100, 103, 105–6; income, not considered as part of, 26; increase in social spending for nonexistent benefits, 117–18; waste and inefficiency in, 9–10, 105–6. *See also* private provision of "public" services
public spending. *See* taxation and government spending

Qaddafi, Muammar, 257
quantity theory of money, 55

Rawls, John, 140–44
Reagan administration, 42, 95, 221
real estate transactions as means of tax evasion, 169
real *vs.* nominal income, 21–25
Reason, 65, 254n20, 320n5, 333n13, 336n17

receipts, requirement to provide, 193, 194n34
redistribution of income. *See* distributist policy
red tape, xii; education vouchers, resistance to, 86–87; government spending "controls," 148–51; salaries, attempts to determine, 152–54; welfare state, bureaucrats and politicians as true beneficiaries of, 98–101
regression fallacy, 160
regulatory burdens, effect of, 175, 230–37, 334–39
La Repubblica, 16n3, 88n7
Republican Party's position on taxation and government spending, 13
responsibility, personal: regulatory threats to concept of, 235–37, 336–39; statism threatening concept of, 60–62
reverse revenue sharing, 301–2, 341n29
Reviglio, Franco, 166–67, 193n32
Reynolds, A., 288n5, 289n6
Reynolds, M., 255n23
Risorgimento, 289
Riva, Massimo, 282n23
Robertson, Dennis, 202
Robertson, Patrick, 268n2
Roberts, Paul Craig, 34
Robinson, Joan, 200–205, 208, 210, 213–14
Robinson, Sir Austin, 201
Romana Recapiti and Rome Post Office, 189–90
Romer, Christina D., 224n15, 272n8, 278n17
Rose, Richard, 16, 104n2, 113–14, 159n4, 166–68, 171, 173
Ross, L., 223n12
Russell, Bertrand, 136
Russia. *See* Commonwealth of Independent States; Soviet Union/former Soviet Union

Sachs, J., 303
Sadowksy, J. S., 270n5
safety and health regulations, threats to freedom posed by, 235–37, 336–39
salaries, attempts to determine, 152–54
Salvemini, Gaetano, 57
Samuelson, Paul, 200
savings levels, 25–26, 135, 181–82, 213, 342
Scheide, J., 295n14
Schoeck, Helmut, 138
Schopenhauer, Arthur, 70, 72
Schuler, K., 285, 297, 307
Schumpeter, Joseph A.: economic liberalism as defined by, 218n1; intellectual climate and policy change, relationship between, 327; Mont Pèlerin Society, comments on, 221n7, 318–19; pessimism as to future of capitalism and free enterprise, xvi, 220, 319, 328; socialism defined by, 220n7; social orders, transformation of, 228n27, 321
Schwartz, Anna J., 224n13, 271n6, 275n12, 278n17, 280n19, 283, 284, 294
secrecy of deposits in Italy, significance of, 165, 182n5, 183n7
"Secret Weapon," 9–10
Seldon, Arthur, 75n8, 104n1, 105n3, 222, 330n5
self-employed persons as tax evaders, 168
Shaw, G. B., 314
Shenfield, Barbara, 157–58, 172n16, 174–75

sick leave, 191
Simmons, Henry C., 241, 255–56
Singer, Fred, 321n6
single economic market possible without common currency, 268
slumpflation (inflation-cum-recession), 26–27
Smith, Adam: classical liberalism, power of, xvi, 235n40, 322, 323; interest *vs.* duty, 86; Keynes and Keynesianism, 216; statism, xiii, 58; taxation, certainty in, 124–25; underground economy, 175–76
smoking restrictions, 236n42, 237, 237n43, 337
social fabric, statist disruption of, 61–62
socialism, x, 218–38; environmentalism, 234–35; evolution of, ix, xiv, xvi, 218–22, 226–29; Keynes and Keynesianism, xiii, 206–10, 222, 223–25; labor market regulation, 230–32; liberalism and socialism, quantitative difference between, 230; moonlighting, 190; statist policy and, 52, 237–38, 320; tax harmonization, 232–34; toleration of market system without acceptance of individual liberty, 229; twentieth century as "century of the state," 219–20
Socialist Party (PSI): education vouchers, acceptance of, 83–89; nationalization aims, 57, 65; statist policy, xii, 54, 57, 65, 320; taxation and government spending, position on, 13
social justice, 136–47; cult of poverty, 137–39; distributionism, 139–46; envy, rationalization of, 137–39; freedom's compatibility with, 146–47; inequalities created by statist policy, 59–60; lofty ideals behind, 137; welfare state, intentions *vs.* results of, 91
social security contributions: invisible taxation, as form of, 18, 167–68; labor costs increased by, 192, 231–32
Il Sole—24 Ore, 88n5
South African Federalism, 341
South America's use of American currency, 161
Soviet Union/former Soviet Union: collapse of communism, x, xiv, xvi, 330–34; emigrating Jews, tax on, 77–78; Federalism, 341; gold standard, 296n16; Orwell's *Nineteen Eighty-four,* 316; real money supply circulating in, 297n17
Spain, 264, 341
Spaventa, Luigi, 202
Spencer, Herbert, 331, 339n23
Spinelli, F., 17n5, 246n11, 247n12, 251n16, 290n9
stabilization policies, 171, 173, 216–17, 223–25
Stalin, Joseph, 64, 139, 219, 314
La Stampa, 282n23
state-owned enterprises (SOEs), 286–87
statist policy, 51–67; awareness of effects of, 15–27; demise of socialism not end of, 237–38; government controls in "free" countries, effects of, 51–52, 63–64, 334–40; intellectual climate and policy change, relationship between, 321–24, 325–27, 342–44; measurement of extent of, 52–53; moral criticisms of, 53–54; move away from, ix, xii, xiv, xvi, 15, 65–67, 318–28, 319–20; rise of, 54, 65–66. *See also* Keynes, John Maynard, and Keynesianism; socialism

steel rod *(tondinisti)* producers, 169
Stein, P., 301n22
Stigler, George J., x, 39n2, 59, 120n13, 142, 199, 200, 324
stock market, 181
Stone, C. C., 244n6
strikes, 56, 191, 192–93
Stroup, Richard L., 234–35n38, 336n17
Studia Diplomatica, 268n2
Suenens, Cardinal, 282
supply-side Keynesians, 202
Sweden, 158–59, 301
Swift, Jonathan, 178
Switzerland: constitutional constraints on deficits, 46; currency competition, 294; Federalism, 233, 259, 302, 341; postal service, Italian use of, 58

tables, charts, and figures: deficit as percentage of government spending and GDP, 19, 34, 37, 38, 95, 122, 250, 328n16; deficit, money supply, and consumer prices, 195; gold prices and consumer price index, Italy, 290–92; government spending as percentage of GDP, 17, 30, 37, 105, 108, 128; interest payments on public debt, 112, 128; marginal propensity for public-sector spending, 33; means of financing government spending, 116; money/income ratio and underground economy, 164, 180, 181, 182, 184n7; per capita cost of government, 1960–1986, 92, 93; per capita GDP, public spending, and per capita income compared, 23; public debt, 39, 40, 111, 112, 128; quantity theory of money, 55; real cost of government, 1960–1987, 35; relationship between deficit and government spending, 36; revised GNP, 187; strikes, work days lost from, 56; tax brackets in Italy, 118; tax burden, size and growth of, 106; tax revenues as percentage of GDP, 31, 32, 93, 105, 106, 128
Taino, Danilo, 133n14
Taiwan, 90
Tanzi, Vito, 157, 158n3, 162–63, 183n7
Tatom, J. A., 119n10
taxation and government spending, x–xii, 1–47; asymmetries in perception of costs and benefits of public spending, 39–41, 42–43, 96–98, 119–23, 249; "balanced budget norm," abandonment of, 122–23; bracket creep (fiscal drag), 11–12, 25, 118–19; evasion of taxes, supposed Italian genius for, 8, 15–16, 20–21; forced labor, taxes on earnings as, 53, 104, 127; GDP, government spending as percentage of, 5, 8, 13, 17, 25, 29–30, 34, 37, 92, 105, 107–8, 115, 124, 128, 340; GDP, tax revenue as percentage of, 4–5, 8, 29, 30–31, 32, 93–94, 105–7, 114, 128; general theory of government growth, 38–42, 95, 119–20; GNP, government spending as percentage of, 193, 301; income tax burden, effect of, 7–10; increases in, 5, 8, 13, 17–19, 24, 29–31, 67, 106–9, 117–18, 171, 328n16; invisible taxation, 16–20, 25, 41, 53, 115–17, 125, 167–68; Italian tax reform, 7–8, 11–14; levels of tax in Italy, 113–15; loss of government revenue from tax evasion and underground

economy, 173–74; monetary constitution for ECCs, 299–301; monetary stability, institutional threats to, 248–54; "money illusion" (increase in nominal per capita income), 21–25; Mont Pèlerin Society, role of, 340–42; per capita cost of government, 1960–1986, 92, 93; political party positions on, 13–14; real per capita cost of government, 1960–1987, 35–36; reasons for lack of Italian resistance to, 15–27; reduction in spending and increase in taxes, 26–27; relationship between, 31–33; reverse revenue sharing, 301–2, 341n29; statism, as measurement of, 52–53; U.S. tax reform of 1986, 7; welfare state, financial crisis caused by, 92–94. *See also* deficits; government growth

taxation, liberty, and the welfare state, 9, 16, 104–28; asymmetries in perception of costs and benefits of public spending, 119–23; bracket creep (fiscal drag), 118–19; deficit, 109–10, 124–25; distributist policy, 125–26; fiscal constitution, need for, 128; forced labor, taxes on earnings as, 53, 104, 127; government growth, analysis of reasons for, 123–25; government spending, rise in, 107–9; inverse relationship between level of taxation and individual liberty, 127–28; invisible taxation, 115–17, 125; moral questions, 125–27; nonexistent benefits, increase in social spending for, 117–18; public debt, 110–12; tax burden, size and extent of, 106–7; tax evasion and tax levels in Italy, 113–15

tax evasion: government revenue, loss of, 173–74; increased taxes as incentive for, 171; monetary statistics, 163; opportunities for, 168–69; redistribution of income from honest to dishonest, viewed as, 173–74; supposed Italian genius for, 8, 15–16, 20–21, 104–5, 113–15, 166–67, 193–94; underground economy, as indicator of, 158, 161–62, 166–69, 193–94

tax harmonization in Europe, 232–34

tax revolts, 4, 11, 13, 27, 67

terrorism, 61

Thatcher, Margaret, 95, 221, 242

Thomas, Ivor, 220n5

Thoreau, Henry D., 137

Thornton, Daniel L., 224n14, 225n17, 271n7, 284

Thurn, M., 161n8

Times, 211, 212, 222

Tobin, J., 223n12

Tocqueville, Alexis de, 101

Toland, John, 219n4

tolerance and dogmatism, 315

tondinisti (steel rod producers), 169

Tory Party, 222

total domestic credit (CTI), 246–47

totalitarianism as presented in Orwell's *Nineteen Eighty-four,* 314–17

total public debt outstanding, 36–37

toy regulations, EEC/EU, 338

trade unions. *See* unions

train timetables, 9–10

Trapp, P., 295n14

Treaty of Rome, x, 272

Trotter, Sir Ronald, 218

Tullio, G., 246n11, 247n12, 251n16

Tullock, Gordon, 87n4, 95, 119, 224n13, 271n6, 304n23

underclass, educational failures leading to growth of, 335, 339–40 underground economy, xiii, 157–95; alternative names for, 157; beneficial nature of "lawlessness" of, 194–95; cash economy, not necessarily operating as, 164–65; causes of existence and growth of, 171; consequences of, 171–76; criminal nature of, 175, 194; definition of, 157–58; economic growth encouraged by, 22; GNP, unmeasured portion of, 157, 159, 160–63, 172, 173, 187; growth and widespread nature of, 158–59; Italian genius for, 178; Italian underground economy, evidence for existence of, 164–71; leisure demands created by, 170–71; monetary statistics used to derive size of, 162–63; tax evasion and, 114–15, 158, 161–62, 166–69, 193–94; types of evidence for existence of, 159–63. *See also* labor market and underground economy; law and legislation; monetary statistics and underground economy

unemployment: inflation, relationship to, 211–12, 222, 271, 284; Keynes' views on effects of, 208–9; Keynes' views on inflation and, 211–12; labor market regulation and, 231–32; underground economy, 170, 172, 188

unification, monetary. *See* common European currency

unions: education vouchers, teachers' unions opposed to, 87; labor costs, high rate of, 192; monetary policy, 253; moonlighting and absenteeism, 190; political process, collective bargaining as, 56; strikes, 56, 191, 192–93; taxation and government spending, position on, 13; underground economy, failure to criticize, 172n16

L'Unita, 316, 317

United Kingdom: deficit, 34; direct pay as percentage of total labor costs, 192; GDP per capita compared to Italy, 22; GDP, tax revenue as percentage of, 93, 105; government spending, ability to control, 95; increase in nominal wages, 192; Labour Party, 206–7, 222; monetary policy, 241–43; money/income ratios compared, 179–80, 181; prediction of dictatorship in, 319; public goods, concept of, 258; socialism in, 222; statist exploitation in, 53; steel rod *(tondinisti)* producers, 169; strikes, 56, 193n30; underground economy, 159, 183n7

United States: common European currency, benefits of, 260, 269; constant monetary growth rule, 295–96; constitutional constraints on deficits, 46; education as public good, 68; Federalism, 233, 259, 302, 341; foreign use of American currency, 161; "Friedman effect," 42; GDP, tax revenue as percentage of, 93, 105; government spending, ability to control, 95; Internal Revenue Service (IRS) report on tax evasion, 161–62; international tender, U.S. currency as, 260, 269, 294; Italian and U.S. deficits compared, 33–35; Italian economy compared, 54; labor market regulation, 230–31; monetary policy, 242, 243, 247–48; money/income ratios compared, 179, 181; Orwell's *Nineteen*

Eighty-four viewed as denouncing, 316; public goods concept and commerce clause, 258–59; redistribution of income, wastefulness of, 59; regulatory excesses, threats to freedom posed by, 235–36n41; single economic market possible without common currency, 268; tax burden compared to Italy, 119n10; tax increases as means of reducing deficit, 3–4; tax reform of 1986, 7; underground economy, 183n7
university professors' salaries, 60, 80, 120, 148–54, 170–71, 189, 325
Urbani, Giuliano, 130n3
U.S.S.R. *See* Commonwealth of Independent States; Soviet Union/former Soviet Union
U.S.S.R. Monitor, 296n16, 304n23

Valitutti, Salvatore, 74n6, 85, 86
Vatican postal service, use of, 58
Vaubel, Roland, 92, 124, 277, 281n20, 293n11, 306
Vietnam, socialism in, 218
vipers of Abruzzi, 91, 177
Visentini, Bruno, 12–13
Vitali, Ornello, 131n8
Voltaire, 175
vouchers, 102–3. *See also* education vouchers

Wagner, Richard E., 44–45, 123, 216, 217
Walker, M., 104n1
Wall Street Journal, 3, 7, 11, 242n1
Wall Street Journal Europe, 111n5, 113n6–7, 231n34, 232n36
Walters, A., 286, 303
Washington Post, 173n17, 236n42, 337
"wedge" (difference between labor costs and take-home pay), 231–32
welfare state, 99–128; asymmetries in perception of costs and benefits of public spending, 96–98, 119–23; bureaucrats and politicians as true beneficiaries of, 98–101; classical liberalism, evolution of, 323; deficits, 94–95; difficulty of disposing of, 98–101; financial crisis caused by, 92–95; GDP and social spending, 98, 99, 105, 107–8, 131; general theory of government growth, 95; increase in social spending for nonexistent benefits, 117–18; intentions *vs.* results of, 90–92; Mont Pèlerin Society, role of, 337, 339–40; size and extent of, 98–99; socialism, evolution of, 236; taxation and government spending, crisis in, 92–94; wastefulness of income redistribution, 59. *See also* taxation, liberty, and the welfare state
Werner plan for monetary unification, 261
West, E. G., 71, 75n8, 81n11
West Germany. *See* Germany
Wicksell, Knut, 44
Wilson, Harold, 134
withholding as invisible taxation, 18
women: protectionist laws, 231n32; underground labor market, 170, 188
workweek, 232

Yavlinsky, Grigory, 296n16
Yeager, Leland B., 281n22
youth and underground labor market, 170, 188

The typeface used for this book is ITC New Baskerville, which was created for the International Typeface Corporation and is based on the types of the English type founder and printer John Baskerville (1706–75). Baskerville is the quintessential transitional face: It retains the bracketed and oblique serifs of old-style faces such as Caslon and Garamond, but in its increased lowercase height, lighter color, and enhanced contrast between thick and thin strokes, it presages modern faces.

The display type is set in Didot.

This book is printed on paper that is acid-free and meets the requirements of the American National Standard for Permanence of Paper for Printed Library Materials, z39.48-1992. ♾

Book design by Rich Hendel, Chapel Hill, North Carolina
Typography by Tseng Information Systems, Inc., Durham, North Carolina
Printed by Edwards Brothers, Inc., Ann Arbor, Michigan, and bound by Dekker Bookbinding, Grand Rapids, Michigan